Inclusive Growth, Full Employment, and Structural Change

Implications and Policies for Developing Asia

Second Edition

Jesus Felipe

A copublication of the Asian Development Bank and Anthem Press

Anthem Press
www.anthempress.com

Asian Development Bank
www.adb.org

This edition first published in 2010 by

ANTHEM PRESS
75–76 Blackfriars Road
London SE1 8HA, UK
or PO Box 9779, London SW19 7ZG, UK
and 244 Madison Ave. #116, New York, NY
10016, USA

and
Asian Development Bank
6 ADB Avenue, Mandaluyong City, 1550
Metro Manila, Philippines

Note:
In this publication, "$" refers to US dollars.

British Library Cataloguing in Publication Data
A catalogue record for this book is available from the British Library.

Library of Congress Cataloging in Publication Data
A catalogue record for this book has been requested.

ISBN-13: 978 0 85728 958 2 (Hbk)
ISBN-10: 0 85728 958 6 (Hbk)

Printed and bound in India

A mis padres (Jesús y María Jesús) y hermanos (Pablo, Carlos, Antonio, Isabel, Víctor, y María Jesús)

Contents

Illustrations

List of Tables

List of Figures

List of Boxes

List of Appendixes

Abbreviations

ADB	Asian Development Bank
AFG	Afghanistan
ASEAN	Association of Southeast Asian Nations
AZE	Azerbaijan
BAN	Bangladesh
BHU	Bhutan
BOP	balance of payments
BPO	business process outsourcing
BSP	Bangko Sentral ng Pilipinas (Central Bank of the Philippines)
CAD/CAM	computer-aided design/computer-aided manufacturing
CAM	Cambodia
CARP	Comprehensive Agrarian Reform Program (Philippines)
CEO	chief executive officer
DDLG	domestic demand–led growth
ELG	export-led growth
EU	European Union
FDI	foreign direct investment
FIJ	Fiji Islands
FY	fiscal year
GBC	government budget constraint
GDP	gross domestic product
GVC	global value chain
HKG	Hong Kong, China
ILO	International Labour Organization
IMF	International Monetary Fund
IND	India
INO	Indonesia
ISIC	International Standard Industrial Classification of all Economic Activities
IT	information technology
KAZ	Kazakhstan

KOR	Republic of Korea
KGZ	Kyrgyz Republic
Lao PDR	Lao People's Democratic Republic
MAL	Malaysia
MLD	Maldives
MNCs	multinational companies
MON	Mongolia
MYA	Myanmar
NEP	Nepal
OBM	original brand manufacturer
ODM	original design manufacturer
OECD	Organisation for Economic Co-operation and Development
OEM	original equipment manufacturer
OLS	ordinary least squares
PAK	Pakistan
PHI	Philippines
PNG	Papua New Guinea
NAIRU	nonaccelerating inflation rate of unemployment
NIEs	newly industrialized economies
PES	public employment services
PIDE	Pakistan Institute of Development Economics
PRC	People's Republic of China
R&D	research and development
SBP	State Bank of Pakistan
SIN	Singapore
SITC	Standard International Trade Classification
SMEs	small and medium-sized enterprises
SOL	Solomon Islands
SRI	Sri Lanka
TAJ	Tajikistan
TAP	Taipei,China
THA	Thailand
TKM	Turkmenistan
TON	Tonga
UNCTAD	United Nations Conference on Trade and Development
UNIDO	United Nations Industrial Development Organization
US	United States

UZB	Uzbekistan
VAT	value-added tax
VIE	Viet Nam
WTO	World Trade Organization

Foreword

World poverty is closely related to unemployment and under-employment. This is especially the case in developing Asia, where about 500 million unemployed and underemployed people have to cope without significant government welfare support. Recently, institutions such as the World Bank and the Asian Development Bank have started using the term *inclusive growth* in setting their policy agendas. In this book, Jesus Felipe argues that if policy makers across developing Asia care about inclusive growth defined as *growth with equal opportunities*, then achieving true full employment should become the paramount objective of Asian governments.

The best strategy to reduce poverty in developing Asia is to introduce a set of policies that will generate full employment. While a number of policy initiatives will be useful—particularly those that target productivity improvements in agriculture and stimulate investment in industry, and those that condition the broader macroeconomic environment (monetary, fiscal, and exchange rate policies)—the key is to coordinate their implementation to ensure that they pull the economy toward full employment.

This policy mix is important because ongoing structural change, the key to development, makes the attainment of full employment a moving target and governments are continually confronted with political and economic choices that at times seem to be conflicting. But at all times, the policy process must aim at ensuring that there are enough jobs available to meet the needs of the labor force.

Agriculture remains the largest employer in many Asian countries, including the two largest developing economies, i.e., India and the People's Republic of China. It is thus clear that any viable development plan must place special focus on agriculture. Any such plan has to involve investment initiatives that improve agricultural productivity and alternative job creation strategies that provide opportunities for rural workers displaced by technological advances. These job creation initiatives must take into account the effects of structural change if full employment is to be achieved. Localized job creation programs will also be necessary to ensure that urban structures are not flooded with workers displaced from the modernized agriculture sector.

The conduct of fiscal and monetary policies at the aggregate level will be crucial in how successful each nation is in achieving the aim of inclusive growth. Ultimately, full employment is the responsibility of the national government. While the private sector makes a significant contribution to employment growth across all economies, it remains a fact that this sector does not provide enough jobs to satisfy the desires for work of the labor force. For this reason, the public sector has a strong role to play as a direct employer in its own right, in addition to providing a policy framework that maximizes private employment growth. When considering the conduct of macroeconomic policy, the neoliberal era has been marked by a focus on low inflation and certain presumptions regarding national budget deficits. During this era, unemployment has become a policy tool to reduce inflation rather than a policy target, and governments have been encouraged to generate budget surpluses. There is a solid body of evidence that shows that this strategy has not delivered sustainable growth in any country, and that it has not contributed in many countries across developing Asia to the generation of the required levels of employment. In this book, Jesus Felipe contends that the policy targets should be realigned to full employment and price stability, and that the size of budget deficit should not be considered a policy target but an outcome of what is required to achieve these other overarching goals.

To make progress toward these goals, budget deficits must be demystified. Jesus Felipe argues, rightly, that the reliance in recent decades on monetary policy to stabilize the business cycle (with the concomitant requirement that fiscal policy becomes passive) has failed to deliver outcomes consistent with the goal of inclusive growth. To remedy this, fiscal policy has to resume primacy among the aggregate policy instruments and be used to ensure that private savings can be financed. Another more conventional way of thinking about this is that when the private sector desires to save some of the national income, aggregate demand will be insufficient to fully employ the workforce unless net government spending fills the spending gap. In this way, the budget deficit serves to provide the spending necessary to generate the income that finances the saving. As a consequence, any particular budget outcome will be market-determined by the desired net saving of the private sector. If the private sector desires to save less, then the resulting budget deficit will be smaller, and vice versa.

What are the limits on the size of the budget deficit? Jesus Felipe maintains that sound fiscal conduct will ensure that aggregate spending (the sum of private and public demand) is sufficient to achieve full employment. If fiscal policy stimulates nominal demand beyond this point, then inflation will necessarily follow. National governments should thus feel comfortable running continuous deficits within this limit, in the knowledge that they are underpinning private saving and also maintaining full employment.

In addition to recognizing the essential role of net government spending in stabilizing aggregate demand, many developing countries also need fundamental fiscal reforms aimed at increasing the efficiency of the public sector so that more resources can be allocated for productive investment and/or direct job creation. The two insights complement each other. Strong fiscal policy is essential but so is an effective use of the resources that the government deploys.

While full employment was an objective of central banks and governments across the developed world between the end of World War II and the 1970s, during the last 30 years this goal has been abandoned. The results of this regime shift in policy practice have been that most societies have been forced by their governments to endure persistently high unemployment and rising levels of underemployment. While the income losses associated with persistent labor underutilization have been huge and dwarf any measured costs of so-called microeconomic inefficiencies, the related social pathologies have also been significant. Increased rates of family breakdown, escalating crime rates, rising drug abuse, and arguably rising political instability and extremism have all been closely tied to entrenched joblessness.

While these costs are disproportionately borne by the most disadvantaged members of our communities, the externalities that arise (for example, crime, terrorism) affect us all. However, the public debate, which has been significantly conditioned by neoliberal commentators, has tended to consider unemployment as a personal issue rather than a systemic failure of the economy to generate enough jobs. In this respect, the debate has placed too much stress on inflation and downplayed the costs of unemployment, which are of a higher order of magnitude than the costs arising from mild inflation levels. Jesus Felipe claims that no rigorous evidence is available to conclude that mild inflation damages the economy to such an extent that would justify to have it as the key economic policy concern; and to induce policy makers to use sustained high unemployment to control it.

Much of the economic debate surrounding inflation has presented wrongly the underlying causality. An inflationary process caused by effective demand hitting full capacity during an economic expansion is significantly different from what happened in the world during 2007–2008. In the first case, the economic bonanza would probably lead to an increase in employment and wages, and necessitate economic policy to dampen nominal demand sufficiently to keep the real economy as close as is possible to full employment.

However, this situation does not describe the 2007–2008 inflation episode in developing countries. The combination of increases in oil and food prices has brought misery to millions of people around the world. The additional problem is that inflation coincided with a major slowdown in the world economy that started in the developed countries (especially in the United States [US]). There is clearly a different approach being adopted by the US Federal Reserve relative to how the European Central Bank saw the problem (at least initially). While the former lowered interest rates significantly in an effort to reactivate economic growth, the latter maintained a firm focus on controlling inflation until late 2008. Only as the global economic crisis deepened significantly did the G20 nations display the semblance of a united strategy aimed at stimulating demand to protect jobs.

Further, the ultimate driver of the increase in oil prices is still not entirely understood. Most likely it was a combination of the control that the suppliers exercised on price with the massive growth in demand coming from the People's Republic of China and India. There is also evidence that financial institutions (hedge funds, etc.) hoarded oil and used it for speculative purposes. What about food prices? Early on it was said that the price increases were due to poor harvests in some key countries, in which case they should be a temporary phenomenon. We were told that the situation was probably leading to inflationary expectations and that sooner or later workers would demand increases in wages. The reality, however, is that central banks do not have solid knowledge about how their own actions affect inflation expectations and how these in turn affect inflation. Little is known about firms' inflation expectations and how, if at all, these beliefs influence pricing decisions. The point being made is that before we can design and implement effective policies we do need to understand the underlying economic and social processes that combine to generate these problems.

As indicated earlier, over the last three decades there has been an important change in the way the public debate constructs unemployment and its causes. Previously, unemployment was thought to result from insufficient aggregate demand—that is, a systemic failure beyond the control of any one individual. In recent times, individuals are deemed to be responsible for their own economic outcomes: people are unemployed because they have not invested in the appropriate skills, because they have not made an effort to search for jobs, or because they have become too choosy in what they might consider doing. Further, the policy structures that were implemented during the full employment period to provide support to workers who were temporarily unemployed are now considered to be complicitous in sustaining unemployment. So, critics of government suggest that welfare provisions are excessively generous and distort individual decision making toward unemployment.

Developing Asia has experienced fast growth rates for decades and is the envy of most other regions in the world. However, Jesus Felipe shows that this perception is lopsided. While high growth is seen as the key parameter for evaluating developing Asia's success, there is abundant evidence that this growth is not translating into sufficient job creation. In particular, labor absorption by industry is low and most of the new employment is being created by services. So this period of development is seeing workers being transferred directly from agriculture into services without an industrial base being developed. This is a significant departure from the development path previously followed by many developed countries and even by the first wave of successful East Asian countries. It is clear that policy makers across developing Asia need to understand these trends to avoid the pitfalls that it is likely to present as time passes.

The book spells out the main constraint that many countries across developing Asia face for their development: a lack of capital equipment and productive capacity. Therefore, the purpose of development must be to increase a country's productive capacity to achieve the full employment of labor. However, rapid structural transformation, competition, and globalization limit the capacity and autonomy of Asia's developing countries to achieve full employment without significant public sector involvement.

Despite the political and technical difficulties in achieving and maintaining full employment, governments across the region should not be deterred. In the final analysis, unemployment and underemployment are states that can be largely prevented by sound government policy. The motivation by policy makers to pursue full employment should be conditioned by the desire to maximize incomes, by the desire to ensure that human rights are maintained, and by the desire to achieve social stability. Allowing high rates of unemployment to persist reflects a diminution of government responsibility and leadership. The decision to pursue full employment policies requires political choices to be made and for the government to engender a sense of collective will. However, over the last three decades governments have progressively tried to undermine this collective approach.

Jesus Felipe takes the view that employment is a human right, and that full employment as an objective of economic policy is firmly entrenched in the United Nations' Universal Declaration of Human Rights (article 23) and in the Charter of the United Nations (articles 55 and 56). Moreover, since 2006, the concept of decent work has been a target of the first Millennium Development Goal (to eradicate extreme poverty and hunger).

But pursuing full employment can also be constructed as a rational public choice for other reasons. An economy running at full employment or "high pressure" maximizes income creation. This leads to more buoyant markets, businesses, investment, and employment. This is an economy that will provide everyone with opportunities.

The late US President John F. Kennedy coined the phrase, "A rising tide lifts all boats," which recognizes the upgrading benefits of the high pressure economy. Governments that use fiscal policy to ensure that their economies stay as close to full employment as possible generate massive advantages: both the strong and the weak prosper, labor participation is strong, unemployment is at the irreducible minimum, labor productivity is high, wages are high, children from disadvantaged families get a chance to transcend poverty, and workers who are displaced by global economic changes are able to be re-absorbed into productive work. In this regard, direct public sector job creation must be a significant part of the national government's responsibilities.

All this means that a fully employed economy delivers great individual and social benefits. Unemployment and underemployment have direct economic costs and lead to poverty, misery, stress, malnutrition, and social injustice. Persistent unemployment and underemployment act as a form of social exclusion that violates basic concepts of membership and citizenship, thus prohibiting inclusive growth. Full employment in the developing world also contributes to political stability, as the consumption of much of the population will be higher than when many people are unemployed. Therefore, it should be an ethical imperative in today's world. As a consequence, a rational person will rightly note that developing countries cannot afford unemployment and underemployment. This construction is eminently more plausible (and evidence-based) than its opposite—that they cannot afford full employment.

Finally, Jesus Felipe also argues that while the private sector is the generator of wealth and most employment in a market economy, governments should be held accountable for their efforts and commitment to achieve full employment. This follows from an understanding of the policy options available to a national government. But it also reflects the observation that when unemployment rises, the public always blames the government rather than the private sector.

Overall, it is clear that governments and the private sector must collaborate strategically to generate a fully employed economy. Both strong investment from the private sector and a strong commitment from the public sector to job creation and public infrastructure development are necessary to achieve this goal.

I view this book as an important contribution in the fields of economic development and policy making in developing countries. Its strength is that it challenges the *status quo* and forces us all to rethink our priorities and reconsider the way we conduct economic policy.

William Mitchell
Centre of Full Employment and Equity (CofFEE)
University of Newcastle, Australia

Preface and Acknowledgments

The only thing we have to fear is fear itself.

—Franklin Delano Roosevelt

I n this book, I expand on my previous work (with Rana Hasan) on unemployment and underemployment in developing Asia, *Labor Markets in Asia: Issues and Perspectives* (2006). Here, I reiterate and stress my view that while economists and social scientists in general have praised developing Asia's unmatched growth record since the mid-1960s, they may have missed the important point that the region is failing to provide employment to its huge and still-growing labor force. Sooner or later this problem will become policy makers' biggest headache.[1] The attainment of full employment, understood amid the problems posed by structural change (or transformation), globalization, and fast technical progress, should be the ultimate goal of economic policy. Figure A reproduces the framework used in *Labor Markets in Asia* to understand and conceptualize full employment and the policies to achieve it. In this book, I move one step forward and analyze the policies to achieve full employment during fast structural change. I view my work as contributing to the concern among policy makers in the developing world that growth has to be inclusive, that is, that it has to provide equal opportunities. In my view, opportunities come through employment.

In early 2008, the International Labour Organization (ILO) announced that as a result of the expected global economic cooling following the turbulence in financial markets, world unemployment would increase. Policy makers have to be aware of this problem and start implementing policies to tackle unemployment as soon as possible. This will require substantial changes in policies and priorities. In my view, this is the biggest challenge that policy makers across much of the region will face in the coming decades. Growth will be useless if it is not accompanied by employment opportunities.

---

[1] Rana Hasan and I estimated that developing Asia is home to about 500 million people who are unemployed and/or underemployed.

Figure A. Framework for Full, Productive, and Decent Employment

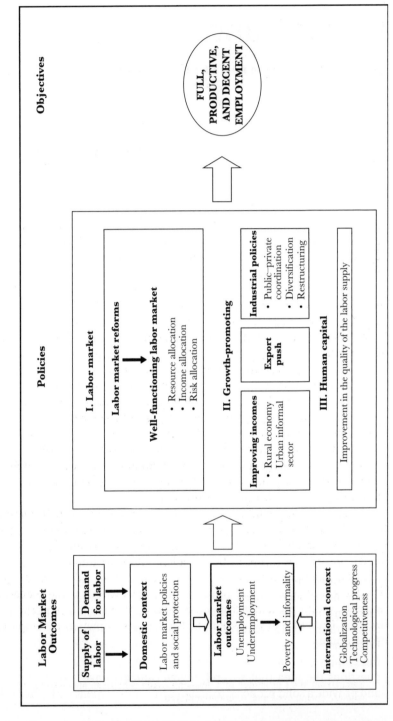

Source: Felipe, Jesus, and Rana Hasan. 2006. *Labor Markets in Asia: Issues and Perspectives.*

I concluded a few years ago that the "development problem," from the point of view of development policy, is an embarrassment, a puzzle that economists have failed to complete and even understand (Felipe 2006). Growth theory adds more and more variables to the discussion, but at the end of the day we do not know how to put all the pieces together. Development is about fundamental change in economic structures, about the movement of resources out of agriculture and into services and industry, about migration to cities and the movement of labor across countries, and about transformations in trade and technology. Social inclusion and change—change in health and life expectancy, in education and literacy, in population size and structure, and in gender relations—are at the heart of the story. The policy challenge is to help release and guide these forces of change and inclusion.

As a consequence of this failure, I have come to the following two conclusions: first, that we know relatively little about the crucial growth questions; and second, that no unique way exists to put all the pieces of the puzzle together. Hence, each country has to find its own way to complete the puzzle. I believe that the different policies I analyze here are important components of the big picture; but each country will have to decide the precise way to implement them and how to proceed.

Part of the problem lies in the complexity of the subject. But economics, as a discipline, must also change in the coming decades. Often, one has to go outside mainstream treatments of development to find challenging and provocative ideas. Mainstream analyses still rely on policy recommendations stemming from the neoclassical model of growth (both in its original formulation and in that of the endogenous growth models developed since the 1980s), in which development is seen simply as a problem of factor accumulation: poor countries are like rich countries, but have less of key factors such as physical and/or human capital. I have written extensively on this issue and I am convinced that orthodox approaches are largely a futile effort. There is a strong movement within the profession expressing discontent with the way standard models, many of which have little to do with reality, are rehearsed over and over again.

During the last 15 years I have been greatly influenced by six critical areas of work: (i) the theoretical work by Frank Fisher (with whom I have collaborated in two papers) on aggregation in production functions, which questions the pillar of neoclassical growth models (the aggregate production function); and the work by John McCombie (with whom I have also been collaborating for 15 years) on the accounting identity critique of production functions estimated with value data; (ii) the work on functional finance and the employer of last resort by Randall Wray and William Mitchell, which questions the idea that sovereign governments have a budget constraint and provide a solid proposal to achieve full employment with price stability;

(iii) the work by Anwar Shaikh reviving the classical research program; (iv) the work by Ricardo Hausmann on structural change; (v) the work by Dani Rodrik questioning free-trade fundamentalism; and (vi) the work by Tony Thirlwall on the balance-of-payments constrained growth.

Although the target of the book is policy makers across developing Asia, I have done my best to write a book that can be read by a wide audience, including readers without grounding on the subject, policy makers in other parts of the world, and scholars. Some readers will find some of my ideas thought-provoking. My efforts have been directed at developing proposals that challenge policy makers' views and compel them to "think outside the box." To support and develop the arguments, I have drawn upon references to a wide body of literature. Some of these references are rather old, but extremely relevant and not outdated. Other references are to recent work (particularly on structural change, economic diversification, and upgrading). The ultimate purpose of the book is to open a debate about the priorities and policies for development in Asia during the next decades. In some areas, I express clear views and opinions; while in others, I simply present different arguments and points of view and let the reader decide.

Underlying my work are two important tenets about how I view policy making in developing countries. The first tenet is that policy makers in developing countries must be capable of undertaking systemic social, political, and economic analyses. These analyses must consider, among other factors, the effects of growth on the environment, the increasing differentiation among developing countries, and the erosion of the core–periphery dichotomy, as well as racial tensions and the political outcomes of elections. As a development practitioner, I feel that globalization—the integration of the world through trade, investment, and technologies such as the internet—has thrown development economics into a quagmire. Globalization has exposed the limitations of the existing models and theories. Development theory needs to revert to the agenda of classical political economy along the lines of Adam Smith, David Ricardo, and Karl Marx, and be grounded on an analysis of historical processes. It cannot continue under the aegis of the neoclassical growth research program. Governance and institutions have become part of mainstream analyses of growth in recent times, but their treatment is similar to that given to any of the other variables that economists include as arguments in the standard aggregate production function, the tool used to analyze growth. Living in the Philippines for many years, I have concluded that development theory cannot be apolitical. Development has a deep political character, as it is shaped by social interests and political projects.

The second tenet is that I do not advocate massive and widespread reforms. Policy makers should set priorities based on an analysis of a country's binding constraints.

Policy making is about choosing economic policies (instruments) in an uncertain environment to achieve some objectives.[2] The choices of both objectives and policies are most often based on a mix of economic reasoning and one's view of the world (including political beliefs); actual circumstances (e.g., high oil prices); assessment of the global environment (e.g., elections and political instability in certain key countries); interpretation of events (e.g., increases in prices amid the weakening of the global economy in 2007–2008); and differentiation between short-run issues and long-run questions. Policy making entails the possibility of choosing contradictory courses of action (e.g., unsynchronized fiscal and monetary policies) and of making mistakes (e.g., due to an incorrect interpretation of events). Moreover, any choice made today (e.g., increasing spending, increasing interest rates, implementing a new educational system, lowering tariffs) will have an impact into the future.

Let me provide an example of what policy makers across developing Asia were dealing with during the first part of 2008. Inflation was rising, mostly because of higher food and energy prices.[3] For example, the price of pork increased in the People's Republic of China (PRC) by about 60% in 2007 and that of vegetables by almost 50%. The PRC's inflation surged to 8.7% during February 2007–February 2008 (however, nonfood prices increased by less than 2% in 2007), the highest in 12 years. And in early 2008, the PRC suffered from severe snowstorms that damaged crops and disrupted traffic. Inflation in India, Indonesia, Thailand, and Singapore was also on the rise (slightly above 4%). Was inflation at these levels a serious problem? Was the fear of returning to the 1970s justified or misplaced? Was it only a temporary phenomenon caused by one-off supply factors? What were policy makers across developing Asia more concerned about, inflation or the possibility of a slowing economy? Central banks were reluctant to increase interest rates when the United States (US) was lowering them to weather its recession. How increases in interest

---

[2]   Harberger defines "good" economic policies as "those that promote the efficient operation of the economy and at the same time intelligently support the process of growth" (Harberger 1998, 203). I am not sure if I completely agree with Harberger, as the term "efficient" in his definition most likely refers to the allocation of resources in terms of microeconomic neoclassical optimality (i.e., equilibrium in production is determined by marginal costs and equilibrium in consumption by marginal utilities; and the operation of the price mechanism clears all markets), and because it designates the growth objective as the key goal.

[3]   It was argued that this was caused by increased demand from fast-growing, emerging economies like the PRC, along with the rise in the price of ethanol, which gobbled up a big chunk of US land dedicated to the corn crop and diverted acreage from wheat. Although the PRC is a big importer of a few agricultural products, such as soybeans, it has been a net exporter of food for many years.

rates would affect food and energy inflation was not clear. What is more certain is that an increase in interest rates would attract capital inflows and push the value of currencies up, helping curb imported inflation (of food and energy products). However, stronger currencies may have a negative impact on exports. And what if growth slows down significantly? Will policy makers reduce interest rates? Will this, however, bring in inflation later?

Countries like India, Thailand, Malaysia, the Philippines, and the PRC resorted in early 2008 to price controls and government subsidies on a wide range of goods (e.g., energy, transport, water, meat, grain, eggs, and cooking oil). For example, in early 2008, to tame the increase in agricultural prices, the PRC government declared that reducing consumer price inflation was a political priority. The government said that it would expand agricultural commodity production, exert strict control on industrial grain use, establish an early-warning system to monitor supply and demand, and strengthen market oversight and price inspections. It also indicated that subsidies for the poor would increase, and that provincial governors and mayors would be held responsible for ensuring basic food supply. Certainly these are political measures that appeal to public concerns (especially low-income urban groups) and address popular discontent that might generate social unrest. However, holding down prices reduces the incentive for producers to increase supply, leading to shortages that can lead to increases in prices despite government measures. In the short run, most likely this measure will be beneficial, as the source of inflation is the increase in energy and food prices, rather than increases in aggregate demand. But in the long run, this is a measure that may hamper the economy. In Malaysia and Indonesia, fuel subsidies account for about 10% of total government spending. And apart from efficiency considerations, if fuel prices are not allowed to increase across Asia, demand will not decrease and will push global oil prices higher.[4] By early 2009, it was clear that inflation was not a problem and that the world economy was spiraling into recession. The question then changed: for how long?

The book is divided into 17 chapters (plus conclusions), each with a question as the title, and each revolves around the central issues of inclu-

---

[4] By December 2008, crude oil prices had declined significantly, to below $50 a barrel. Inflation started taking on a secondary place in discussions (headline consumer prices seem to have peaked) when a number of central banks around the world decided to lower interest rates, acknowledging that a recession is the most serious problem the world faces. Given that in the span of 6 months the price of oil declined by about $100, it is difficult not to think that there had been an important element of speculation during 2007 and first 6 months of 2008. Evidence that this was the case is provided by Wray (2008a).

sive growth, full employment, and structural change. It would have been much more difficult and challenging to organize the book by countries. Probably the PRC and India would have accounted for the bulk of it. Some readers may argue that I have omitted important topics, such as aging, global health risks, environment and climate change, energy, the informal economy, and ethics. No doubt these topics are important, but the book would have been excessively long. These topics deserve another book.[5] I do not discuss either the financial turmoil that started in 2007, except for some quick references that I make in some parts of the book. The reason is that I do not know yet how the crisis will damage the world economy and the changes that it will bring.[6] The standard argument is that this is a crisis that started in the US, the result of two decades of easy-money policies coupled with the development of innovative financial products that fueled the US's "ownership society" (based on the idea that every American family would own a home). Since the 1980s, Americans have consumed more than they produced. In retrospect, this is the "chronicle of a death foretold." Only time will disclose its full implications.[7]

Chapter 1 defines inclusive growth. I use throughout the book the term "inclusive growth" because it is making its way into policy makers' language despite the lack of a unanimously accepted definition. The key issues are (i) what should policy makers' objectives be? and (ii) what policies should they implement? I will argue strongly that the key to inclusive growth is full employment. My position is that governments should not simply provide a series of public goods, as many argue, but ensure the full employment of labor. This is a much more ambitious and serious role that does not imply a bigger government.

Chapter 2, on the main problem of developing countries, and chapter 3, on the concept of full employment, contain the foundation of my arguments. Chapter 4 contains a discussion of why growth tends to be unstable, based on the Harrod–Domar model. Starting in chapter 5, chap-

---

5   The interested reader can see the excellent essays in Quibria (1995) and Quibria and Dowling (1996). See in these volumes Dasgupta (1995) on the environment and Kapur (1996) on ethics and values.

6   By the end of 2008, it became clear that the financial crisis was affecting developing Asia. Initially, the region was well positioned to weather the global crisis. Economies across the region had learned the lessons of the 1997–1998 financial crisis and banks were well capitalized, highly liquid, and with low rates of nonperforming loans. Moreover, central banks had accumulated large amounts of reserves. But as the crisis deepened in the US and Europe, the effects began to be felt, especially through real-sector channels. Given Asia's dependence on exports, the rich world's recession hurts Asia.

7   Wray (2008b) is critical of the orthodox view of the causes of the current global financial crisis. He argues that US current account deficits and federal budget deficits are sustainable, so the US does not need to adopt austerity.

ters where I make policy proposals (in chapters 5, 6, 8, 12, 14) have been labeled "Full Employment I, II, III, IV, and V" respectively. Chapter 5 is on the role of agriculture, and chapter 6 on the role of investment. Chapter 7 is on the need to plan development. Chapter 8 discusses the role of industrial policy. Chapter 9 analyzes the record of structural transformation and industrialization in developing Asia. Chapter 10 presents a modern analysis of why economic diversification is important. Chapter 11 is on inflation. Chapter 12 discusses how fiscal and monetary policies can be consistent with inclusive growth. Chapter 13 discusses the technical problems in achieving and maintaining full employment in economies undergoing structural change. Chapter 14 discusses the role of the public sector as employer of last resort. Chapter 15 summarizes my views on globalization and competitiveness and their relationship with inclusive growth. In chapter 16, I review recent discussions about the need to shift from export-led growth to domestic demand–led growth and what this implies and entails. Chapter 17 offers a discussion of externalities, knowledge, and education. Finally, chapter 18 summarizes the main arguments.

Writing this book has been a most rewarding personal experience from which I have learned a lot. For this reason, I want to close this preface with the always pleasant task of thanking those who in many ways have contributed to the improvement of the original manuscript. I am deeply grateful to Luis Cañete, David Dole, Nimal Fernando, David Garrigos, Tun Lin, Saby Mitra, Safdar Parvez, Sukhumarn Phanachet, Raquel Rago, Sona Shrestha, Ramesh Subramaniam, Joey Tan, Alex Warren Rodríguez, and Juzhong Zhuang for useful discussions, comments, and suggestions about different chapters and versions of the original paper that led to this book, titled *Macroeconomic Implications of Inclusive Growth: What are the Questions?* This does not necessarily mean that they share all the views expressed. In fact, many of their comments (and, in particular, disagreements) were tremendously useful and helped me polish the arguments and make them more comprehensible. Joseph Lim and Gemma Estrada helped me with the data on structural change. Conversations and joint work with Ricardo Hausmann, Cesar Hidalgo, and Bailey Klinger were also very useful and aided me to fully grasp their recent path-breaking work on the implications of structural transformation, diversification, and upgrading using network theory. Michael Hobday provided me with the material on global value chains. Work with my colleague Norio Usui during the last 2 years, especially on growth diagnostics, public finance, and structural change, also helped me polish the arguments. Mathew Forstater, Warren Mosler, and especially Randall Wray and Bill Mitchell helped me understand the details of the public sector as employer of last resort as well as of the functional finance approach, and the true meaning of budget deficits and surpluses. Conversations and discussions on growth during the last 15 years with my coauthor John McCombie, as well as with Tony Thirlwall, have helped me shape my views on many issues in growth and development. John's great generosity during all these years has made our collaboration a most rewarding experience for which I shall always be grateful. I am deeply indebted to all of them, although I am solely responsible for the content, in particular, for any remaining errors.

Also, participants at the workshop on Policy Implications of Inclusive Growth organized by the Asian Development Bank's (ADB) Central and West Asia Department on 28 September 2007, and at a seminar organized by the Philippine Institute for Development Studies (Manila, Philippines) on 7 December 2007, made very helpful suggestions. And participants in the lecture I gave on Long-Run Growth Drivers and Economic Policy at Singapore's Ministry of Trade and Industry on 20 June 2008, where I presented some of the issues that I discuss in this book, also made very useful remarks.

Many of the ideas in this book started maturing during my years in the Economics and Research Department of ADB. Ifzal Ali, ADB's chief economist from 2002 through 2008, provided the department with an excellent environment to be creative and carry out independent work. His lack of dogmatism and his openness to different ideas made me respect him deeply. He retired from ADB in October 2008, after more than 20 years of service. I wholeheartedly wish him the best.

Discussions over many lunches, dinners, and coffee sessions with my colleague and friend Joao Farinha-Fernandes were instrumental in keeping my arguments judicious. Rana Hasan has also been a source of inspiration and friendship during many years. I have learned a lot from him on employment issues and development in general. Both are outstanding individuals who possess great human qualities that I admire. Living and working in developing Asia is a fascinating and most satisfying experience that we enjoy and share.

Finally, Juan Miranda (director general, Central and West Asia Department, ADB) and Xianbin Yao (director general, Regional and Sustainable Development Department, ADB) were always very supportive, and, since the inception, they encouraged me to develop the ideas in the book.

My gratitude also goes to my assistants Arnelyn May Abdon and Damaris Yarcia, who patiently copy edited the manuscript.

To conform with ADB's rules and policies, I use "[Taipei,China]". This has affected the references to some work. My apologies to the authors.

My employer, ADB, has provided me with the opportunity to learn about developing Asia. I am very grateful. Nevertheless, the views expressed in the book are solely mine and do not necessarily reflect the views or policies of ADB, its executive directors, or those of the countries that they represent.

Jesus Felipe

Central and West Asia Department
Asian Development Bank
Manila, Philippines

Cambridge Centre for Economic & Public Policy
University of Cambridge
Cambridge, United Kingdom

Centre of Full Employment and Equity (CofFEE)
University of Newcastle
Australia

Centre for Applied Macroeconomic Analysis (CAMA)
Australian National University
Canberra, Australia

Manila, July 2009

Executive Summary

This book discusses the implications for macroeconomic policy of the term inclusive growth, understood as growth with equal opportunities. This is a term that, in different ways (e.g., harmonious society, sufficient economy), is making its way into the policy discourse in many countries in Asia, and multilateral organizations such as the World Bank and the Asian Development Bank have also started using it. To achieve inclusive growth, Asian governments must commit efforts and resources to the pursuit of the full employment of labor to provide jobs to the 500 million unemployed and/or underemployed people in the region. The book discusses the different aspects of the link between inclusive growth and full employment, and offers a menu of policies that will have to be tailored to each country's circumstances.

A summary of the main arguments is as follows:

(i)   The most salient feature of developing Asia's labor markets is the considerable underutilization of labor, which manifests itself in unemployment and underemployment. Having a job that pays a decent salary is the most basic measure of a person's living standard. For this reason, Felipe and Hasan (2006, 2) argue that "improving labor market opportunities for workers is the key to reducing poverty and improving standards of living for the large majority of Asia's workers and their families. Poverty reduction requires helping people as workers." A high-employment economy is the best single tool for fighting poverty.

(ii)   The main cause of unemployment and underemployment in developing countries is lack of capital equipment and productive capacity. Therefore, the purpose of development must be to increase a country's productive capacity. Only sound policies geared toward full employment will create the foundation for inclusive growth.

(iii)   Unemployment and underemployment as the fundamental causes of lack of inclusiveness are unethical states of a malfunctioning economy. They ultimately are the result of a lack of collective will to make political choices that favor maintaining adequate levels of demand.

(iv)   The most important way in which a person can participate in society and contribute to its progress is through a productive and decent job.

(v)   Full employment means, ideally, zero involuntary unemployment as well as zero part-time employment.

(vi)   In developing countries, the objective of achieving full employment has to be complemented with the objectives of creating productive employment (i.e., employment that is not underutilized) and ensuring decent employment (i.e., employment that provides living wages—determined by local conditions, benefits, reasonable job security, and a healthy work environment).

(vii)   Full employment requires the government's commitment to attaining and maintaining it. Achievement of this objective must be the government's mandate and responsibility, and governments should be evaluated and held accountable. Ensuring full employment is the most direct way to achieving the ultimate objective of economic policy, to improve the long-run well-being of *all* the people in the country, especially the most disadvantaged. And maintaining the economy as close as possible to full employment will lower safety net expenditures.

(viii) While the private sector is the generator of wealth in a market economy, it cannot be entrusted with the achievement of full employment, because it is not a component of its overall objective function. The private sector has neither the commitment nor the tools to achieve it. Full employment requires close coordination between private and public sectors.

(ix)   Achieving full employment will require the synchronization of different policies (agricultural, monetary and fiscal, exchange rate, trade, and industrial). Piecemeal approaches will not work because the policies directed at the achievement of full employment have to take into account a country's overall economic conditions. This means that one must think in a systemic and coordinated way: that is, policies that influence the achievement of inclusive growth cannot be devised independently. The policies discussed in this book are (a) the expansion of agricultural production (chapter 5); (b) a coherent public investment plan that determines not only the amount but also the composition of investment across sectors (chapter 6); (c) an industrial policy program for productive diversification (chapter 8); (d) fiscal, monetary, and exchange policies geared toward full employment (chapter 12); and (e) governments (the public sector) willing to act as employers of last resort when necessary (chapter 14).

(x)   In pursuing full employment, the government will have to set priorities and deal with constraints.

(xi) The key to growth is structural transformation aimed at upgrading production and export structures, industrializing, and diversifying. Structural transformation is policy induced and not the result of market forces. It requires the government and the private sector to be aware of the information and coordination problems that inhibit investment. They have to work together.

(xii) Achieving inclusive growth-*cum*-full employment in a developing economy undergoing structural transformation, and where fighting inflation is often the central objective of policy making (and with the constraints imposed by globalization and competitiveness), is extremely difficult because of technical and political reasons, as argued by Karl Marx, Michal Kalecki, Milton Friedman, and Luigi Pasinetti. On the other hand, John Maynard Keynes, John Kenneth Galbraith, and William Vickrey thought that a market economy could achieve it, as the government has the tools and mechanisms to steer the economy in that direction.

1

What Is Inclusive Growth?

We need to make growth more inclusive—to expand access to opportunities so that all can participate, regardless of their individual circumstances.

—Haruhiko Kuroda, ADB's President (2008)

During the last few years, terms such as "harmonious society" in the People's Republic of China (PRC), "sufficient economy" in Thailand, and similar terms in other countries across Asia, have made their way into the discourse of policy makers. The message in all cases is similar: development is more than growth. The Commission on Growth and Development (2008) in its *Growth Report* also echoes the same sentiment. The Government of India, for example, boasts to have fostered "inclusive growth." By this it means that the budget has increased allocations to school meals or rural road-building.[1] The high-growth policies implemented across the region since the 1960s were successful and led to increases in per capita income and dramatic reductions in poverty, contributing to closing the gap with the developed world. But today a feeling has spread that policies and objectives need to be revised as citizens across Asia demand more than growth. Inequality, productive and decent employment, the environment, health, and climate change are becoming increasingly important in the agendas of policy makers. Institutions such as the World Bank and the Asian Development Bank also acknowledge the issue and argue that growth and globalization have to be *inclusive*.[2]

What is inclusive growth? Although the term has not been formally defined, Ali and Zhuang (2007, 10) claim that a consensus is emerging as to what it means: "growth with equal opportunities." In a related paper, Ali and Son (2007, 1–2) further argue that inclusive growth is "growth that not only creates new economic opportunities but also one that ensures equal access to the opportunities created for all segments

---

[1]   *The Economist* 2008c.
[2]   For example, World Bank President Robert Zoellick argued in October 2007 that the challenge of globalization is to make it inclusive.

of society. Growth is inclusive when it allows all members of a society to participate in, and contribute to, the growth process on an equal basis regardless of their individual circumstances" (Box 1.1 and Table 1.1 on the PRC).

In this book, I discuss the implications of inclusive growth for policy making in developing Asia. *If* the term inclusive growth is a useful concept, how should it be interpreted in developing policies? What sort of policies should be implemented to achieve it? What are the constraints and trade-offs? And finally, can it be achieved? The *central argument of the book* is that in order to achieve inclusive growth, governments must commit efforts and resources to the pursuit of full employment. The most significant way for a person to participate in society as a valuable member is through a productive and decent job. Moreover, maintaining the economy as close as possible to full employment will lower the need to dedicate resources to set up safety net expenditures. In the final analysis, full employment is the most direct way to improve the long-run well-being of *all* the people in the country. The questions into which the book is divided discuss different aspects of the link between inclusive growth and full employment and, in so doing, offer a menu of policies that will have to be tailored to each country's circumstances (some proposals may not even apply to some Asian countries). All this implies that governments must set objectives and policies aimed at achieving inclusive growth (Stiglitz 1998).[3] As modern economic theory and historical experience show, markets are the best way to organize the production of goods and services, but in some instances they fail to produce efficient outcomes (e.g., as a result of the existence of public goods, externalities, imperfect information, technology). But of all the market failures, none is perhaps more important for its social consequences than the failure of an economy to utilize its resources fully, especially employment. This is a key tenet of this book.

Does this mean that growth is not important? No, certainly not. Growth is fundamental for developing countries. One of the main themes of this book is the relationship between growth and structural change. This is how

---

[3]   The fact that I link inclusive growth with full employment does not mean that I disregard other very important questions. For example, the role of investment in nutrition, health care, and basic education, all of them key to a more productive workforce in the future, must also be considered. One of the fundamental prerequisites for successful inclusive growth is investments in helping the people both create and take full advantage of the opportunities arising in development. These investments should be part of all government's commitment to deliver inclusive growth, as malnutrition and diseases may have lifelong consequences, and affect the prospects of an entire generation. These types of investments are also necessary and valuable for social and political reasons, as they contribute to society's quality of life (Galbraith 1997). Empirical evidence shows that feeding young children (up to 3 years old) with a high-energy, high-protein supplement leads to increased economic productivity in adulthood, and to about 40% higher wages on average (Hoddinott et al. 2008).

Box 1.1. The People's Republic of China's Harmonious Society: The 11th Five-Year Plan

In March 2006, the National People's Congress of the People's Republic of China endorsed the 11th Five-Year Program, 2006–2010, which builds on a gradual shift in the government's emphasis since 2003 toward policies aimed at achieving balanced, equitable, and sustainable development. This plan, officially called a "program," generally provides indicative targets, rather than fixed targets, and gives attention to standards of living and the environment as well as to the economy. Of 22 goals, only 2 relate to economic growth—total gross domestic product (GDP) and per capita GDP—and 4 to changes in economic structure—share of services in the economy and in employment, spending on research and development, and the urbanization rate. The other 16 relate to population growth, use of resources, the environment, and standards of living (Table 1.1). The primary economic target is an average GDP growth rate of 7.5% over the next 5 years (compared with actual average growth of 9.5% over the past 5). Key goals are to reduce both energy consumption and discharge of major pollutants.

There is a stronger emphasis on rural development. The government pledges to raise farmers' incomes and promote public services in the countryside. In addition to abolishing the agricultural tax at the start of 2006, it will eliminate all tuition fees for 9 years of compulsory education in rural areas in 2007, and trim local government bureaucracies. It will increase subsidies for farmers who grow grain, and will continue to set prices for grain purchases as a support measure.

For industry, the focus is on strengthening its structure rather than on increasing its size. In the environmental area, the authorities will push industries to upgrade equipment and technology and eliminate processes that waste energy, water, and raw materials. They will also make efforts to expand services. Recognizing a lack of technological innovation, the government will invest $8.9 billion in 2006 to encourage innovation, up nearly 20% from 2005. In education, the government will expand the secondary vocational education system to about the same size as the general secondary education system; increase enrollment rates for senior secondary education and higher education to 80% and 25%, respectively; and extend the availability of 9 years of compulsory education to all regions.

Source: Asian Development Bank 2006a.

I understand the story of the successful developing Asian countries. Understanding the dynamics of structural change is essential for comprehending the difficulties in achieving full employment. However, the elasticity of employment with respect to output in many parts of Asia is not particularly high, and in some cases it has even decreased (Felipe and Hasan 2006, chapters 3 and 4). What does this mean? To cite Felipe and Hasan (2006, 113) in discussing the PRC's employment elasticity: "In the 1980s, it took a 3% growth rate of output to induce a 1% increase in employment. By the 1990s, however, it took more than twice as much growth—about 7.8%, to achieve the same result." In the same vein, the United Nations Conference on Trade and Development (UNCTAD) has also recently claimed that although "most developing economies have seen strong growth in employment or even succeeded in stabilizing or slightly reducing unemployment rates . . . open unemployment in developing countries is much less responsive to high growth rates than it is in developed countries. . . . The main reason for the low impact of growth on open unemployment in many developing countries and emerging market economies could be the huge reserves of labour that enter the formal economy only after a longer phase of rising demand for labour and increasing wages. As some emerging countries—including [the People's Republic of] China—show, the process of integrating such reserves of labour into more formal labour markets may take many years of fast growth" (2007, II). This is of utmost importance because, as Figure 1.1 shows, the labor forces of many Asian countries will increase significantly in the next two decades.

Indeed, the expectation that labor could be released from agriculture and rapidly absorbed by industry has largely not been realized during the last 15 years. While the share of employment in agriculture has declined in much of developing Asia, labor has found new employment in the service sector (formal or informal) in relatively low-productivity occupations, mostly in trade and personal services. In other words, today, a high-growth economy does not necessarily generate the level and quality of employment that many Asian countries need. And without creation of employment, reduction of poverty will be very difficult. If growth is inclusive, it has to lead to a decrease in poverty; in particular, a faster decline in poverty should be observed for a given growth rate. The empirical evidence, however, indicates that, with the exception of East Asia, the degree of inclusiveness of Asian growth is relatively low (Pasha 2007). This is especially true in South Asia.

A preliminary conclusion is that policy makers should, perhaps, reverse the causality between growth and employment, and start thinking that a full-employment economy has a lot of virtues, and that full employment is what will lead to high growth, rather than the other way around.

I close this first chapter with the question of whether or not we need the adjective "inclusive." Many may argue that, one way or another, growth

Table 1.1. People's Republic of China: Key Indicators of Economic and Social Development, 2005–2010

Item	Indicators	2005	2010	Target	Type of target
Economic growth	GDP (CNY trillion)	18.2	26.1	7.5%	Indicative
	Per capita GDP (CNY)	13,985	19,270	6.6%	Indicative
Economic structure	Share of services sector value-added in GDP (%)	40.3	43.3	[3 pp]	Indicative
	Share of employment in services sector (%)	31.3	35.3	[4 pp]	Indicative
	Share of research and development spending in total GDP (%)	1.3	2.0	[0.7 pp]	Indicative
	Urbanization rate (%)	43	47	[4 pp]	Indicative
Population, resources, and environment	Population (billions)	1.308	1.360	<0.8%	Maximum
	Energy consumption per unit of GDP	–	–	[20%]	Reduction
	Water consumption per unit of industrial value-added	–	–	[30%]	Reduction
	Coefficient of effective use of water for irrigation	0.45	0.50	[0.05]	Indicative
	Rate of use of solid industrial waste (%)	55.8	60.0	[4.2 pp]	Indicative
	Total area of cultivated land (100 million hectares)	1.22	1.20	(0.3)	Minimum
	Total discharge of major pollutants	–	–	[10%]	Reduction
	Forest coverage (%)	18.2	20.0	[1.8 pp]	Minimum
Public services and standards of living	Years of education per capita	8.5	9.0	[0.5]	Indicative
	Coverage of urban basic old-age pension (100 million)	1.74	2.23	5.1	Minimum
	Coverage of rural cooperative medical care system (%)	23.5	>80.0	>[56.5]	Minimum
	New jobs created for urban residents (10,000)	–	–	[4,500]	Indicative
	Number of rural laborers transferred to nonagriculture sectors (10,000)	–	–	[4,500]	Indicative
	Urban registered unemployment rate (%)	4.2	50.0	–	Indicative
	Per capita disposable income of urban residents (CNY)	10,493	13,390	5%	Indicative
	Per capita net income of rural residents (CNY)	3,255	4,150	5%	Indicative

– = data not available, CNY = yuan, GDP = gross domestic product, pp = percentage points.

Note: (i) GDP, per capita disposable income of urban residents, and per capita net income of rural residents are at 2005 prices; (ii) changes in [ ] refer to cumulative figures for 2006–2010; (iii) major pollutants refer to sulfur dioxide and chemical oxygen demand.

Source: Asian Development Bank 2006a.

benefits the average citizen and, therefore, this adjective is superfluous. The reality, however, is that large segments of society feel that their living standards are deteriorating vis-à-vis those of some privileged groups, so that the gap is widening. In many cases, societies are failing to transform themselves fast enough to provide sufficient productive and decent employment to the increasingly large labor forces. For these reasons and at the risk of laboring the obvious, the adjective "inclusive" plays a role, if only to alert policy makers of the nature and magnitude of the problem.

A telling example is that of the Philippines. In 2007, the country registered its highest economic growth in three decades, 7.3%. However, this growth does not appear to be benefiting the majority of Filipinos. In fact, poverty has increased. Obviously the mere quantity of economic activity, as measured by a common indicator like GDP growth, taken alone, "says virtually nothing about whether life for the common Filipino is getting better or worse. It ignores the distribution of income and makes no distinction between workers with top-paying jobs and those workers who can barely eke out a living. It ignores the fact, for instance, that the record remittances which makes economic figures so rosy have a heavy social toll in terms of broken families. The booming mining industry which the government touts? That has environmental costs, too, which should count for something when you're calculating economic balance."[4]

Figure 1.1. Percentage Change in Labor Force Projections, 2005–2030

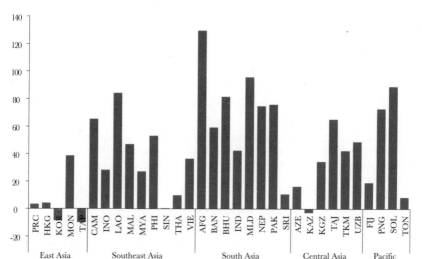

Source: Felipe and Hasan (2006, Table 2.1).

---

[4]   Herrera, Ernesto. 2008. More Than Common Economic Indicators. *The Manila Times.* 18 March.

2

What Is the Main Constraint
that Developing Countries Face?

If the maximum capacity of equipment is inadequate to absorb the available labour, as will be the case in backward countries, the immediate achievement of full employment is clearly hopeless.

—Micha Kalecki (1944, 43)

The fundamental problem of most developing countries is the unemployment and underemployment of an important segment of the labor force. The cause of this problem is the shortage of capital equipment and productive capacity, the latter understood as potential production (Box 2.1).[1] This view is very much consistent with the analyses of the classical authors and with the modern treatment in terms of growth diagnostics of Hausmann, Rodrik, and Velasco (2005). See Box 2.2.

Suppose the quantities produced of two goods x and y might be represented by point p in Figure 2.1, inside the curve. In this case, some of the

---

[1] I will not discuss (at least in detail) classical unemployment, i.e., unemployment resulting from wage rigidity, as I do not believe this is the main cause of unemployment and underemployment in most developing countries (Felipe and Hasan 2006, chapter 3). Even in developed countries, consultants and business insiders from the McKinsey Global Institute (cited by Solow [1997]) do not classify labor-market rigidities as an important causal factor in the failure of six industries (automobiles, house building, telecommunications, retail trade, consumer banking, and computer software) in France and Germany to create more jobs. Lewis (2004), founding director of the McKinsey Global Institute, makes the same point. And neither will I discuss what could be referred to as Schumpeterian unemployment, derived from sluggish innovation. Surely developing countries do not invest in research and development and the level of scientific education is very low. But these are not the ultimate causes of unemployment and underemployment in these countries.

Figure 2.1. Economy with Underutilized Resources

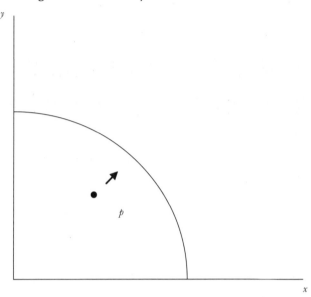

Source: Author.

Box 2.1. The Production Possibility Frontier

Economic growth, as it occurs in practice, is an intricate process. To understand this, we must start with the notion of a *country's productive capacity*. This is the maximum amount of goods and services that can be produced with the existing factors at the prevailing state of technology. This implies that the output of any particular commodity that the country can produce with the available resources can be increased only by reducing the output of other goods. Economists represent this trade-off through what is called the country's *transformation curve*, or *production possibility frontier*, by referring to two commodities. Thus, the country's transformation curve represents the maximum quantity of one commodity (e.g., x) that can be produced for a given quantity of the other (e.g., y). Figure 2.1 shows this curve. It illustrates the supply of these two goods by showing the combinations that can be produced with the economy's resources. The transformation curve shows all possible combinations. While combinations inside the curve are possible, combinations outside the curve cannot be produced because not enough resources are available.[a]

[a] The transformation curve is concave because goods x and y use inputs in different proportions.

Source: Author.

Box 2.2. The Growth Diagnostics Methodology

During the late 1980s, international institutions started recommending to developing countries a reform package that became known as the Washington Consensus. The reform package was based on three key concepts, namely, "stabilization," "liberalization," and "privatization," and included fiscal discipline, reorientation of public expenditures, tax reform, financial liberalization, unified and competitive exchange rates, trade liberalization, openness to foreign direct investment, privatization, deregulation, and secure property rights. However, toward the end of the 1990s, it became clear that the reform package advocated by the Washington Consensus could not work without being supplemented by a solid governance and institutional foundation. Then, the initial reform list advocated by supporters of the consensus was augmented with a series of so-called second-generation reforms that emphasized institutions and governance. The augmented Washington Consensus reform package did not work either, as countries that adopted and implemented comprehensive reform packages reaped small benefits. In recent years, economists have observed that countries that implemented well-focused reforms in key areas accelerated growth. The People's Republic of China, India, and Viet Nam are good examples.

In a recent paper, Hausmann, Rodrik, and Velasco (2005) advocate a new methodology to study what constrains growth. It departs significantly from traditional approaches and is known as the "growth diagnostics approach." It provides a framework for formulating hypotheses on what may constrain a country's growth. This approach views economic growth as the result of optimization under constraints, and seeks to identify the most binding constraints (whose removal would allow a growth spurt) by estimating shadow prices—a higher shadow price reflects scarcity of the resource, indicating that the resource constrains growth. Hausmann, Rodrik, and Velasco (2005) propose a decision tree where low levels of private investment and entrepreneurship are seen as the key problem. The tree takes researchers through different branches to determine the root causes of the problem, i.e., the binding constraints to economic growth. At the very top of the decision tree is the question of whether private investment is held back by lack of access to finance (i.e., there are many projects but entrepreneurs cannot finance them at reasonable cost) or by low returns (i.e., there is plenty of credit but entrepreneurs do not find profitable investments). The two constraints have different implications. Rodrik and Subramanian (2008) indicate that investment in many economies is constrained by low returns and not by access to finance due to high cost. In these economies, external finance does not help (as, in these economies, credit is available), so the effect of capital inflows is to boost consumption, while investment is unaffected.

available resources are clearly not fully utilized (e.g., people are unemployed). Under these circumstances, growth requires higher utilization of the country's production capacity. The country has to try to get closer to the transformation curve. This is the typical problem that most developing countries suffer from.

This does not mean that developing countries do not suffer from inadequacy of effective demand or from allocative efficiency problems.[2] Indeed they do. The problem of markets—that, because of their small internal demand, there will be no outlet for the products of the newly built factories—may limit developing countries' growth rate. Hence, industrialization will prove impossible unless it is oriented toward external markets (even though this problem could potentially be solved if investment were sufficiently high, as this would generate demand for consumption goods).[3] Likewise, effective demand problems can become the binding constraint on production in developing countries at a fairly advanced stage of industrialization (e.g., Malaysia, Thailand, the People's Republic of China) as they can be "balance-of-payments constrained" (McCombie and Thirlwall [1994]; also see section on *Export-Led Growth and the Balance-of-Payments Constraint* in chapter 16 of this book).[4]

Allocative efficiency problems are also present in developing countries. The combination of goods and services being produced in developing countries is often not the one that maximizes the value of output at the prevailing prices. In Figure 2.2, *p'* is on the transformation curve. The

---

[2] Certainly developing countries do have many other candidates for fundamental problems. McCombie and Thirlwall (1994) discuss the importance of the balance-of-payments constraint. Easterly (2002) emphasizes lack of incentives and argues that good policy must provide the right economic incentives. Rajan and Zingales (2003) stress the importance of financial development. The literature is not short of candidates. However, I strongly believe that the starting point for analyzing developing economies should be their lack of productive capacity.

[3] For productive capacity to be fully utilized there must be sufficient effective demand. Classical (and neoclassical) economists considered this to be the case due to their belief in Say's Law (i.e., supply creates its own demand). Hence, they concluded that the level of production would correspond to productive capacity. The belief in Say's Law ultimately derives from the view that markets function efficiently and competitively so that the prices of all factors and goods speedily adjust to their equilibrium level at which demand equals supply. On these assumptions, all factors of production are fully utilized. Market forces allocate the resources available at any time optimally so that the total value of all goods and services produced in an economy is the maximum that can be attained.

[4] Even in these cases one must be careful not to confuse bottlenecks in some markets with a generalized problem of effective demand. If anything, the People's Republic of China, for example, still suffers from weak domestic demand, and while a few isolated bottlenecks are present in the economy, in general, plenty of inputs, mostly labor, are available to increase production.

Figure 2.2. Growth Due to Improvements in Allocative Efficiency

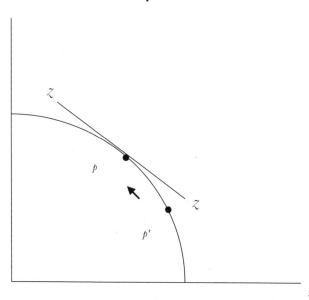

Source: Author.

problem is that the combination of goods and services produced may not be the optimal one, in the sense that it may not maximize the value of total output at the prevailing prices. The relative price of the two goods is shown by line ZZ. Point p is the combination of the two goods that maximizes the value of the goods at these prices. How will growth occur now? By moving from p' to p, i.e., by producing a different combination, even with constant productive capacity. Growth in this case is said to be due to improvements in allocative efficiency. This is a problem that affects mostly developed countries, and their efforts are directed toward eliminating this inefficiency, e.g., through reforms in product and factor markets. Growth, therefore, might occur, even at a constant productive capacity, by producing a different combination of goods and services (which, at the prevailing prices, would lead to a higher output).[5]

But while these problems are pervasive in most developing countries, they are not as important as the lack of productive capacity that prevents the fuller utilization of resources. Indeed, considering the national economy as a whole, the major obstacle to the development of many poor countries

---

[5] This was the problem of the former Soviet Union, namely, the lack of market signals guiding production decisions (and also because the budget was severely misallocated toward military expenditures).

in developing Asia is the shortage of productive capacity.[6] This is obvious in policy discussions in countries like India, Pakistan, or the Philippines, where there are constant references to the "low investment" problem. This constraint prevents the elimination of unemployment and underemployment, even when an increase in demand would make the expansion of output profitable.[7]

Developed economies, and a number of semi-industrialized economies, possess adequate capital equipment for the existing labor force. This allows them to generate high labor productivity and, consequently, a high income per capita, provided capital is fully and productively utilized.[8] The problem in many developing countries is different. Their capital equipment, however small, may be underutilized. The problem is that even if equipment were fully utilized, it would not be capable of absorbing the available labor force, leading to low capital–labor ratios. In other words, the problem of many developing countries is the *deficiency* of productive capacity rather than the *anomaly* of its underutilization (Kalecki 1966a). Hence, most developing countries are often below full employment. Most likely, the poorer the country, the more important the problem of lack of productive capacity will be; while the more advanced the country, the more important the problem of lack of effective demand will be. From this point of view, the objective of development is to increase productive capacity, and economic development may be described as a generalized process of capital accumulation-*cum*-structural change.

There is a third possibility to grow in the production possibility frontier framework. This would be an outward shift in the transformation curve. Many growth theories (e.g., the neoclassical model) have concentrated on growth explanations of this type. These theories assume that the countries allocate their available resources efficiently. The problem, therefore, is how

---

[6]   In *The General Theory*, Keynes (1936) was certainly thinking of the developed countries (e.g., England) and yet he argued: "I see no reason to suppose that the existing system seriously misemploys the factors of production which are in use. There are, of course, errors of foresight.... When 9,000,000 are employed out of 10,000,000 . . . there is no evidence that the labour of these 9,000,000 is misdirected . . . The complaint against the present system [is that] tasks should be available for the remaining 1,000,000 men. It is in determining the *volume*, not the *direction*, of actual employment that the existing system has broken down" (Keynes [1936, 379]; italics added).

[7]   It is important to note, however, that increasing productive capacity does not guarantee full employment. See chapter 4 in this book.

[8]   One could visualize this chain through the following two identities for income per capita (Y/P) and labor productivity (Y/L) : (i) $(Y/L) = (Y/K) \times (K/K^*) \times (K^*/L)$, where (Y/K) is capital productivity measured in terms of the actual or utilized level of capital (K), (K/K^*), denotes the level of utilization of the existing capital $(K^*$ is the trend of the capital stock), and (K^*/L) is the trend of the capital-labor ratio; and (ii) $(Y/P) = (Y/L) \times (L/P)$, where (L/P) is the employment–population ratio.

to expand the frontier. The truth is that whether productive capacity is fully utilized or not, for economic growth to be sustained over a long period, productive capacity must be expanded. This will result from a dynamic interaction between capital accumulation and technological progress.

The analysis in the previous paragraphs implies that the objective of public policy in developing countries should be to increase productive capacity to attain the full employment (defined as a situation such that no one who is ready and willing to work for an appropriate wage is without a job; chapter 3) of the labor force. Full employment must be the basic measure of a socially just economic policy. This is not an easy objective and it will be discussed in detail. But it will be very difficult (and even almost pointless) for a government that does not place this objective at the top of its agenda and that does not aim at achieving it, to set ambitious objectives for reducing inequality and poverty, and for achieving inclusive growth. What this means is that a society must achieve a "steady expansion of the economy and therewith a steady and reliable increase in the number of workers employed" (Galbraith 1996, 33). This is even more compelling in developing countries, because the ultimate cause of lack of inclusive growth is the nonexistence of adequate employment opportunities (Felipe and Hasan 2006, chapter 1). Therefore, unless governments make full employment their priority, much of their efforts to make growth inclusive will be futile.

A useful framework to conceptualize these arguments is through Boyer's (2006) adaptation to the analysis of factors limiting employment creation of Hausmann, Rodrik, and Velasco's (2005) growth diagnostics approach. This is shown in Figure 2.3. Unemployment is Keynesian if the limiting factor is effective demand; classical if the problem is one of wage-productivity discrepancy; and Marxist if the scarcity of productive capacity is the cause of low employment. The root cause is obviously not the same in all countries. That is why the framework in this tree diagram is useful. For example, unemployment may be related to an overvaluation of the domestic currency; or to an excessively high interest rate. In these cases, wage flexibility may not lead to employment creation as it is not the relevant constraint. The argument underlying the chapter (and the rest of the book) is that, very often, the main cause preventing employment creation in developing countries lies in the third explanation, i.e., insufficient productive capacity, combined with lack of effective demand in some cases.[9]

---

[9]   The reader will note that at times I draw upon Keynesian arguments, i.e., lack of demand, to explain unemployment. This may be due to, for example, an inadequate policy mix or to high uncertainty. As I noted above, lack of effective demand can certainly be a constraint in developing countries.

Figure 2.3. What are the Factors Limiting Employment?

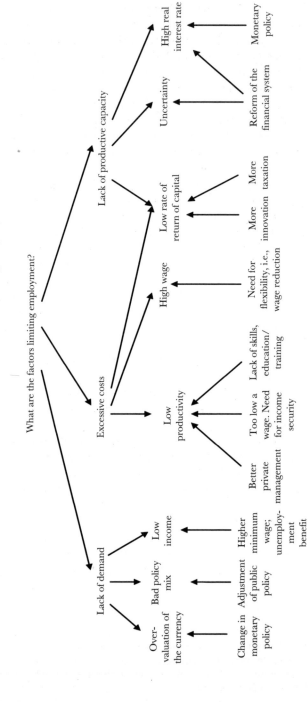

Source: Boyer 2006, Figure 9.

I do not want to close this chapter without a word of caution. The role of investment in development is neither well understood nor even agreed upon by economists. While the proposition that investment is key for growth seems obvious, the empirical evidence is not conclusive. For example, Easterly (2002, 39–42) and Oulton and O'Mahony (1994) claim that capital does not play any special role;[10] while Prichett (2003a, 217–221), claims that, "except for the causality issue, the role of physical investment in growth is well understood" (2003, 217). On the issue of causality, Blomstrom et al. (1996) used causality tests and found that a faster growth rate of GDP causes a higher investment–output ratio and not vice versa. If this is true, the implication is that investment is not a key determining exogenous variable in the growth process. Once growth is underway, the resulting profits will cause the investment rate to increase in a Keynesian fashion. As Kaldor (1970) pointed out, Henry Ford did not build up his automobile business from high initial savings, but from the profits his factory generated. Moreover, as argued by Hausmann, Rodrik, and Velasco (2005), investment matters for purposes of *igniting* growth. However, if the country's objective is *sustaining* growth, then the problem is one of developing institutions. Felipe and Usui (2008) elaborate on the issue and show that, historically, higher growth has been possible without a high investment share; and that a high investment share does not lead in all cases to a higher growth.

Finally, Lewis (2004) criticizes the view that capital accumulation is the key to growth and development, as well as the public debate around the prescription that what poor countries need is more capital. He makes two crucial points: (i) capital *does not* automatically increase labor productivity, and (ii) what capital *does* is to increase the capacity for long-run growth. This means that developing countries could increase their performance dramatically without any significant increase in capital. To become rich, however, they need additional capital. The problem in most developing countries lies in the efficiency with which the existing capital is used. To see this, one can think of the role of capital accumulation in a

---

[10] Easterly (2002, chapter 2) warns against "aid for investment" as a development strategy that has failed and questions (on empirical grounds) the investment–growth connection. His warning should be kept in mind. This does not mean, however, that investment does not matter. The point is that many other things matter too. One should also be careful about making estimates of investment requirements to achieve a growth rate and using these as the basis for pushing investment (and foreign assistance). He concludes: "Rather than worrying about how much investment is 'needed' to sustain a given growth rate, we should concentrate on strengthening incentives to invest in the future and let the various forms of investment play out how they may" (Easterly 2002, 42). My emphasis is on the role that investment plays for long-run growth and as a mechanism to achieve full employment.

growth-accounting exercise. The growth rate of the capital stock can be written as the product of the investment share and capital productivity.[11] This means that capital accumulation depends on two factors: one is the amount of investment (as a share of output), and the other one is the productivity with which capital is used. While Hausmann, Rodrik, and Velasco (2005) would argue that developing countries need higher investment, Lewis's point is that their performance could improve substantially through an increase in capital productivity. Moreover, Lewis insists that "improving the rules and regulations governing competition would improve not only labor productivity *but also capital productivity*" (2004, 251; emphasis added).[12] Naturally, in the long run, and to become a rich country, developing countries with spare labor capability (i.e., labor surplus) need to build offices and manufacturing plants where these workers can work. That is, countries need to increase the capacity to produce goods and services. Lewis remarks: "Of course, the total capital required to increase capacity depends on the efficiency with which the capital is employed" (Lewis 2004, 250). Therefore, Lewis seems to reverse the role of capital in development vis-à-vis Hausmann, Rodrik, and Velasco (2005): in the short run, developing countries do not need more capital; what they need is to use more efficiently the capital they have. To achieve this, reforms of the rules and regulations governing competition are the key. It is in the long run, on the other hand, that developing countries will need more capital. I will return to the question of investment in chapter 6.

---

[11]   Algebraically: $\hat{K} = (\Delta K / K) = (I / K) = (I / Y) \times (Y / K)$, where $\hat{K}$ is the capital stock, (I / Y) is the investment share and (Y / K) denotes capital productivity.

[12]   In chapter 6, I shall argue that the empirical evidence shows that capital productivity tends to decline as countries develop.

3

Why Full Employment and Who Should Be Responsible for Trying to Achieve It?

For conservatives who believe that the unemployed have chosen not to work, the mystery of the unemployed's profound unhappiness is a matter for psychologists more than economists.

—Joseph Stiglitz et al. (2006, 42)

F ull employment is a widely used term, although often different people mean different things. There are two important issues to consider. The first one concerns the resource the term refers to. In my discussion, full employment refers to labor. Underutilization of plant and equipment is not the problem that developing countries face, as noted above. The second issue regards the level to which "full" refers to. During the last three decades, the term "full employment," as used in orthodox circles, refers to the nonaccelerating inflation rate of unemployment (NAIRU), one of the most powerful notions in economic policy since the 1970s. This is the level of unemployment that is associated with price stability, even if many workers ready and willing to work are unemployed. The basic proposition underlying the NAIRU is that policy makers cannot use deficit spending or an increase in the money supply to reduce unemployment below some "equilibrium" rate, except at the cost of accelerating inflation. This is an important departure from the Keynesian view that inflation poses a problem only when the economy approaches full employment.[1]

---

[1] To be precise, the NAIRU is that level of unemployment where the labor market is said to be in equilibrium. This occurs at the so-called natural rate of unemployment. Here, actual and expected rates of inflation are equal (i.e., inflation is fully anticipated). At this point (i.e., the natural rate of unemployment), the Phillips curve is vertical, with no long-run trade-off between unemployment and wage inflation. In the NAIRU view, the Phillips curve is only a short-run relationship. Models of inflation targeting, for example,

Full employment in the framework of the NAIRU obviously places fighting inflation (as a macroeconomic objective) above combating unemployment. Indeed, the view that price stability requires maintaining a pool of unemployed means that the fiscal and monetary brakes have to be slammed as soon as economic growth causes unemployment to drop below a certain level. Many policy makers and politicians also seem to have accepted this concept and hold the view that there is a natural rate of unemployment that is invariant to aggregate spending.[2] They argue that this natural rate can be reduced only through supply-side measures: deregulation, privatization, and welfare reforms (e.g., cutting the minimum wage, eliminating unemployment benefits), or upgrading the skills of workers. For those who view the economy through this lens, supply-side measures are the only way to reduce unemployment. Moreover, when this is close to the NAIRU, the monetary authorities must take prompt anti-inflationary measures to prevent the economy from overheating, otherwise inflation will not only grow but will also accelerate (I will take up these issues again in chapters 11 and 12). However, low unemployment might also lead in some situations to low inflation (Eisner 1995). Indeed, low unemployment is most likely associated with a more efficient use of resources. Increases in wages derived from low unemployment may encourage the substitution of capital for labor and raise anticipated future productivity, which would lower inflation. With profits high, firms may decide to keep prices low to prevent others from entering the market.

Full employment in my discussion, on the other hand, refers to zero involuntary unemployment. It means that no one who is ready and willing to work for an appropriate wage is without a job. This also means zero involuntary part-time employment, a type of underemployment pervasive across the developing world.[3] In developing countries, the latter aspect is very important, because underemployment is a much more serious problem than open unemployment. For this reason, the goal of full employment in developing countries is about reducing underemployment as well as reducing unemployment (Felipe and Hasan 2006, chapter 1). Felipe and Hasan (2006, chapter 1) distinguish four types of underemployment: (i) working limited

---

associate full employment with the NAIRU. For a succinct (critical) review of the theory underlying the NAIRU, see Espinosa-Vega and Russell (1997).

2   Even in developing countries with unemployment and very high underemployment, some economists and policy makers use the NAIRU theory.

3   Ideally, I am thinking of full employment à la Beveridge (1944), that is, full employment holds when there are at least as many unfilled job openings as there are unemployed individuals seeking work. Society's responsibility is to create more positions than job seekers, so that firms do the search for workers, not the other way around. Certainly this is very unrealistic given the conditions in developing countries. I use this idea simply as a target.

hours; (ii) high-skilled workers being forced to take up low-paying jobs; (iii) overstaffing; and (iv) workers carrying out their work with very little capital. Therefore, the objective of full employment must be complemented with that of generating *productive* employment.[4]

Likewise, the objective of policy making must also be to generate *decent* employment (i.e., employment that provides living wages, benefits, reasonable job security, and a healthy work environment).

The point of departure of my arguments is that the free-market institutional system does not guarantee full employment in a developing country. Traditional neoclassical theory puts forward an explanation of how, under certain conditions, a market economy will tend toward full employment through the workings of the price mechanism. However, the assumptions necessary to derive this result do not hold, and therefore this theory is not too useful. As Keynes (1936) showed, even with flexible wages an economy has a tendency toward unemployment (especially if there is a declining demand), because a given level of employment short of full employment may be the most profitable for entrepreneurs. To show this, he demolished the classical notion of "supply curve of labor" and of an aggregate labor market, and showed that an excess of unemployment could not be expected to drive down real wages.[5] Keynes showed that even with high unemployment, the employed workers would resist reduction of their nominal wages; and even in case this opposition failed, the subsequent reduction in nominal wages would bring down prices, leaving real wages unchanged.[6] Contrary to theories with classical roots, where employment is determined by wage bargaining between workers and employers, Keynes argued that it is determined by the existing effective demand, which depends on the propensity to consume and on the rate of capital expansion. The analysis of the "labor market" as if it behaved like the market for oranges is fallacious. For

---

[4] Naturally, the question to consider here is the meaning of productive. Is flipping hamburgers (a job created by the private sector) more productive than cleaning streets or taking care of the elderly (jobs created by the public sector)? Does productivity (simply) reflect the technical conditions of production, as in neoclassical economics (a low wage is the reflection of a low marginal productivity), or is it socially determined?

[5] Keynes argued that labor supply and demand cannot be modeled in terms of the real wage, for workers care about relative wages as well as real wages. This introduces an asymmetry between nominal wage cuts and nominal price increases. Moreover, workers cannot negotiate their own real wages, because money wages and price level are interdependent. These two objections undermine the notion of the labor supply curve.

[6] Felipe and McCombie (2008a, 2008b) show that empirical estimations of the neoclassical "labor demand curve," that is, the (inverse) relationship between the level of employment and the wage rate (used to show since the 1930s that both variables are indeed inversely related) are driven by an accounting identity that forces such inverse relationship. This invalidates the standard interpretation of the labor demand curve and, in particular, renders empirical estimates pointless for policy.

this reason, Galbraith (1997, 15) speaks of a "job structure," that is, "a historically, socially, and politically specific set of status and pay relationships in the economy, within and between firms and across industries." The elements of a job structure are much more complex than the simple supply-and-demand characterization of textbook analyses. Wages are not determined by the workings of supply and demand, but by a complex process of comparisons within and across occupations and industries, as well as the qualifications of the worker. Once the notions of supply and demand of labor (as in the market for oranges) are questioned, the idea of the NAIRU crumbles. Aggregate employment is determined not by the supply and demand for labor, but by aggregate demand for output.

Even if full employment could never be achieved due to the failure of the market mechanism to attain it (or for the reasons discussed later in chapters 6 and 13), this should not be a justification not to pursue it by other means, e.g., government involvement and commitment to it. Only during a boom does capitalism come close to full employment. Therefore, the right remedy for the business cycle is to be found, in Keynes's view, in "abolishing slumps and thus keeping us permanently in a quasi-boom" (1936, 322).[7]

Before I move on to the justification for full employment, let me make two digressions. The first is that inclusive growth is obviously related to inequality. In this sense, inclusive growth essentially means broad-based, or equitable, growth, which implies rising living standards for all socioeconomic levels.[8] A widespread perception holds that the more unequal the distribution of income, the more dysfunctional a society becomes, and the worse its prospects for growth and development in general. Therefore, as *excessive inequality* is inherently damaging, society will need to take care of those groups that are left behind.[9] Judging by optimality, if the incomes of some segments of the population accelerate without the rest of the population being worse off, overall welfare would be enhanced. However, this is not acceptable socially and morally

---

[7] It is often argued that Keynesian economics has little to offer to developing countries in terms of economic policy. This is utterly incorrect. See Thirlwall (1987, 2007).

[8] For an excellent introduction and review of income distribution in Asia, see Fields (1995). Harberger (1998) argues that "good" economic policies produce long-term benefits for all or nearly all segments of society. Hence, attaching the qualifier "equitable" to growth does not add anything. I do have some disagreements with this view, especially because Harberger defines "good" economic policies as those that promote the efficient operation of the economy (1998, 203). I have already expressed my view that the world is such that markets do not operate efficiently. Unemployment and inequalities are a fact of life. Moreover, I do not believe they can be eradicated by pursuing policies that seek the efficient operation of the economy. For this reason, I believe that governments must promote equity (see Stiglitz 1998).

[9] The point at which inequality becomes, technically speaking, "excessive" is difficult to determine. Rather, this is something that is perceived by the different groups of society. On this, see Asian Development Bank (2007a), in particular section 2.

(Sen 1999). In chapter 24 of *The General Theory*, Keynes (1936, 374) argued as follows: "I believe that there is social and psychological justification for significant inequalities of incomes and wealth, but not for such large disparities as exist to-day." Keynes believed that some activities justify the accumulation of wealth. But he clearly argued that "it is not necessary for the stimulation of these activities and the satisfaction of these proclivities that the game should be played for such high stakes as at the present" (1936, 374).

I believe that neither human nature nor the market system is consistent with equality, and that development is inherently not egalitarian. People have different commitments to excelling in the business of making money. This should be acknowledged. And capitalism as an economic system rewards, or so the argument goes, according to one's contribution to the product (the marginal theory of factor pricing). Hence, this need not be *unfair*. However, it can lead to a highly unequal and socially adverse distribution of income, especially when one's talents are unclear or when compensation bears little relationship to the contribution to the product. Excessive inequality can be neither accepted nor intellectually justified, much less be regarded as a "moral entitlement" (Galbraith 1996, 61).[10]

If inequality is a fact of life, the forces that drive the distribution of income must be understood to design an adequate policy on income distribution. Some individuals do work "harder" than others under the same set of opportunities and they should be rewarded for that. But this is not the main reason underlying the huge income inequalities pervasive in many societies.[11] For example, today, the modern corporate and financial world rewards a group of privileged people through astronomical salaries, stock options, and at times, illegal means, in a disproportionate manner. Are the high inequalities observed today across much of developing Asia (Asian Development Bank 2007a) the result of *individual effort* (Roemer 2006)? While Roemer's arguments do have weight and in some cases effort may be more important than *circumstances* in explaining inequality (although disentangling effort and circumstances is difficult), inequalities in many developing countries cannot be readily justified as the result of individual effort, much less supported with hard empirical evidence. Chief executive

---

[10] Akerlof (1982) argued that wage rates that are not a "fair" reflection of a firm's ability to pay will result in poor worker morale and, hence, lower productivity.

[11] Chapter X in Book I of the *Wealth of Nations* (Smith 1776) contains a discussion of "Inequalities arising from the nature of the employments themselves." Smith discusses five reasons: (i) "the agreeableness or disagreeableness of the employments themselves"; (ii) "the easiness and cheapness, or the difficulty and expence [*sic*] of learning them"; (iii) "the constancy or inconstancy of employment in them"; (iv) "the small or great trust which must be reposed in those who exercise them"; and (v) "the probability or improbability of success in them."

officers (CEOs) and highly educated knowledge workers belong to a narrow aristocracy. Are their high wages and other benefits exclusively the result of returns to education?[12] If this were the case, it would suggest that nobody is to blame for rising inequality, as this would be the result of demand and supply at work. The super-high paychecks of some CEOs (whose talent may be dubious) are then easily justified. The way to mitigate inequality would then be to improve the educational system. In my view, however, these inequalities, supposedly the result of individual effort,[13] are more the consequence of power relations than of market forces.[14]

The second digression is that diametrically different views about the world, namely, those of Karl Marx and Milton Friedman, come to the same conclusion: unemployment is functional to a market (capitalist) economy, the result of class struggle over the distribution of income, and political power (Pollin 1998). Marx called unemployment the *reserve army*, while Friedman (1968) called it the *natural rate*. Both held that high unemployment in capitalist economies occurs when workers have the capacity to use their bargaining power.[15] The difference in their theories lies in how they reached the same conclusion: Friedman (and other orthodox economists) argued that workers demand more than they deserve, while for Marx capitalists use unemployment as a weapon to prevent workers from getting their fair share.[16]

---

[12] Dew-Becker and Gordon (2005) have argued that the biggest cause of increased wage inequality in the US has not been a rise in returns to education and skills, but the result of increased payments to superstars such as baseball players and out-of-control pay raises for chief executives. Think also of how lucky some workers in India are as a result of outsourcing from developed countries, which has automatically increased their salaries.

[13] I do believe, on the other hand, in the individual effort and talent of opera singers such as Placido Domingo or Luciano Pavarotti. The latter died on 6 September 2007.

[14] For this reason, Galbraith (1996, 63–65) proposes some basic policies to address income inequality: (i) a support system for the poor; (ii) the need to deal with the tendencies of the financial world, e.g., insider trading, speculative behavior; (ii) the need for stockholder and informed public criticism to address the personal income maximization of corporate management; (iv) the removal of tax concessions to the affluent should they exist; and (v) a progressive income tax.

[15] Eisner (1997) noted that, "I have only half jokingly accused [financial and business circles] of being closet Marxists, wedded to the notion that a 'reserve army' of unemployed is necessary for a private-profit economy to function successfully . . . economists over the last several decades have most unfortunately offered modern rationalizations in seemingly rigorous theory of this old bit of Marxian dogma. The seeds were planted in the enshrinement of the old Phillips curve."

[16] Galbraith has argued that, "Unemployment has, in fact, some socially and economically attractive effects: services are well staffed by eager workers forced thereto by the lack of other job opportunity; employed workers, fearing unemployment, may well be more cooperative, even docile, as may their unions. And even more significantly, for most citizens, including those with influential political voice, joblessness is not a threat" (1996, 45).

But both Marx and Friedman thought that full employment was not attainable.[17]

Unfortunately, the goal of creating a full-employment economy has been abandoned by most central banks of developed countries, national governments, and international organizations (with the exception of the International Labour Organization), although all of them talk today about the seriousness of the unemployment–underemployment problem.[18] Why have policy makers abandoned this goal? Between World War II and the early 1970s, the so-called Golden Age of Capitalism, governments and central banks in most advanced Western nations were committed (in different forms and degrees) to this goal, and most central banks were integrated into their governments' macroeconomic policy apparatus. They manipulated their spending levels (fiscal policy) and could adjust interest rates and the availability of credit (monetary policy) to maintain a level of aggregate demand close to full employment. This period featured a tactical accord between the social classes, in which progressive taxation financed an expanding welfare state and a set of social rights, which in turn translated into a relatively low degree of social confrontation.[19] During much of this

---

[17] Reminiscent of Marx's ideas concerning the reserve army of labor, Shapiro and Stiglitz (1984) developed a shirking model that stresses the difficulties of monitoring workers' on-the-job effort to explain the persistence of involuntary unemployment. In essence, if firms pay more than the going wage, workers will work harder because the cost of being fired for shirking increases. When all firms do this, increased wage levels result in unemployment. On the other hand, employers will not reduce wages to the market clearing level because this will result in lower work effort. Shapiro and Stiglitz conclude that persistent unemployment may actually be required in a market economy as a "worker discipline device". However, their argument is not identical to Marx's. Marx argued that the reserve army is the result of rising labor intensity via mechanization. This exerts downward pressure on the wage rate. However, in Shapiro's and Stiglitz's model, unemployment is supposedly generated by the firm's need to raise wage rates above the market clearing level in order to induce workers not to shirk.

[18] Ironically, one of the roles envisaged for the International Monetary Fund (IMF) in 1944, when it was set up, was to help finance the external gap (i.e., trade deficit) when the market does not close it, so as to guarantee that full-employment policies can be pursued. Developing countries do not have an open commitment to full employment. At most, they acknowledge the employment problem. As an example, Felipe and Hasan (2006, 497, endnote 44) indicate that the main objective of the Central Bank of the Philippines, as stated by the central bank itself, is to ensure price stability. Objectives such as balanced and sustained growth and employment are secondary to the main objective. And these other objectives do not have quantified targets.

[19] In the context of the 1930s and 1940s in Europe, Kalecki (1943) argued that the unemployment problem had two solutions. One was the authoritarian solution in the form of fascism, which replaces the discipline of unemployment by the direct repression of the working class by force. The other was the democratic solution (which he favored), in which trade unions cooperate with employers in return for income redistribution and other egalitarian measures. This type of cooperation became widespread in Northern

period, wages increased hand in hand with productivity, and full employment and expanding social benefits gave workers the upper hand in wage bargaining, while the rapid pace of investment in new technologies kept inflation in check. Governments were willing to maintain levels of aggregate demand that would create enough jobs to meet the preferences of the labor force. In the late 1960s, this state of affairs started to change and, in the mid-1970s, the failure of the Organisation for Economic Co-operation and Development (OECD) economies to contain inflation following the oil shocks led to the downfall of full employment as an objective, as governments became convinced that low unemployment and low inflation were incompatible. As a consequence, intellectual support for these policies vanished and opposition arose to the use of budget deficits to maintain full employment. Friedman's notion of the natural rate of unemployment was instrumental in this change of focus. The result was a battle that led to the victory over inflation, but at the cost of sluggish growth, high unemployment, and increased income inequality in many parts of the world.

Despite this state of affairs, I believe that several powerful reasons exist today to argue the case for full employment, if key institutions in developing countries, as well as multilateral lending institutions, are serious about reducing poverty, making growth inclusive, and achieving the Millennium Development Goals. First and foremost, an economy running at full employment creates high overall purchasing or spending power. This leads to more buoyant markets, businesses, investment, and employment. "These promote the social cohesion and economic progress that make democratic mixed capitalism such a wonderful system when it works well" (Blinder 1988). A full-employment economy will provide everyone with opportunities. Second, an economy operating at full employment can deliver great individual and social benefits. Unemployment and underemployment cause not only direct economic costs (e.g., loss of potential output and income, lower tax revenues due to a lower tax base, deterioration of labor skills and productivity) but also social costs such as poverty, misery, malnutrition, and injustice (Rawls 1971; Sen 1999). Persistent unemployment and underemployment lead to social exclusion and violate basic concepts of membership and citizenship, and thus they do not allow inclusive growth. Third, employment is a right, and full employment as an objective of economic policy is found in the International Covenant on Economic, Social and Cultural Rights; the International Covenant on Civil and Political Rights; the International Labour Organization

---

Europe after World War II. Sweden, for example, implemented policies that kept the economy close to full employment with low inflation and provided decent wages between 1951 and 2000. The key to its success was the development of a system based on cooperation among different groups. In the absence of this cooperation, employers and the financial sector will turn against full-employment policies.

Conventions; the Charter of the United Nations (article 55 and 56); and the United Nations' Universal Declaration of Human Rights (article 23). In the United States (US), *high* employment is a mandate of the Federal Reserve. The Humphrey–Hawkins Full Employment and Balanced Growth Act of 1978 lists high employment, balanced growth, and price stability as specific policy goals.[20] Fourth, since 2006, decent work is a target of the first Millennium Development Goal, namely, to eradicate extreme poverty and hunger. Fifth, full employment in the developing world contributes to political stability, as the levels of consumption of large segments of the population will be higher than when unemployment is widespread. Moreover, peace and prosperity in the developed world also depend on the well-being of the people in the developing world. And lastly, full employment should be an ethical imperative in today's world. The benefits of full employment outweigh the costs of its achievement. It benefits everyone, including (contrary to Marx) capitalists. These may end up getting a smaller share (in percentage) of the pie, but the size of the pie will be growing possibly faster than with significant levels of unemployment. Therefore, it is more rational to argue that developing countries cannot afford unemployment and underemployment, than to suppose that they cannot afford full employment. In the words of Paul Krugman (1999, 15): "An unsold commodity is a nuisance, an unemployed worker a tragedy; it is terribly unjust that such tragedies are created every day by new technologies, changing tastes, and the ever-shifting flows of world trade." Expressing a similar sentiment, Alan Blinder (1987, 33) stated that "high unemployment represents a waste of resources so colossal that no one truly interested in efficiency can be complacent about it. It is both ironic and tragic that, in searching out ways to improve economic efficiency, we seem to have ignored the biggest inefficiency of them all." For this reason, full employment must be the natural point of reference for economic policy and for evaluating a government's performance.[21]

---

[20] The Employment Act of 1946 commits the US to the goal of "maximum employment, production and purchasing power." Most likely, although the term was not used, it meant "full employment." The Humphrey–Hawkins Act refers, on the other hand, to "high" employment, not to "full." In practice, the US government has never adopted policies that guarantee the latter outcome. Rather, it has adopted a variety of "supply-side" policies and some "demand-side" policies in the hope that markets would operate at a sufficiently high level to ensure high employment. Since the market has not done this, the government has been forced to supplement these policies with various "welfare" programs.

[21] The former Soviet Republics of Central Asia present a peculiar case. After the break-up of the Soviet Union, most of these republics went into recession and their industrial sectors collapsed, causing massive unemployment. One way to cope with it was a shift of many industrial workers to agriculture and services. The experience of these countries cannot be taken as evidence that the pursuit of full employment is the wrong policy. The pursuit of full employment was not what caused their collapse.

Finally, if full—as well as productive and decent—employment is a desirable state of the economy (so that it must be the basic measure of a just society, and *the* goal of economic policy), we have to ask, who should be responsible for achieving it and for keeping the economy as close as possible to it? Unemployment and underemployment may be the result of skills mismatch or of particular problems with the individuals who are unemployed. Today, this is a widely held view of the cause of unemployment and underemployment. Policies to solve them target directly those affected through, for example, training (chapter 17). But if the problem is job shortage because the economy does not generate employment for all those in the labor force and willing to work, i.e., a systemic failure of the aggregate economy to create enough jobs, then training will not do much. In a market economy, the private sector must be the generator of wealth and employment. To do this, the private sector must operate in an enabling environment, which the government must provide. However, this role of the private sector is compatible with the existence of significant involuntary unemployment and underemployment. Who is, therefore, ultimately responsible for the achievement of full, productive, and decent employment? *Unfortunately*, society makes the government responsible. The reality is that if at the end of the year unemployment has increased in a country, the government, not the private sector, is blamed for it.[22] And indeed, many governments make promises about reductions in unemployment and creation of employment during election campaigns (while they do not create these jobs). For these reasons, the private and public sectors must coordinate their actions and understand each other's role in employment generation (and the elimination of unemployment). I will take up this issue again in chapter 6 in the discussion of the role of investment; in chapter 12 in the discussion of the role of fiscal policy; and in chapter 14 in the analysis of the public sector as employer of last resort.[23]

Developing Asia's Employment Record

As noted in chapter 1, many countries across developing Asia are not generating enough employment in the secondary sector to absorb the labor

---

[22]   In November 2008, the Big Three American car makers—Ford, General Motors, and Chrysler—asked the US government for help to deal with the recession. German car maker Opel also appealed to the German government.

[23]   Pollin (1998) tells the story of a visit to Bolivia in 1990. There, he was told that the country did not suffer from any employment problem: people begging, shining shoes, or hawking in the streets were indeed employed.

force (Felipe and Hasan 2006). Many of the new entrants into the labor market are being absorbed by low-productivity service activities. For example, Mehta et al. (2007) document that in 1991, about 14.4% of the total male nonagricultural employment in the Philippines consisted of male drivers. By 2004, this had increased to 17.5%. Also, in 1991, 10.3% of the total female nonagricultural employment in the Philippines consisted of household servants. By 2004, the figure was 11.6%.

Why have many countries failed to absorb employment in the course of capital-intensive industrialization? A first reason is the high rate of population growth in many developing countries, in contrast to today's developed countries. A second explanation lies in the industrialization strategies followed by some countries, including India (Kochhar et al. 2006). Although the intention was to promote industries that would maximize the absorption of labor (either by developing labor-intensive industries or by choosing the most labor-intensive techniques possible in each industry), Indian manufacturing development became fairly capital intensive through policies for capital deepening. Recent work by Basu and Mallick (2007) concludes that there has never been a trickle-down effect in India. This is the result of introducing labor-saving techniques that prevented growth from reducing poverty. When poverty fell during the 1970s and 1980s, it was the result of government anti-poverty measures, together with a more equitable distribution of credit and inputs to small and marginal farmers.

Third, for a large number of commodities, capital and labor cannot be readily substituted for each other in their production. Hence, the manufacturing technology does not vary much between industrial and developing countries. Fourth, the market price of factors of production in developing countries often fails to reflect relative abundance. This is due to distortions in the form of, for example, subsidies to capital, and to the encouragement of high wages in modern industries. The cheaper capital is made relative to labor, the more capital intensive the technique will be. Fifth, although money wages may be lower in developing countries, unit labor costs (efficiency wages), that is, the nominal wage rate divided by labor productivity, may differ little. In these circumstances, it is profitable to use a relatively capital-intensive technique.

Sixth, most developing countries find themselves today in a peculiar situation, namely, that old-fashioned, labor-intensive techniques would be advantageous for them given their labor abundance. However, these technologies do not exist today, because they are not produced any longer by the industrialized countries. Thus, the only technologies available to developing countries are, essentially, the same as those in developed countries (Felipe and Hasan 2006, chapter 3). However, these tend to be highly capital intensive (i.e., labor saving). Certainly, old technologies do exist in the form of secondhand equipment that can be purchased. But firms often do not buy old equipment because its maintenance requires spare parts that are not produced any longer, and because the technicians running the equipment in question will most likely know how to use only the most up-to-date methods. This argument relates to the thesis of the so-called *advantages of backwardness* (Gerschenkron 1962), the idea that latecomers do not have to develop new techniques at great cost. However, the contemporary developing countries suffer the disadvantage of having to use technologies developed by advanced countries, which are *inappropriate* for the developing countries' factor endowments. On the other hand, today's developed countries industrialized along much more labor-intensive lines. The trend during the last part of the 20th century and at the beginning of the 21st has been toward greater mechanization.

A final reason that explains the adoption of capital-intensive techniques by developing countries is that due to the shortage of skilled labor, and to prevent breakdowns, neglect of maintenance, and other problems that would decrease the productivity of capital, firms prefer operations that are "machine paced" as opposed to "operator paced" (Hirschman 1958); that is, given a shortage of skilled labor, a capital-intensive technology enables firms to economize on a scarce factor of production.

The result, in the words of Raj (1978, i), is that "there is little prospect (except in a few countries) that expansion of manufacturing industries and productive services will be high enough to absorb the growing labor force. There is therefore general recognition now that a large part of the additional employment opportunities needed has to be generated within agriculture itself, at any rate in the next one or two decades." Therefore, other developing Asian countries will find it rather difficult to emulate the successful economies of East and Southeast Asia, as the initial conditions that led to the industrialization of these economies during the 1970s and 1980s cannot be reproduced today. Moreover, the globalization that started in the 1990s sets a very different international scenario, with the possibility of a race to the bottom. The option being used by many firms in developing Asia is to link themselves to global value chains. These issues are discussed in chapter 15.

4

Why Is Growth *Unstable?*

One of the oldest unresolved dilemmas in economics is whether market economies are naturally stable, or whether they need to be stabilized by policy. Classical and neoclassical models argue that a market economy can look after itself and that, in the absence of egregious government interference, it would gravitate naturally to full employment, greater innovation, and higher growth rates. However, Keynes emphasized the flimsiness of the expectations on which economic activity in decentralized markets is based. While the dominant intellectual paradigm since the 1970s has adhered to the idea that a market economy gravitates toward full employment, the historical record shows that the regime of the 1950s and 1960s was more successful than what followed afterwards. Indeed, other than the exceptions of the People's Republic of China (PRC), and perhaps a few more developing countries recently (e.g., India, Viet Nam), economic growth was faster and much more stable in the Keynesian golden period; its fruits were more equitably distributed and social cohesion and moral habits better maintained.

Modern analysis of economic growth started with the so-called Harrod–Domar model (Harrod 1939, Domar 1946).[1] This model has Keynesian and classical (mostly Ricardian) features. It is important to understand this model because subsequent modern growth models provide different solutions to the so-called *Harrod–Domar knife-edge problem* (discussed below). Moreover, I believe that, despite being "old," it is still useful because it contains a fundamental feature of the experience of many developing countries, including those in developing Asia: the instability of growth. Indeed, a review of the world experience leads to the conclusion that growth is far from stable. For this reason, I consider this model an important thinking tool. Some may disagree with my view that the world experience at large is characterized by the instability of growth. For example, the United States (US), and in general the developed world, has had few downturns since 1979–1980, and these have been both short and shallow. Likewise, growth in the developing world has increased and African and Latin American

---

[1] The interested reader on Harrod's work can see the essays in Rampa et al. (1998).

economies are performing better. But the reality is that not all developing countries have done well. Indeed, episodes of high and sustained growth are not the norm across the developing world. Rather, these are concentrated in a few countries. Growth in many developing countries is characterized by boom–bust episodes. And crises continue affecting the developing countries (think of Mexico 1995, East Asia 1997, the Russian Federation 1998, Argentina 2001), and when these countries are hit, the effects tend to be severe.[2]

As I mentioned in chapter 2, for productive capacity to be fully utilized, sufficient effective demand must exist for the goods and services produced. Classical economists acknowledged this, but they believed in Say's law (i.e., supply creates its own demand, with the consequence that all that is produced is sold), and hence equated the actual level of production with the country's productive capacity. The belief in Say's law was, in turn, a consequence of the assumptions that markets work efficiently, especially factor markets, and that prices (wages) speedily adjust to their equilibrium levels at which demand equals supply. Certainly classical economists were aware that resources were not always fully utilized, especially labor, but unemployment was explained as a result of either frictions in the labor market, voluntary idleness, or wages failing to adjust to their equilibrium level, for example, due to trade union pressures.

One key feature of Keynesian economic theory is the distinction between decisions to save, made by the holders of wealth, and decisions to invest, made by entrepreneurs. Investment, in this context, refers to decisions to purchase new capital goods, while saving refers to decisions to refrain from consuming a portion of income. Entrepreneurs' decisions to invest can help determine the actual growth path of an economy. This implies that investment expenditures are independent, in the sense that they do not adjust passively to savings decisions.

In Keynesian analysis, the achievement of full employment equilibrium requires that a certain amount of net investment be undertaken to bring total effective demand to the level of full capacity utilization. Domar (1946) argued that investment plays two roles: (i) the total level of investment determines the total level of effective demand through the operation of the multiplier, and (ii) the new investment represents an addition to existing productive

---

[2] Writing these pages in 2007–2008 during the subprime market and housing crises in the US, it is difficult not to think that growth is unstable. This is the third major shake-up of the system in the last 10 years. The previous two were the Asian and Russian financial crises (1997–1998) and the US dot-com crisis (2001). All three were caused by irrational exuberance as well as regulatory failures in the finance sector. It is true though that at times and for significantly long periods, growth has been stable and steady (e.g., developed countries between the 1950s and the early 1970s; or the experience of East Asia between the 1960s and the 1990s).

capacity. Since there is no reason why these two effects should necessarily be compatible with the maintenance of full-capacity utilization, Domar therefore studied the conditions that the economy should satisfy in order that effective demand and productive capacity may expand at the same pace through time.[3] Note that if Say's law holds at all times, this will not be an issue because whatever the changes in aggregate supply brought about by investment, aggregate demand will always be equal to it. But if this assumption is rejected (one of Keynes's key points), demand will not necessarily keep pace with productive capacity.

In his seminal paper, Domar (1946) showed that to keep effective demand and productive capacity moving together in the long run, investment has to expand at the percentage rate given by the ratio of the savings rate (s) and the capital–output ratio (k), that is, $g = \frac{s}{k}$.[4] When this happens, net income, consumption, and the stock of capital will all grow at the same percentage rate given by the ratio of these two variables. Domar's condition is not a description of what it actually happens in the economy, but a condition that must be satisfied for productive capacity to be fully satisfied. The condition requires the constancy of the savings rate and of the capital–output ratio.[5]

Domar (1946) made no distinction between full utilization of productive capacity and full employment of the labor force (he assumed they coincide). While this can be defensible in the short run, it cannot be justified over the long run. This means that Domar's condition ($g = \frac{s}{k}$), although ensuring an equal growth of effective demand and of productive capacity, does not necessarily ensure maintenance of full employment of the labor force as time goes on. Harrod (1939) assumed that the labor force grows at the rate n and technical progress at the rate λ. Both are exogenously given. He defined the "*natural* rate of growth" (g_n) as the sum of the growth rate of labor and that of labor-augmenting technical progress, that is, $g_n = n + \lambda$.

---

[3] The basic results of the model were shown by Harrod (1939). He was the first to find what has become known as the "Harrod–Domar equation." Domar's (1946) model is an extension, but for our purposes, the extensions are not essential.

[4] This result derives from the solution of the model: new investments (I) have to expand through time according to the equation $I(t) = I(0)e^{(s/k)t}$, where s is the saving rate, k is the required capital–output ratio, and t is time (0 denotes the initial-period value of investment).

[5] This simple framework has been used extensively in the literature. Multilateral development institutions, for example, have used it to determine the required investment rate for a target growth rate (Easterly 2002, 28–29), i.e., $s = g\,k$; and statements like "given a capital–output ratio of 2.5, the achievement of a growth rate of 6% requires capital resources equivalent to 15% of GDP" have been made on countless occasions. This distorts the spirit of the model.

This represents the maximum sustainable rate of growth that technical conditions make available to the economic system as a whole, i.e., it defines the growth rate of productive capacity or the long-run full employment equilibrium growth rate. It also sets the upper limit to the growth rate that an economy can achieve in the long run. At that point, cumulative expansion in Harrod's analysis reaches a sticky end.

Harrod also introduced the notion of the "*warranted* rate of growth" (g_w). This is the rate of growth necessary to absorb society's saving in investment projects. Domar's equilibrium condition requires, therefore, equality between the warranted growth rate (g_w) and the rate at which investment has to move so as to keep effective demand and productive capacity moving together (g), i.e., $g_w = g = \dfrac{s}{k}$. If the actual growth rate exceeds the warranted rate, chronic labor shortages, wage increases, and inflation would disrupt growth. This situation implies that the actual capital–output ratio is smaller than the one required by the economy, resulting in a shortage of equipment and an incentive to invest more. Firms will demand more equipment and materials than are available. The effort to satisfy this demand will cause output to rise faster than previously. The consequence is that actual growth will deviate even further from the warranted growth until the latter hits the natural rate, when all available labor has been absorbed. This means that the long-run question for an economy is that of the relation between warranted and natural growth rates; or, in different terms, that of the relationship between the growth of capital and the growth of the labor force (measured in efficiency units).

On the other hand, if the actual growth rate falls short of the warranted rate, the economy will slip into increasing unemployment, stagnation, deflation, and an overall chronic depression. This situation implies that the actual capital–output ratio is greater than the one required by the economy. In this case, the actual rate of growth is not sufficient to stimulate investment demand to match the amount of saving at full-employment equilibrium. There is too much capital and saving. Firms will demand less equipment and materials than currently available, and this will depress output through the multiplier and accelerator effects. This will make the shortfall of actual growth in relation to warranted growth still greater, so that the former, far from returning to equality with the latter, will deviate from it even more. Summing up, the warranted growth path is fundamentally unstable, because deviations of the actual from the warranted growth rate do not disappear automatically, but cause even larger disparities.

However, as noted above, the long-run question for an economy lies in the relation between natural growth rate (g_n) and the warranted growth rate (g_w). Harrod (1939) argued that the two growth rates would be equal (a situation referred to as a "golden age") only by accident because in reality the natural growth rate (g_n), savings rate (s), and capital–output ratio (k) are constant. Any discrepancy between the actual growth rate and the warranted rate would take the economy further away from equilibrium. This situation is referred to in the literature as the *Harrod–Domar knife-edge problem.* The most fruitful way to understand Harrod's relationship $n + \lambda = \dfrac{s}{k}$ is as an equilibrium condition, although it immediately raises the problem that for the expression $n + \lambda = \dfrac{s}{k}$ to be an equation, at least one of the three magnitudes must be a variable.

Full employment of the labor force *and* full utilization of productive capacity will take place only if both rates of growth are equal, i.e., if $g_n = g_w$, or $n + \lambda = \dfrac{s}{k}$. When the natural growth rate is smaller than the warranted growth rate, full employment will prevail, but with accelerating inflation. This case will result in a chronic tendency toward depression as the actual rate of growth is not sufficient to stimulate investment demand to match the amount of saving at full-employment equilibrium. But when the natural rate exceeds the warranted rate, the economy will be growing at an ever-increasing rate of unemployment (not voluntary, but structural, caused by insufficient capital for workers to work with), with a tendency toward demand inflation because the actual rate of growth will tend to exceed investment to match saving. As the growth of the capital stock falls short of the growth of the effective labor force, unemployment will surface. This seems to be the historical experience of many developing countries (Thirlwall 2007). What can developing countries do in these circumstances (i.e., unemployment and inflation)? First, they could reduce the growth rate of the labor force by implementing measures to control population growth. Second, they could reduce the growth rate of labor-augmenting technical progress, although this would certainly affect the living standards of those working, and therefore is problematic. A third policy option is to induce a rise in the savings ratio, for which monetary and fiscal reforms are necessary. Finally, a reduction in the capital–output ratio (i.e., an increase in capital productivity) will also contribute to bringing natural and warranted growth rates in line.

The conclusion is that a free-market capitalist economy does not have an automatic tendency toward a full-employment equilibrium growth path. Nothing guarantees that supply will equal demand. However, in Harrod's model, a government sector can be incorporated, whose expenditure and taxes can be manipulated to keep natural and warranted growth rates permanently in line, along with a monetary authority that can operate on the savings rate and the capital–output ratio. These two policies could potentially lead to the attainment of full employment and maximum growth as allowed by the productive potential of the economy.

The growth literature evolved after the Harrod–Domar model. Two different solutions to the knife-edge problem were proposed. One solution was the so-called Keynesian approach. Pasinetti (1962) argued that the saving rate could not be considered a constant, as it is a weighted average of the saving propensities of the various categories of savers (workers and capitalists). Therefore, a change in the functional distribution of income between wages and profits would bring natural and warranted growth rates in line. The other solution to Harrod–Domar's knife-edge problem was that provided by Solow (1956). Here the capital–output ratio is the equilibrating variable. The mechanism through which equilibrium is achieved is competition. In this model, the system can evolve by itself, without government intervention, to a steady-state situation.

5

What Is the Role of Agriculture in the Process of Structural Change and in Delivering Full Employment? Full Employment I

Any discussion of development must start with a consideration of the state and prospects of agriculture. If this sector cannot be transformed, there can be no genuine revolution of economic growth. The World Bank's (2008) *World Development Report* highlights the importance of this sector for development. As the food crisis that erupted in early 2008 (labeled "a silent tsunami" by the United Nations' World Food Programme) showed, the international community cannot neglect agriculture, for this crisis may bring obstacles to globalization (food markets are in turmoil, protests are growing, and trade and openness can be undermined).

Agriculture is still the largest employer in many developing countries in Asia, including Bangladesh, Cambodia, the People's Republic of China (PRC), India, Indonesia, Pakistan, Papua New Guinea, Thailand, and Viet Nam (in 2000–2004, agriculture was still the largest employer in developing Asia in 12 out of 23 countries for which data were available). And in many other countries in the region, although it is not the largest employer, it still employs a very significant share of the labor force.

Figure 5.1 shows the generalized tendency for agricultural output and employment shares to decline as countries become richer. This is also the case across much of developing Asia. Especially significant have been the declines in output that occurred in the PRC and India: in the former from about 32% in the 1970s to about 13% in 2000–2004, and in India from about 42% to about 23% during the same period. The share of employment

Figure 5.1. Agricultural Output and Employment Shares vs. Per Capita GDP, 1970–2004 (All countries in the world)

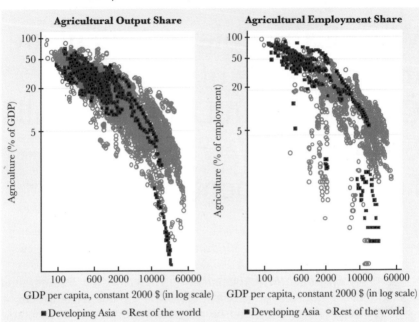

Source: Word Development Indicators Online (World Bank 2006).

in agriculture has also declined across most of developing Asia, except in Central and West Asia. This is the result of the convulsion that this region underwent after the collapse of the Soviet Union. Figure 5.1 also indicates that, in general, the decline in agricultural employment has occurred at a much slower pace than that in output. Tables A5.1 and A5.2 at the end of the chapter provide total and sector growth rates and output and employment shares.

As stated above, the objective of development has to be the increase in productive capacity; but this occurs during the structural transformation of the economy, that is, the shift of resources (e.g., labor) from activities with low productivity, traditionally agriculture, into activities with high productivity, such as industry and services (Asian Development Bank 2007b; Felipe and Estrada 2008; Felipe et al. 2007). Both problems, i.e., the increase in productive capacity and structural change, have to be understood as a joint question. Ultimately, development will occur only if a poor country has the capacity to transfer a large portion of its labor force from agriculture (in particular from farming activities) into industry and services. (Box 5.1 on structural change and Figure 5.2 for a summary of causes and outcomes.) In this

Box 5.1. Structural Change

The successful Asian economies (i.e., Hong Kong, China; the Republic of Korea; Singapore; Taipei,China; Malaysia; Thailand; or the People's Republic of China and Viet Nam more recently) present two main differences between three decades ago and today. First, they are significantly bigger. Second, they are significantly different. Indeed, what sets the performance of the successful Asian economies apart from that of many other countries is not only their high growth rates but also their fast and intense structural transformation: their output and employment structures changed dramatically; resources were transferred to higher-value-added sectors (i.e., from agriculture to industry and services); production diversified; firms learned how to produce and export a more sophisticated and technologically advanced range of products; and their levels of labor productivity increased significantly.

Except for those countries well endowed with natural resources such as oil, growth is always linked to the structural transformation of the economy. Indeed, the growth experience of the developed economies since the 19th century reveals that growth was associated with changes in the structure of the economy. More recently, the experience of the successful Asian economies also shows that high growth has been associated with deep changes in the structure of these economies. Many economists see the development of a modern industry sector as the key for propelling structural transformation.

Growth and structural transformation are related in a circular way, since countries do not grow by simply reproducing themselves on a larger scale. Generally (unless all sectors of the economy grow at identical rates), countries become different as they grow, not only in terms of *what* they produce but also in terms of *how* they do it, i.e., by using different inputs, including new methods of production. The successful economies have generated new activities characterized by higher productivity and increasing returns to scale. The transition across different patterns of production and specialization involves upgrading to higher-value-added activities within each sector through the introduction of new products and processes. These changes entail far-reaching transformations in terms of, among other things, economic geography and the skill content of output. The countries that can sustain multiple transitions across different stages of their structural transformation will grow successfully.

Source: Author.

Figure 5.2. Structural Change: Causes and Outcomes

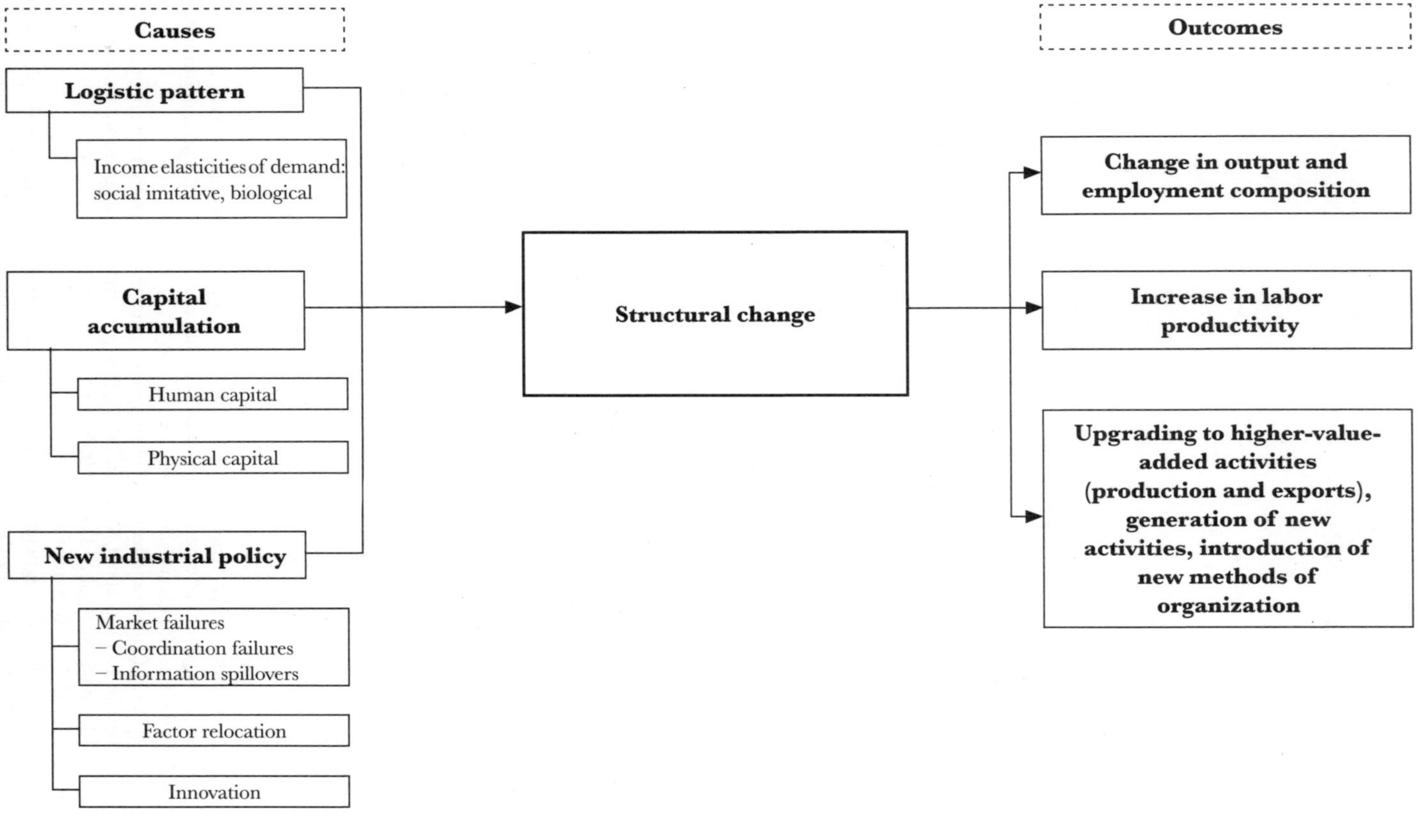

Source: Author.

chapter, I consider the role of agriculture. In chapter 8, I consider a second aspect of structural change, the role of industrial policy. And in chapter 10, I discuss the upgrading aspect and the role of manufacturing and exports.

What caused the food crisis that hit developing Asia in early 2008? It was a combination of factors, the most important of which was probably the diversion of a large part of the United States' (US) corn crop to ethanol production (which has boosted demand for other staples, such as rice).[1] Other factors—supply shocks that affected a large producer and exporter of rice like Viet Nam (because of very cold weather and pest infestation); the November 2007 cyclone in Bangladesh that destroyed about 800,000 metric tons of rice (and which forced the country to import about 2.4 million metric tons from India); a drought in Australia; and rising long-term demand in countries such as the PRC as a result of prosperity (i.e., people eat more and better)—also have contributed.[2] Bad policies (e.g., export bans in some countries) have made things worse and productivity growth has reached a plateau, the result of lack of investment in agriculture. For this reason, the food crisis is not expected to be a temporary phenomenon.[3]

In much of Asia, rice farming remains small-scale and inefficient. Despite the obvious importance of agriculture for development, it has been neglected for decades. For example, in 1980, 30% of the World Bank's annual lending went to agriculture projects. By 2007, this share had declined to 12% (adjusted for inflation, the World Bank cut its agricultural lending to $2.0 billion in 2004 from $7.7 billion in 1980). Today, the overall proportion of official development assistance going to agriculture is only 4%. Why has this occurred? One reason is countries' attempt to emulate the experience of the East Asian countries.

At the time these countries started growing in the 1970s, the prevailing view was that a significant amount of labor would be transferred from agriculture into industry and services (following Lewis's [1954] model). Likewise, there was some degree of export pessimism with regard to agriculture (following Prebisch's [1959] work).

---

[1]   For example, almost all the increase in global corn production between 2004 and 2007 in the US was dedicated to biofuel production. Between 1980 and 1996, annual US ethanol production increased from nil to about 1 billion gallons. Since 1996, production has increased very fast, reaching 8 billion gallons in 2006. By law, in 2008 the US has to use 9 billion gallons of ethanol. The forecast is that production will continue increasing and will reach 12 billion gallons in 2016.

[2]   In the PRC, for example, meat consumption per capita increased from about 20 kilogram (kg) in 1980 to about 50 kg in 2007. This puts tremendous pressure on water: while 1 kg of wheat requires 1,000–2,000 liters of water, the production of 1 kg of beef requires 10,000–13,000 liters of water.

[3]   As of July 2009, agricultural prices were above their 2006 average despite the world recession, suggesting that there is a mismatch between supply and demand.

The prospects of achieving fast growth in the exports of labor-intensive manufactures were much better. The experience of East Asia seemed to corroborate these views. This led other countries in the region, especially in South Asia, to also push the export-led growth route. The consequence was the neglect of agriculture in favor of industrialization, although in many cases this strategy did not succeed to the extent that it had previously succeeded in East Asia. This is most obvious in India, where the decline in public infrastructure in rural areas has led to the sector's stagnation. In Viet Nam, large agricultural areas are being lost in the name of industrialization. According to the Ministry of Agriculture and Rural Development, the country loses about 40,000 hectares (ha) of rice fields a year to construction of cities, highways, and industrial zones. And in Thailand, the amount of land under cultivation declined by more than 13% between 1995 and 2005. This means that Asia's food crisis may not end soon and its solution may require international cooperation.

What the situation in 2008 revealed was serious market failures.[4] The significant increase in prices was the result of shifts in demand not accompanied by shifts in supply. For decades, food prices were low and they were subsidized in the developed countries. Now, prices are increasing and governments (also in the developed countries) are subsidizing the production of biofuels. Moreover, since the 1980s, governments have been reducing spending on green-revolutionary technologies, thinking that the food problem had been solved. During the 1980s and 1990s, the developed countries dumped large agricultural surpluses on the markets, depressing world prices.

In the 1960s, population growth was faster than food production, putting at risk many poor countries. At that time, an important joint effort between developing and developed countries culminated with the Green Revolution. Countries like India and Pakistan embraced new plant varieties, irrigation projects, and fertilizer programs. Yields soared and between 1970 and 1990, the peak of the Green Revolution, the food supply grew faster than world population. By the 1980s, the threat of starvation had disappeared from most of the world. At the same time, Europe and the US offered their farmers heavy subsidies that encouraged production, and grain became abundant. The result was that prices fell, and many poor

---

[4] By July–August 2008, it was obvious that the Doha Round of trade had collapsed. Some economists have argued that this is a tragedy. In their view, a Doha deal would contribute to fairer trade by eliminating all farm export subsidies in the rich world. However, if the US and the European Union (EU) wanted to reduce farm support, they could do so without having to ask in exchange for market access to developing countries in a multilateral forum. This is not to say that a successful round will not bring important benefits to developing countries.

countries, instead of developing their own agriculture, turned to the world market to buy cheap rice and wheat. However, after 1990, the growth rate of the food supply fell again below that of population. In 2004, the world economy started growing faster, at about 5% a year, and the numbers of people desiring to improve their diet also increased. The world began to use more grain than it was producing, cutting into reserves, and prices started rising. The situation got out of control in 2008.

On the state of agricultural research, the example of the International Rice Research Institute, located in the city of Los Baños in the Philippines, is truly revealing. In the 1980s, the institute employed five entomologists, overseeing a staff of 200. Today, it has one entomologist with a staff of 8. Researchers at the institute claim that they know how to create rice varieties resistant to insects that damage rice paddies in East Asia, occurring at a time of scarcity and high prices (these insects have become resistant to old insecticides). Budget cuts have prevented them from doing so.

My view is that if growth in developing Asia is to be inclusive, then agriculture will have to be given priority. Thailand's labor productivity in agriculture is estimated at about $1,650. In the US, it is about $40,000. Labor productivity in agriculture in the Philippines, Indonesia, Myanmar, the PRC, India, Nepal, Bangladesh, and Cambodia barely reaches $1,000. There is no doubt that if developing Asian countries upgraded their agricultural practices only to the level of Thailand, millions of people would be lifted out of poverty. Another problem is the fragmentation of holdings as a consequence of population growth. In the PRC and Bangladesh, average farm size has fallen from about 1.5 ha in the 1970s to about 0.5 ha now. Improvements in agriculture will require deep understanding of the transformation that agriculture can potentially undergo. One such transformation is the increasing importance of commercialization and the role of supermarkets.

Given that I have argued that unemployment and underemployment of resources are developing countries' most important problems, one could think that the solution may lie in reallocating the labor force out of agriculture toward more productive activities. I have in mind, for example, labor-intensive building and construction, although some industry and services activities could also serve the same purpose. The preliminary answer is yes; indeed, this is (part of) the solution. This encounters, however, an important obstacle.

The problem policy makers would face to make this a feasible solution is the bottleneck of supply of necessities (resulting from the low elasticity of agricultural production) that would arise (Kalecki 1966a). Indeed, an increase in employment outside agriculture creates additional income (wages) and, given that workers spend a considerable part of their wage bill on food, if there is no concomitant increase in agricultural output, food inflation will show up. The slow development of agriculture compared with general economic growth leads to an inadequate supply of foodstuffs and an increase in their prices. This indicates that one important reason underlying the inflation pressure experienced in the course of rapid economic development results from basic disproportions in productive relations. Inflation poses a real danger to developing countries for it leads to real wage reductions.[5] As I will argue, declines in real wages should not be acceptable and should be considered unethical.[6]

This implies that the limit to the increase in employment outside agriculture is determined by the possibilities of increasing marketable agricultural output. Since this is restricted in the short run, it prevents a rapid increase in employment. And as a consequence, the growth rate of agricultural output constrains, in many developing economies, the growth rate of overall output. Even if a large part of those employed in the new activities were effectively underemployed peasants, inflationary pressures would remain. The reason is that the demand for necessities would increase, either because wages in the new employment would be higher than in the countryside, or because the income of the peasants who remain in the countryside would increase.

How could policy makers avoid such inflationary pressures (more will be said on inflation in chapters 11 and 12)? Perhaps the first obvious measure would be to tax necessities (mostly consumed by low-income groups) to contain food inflation. This, however, is not a solution if policy makers aim at achieving inclusive growth. Indeed, increasing employment at the expense of a decrease in real wages should not be acceptable as a policy option, for it amounts to taxing the poor rather than the well-off on the grounds that the latter would not reduce their consumption despite the imposition of a tax (apart from the fact that it limits the expansion of the market for mass consumption articles, an important factor of industrialization).[7] Nevertheless, taxation of the upper-income groups would probably only slightly depress the demand for food, and hence inflationary pressures would remain.[8]

---

[5]   It also leads to capital flight, currency speculation, political tensions that are dangerous for the ruling groups, and low investment.

[6]   Of course, increases in agricultural prices can help agricultural workers and the rural poor. Policy makers will therefore have to evaluate this distributive effect.

[7]   I have in mind inflation that is constantly eroding the purchasing power of wages, especially those of the poor. Of course, the effect of inflation on workers depends on how their wages adjust. The reality is that in many developing countries, due to lack of organized labor, indexation is not the norm. Stiglitz et al. (2006, 17–26) argue that moderate inflation does not seem particularly bad for growth. Certainly all groups who live on fixed income (e.g., retirees) are affected by inflation. The rich and wealthy are also affected by inflation as they tend to hold financial assets whose worth is eroded as a result of sustained increases in prices.

[8]   When the wealthy in developing countries increase their consumption, they spend a sizable share on imported goods.

Imports of food can also help relieve the problem. These, however, will require that the country in question export enough to pay for its imports. Otherwise, it will run a trade deficit. For this reason, in general, the increase in food supply will depend on domestic output.

If the increase in food supply will largely depend on increasing domestic output, policy makers will have to plan an increase in the supply of food (i.e., an increase in agricultural output) and, in general, of consumer goods that matches the demand for them. Therefore, an increase in agricultural output is crucial for many developing countries to initiate economic development. This policy also matters because many developing countries today have a higher density of population on their land than most developed countries had at the time they underwent structural transformation and modern growth. The developing countries are also experiencing higher population growth than the developed countries ever experienced (Booth and Sundrum 1984; Khan 1996). Unlike what occurred in Western Europe, demographic changes in developing countries today are being driven by the diffusion of modern medical knowledge and public health technology (Nerlove 1996). The question of population growth deserves utmost attention and an array of different solutions, ranging from promoting social development and education (e.g., making contraceptive measures available) to legal and economic pressures to reduce the birth rate. Box 5.2 discusses the Philippines' population policy.

For this reason, a complementary policy is to prevent large-scale migration from the countryside into urban areas. Arthur Lewis (1978, 241) pointed out: "the only way to avoid mounting urban unemployment is to persuade more people to remain in the countryside . . . our agricultural economics is based on the assumption that numbers in agriculture will decline as economic development proceeds; our policies are therefore set towards helping to reduce the number of men per acre. Instead we shall need for the next three or four decades agricultural policies aimed at absorbing more men per acre."

Agricultural output can grow through the following means (Briones and Felipe 2007): (i) expansion in area planted, (ii) increases in yield, and (iii) a reallocation of resources toward agricultural products with greater value added. The first avenue, which was the traditional means of supporting population expansion, has narrowed considerably in most Asian countries in recent years.[9] The amount of good, productive land is falling.

---

[9] Given the World Bank's renewed interest in agriculture, the four key elements that it proposes for a comprehensive approach to agricultural growth may be summarized (World Bank 2008): (i) improvement of producer incentives, including the removal of subsidies, as these tend to benefit richer farmers more; (ii) provision of quality key public goods, such as infrastructure and human capital; (iii) development of stronger institutions to support an adequate rural investment climate (e.g., better access to rural

Box 5.2. Philippine Population Policy

Despite claims of its apparent weaknesses, the Philippines has had a population policy since the 1970s. During the Marcos regime, the Population Commission, which was created in 1971, and the Department of Agriculture designed two modules for the Integrated Planning for Improved Living Program, aimed at incorporating the concepts of family and population planning in the home extension education program of the then Bureau of Agricultural Extension (now called Agricultural Training Institute) of the Department of Agriculture. With its more than 800 female family-extension workers, who regularly carried out village-to-village training and information on family and community development, this bureau achieved some success by handing out free contraceptives, mostly to women in the rural areas.

After the fall of the Marcos government, the family planning program continued with the Aquino administration, but began to weaken. The family planning functions were eventually transferred from the Population Commission to the Department of Health in 1989. The program further waned in the mid-1990s with the devolution of some national government functions to the local governments, including some of the functions of the Department of Agriculture. With a limited budget and the lack of an integrated national population program, the local governments showed little interest in population growth. In 1993, with the arrival of President Ramos and in preparation for the 1994 International Conference on Population Development in Cairo, the Population Commission, which continued its task of formulating the country's population program, established the program called Integrated Population Concept on Agriculture and Home Extension, to be jointly funded by the Food and Agriculture Organization and the United Nations Population Fund. However, this program was ineffectively pushed and as a result failed to reduce the growth of the population, which already reached 68.5 million in 1995.

A key factor behind the lack of state commitment to the population programs was the opposition of various women's and Catholic Church organizations to the population policies in the 1990s. Through the so-called Third World Network, these organizations proposed that the population policy be closely integrated with the distribution and use of the resources of the country, as well as of the world, as the program promotes women's empowerment. The government's Medium-Term Development Plan for 1992 to 1997 thus attempted to integrate population and development policies, but was viewed by many with skepticism for being merely a part of the country's structural program with the World Bank. A study in 1997 by the Population Commission further

continued on next page

Box 5.2 (continued)

showed that young people's attitudes about sex and family had not been influenced by previous family planning programs.

During the Estrada administration, population policy became more focused by assisting married couples to reduce unwanted fertility and by meeting their demand for contraceptives. In addition, the government expanded the resources available for family planning through budgetary appropriations for the purchase of contraceptives, which had previously been available only because of donations from international agencies. Again, this initiative did not progress.

Many politicians and academics have criticized the Arroyo government for its ambivalence on the population question. The government faces opposition from the powerful Catholic Church (Teves 2008) and pro-life groups. In the southern Philippines, the Church has even said that it would deny communion to government health workers who want to implement a safe-motherhood program through the Department of Health. In stark contrast to the aggressive stance of the Estrada government, the Arroyo administration sees the population issue as primarily a health intervention problem and as a means to help couples achieve their fertility preference. Aside from the lack of financing, the Arroyo government's family planning program has emphasized the improvement of reproductive health at the expense of what others see as its main goal—the reduction of fertility.

A number of researchers (e.g., Herrin and Pernia [2003]) have attributed the failure of these programs to the opposition of the Catholic Church to the use of contraceptives. Likewise, ignorance (e.g., rumors that the birth-control pill could cause psychological illnesses) and scare tactics are widespread among poor people. However, these studies have seldom noted the other factors that are necessary for effective population programs. Schultz (1994) observed that, despite the controversial treatment of family planning as exogenous, it is statistically insignificant in estimates using cross-country data when this variable interacts with education, nutritional inputs, natural resources, and other socioeconomic variables affecting the costs and benefits of bearing and raising children. Mellor (1998) noted that while family planning programs are effective, these are not independent of other socioeconomic policies, and failure to consider their endogeneity will lead to either underestimates or overestimates of program effectiveness.

Source: Felipe and Hasan 2006.

Growth in arable land has usually been much slower than growth in population, and in countries like the Republic of Korea, Japan, and Bangladesh, the arable land area has even shrunk. In other countries, growth in arable land area is unlikely to continue even at the low rates observed, given that most of the remaining uncultivated lands are less suitable for agriculture. The Green Revolution of the 1960s and 1970s included the expansion of irrigation. However, today, the amount of irrigated land is very limited. A certain "technological fatigue" has set in as the benefits of the Green Revolution have vanished. Second, yields of new crop varieties have reached a plateau and in many developing countries remain substantially lower than potential yields possible with best cultivation practices. Nevertheless, yields may still be increased in many countries by using better fertilizers, new machinery, better irrigation, and new seeds. Sustained growth of agriculture requires increasing agriculture's value added on the same amount of land, and for this, science and technology are crucial.[10] This is also the only way for employment generation in agriculture to keep pace with population growth, while increasing labor productivity. Such increases can be achieved by raising the yield of major crops and by adopting genetically modified strains (e.g., of corn and wheat), although they are expensive and politically controversial.[11] Finally, agricultural output can also increase by allocating land and labor toward agricultural products that produce more value added per unit area.[12]

The policies discussed in the previous paragraph are also important because increasing agricultural output is a prerequisite for industrialization. Intensive cultivation of the land will lead to a higher transfer of labor from agriculture into industry and services. Up to a point, a higher output per acre can be produced with fewer people without introducing labor-saving techniques. And simultaneously, the higher supply of food will make it possible to feed the population and dampen down the inflation

---

financial institutions and improved property rights); and (iv) provision of the mechanisms to ensure sustainable use of natural resources.

[10]   See, for example, the report on Pakistan by the Pakistan Institute of Development Economics (PIDE) (2006), where it is claimed that agriculture suffers from low-productivity crop yields. This is due to, among other reasons, lack of seed varieties, drought and high-temperature stress, soil nutrient mining, and high salinity and waterlogging of soil. PIDE (2006, 23) argues that sustained growth in agriculture of 5%–6% is needed in Pakistan to ensure rapid growth. In terms of strategies, the document proposes to diversify agricultural production toward high-value crops, increase the level of investment in agricultural research, develop the human resource base, and improve infrastructure (PIDE 2006, 23).

[11]   See *The Economist* (2008b).

[12]   The nutritional value of agricultural output also has to increase. As noted in the text, greater value added could be achieved by producing cash crops for exports, but this will not reduce the inflation pressure. It may well increase it.

problem. Techniques that increase the productivity of land will also raise the productivity of labor. On the other hand, techniques that raise the productivity of labor (e.g., large-scale mechanized farms) without increasing the productivity of land do not help solve the problem of unemployment and underemployment. These techniques would increase agricultural production, a part of which would be sold to the cities, thus helping create employment there. However, they would exacerbate unemployment and underemployment in rural areas and induce migration to the urban areas.

Introduction of small-scale irrigation projects, application of fertilizers, introduction of improved seeds, proper use of manure, and similar techniques that do not rely on the introduction of heavy equipment would deliver appreciable results quickly. The main problem with implementing them is the prevailing agrarian conditions in many poor countries (e.g., lack of affordable credit to small peasants, the existence of disguised tenancy without security of tenure), which discourage the growth of agricultural production. Overcoming these institutional impediments requires government action in the form of deep social and structural changes. Bardhan has argued that this is not so simple: "The political stumbling blocks to beneficial institutional change in many poor countries may have more to do with distributive conflicts and asymmetries in bargaining power" (Bardhan 2001, 277).[13] These distributive conflicts lead to the persistence of dysfunctional institutions. High growth of agriculture as a precondition for noninflationary redeployment of the labor surplus requires, in most cases, deep institutional changes, especially in the areas of land reform (Rashid and Quibria 1995) and the credit system (Basu 1995). Rashid and Quibria (1995) argue that land reform continues being a pending issue in many developing countries. The incomplete and endless process in the Philippines is a case in point (Box 5.3). The problem with land reform is that it is not endogenous, but imposed, as it was in the Republic of Korea (by a military government) and Taipei,China (by a foreign military power). Rashid and Quibria argue that land reform is not a magic solution for poverty alleviation. If the latter is the objective, it can be achieved through land-contingent poverty alleviation schemes; on the other hand, if the goal is to achieve economies of scale, then associative farming could be the solution. Basu (1995) notes that the formal credit market often excludes the poor, who cannot borrow from cheaper sources of credit and have to borrow at high interest rates, often from rich local moneylenders and powerful land-

---

[13] Rajan (2009) argues that a key impediment to development is that underdeveloped economies are divided into constituencies that prefer idiosyncratic pathways to reform rather than a collectively beneficial one. Competitive rent preservation ensures that no comprehensive reform path may command broad support.

lords. Expanding the availability of credit requires grassroots activism and carefully designed government policies.

Some countries develop self-reinforcing mechanisms that perpetuate socially suboptimal institutions. Some initial adopters chose these institutions at some point in the past because they suited their interests, but then the whole system became "locked in." One may wonder why these institutions are not changed. The answer would seem to be that powerful vested interests make institutional change politically difficult in terms of distributive conflicts and asymmetries in bargaining power (e.g., Haque [2006] and Siddiqa [2007] on Pakistan; and Aldaba et al. [2005] on the Philippines). The tenacity of vested interests, the difficulty of mobilizing collective action to bring about institutional change, and the differential capacity of different social groups for mobilization and coordination are long-lasting barriers to economic progress (Bardhan 2001).

Box 5.3. Land Reform Programs in the Philippines

Land reform has a long history in the Philippines. A series of republic acts even before the martial law period mandated the redistribution of large rice and corn estates, the shift from share tenancy to leasehold, and the establishment of an administrative institution for implementation.

Despite previous attempts, however, it was Presidential Decree 27 of 1972, or the Land Reform Program, that initiated and enforced a large-scale program of land reform. The objectives of the program were (i) the conversion of tenants into owners of the land they were tilling for rice and corn, (ii) the introduction of a system to allow tenants to purchase tenanted land by installments, and (iii) the establishment of a rental ceiling to ensure a higher income to remaining tenants. The program was applied to rice- and corn-tenanted areas (1.01 million hectares [ha]).

Under the program, lands in excess of a 7 ha retention limit (with another 3 ha for each legal heir) were to be transferred to tenants. This was undertaken by Operation Land Transfer. Meanwhile, the reform of the tenure system was implemented through Operation Leasehold. In its first 14 years (1972–1986), the Land Reform Program achieved 48% of its target, distributing 539,000 ha of land. This success can be attributed partly to the extensive irrigation program of the government and the introduction of modern crop varieties during the period.

Nevertheless, the program failed to alleviate rural poverty for several reasons. First, the program exempted 368,000 ha of sugarcane land, 2.15 million ha of coconut land, and 1.8 million ha of other cropland. Second, the landowners

continued on next page

Box 5.3 (continued)

took many measures to evade the redistribution, such as subdividing the land to their relatives, selling or mortgaging their land, and shifting to cash crops from rice and corn. Third, a land reform program by itself and without other inputs cannot boost agricultural production. Presidential Decree 27 was centered on land reform or redistribution of land rather than agrarian reform or the provision of adequate infrastructure and inputs.

Many of the problems raised against the previous land reform programs were addressed by the Comprehensive Agrarian Reform Program (CARP), or Republic Act 6675 of 1987. This program covers all agricultural land, including public lands, for a total scope of 8.2 million ha. It also incorporates extensive support services to boost the productivity of the new landowners. Under CARP, owners of private agricultural lands are subject to a 5 ha retention limit. Land awardees meanwhile are to receive no more than 3 ha in the form of a Certificate of Land Ownership Award. Awarded lands are officially acquired with funding by the Land Bank and are amortized by beneficiaries over a 30-year period. Repayment terms are leniently set at 6% per year, with a further minimum rate set at 10% of the average value of harvest. Under CARP, the transfer of land ownership need not eliminate the former landowner from productive access to land. In the case of commercial agriculture, former owners are allowed to enter joint ventures, corporate farming, or leaseback arrangements with land awardees.

Aside from redistribution, land reform also involves various land market restrictions: land under coverage cannot be sold or transferred unless by inheritance. The prohibition applies even to beneficiaries for a period of 10 years. Share tenancy continues to be prohibited, while location-specific rental ceilings are also imposed.

The pace of land distribution has been slow. Between 1987 and June 2002, only about 5.7 million ha, or about 70% of the target area of 8.2 million ha, was distributed (Department of Agrarian Reform 2002). The redistribution of the remaining 1.4 million ha of private lands is expected to be prolonged. This slow pace of the program prompted Congress to give CARP a 10-year extension after the government failed to complete its land transfers. According to Llanto and Ballesteros (2003, 15), aside from the lack of financing, the problems of CARP are cumbersome land valuation (leading to conflicts on "fair market value"), slow land surveys, the difficulty of coordinating land reform–related activities, and numerous loopholes in the law (e.g., land use conversions).

In September 2004, President Gloria Macapagal-Arroyo further complicated matters by signing into law Executive Order No. 364, which transformed the Department of Agrarian Reform into the Department of Land Reform. This law makes the newly transformed department responsible for all types of land reform, i.e., agrarian reform, urban land reform, and ancestral domain reform.

continued on next page

Box 5.3 (continued)

The government sees this move as a means of streamlining the bureaucracy. However, given the limited budget of this department, an overall increase in its functions may only reduce further the budget for agrarian reform beneficiaries.

Continued delays in land reform implementation might also have contributed to the decline in investments, particularly in agriculture. The declines are attributed to two factors. The first is the depletion of bank credit for agriculture, as the uncertainty due to CARP has eroded the collateral value of land. The second is the delay in CARP implementation, which keeps land in the hands of persons who may eventually lose it and so fail to recover the value of invested capital, thus diminishing investment incentives. A study by Habito et al. (2003) looked into the causes of depressed investment, among other things. Using farm-level data, the study showed that the delay in the implementation of land reform is more significant than the erosion of collateral values. Hence, the failure to complete land reform can account to some extent for the lack of investment incentives in the countryside.

Source: Felipe and Hasan 2006.

Table A5.1. Total and Sector Growth Rates by Decade

	1970s				1980s				1990s				2000–2006			
	GDP	Agri-culture	Industry	Services	GDP	Agri-culture	Industry	Services	GDP	Agri-culture	Industry	Services	GDP	Agri-culture	Industry	Services
China, People's Republic of	5.90	2.39	8.22	5.79	9.23	5.14	10.05	11.93	9.53	4.23	12.10	8.91	9.29	3.95	10.09	9.93
India	2.52	0.31	3.84	4.45	5.71	4.18	6.57	6.28	5.53	2.95	5.60	7.34	7.07	2.77	7.43	8.55
Newly Industrialized Economies																
Hong Kong, China	8.73	–	–	–	6.97	–	–	–	3.66	–	–	–	4.63	(0.95)	(3.20)	6.03
Korea, Republic of	7.95	3.69	13.57	6.32	7.32	1.58	8.98	7.23	5.96	0.96	6.41	5.76	4.53	(0.16)	5.91	3.85
Singapore	8.40	2.75	9.13	8.38	7.18	(3.74)	6.17	7.75	7.32	(3.49)	8.13	7.14	4.52	1.65	3.90	4.97
ASEAN-4																
Indonesia	7.48	4.15	9.80	8.41	6.14	4.01	7.08	6.62	4.51	2.06	5.67	4.53	4.74	3.27	4.12	5.99
Malaysia	7.56	4.96	8.29	8.63	5.65	3.46	6.44	6.01	6.88	0.11	8.06	7.74	4.61	3.16	4.03	5.48
Philippines	5.81	3.93	7.89	5.02	1.89	1.50	0.58	3.41	2.71	1.45	2.40	3.63	4.50	3.58	3.30	5.76
Thailand	6.80	4.06	9.40	6.63	7.02	4.39	8.67	6.82	4.94	0.42	6.91	4.50	4.93	(1.38)	5.92	5.12
Other Southeast Asia																
Cambodia	–	–	–	–	–	–	–	–	7.11	4.59	12.60	6.51	8.95	6.05	12.97	8.26
Lao PDR	–	–	–	–	3.86	3.86	6.14	2.74	6.18	4.86	11.24	5.44	6.27	2.77	11.56	6.41
Viet Nam	–	–	–	–	4.36	3.03	5.19	5.53	7.14	3.82	9.96	7.39	7.34	3.76	9.75	6.73

continued on next page

Table A5.1 (continued)

	1970s				1980s				1990s				2000–2006			
	GDP	Agri-culture	Industry	Services	GDP	Agri-culture	Industry	Services	GDP	Agri-culture	Industry	Services	GDP	Agri-culture	Industry	Services
Other South Asia																
Bangladesh	0.82	(0.31)	1.26	2.15	3.17	1.58	4.41	3.72	4.69	3.32	6.75	4.15	5.49	2.79	7.49	5.64
Bhutan	–	–	–	–	7.13	4.84	14.89	6.59	6.21	3.33	8.28	7.25	7.35	3.07	8.97	7.45
Maldives	–	–	–	–	–	–	–	–	–	–	–	–	6.48	–	–	1.37
Nepal	3.59	1.09	6.17	4.63	3.95	3.47	7.30	3.46	4.75	2.42	6.97	5.97	2.73	3.07	1.59	1.37
Pakistan	4.04	1.84	5.40	6.05	6.62	4.24	7.86	6.52	3.88	4.05	4.56	4.43	5.01	2.22	7.07	5.76
Sri Lanka	4.15	2.36	3.39	5.00	4.04	2.25	4.11	5.12	5.12	2.49	6.54	5.43	4.41	0.81	3.48	4.93
Central Asia and Mongolia																
Armenia	–	–	–	–	–	–	–	–	(4.99)	0.10	(13.74)	(10.47)	11.71	6.78	14.38	11.77
Azerbaijan	–	–	–	–	–	–	–	–	(7.04)	(4.26)	(4.67)	(6.05)	15.49	6.62	18.37	8.76
Kazakhstan	–	–	–	–	–	–	–	–	(5.05)	(7.41)	(10.56)	(1.83)	9.90	4.84	10.70	10.18
Kyrgyz Republic	–	–	–	–	7.75	7.18	10.14	5.38	(4.05)	0.70	(11.13)	(2.08)	3.54	2.40	(1.35)	6.39
Mongolia	–	–	–	–	5.80	2.52	6.89	7.99	1.38	2.64	(0.14)	(1.29)	6.07	0.97	7.67	7.44
Tajikistan	–	–	–	–	2.11	(1.60)	5.56	3.48	(10.51)	(7.98)	(10.23)	(4.60)	8.58	8.97	10.57	6.72
Turkmenistan	–	–	–	–	3.06	5.41	(3.05)	7.33	(4.31)	(3.92)	(5.06)	(4.00)	–	–	–	–
Uzbekistan	–	–	–	–	5.75	2.85	8.82	1.27	(0.37)	1.05	(3.07)	(1.36)	5.56	6.31	3.91	6.01

continued on next page

Table A5.1 (continued)

	1970s				1980s				1990s				2000–2006			
	GDP	Agri-culture	Industry	Services	GDP	Agri-culture	Industry	Services	GDP	Agri-culture	Industry	Services	GDP	Agri-culture	Industry	Services
Pacific																
Fiji Islands	5.52	3.35	3.93	7.50	0.65	2.07	0.19	0.99	2.84	0.04	4.12	3.43	2.56	0.87	1.87	2.87
Kiribati	–	–	–	–	(4.67)	0.15	(5.24)	(1.01)	5.15	(1.52)	8.44	5.37	1.88	9.61	0.36	0.95
Marshall Islands	–	–	–	–	8.24	–	–	–	(0.68)	–	–	–	3.14	–	–	–
Micronesia, Federated States of	–	–	–	–	2.31	–	–	–	1.06	–	–	–	0.20	–	–	–
Palau	–	–	–	–	–	–	–	–	0.78	–	–	–	–	–	–	–
Papua New Guinea	3.03	–	–	–	1.74	2.09	0.36	2.41	4.48	3.24	7.70	1.54	1.90	1.67	(2.78)	1.46
Samoa	–	–	–	–	(0.31)	–	–	–	2.76	0.26	(0.56)	12.64	3.91	(2.51)	5.31	5.45
Solomon Islands	5.29	–	–	–	5.65	–	–	–	3.14	–	–	–	2.15	–	–	–
Timor-Leste	–	–	–	–	–	–	–	–	–	–	–	–	0.75	4.27	(5.47)	0.20
Tonga	–	3.73	11.70	4.58	2.33	0.79	3.14	2.41	2.04	1.77	3.02	2.25	2.37	0.33	3.41	3.19
Vanuatu	–	–	–	–	1.30	0.58	1.26	1.66	3.72	1.97	0.93	4.75	3.14	–	–	–
Total	5.60	2.05	8.07	5.85	6.90	4.09	7.90	7.76	6.62	3.12	8.53	6.80	1.67	(0.79)	(4.29)	1.67

Note: Annual growth was calculated using exponential growth rate. The 1970s figures for Nepal refer only to 1973–1979. The 1980s figures for the Lao PDR refer only to 1984–1989; for the Kyrgyz Republic, Turkmenistan, and Uzbekistan, 1987–1989; for Tajikistan, 1985–1989; and for the Marshall Islands, 1982–1989. The 1990s figures for Cambodia and Solomon Islands refer only to 1993–1999; and for Kazakhstan, 1992–1999. Kiribati sector figures are up to 2004. Vanuatu and Papua New Guinea sector figures are up to 2003. The Fiji Islands and Tonga sector figures are up to 2005.

– = data not available, ASEAN = Association of Southeast Asian Nations, GDP = gross domestic product, Lao PDR = Lao People's Democratic Republic.

Source: Directorate General of Budget Accounting, and Statistics. http://eng.stat.gov.tw, downloaded 13 September 2006; World Bank, World Development Indicators online database, downloaded 4 August 2006.

Table A5.2. Output and Employment Shares by Sector and Decade

	Output shares												Employment shares								
	1970s			1980s			1990s			2000–2006			1980s			1990s			2000–2006		
	Agri-culture	Ind-ustry	Ser-vices	Agri-culture	Ind-ustry	Ser-vices	Agri-culture	Ind-ustry	Ser-vices	Agri-culture	Ind-ustry	Ser-vices	Agri-culture	Ind-ustry	Ser-vices	Agri-culture	Ind-ustry	Ser-vices	Agri-culture	Ind-ustry	Ser-vices
China, People's Republic of	32.33	44.54	23.13	29.31	44.60	26.09	20.33	45.50	34.17	13.23	46.06	40.71	63.87	20.24	15.89	54.15	22.63	23.22	49.78	21.95	28.28
India	42.28	22.43	35.30	34.61	26.14	39.25	29.42	26.92	43.65	20.43	26.66	52.91	67.00	15.50	17.50	63.30	16.70	20.00	59.80	18.00	22.20
Newly Industrialized Economies																					
Hong Kong, China	–	–	–	0.52	30.28	69.20	0.16	18.06	81.78	0.07	11.19	88.74	1.35	44.60	54.05	0.55	28.28	71.17	0.27	17.71	82.02
Korea, Republic of	26.16	29.82	44.02	13.43	39.20	47.37	6.64	41.39	51.98	3.96	39.70	56.34	26.78	31.12	42.10	12.97	32.88	54.15	9.13	27.49	63.38
Singapore	–	–	–	–	–	–	0.18	34.75	65.07	0.10	33.83	66.00	0.84	36.08	63.08	0.26	31.80	67.94	0.26	26.88	72.76
Taipei,China	11.60	40.58	47.82	6.13	42.98	50.89	3.16	34.16	62.68	1.79	27.29	70.92	16.98	41.97	41.05	10.79	38.82	50.39	7.33	35.72	56.95
ASEAN-4																					
Indonesia	34.02	30.07	35.91	23.18	38.12	38.70	17.91	41.77	40.32	14.95	44.89	40.16	55.90	11.46	32.64	46.73	12.58	40.69	44.56	17.92	37.52
Malaysia	27.39	33.09	39.52	20.30	39.00	40.70	13.15	42.54	44.31	8.90	49.83	41.27	31.64	24.14	44.22	20.35	31.60	48.05	15.58	32.04	52.38
Philippines	29.49	34.53	35.99	23.87	36.81	39.33	20.35	32.49	47.16	14.81	32.11	53.08	49.59	14.50	35.90	43.05	15.92	41.03	36.71	15.72	47.57
Thailand	25.67	27.57	46.76	17.92	31.99	50.08	10.38	39.73	49.89	9.68	43.40	46.93	65.42	12.05	22.53	54.62	16.95	28.44	45.21	19.54	35.24
Other Southeast Asia																					
Cambodia	–	–	–	60.55	13.42	26.03	46.60	15.94	37.47	34.95	25.62	39.42	–	–	–	76.37	4.36	19.28	68.45	10.52	21.03
Lao PDR	–	–	–	–	–	–	56.52	19.15	24.33	49.08	25.65	25.26	–	–	–	85.40	3.50	11.10	–	–	–
Myanmar	42.71	12.60	44.70	50.54	11.98	37.48	60.05	9.68	30.27	54.87	11.89	33.25	66.07	10.52	23.41	67.08	10.25	22.67	–	–	–
Viet Nam	–	–	–	41.43	26.30	32.27	30.24	28.90	40.86	22.66	38.98	38.36	–	–	–	69.31	12.38	18.48	61.78	14.96	23.26

continued on next page

Table A5.2 (continued)

	Output shares												Employment shares								
	1970s			1980s			1990s			2000–2006			1980s			1990s			2000–2006		
	Agri-culture	Ind-ustry	Ser-vices	Agri-culture	Ind-ustry	Ser-vices	Agri-culture	Ind-ustry	Ser-vices	Agri-culture	Ind-ustry	Ser-vices	Agri-culture	Ind-ustry	Ser-vices	Agri-culture	Ind-ustry	Ser-vices	Agri-culture	Ind-ustry	Ser-vices
Other South Asia																					
Bangladesh	–	–	–	31.60	21.17	47.24	27.13	23.94	48.93	22.11	26.54	51.35	68.24	16.19	15.56	67.04	11.71	21.25	58.23	12.22	29.55
Bhutan	–	–	–	51.02	20.41	28.57	40.04	31.09	28.88	26.95	37.85	35.20	–	–	–	–	–	–	–	–	–
Maldives	–	–	–	–	–	–	–	–	–	–	–	–	–	–	–	24.61	24.04	51.35	16.53	22.92	60.55
Nepal	67.44	10.11	22.46	56.02	14.20	29.78	43.49	20.92	35.59	38.96	21.14	39.89	–	–	–	79.56	3.65	16.79	–	–	–
Pakistan	33.78	22.79	43.43	28.55	23.27	48.19	26.13	24.36	49.50	23.24	24.54	52.22	52.07	20.03	27.90	47.71	18.59	33.71	46.33	18.95	34.72
Sri Lanka	28.97	26.08	44.96	27.23	27.02	45.75	23.64	26.36	49.99	18.65	26.59	54.76	50.14	19.71	30.15	42.04	22.69	35.26	36.15	24.58	39.27
Central Asia and Mongolia																					
Armenia	–	–	–	–	–	–	34.41	36.53	29.06	24.02	38.71	37.31	–	–	–	37.32	23.81	38.87	45.63	16.74	37.63
Azerbaijan	–	–	–	–	–	–	26.60	35.60	37.80	13.22	54.12	32.66	34.37	30.37	35.25	38.08	19.84	42.08	40.01	11.45	48.53
Kazakhstan	–	–	–	–	–	–	14.61	34.82	50.57	8.03	38.87	53.10	35.55	26.46	38.00	23.15	26.80	50.04	35.43	16.53	48.03
Kyrgyz Republic	–	–	–	32.72	–	–	40.76	27.48	31.75	35.29	24.60	40.11	–	–	–	43.13	18.71	38.16	44.78	10.37	36.73
Mongolia	–	–	–	17.36	27.30	55.34	33.73	24.90	41.37	25.96	31.30	42.74	–	–	–	47.09	21.84	31.07	–	14.77	40.46
Tajikistan	–	–	–	32.06	40.11	27.83	31.19	36.43	32.37	24.93	35.51	39.56	–	–	–	57.76	19.96	24.77	–	–	–
Turkmenistan	–	–	–	27.77	37.06	35.17	23.49	45.50	31.01	22.12	42.48	35.39	–	–	–	44.77	–	–	–	–	–
Uzbekistan	–	–	–	29.34	35.54	35.13	32.79	30.11	37.10	31.81	25.06	43.13	–	–	–	42.50	20.94	36.56	34.40	20.30	45.30
Pacific																					
Fiji Islands	24.72	21.88	53.40	20.38	20.97	58.66	19.05	25.68	55.27	15.85	26.25	57.90	–	–	–	2.22	35.39	62.35	–	–	–
Kiribati	19.06	52.28	28.66	29.66	7.81	62.53	21.29	6.38	72.32	7.62	12.67	79.71	–	–	–	9.61	13.86	76.53	–	–	–
Marshall Islands	–	–	–	–	–	–	14.45	14.59	70.96	10.93	20.82	68.25	–	–	–	–	–	–	–	–	–
Micronesia, Federated States of	–	–	44.54	–	–	–	–	–	–	–	–	–	–	–	–	–	–	–	–	–	–

continued on next page

Table A5.2 (continued)

| | Output shares | | | | | | | | | | | | Employment shares | | | | | | | | |
| | 1970s | | | 1980s | | | 1990s | | | 2000–2006 | | | 1980s | | | 1990s | | | 2000–2006 | | |
	Agri-culture	Ind-ustry	Ser-vices	Agri-culture	Ind-ustry	Ser-vices	Agri-culture	Ind-ustry	Ser-vices	Agri-culture	Ind-ustry	Ser-vices	Agri-culture	Ind-ustry	Ser-vices	Agri-culture	Ind-ustry	Ser-vices	Agri-culture	Ind-ustry	Ser-vices
Papua New Guinea	32.45	28.00	39.55	32.21	27.48	40.32	28.75	37.02	34.22	37.58	39.58	22.84	–	–	–	–	–	–	73.33	3.65	23.02
Palau	–	–	–	–	–	–	11.14	11.06	77.80	3.46	17.05	78.43	–	–	–	–	–	–	–	–	–
Samoa	–	–	–	–	–	–	19.63	26.94	53.43	14.42	26.93	58.65	–	–	–	–	–	–	–	–	–
Solomon Islands	–	–	–	–	–	–	–	–	–	.			–	–	–	26.68	13.65	59.15	–	–	–
Timor-Leste	–	–	–	–	–	–	43.15	16.77	40.08	28.67	15.23	56.10	–	–	–	–	–	–	–	–	–
Tonga	44.65	12.29	43.06	37.91	14.20	47.89	33.63	14.79	51.58	28.93	16.31	54.76	–	–	–	37.13	–	–	–	–	–
Vanuatu	21.95	6.05	72.00	22.70	9.30	68.00	16.84	10.40	72.76	15.19	9.04	75.42	–	–	–	–	–	–	–	–	–

– = data not available, ASEAN = Association of Southeast Asian Nations, Lao PDR = Lao People's Democratic Republic.

Note: The main data source is the World Bank's *World Development Indicators* (WDI). Agriculture includes agriculture, fishery, and forestry. Industry includes manufacturing, mining, construction, and utilities. Services include transport, trade, finance, public administration, and others. Sector shares are computed in nominal terms. It is important to add that we checked the quality of the data of this database and found some problems. We calculated the number of cases where the change between 2 consecutive years in the share (both output and employment, for each sector) was larger (i.e., increase in the share) or smaller (i.e., decrease in the share) than 5 percentage points. Except in extreme circumstances, e.g., wars or natural disasters, sector shares cannot change by this much between 2 years. We discovered that there were plenty of such cases for output, and substantially fewer for employment.

Figures for the output shares: Hong Kong, China; Cambodia; Bangladesh; and Fiji Islands are up to 2005. Turkmenistan, Papua New Guinea, and Tonga are up to 2004. Vanuatu are up to 2003.

Figures for the employment shares: The People's Republic of China figures are for 2000 only. Hong Kong, China; the Republic of Korea; Indonesia; the Philippines; Thailand; and Azerbaijan figures are for 2000–2005. Singapore agriculture shares are for 2000–2004 while industry and services shares are for 2000–2005. Cambodia figures are for 2000–2001 and 2004; Viet Nam and Mongolia for 2000–2004; Bangladesh for 2000 and 2003; Maldives for 2000 only; Pakistan for 2002–2004; Sri Lanka and Armenia for 2002–2003; and the Kyrgyz Republic for 2000–2004.

Source: Asian Development Bank, Statistical Database System, accessed 14 September 2006; Directorate General of Budget, Accounting, and Statistics (various years), Statistical Yearbook of [Taipei,China]; National Bureau of Statistics (various years), China Statistical Yearbook; Sundrum (1997) and Chadha and Sahu (2002), cited in Anant et al. (2006); World Bank, World Development Indicators online database, accessed 13 March 2008.

6

What Is the Role of Investment in Delivering Full Employment? Full Employment II

Mass poverty of the kind seen in rural Tamil Nadu and elsewhere cannot be viewed as a "pocket phenomenon" or as a mere aberration of the system. It is a reflection of the total malfunctioning of the economic order. . . . Hence, any attempt to analyse the problem in terms of one or two variables such as low capital formation or absence of policy measures to ensure adequate distribution of income must be viewed with suspicion. . . . There is no comprehensive theory which details the working of an economy such as that of Tamil Nadu.

—John Kenneth Galbraith (1979, 43)

As discussed in chapter 5, given that a large share of output or of the labor force is still in agriculture in many Asian countries, any development program will have to consider the situation in this sector. The traditional literature on structural change argues that the key to the development of agriculture is the transfer of resources, labor particularly, into industry and services. I have argued that insofar as the other sectors of the economy do not absorb fully the surplus labor in agriculture, conditions must be improved in the countryside to achieve full employment of the labor force. The transfer of labor to other sectors requires investment (to lift the capacity constraint discussed in chapter 2) for industrialization. The first issue (investment) is discussed here, while industrialization is discussed in detail in chapters 7, 8, 9, and 10.

Kalecki (1944) distinguished three ways to achieve and maintain full employment: (i) by government spending on public investment (e.g., schools, hospitals, highways) or on subsidies to mass consumption (e.g., family allowances, reduction of indirect taxation, subsidies to keep down the prices of necessities); (ii) by stimulating private investment (e.g., through a reduction in the rate of interest, lowering of income tax, or other measures assisting private investment); and (iii) by redistributing income from higher to lower income classes. Kalecki favored the first and third methods.

A dynamic economy requires increases in the growth rate of the capital stock (i.e., capital accumulation) in the form of, among others, investment in public transportation and in public utilities. These increases can be achieved in two ways. The first one is to increase the productivity with which capital is used.[1] This route, however, is very difficult, for the empirical evidence shows that capital productivity tends to decline in the long run (Foley and Marquetti 1999; Foley and Michl 1999; Marquetti 2003; Felipe et al. 2008). It seems that development entails increases in labor productivity combined with decreases in capital productivity.

The second mechanism to increase the growth rate of the capital stock is to increase the investment share in output. This is the basis for a policy of industrialization, and is the one followed by the successful East and Southeast Asian economies (see, for example, Lau 1990 on the Republic of Korea and Taipei,China), and the People's Republic of China (PRC) (Wang and Li 1995). The importance of investment for development is crucial.[2] There is no lack of candidate projects: schools, hospitals, transport, power, and telecommunications are all underserved in much of developing Asia. Investment, as noted in chapter 4, plays a dual role. On the one hand, investment expenditures are a source of demand when they are incurred. And on the other hand, investment increases the productive capacity of the economy in the long run. This second role is the one I consider here.[3]

---

[1]   Recall (chapter 2) that the growth rate of the capital stock $(\hat{K})$ can be expressed as $\hat{K} = (\Delta K / K) = (I / Y) \times (Y / K)$, where (I / Y) is the investment-to-GDP ratio and (Y / K) is capital productivity.

[2]   And not only for development. In early 2008, as the news about the possible recession in the United States increased following the problems in the subprime loan and housing markets, Paul Krugman wrote an article in the *New York Times* asking the American administration to implement a large public investment program (e.g., to repair the country's infrastructure) to tackle the looming recession. The key objective? To avoid unemployment and a subsequent "jobless recovery."

[3]   Kalecki (1939, 148–149) in his discussion of "what causes periodical crises?" argued that investment is both an expenditure and an addition to capital accumulation. The tragedy of investment is that it causes crises because it is useful. The basic contradiction underlying investment lies in the different time horizon of the effects of investments on demand and on capacity; that is, while the impact of demand is exhausted in a short time, that of capacity lasts longer.

How did the successful Asian countries increase their investment-to-gross domestic product (GDP) ratios? While savings in Asia have traditionally been high, it is important to stress that *investment finances itself*. This means that investment, as it is carried out, creates its counterpart in savings. The implication is that "there are no financial limits, in the formal sense, to the volume of investment" (Kalecki 1954, 25), which implies that investment causes savings, and not the other way around. As Vickrey argued (1993, 6), "If some genius invents a new product or process and obtains a credit or borrows the funds needed to finance the capital involved in its production, this added real wealth is *ipso facto* someone's savings. Instead of Say's law, we have 'Capital formation created its own saving'." And further, "Attempted saving, with corresponding reduction in spending, does nothing to enhance the willingness of banks and other lenders to finance adequately promising investment projects. With unemployed resources available, saving is neither a prerequisite nor a stimulus to, but a consequence of capital formation, as the income generated by capital formation provides a source of additional saving" (Vickrey 1996, 195).

To understand how the Asian countries managed to increase significantly their investment shares and accumulate capital, the relationship between the labor share, real wage rates, and labor productivity should be considered.[4] During full employment, labor productivity rises, and if the labor share is approximately constant, real wages will have to increase. But the labor share might decrease and yet workers see their real wages increase. This will happen if productivity increases rapidly but such increases are not passed on to wages one-to-one (but these nevertheless increase fast too). Under these circumstances wages will increase by a lesser amount than labor productivity and thus the labor share will decrease.[5] Workers, although they see their share in total income decrease, will tolerate the situation, as happened in the past in a number of Asian countries. The lack of militancy in the labor force also contributed to workers' acceptance of

---

[4]   Algebraically, the relationship is as follows: $s^L = \dfrac{W_n}{Y_n} = \dfrac{w_n \times L}{Y_n} = \dfrac{(w_n/P_w) \times L}{(Y_n/P_Y)} \times \dfrac{P_w}{P_Y} = \dfrac{w_r \times L}{Y_r} \times \dfrac{P_w}{P_Y}$, where the subscript n denotes nominal values and the subscript r denotes real values. W is the overall wage bill, Y is output (hence s^L is labor's share), w is the wage rate, L is employment, and (P_w/P_Y) is the ratio of the wage-to-output deflators.

[5]   From the definition of the labor share, the growth rate of the labor share is $\hat{s}^L = \hat{w}_r - \hat{q} + (\hat{P}_w - \hat{P}_Y)$, where the symbol ^ denotes growth rate, and q is labor productivity (i.e., Y_r/L). If $\hat{q} > \hat{w}_r$ (assuming the growth of the deflators is approximately similar), $\hat{s}^L < 0$, i.e., the labor share will decline. Of course, in practice, the labor share cannot decline beyond a limit. This is because, first, labor unions would not accept a constantly dwindling share in total output. And second, because as countries develop (and the service sector dominates the economy), productivity increases become smaller, which allows smaller increases in real wages.

the situation, partly because of a substantial labor surplus in the economy, and partly because of repression by state agencies. Indeed, authoritarianism helped repress labor and other popular movements, thereby lowering the costs of industrial capital accumulation.[6] I elaborate upon this question in chapter 9.

Naturally, the counterpart of the decrease in the labor share was the increase in the capital share. A good deal of evidence suggests that capital accumulation for industrialization is largely financed by profits in the form of retentions, rather than by household savings (Akyüz and Gore 1996). Indeed, according to Arthur Lewis (1954, 157), "the major source of savings is profits, and if we find that savings are increasing as a proportion of the national income, we may take it for granted that this is because the share of profits in the national income is increasing." Over the long run, a high rate of retained profits tends to be associated with a high rate of corporate investment. Using data for 30 developing countries for the 1980s, Ros (2000, 79–83) showed that there is a strong relationship between a high savings rate, a high share of manufacturing output in GDP, and a high profit share in manufacturing value added in East Asia (Box 6.1).

Monetary policy also contributed to capital accumulation: interest rates were kept relatively (and often artificially) low to maintain cheap lending.[7]

A key aspect of this strategy, i.e., the increase in the share of investment, should be emphasized. This is that real wages must not fall. This requires both a high rate of labor productivity and stable prices of essential consumer goods, which implies that their supply must rise in step with their demand. Maintenance of stable prices will also require that investment in the different sectors of the economy, particularly in capital and consumer goods, be undertaken in the right proportions. And finally, it will also necessitate, as already noted, the adjustment of the rate of growth of employment to the limit set by the increase in food supply and articles of mass consumption in general. Certainly all this is not easy. Maintaining the purchasing power of wages is also important because declines in real wages limit the expansion of the market for mass consumption articles. However, because I consider the objective of full employment as the basic measure of a socially equi-

---

[6] In the Republic of Korea, real wages in the manufacturing industry rose rapidly through the 1960s and 1970s (see Hamilton [1986] and Deyo [1987]).

[7] In recent years (since approximately 2001), many Asian developing countries have become international net creditors. Now an ample cushion of foreign exchange reserves bolsters the confidence of financial markets and domestic households. This means that spending programs can be financed with high rates of internal savings. This requires careful thinking about the growth model to follow, in particular about a possible reorientation from export-led growth toward domestic demand–led growth (see chapter 16), as well as about the implications for inflation and real exchange rates.

Box 6.1. The People's Republic of China's Development Model: Does It Need Rebalancing?

For years economists have been debating whether the People's Republic of China's (PRC) astonishing growth rates of about 10% per annum can be maintained. The profession seems to be divided between those who argue that it can be sustained for years to come, as the country has an almost unlimited labor supply that guarantees the country's (price) competitiveness for a long time;[a] and those who argue that the model is showing signs of wear. This latter group argues that the PRC has to change its growth model and shift from investment and exports to a more domestic consumption–led model and, overall, to promote balanced growth in multiple sectors. The reason is that the PRC has been investing too much and too fast in its export-oriented manufacturing sector. The main source of this investment is retained profits. The implication is that the share of household consumption in total output has been declining and now stands at a low 36% (in the US it is over 70%), down from over 60% in the 1950s (Asian Development Bank 2006a, 123). This is the reflection of an also declining share of total wages in output, from almost 55% in the early 1990s to less than 40% recently (Kuijs 2007; Kuijs and He 2007).[b] This situation poses a conundrum: how can labor, as a class, accept a permanent decline in its share in output? The answer is that it is possible provided certain conditions are met. The PRC's spectacular boom is driven by massive productivity gains and increasing profits in manufacturing. These profits are reinvested, which generates further manufacturing capacity (Felipe et al. 2008). It has been estimated that annual productivity growth in the PRC's manufacturing sector grew at an average 20.4% per annum between 1995 and 2003.[c] This allows very large wage rate increases, of about 15.0% per annum,

---

[a] Moreover, labor laws in the PRC have been for decades very lax. Although on paper they provide minimum guarantees to workers, in practice they are, like in many other developing countries, routinely violated. This has made labor very cheap. From 1 January 2008, workers who have been with a company for 10 years or signed two fixed-term contracts will be entitled to 1 month's severance pay for every year worked. The law also requires employers to consult an employee representative congress, usually a branch of the official All China Federation of Trade Unions, on any changes to matters including hours, benefits, and compensation. The new law closes a loophole that allowed companies to dismiss workers on temporary or fixed-term contracts without compensation, or even employ them without a formal contract altogether, often through third-party labor agencies. The result of this new labor law is that employers have already started complaining about it on the grounds it will enhance the bargaining power of workers, and that it will raise labor costs and make hiring more complicated.

[b] I must admit that my own estimates of the factor shares differ significantly from these. In Felipe et al. (2008), I report an increase in the labor share (and consequently a decrease in the share of capital). I argue that what characterizes the PRC economy is the very high level of reinvestment of profits.

[c] These huge productivity gains are significantly more important in explaining the competitiveness of the PRC's manufacturing than the possible undervaluation of the exchange rate or government subsidies.

continued on next page

Box 6.1 (continued)

which explains the decline in the labor share in output (i.e., declines in unit labor costs). This means that, as a class, labor may be willing to accept this situation as long as wage rates continue increasing.[d]

But what happens to consumption? Aggregate consumption can be characterized as an income share–weighted consumption function.[e] As the share of total income that goes to (capitalists') investment is increasing, workers have a lower income share, and because workers spend more and capitalists less on the margin, the overall marginal propensity of the economy to consume declines, implying that total consumption declines. This can lead to an underconsumption crisis. If this process continues, the PRC may reach a situation in which production is profitable, but the profits embedded in output cannot be realized due to deficient demand. This may eventually lead to reductions in capacity utilization, profit rates, investment, income, production and, finally, in employment. The PRC's policy makers should be aware of this chain of events. Indeed, the PRC's key problem for the next decades will be employment generation, the key to political stability. And this requires an "aggressive" growth model.

Therefore, the key challenge for the PRC's policy makers is to maintain a growth model whose ultimate outcome is employment generation while avoiding an underconsumption crisis. It is in this sense that the PRC needs to find balance and maintain harmony. Economic reforms should have this as their background. Increases in spending in social infrastructure, such as education, health care, and the environment, will be important in this rebalancing.[f]

---

[d] Of course, until labor costs, a widely used measure of how competitive an economy is, are nothing but the share of labor in value added (Felipe 2007). This has very important implications for policy analysis for, under this view, the competitiveness of an economy is a question of income distribution.

[e] $C = a + mpc_L\left(1 - \frac{\Pi}{Y}\right)Y + mpc_K\left(\frac{\Pi}{Y}\right)Y$, where C is consumption; mpc_L and mpc_K are the marginal propensities to consume of labor and capital, respectively (and usually $mpc_L > mpc_K$); and $\left(\frac{\Pi}{Y}\right)$ and $\left(1 - \frac{\Pi}{Y}\right)$ are the shares of profits and wages in total income (Y). The overall mpc of the economy is a weighted average of the two marginal propensities.

[f] In 2007, private consumption in the PRC accounted for a bigger slice of GDP growth than investment for the first time in 7 years (see *The Economist* [2008a]).

table economic policy, the constraint that real wages should not decrease could pose a problem. For this reason, the lower acceptable limit for society should be stable real wages for the better-off workers and increased real wages for the bottom workers. To be more precise, inclusive growth should favor policies that encourage faster wage growth for low-paying jobs than for highly paid work. This means that, at the low end, wage growth will exceed productivity growth, while at the high end, productivity growth will exceed wage growth. This proposal is consistent with the idea of broad-based growth, which should translate into development efforts directed toward raising the standard of living of those at the bottom. This policy implies that, most likely, prices will grow in the low-wage sector as costs rise. Preventing inflation will require some constraint on prices and wages in the high-wage sectors (Kalecki 1966a; Minsky 1965, 1968, 1973).

What is the impact of this development strategy (the increase in the profit shares) on consumption? Given that workers have a high propensity to consume, the decrease in the labor share will affect overall consumption. How should policy makers proceed, i.e., what consumption categories should be reduced? To accomplish this in a fair manner, policy makers would have to restrain the consumption of nonessentials (something that is politically difficult) through the imposition of appropriate taxes. In these circumstances, an acceleration of income (induced by the acceleration of investment) will be accompanied by an increase in the supply of necessities adequate to prevent inflationary pressures. Thus, a higher investment share in output will be offset by a decline in the share of nonessential consumption via direct and indirect taxation of the upper classes. At what point is the share of investment too high and that of consumption too low? This is difficult to ascertain, but signals will be apparent (Felipe et al. 2008). Profitability may decrease precipitously, leading the economy into a profitability slump. On the other hand, if authorities are not careful and the share of consumption of essential goods goes down, the problem might be underconsumption (as discussed in Box 6.1).

There are, however, three important potential obstacles to the increase in investment (Kalecki 1966a). The first obstacle is that the investment goods sector (e.g., construction) may be already running at close to or full capacity and thus may not be able to increase its output. The second and third obstacles—namely, the inflationary pressures derived from increases in investment, and that in a market economy the private sector is the generator of wealth—need some elaboration.

The second obstacle derives from a problem discussed previously. This is that an increase in investment will probably lead to an increase in employment, and this raises the question of how to secure an adequate supply of necessities to cover the higher demand. This increased demand will induce inflationary pressures as the supply of necessities (especially food) is limited.[8] But this has an additional implication. Suppose that the economy is capable of increasing investment. This will lead to more employment and to a higher total *nominal* wage bill. However, the overall wage bill in *real* terms will remain unchanged as a result of the increase in the price level. What is the implication? That although the level of employment will have increased (certainly a positive outcome), the real wage rate (i.e., wage per worker) will have declined, and this is an unfair way of financing the acceleration in growth. The conclusion is that the increase in investment under conditions of an inelastic supply of food will cause both a fall in real wages and an acceleration in prices. For this reason, expanding food production in parallel to industrial development is essential. Investment in public transport and public utilities should be accompanied by measures to expand agricultural production, such as land reform and easy credit to farmers (chapter 5). Chapter 13 provides a discussion of the obstacles to the achievement and maintenance of full employment during structural change.

This discussion means that inclusive growth cannot throw the costs of capital formation on the wage earners and in general on the poor. In a command economy, investment is financed out of the incomes of state institutions and not out of the savings of private individuals (Dobb 1959); in countries that have followed the capitalist path of development (i.e., where savings and investment decisions are distinct), who bears the cost of capital accumulation is an important political economy question that needs to be answered. Just as governments must be accountable for their actions, policies, goals, and ultimately for their performance and capacity to deliver, the domestic upper and business class of developing countries—in many cases a relatively small group of individuals and families—must also be made ethically and politically responsible for the development of the country.[9] Domestic investment often depends on the decisions of a small group of businessmen. But as long as private investment cannot be enforced, the public sector will have to cover the gap up to full employment. Many developing countries, however, cannot enforce the tax collection system; tax evasion, therefore, is rampant, and instituting progressive financial reforms is an uphill battle.[10] Under these circumstances, the funds for investment

---

[8]   Of course, inflation may not show up if entrepreneurs are unwilling to expand their capital expenditures.

[9]   Haque (2006) refers to 22 controlling families in Pakistan. See Coronel et al. (2004) for an in-depth analysis of how a group of wealthy families dominates politics in the Philippines.

[10] One such case is the Philippines, where collecting direct taxes is a serious problem. In 2005, the Government of the Philippines extended the value-added tax (VAT) to energy products previously exempt. And in 2006, it raised the VAT rate on all taxable products (including energy) from 10% to 12%. Given that most energy is consumed by

are hard to extract. Therefore, both agriculture and manufacturing fail to develop efficiently, and growth of total output is swallowed up in growing consumption. I will return to this question in chapter 12, and argue that developing countries' governments can finance their investment needs by spending.

Third and final, as noted above, in a market economy the private sector is the generator of wealth. However, in many developing countries, the private sector may not collaborate due to low profitability, large uncertainty, high cost of investment, or because firms do not reinvest their full savings out of profits. The underlying reasons can be analyzed through the growth diagnostics approach (Box 2.2 in chapter 2). Recall that the basic problem is to identify if a low private investment share is due to the high cost of investment or to low returns. One possibility is, of course, to identify and relax the binding constraint on private investment. But perhaps doing this is not easy and may not be enough to increase private investment to the necessary levels. For this reason, a policy of stimulating exclusively private investment may not be satisfactory. In these circumstances, the government will clearly have to step in to reach the desired level of investment. Government investment should not replace or crowd out private investment, but complement it because it is insufficient. Indeed, the most effective and egalitarian way to achieve full employment is through a program of public investments targeted carefully at location-specific high-employment activities. For this reason, the government will have the responsibility to provide a large volume of public sector investment, e.g., in infrastructure. This, I must stress, is not to deprive the private sector from being active in the economy; quite the opposite. The private sector has to invest in whatever activities it finds profitable. This is the way a market economy will prosper, although this does not guarantee the full employment of the labor force.

In many developing countries, the private sector cannot be relied upon to undertake a sufficient amount of investment in the areas that a developing country may need. The reason is that nobody can force this sector to undertake such investments. Moreover, in some developing countries the business class does not play, on a large scale, the role of dynamic entrepreneur that it should (contrary to what occurred in today's developed countries at the time they underwent deep structural changes), driven by "animal spirits" (i.e., a spontaneous urge to action and willingness to take risks), using Keynes's (1936) terminology. In some cases, this is due to the consequence

---

the wealthier groups, and because the government used part of the proceeds from the VAT to reduce taxes on kerosene and to increase spending on infrastructure and social services, the negative effects on the poor were somewhat reduced. Nevertheless, the VAT is not a progressive tax and the big loophole is in direct taxation.

of a poor investment climate (e.g., difficulties in opening a new business), the result of government-imposed constraints. In other cases, some oligo-polistic sectors of the economy favor privileged groups that enjoy rents, groups that lobby to perpetuate the situation. The problem is neither the high cost of investment nor low returns (in the growth diagnostics termi-nology of Hausmann, Rodrik, and Velasco [2005]) but the desire by these groups to maintain their privileges. Investment takes place in the areas these groups control and at the pace that suits them. They might be unwill-ing to expand capital expenditures, simply because not doing so favors their objectives.

The private sector's capacity for entrepreneurship must be nurtured and developed, since the driving force in a capitalist economy is the deci-sion to invest, and the rate of capital accumulation (and the demand for labor) depends on it. But the objective of the private sector is not to maxi-mize employment and, hence, as noted in chapter 3, it *cannot* be and should not be made responsible for achieving full employment.

As I noted at the start of the chapter, Kalecki (1944) also favored the increase in private consumption as a complementary mechanism to achieve full employment. As Kalecki (1944) argued, public and private investment should be carried out only to the extent to which they are considered use-ful. If the effective demand that they generate fails to provide full employ-ment, then the gap should be filled by increasing consumption and not by undertaking further investment, which most likely will be unproductive. This (i.e., promoting consumption) is the advice that some Asian countries (e.g., Thailand, Malaysia, the PRC) are receiving today, to shift their growth strategy from investment-driven (and export-led growth) to domestic demand–led growth by activating private consumption through, for exam-ple, decreases in indirect taxation, opening markets to induce price compe-tition, or developing the credit card market (chapter 16). As argued above, a number of East and Southeast Asian countries relied on investment for decades and this strategy paid off. Now, the argument goes, it is about time to shift strategy. Many other countries in the region, however, still would benefit considerably from an increase in investment (this is a constant topic of debate in countries like India, Pakistan, or the Philippines), not to gener-ate effective demand, but in order to accelerate expansion of productive capacity indispensable for the rapid growth of output.

Stimulation of private investment (the second of Kalecki's methods to achieve full employment) through, for example, reductions in interest and/ or tax rates or through subsidies to private investment, will not deliver full employment. If the economy is already in a boom, measures to stimulate investment further will be pointless. And in a slump some of these measures may not work, e.g., reductions in interest rates may be ineffective if there is excess capacity. Private investment depends, especially in developing countries, on expectations and political stability. A one-time reduction in interest or tax rates does not eliminate a downturn. Policy makers would have to lower them successively and continuously to keep investment going.[11]

A final comment on investment is that Keynes (1936, chapter 24) argued that since investment causes saving (and not the other way around, as in classical theory) and investment is promoted by a low interest rate, low interest rates should be maintained. However, he continued, since banking policy will probably not be sufficient by itself to determine an optimum rate of investment, a "somewhat comprehensive socialization of investment will prove the only means of securing an approximation to full employment; though this will need not exclude all manner of compromises and of devices by which public authority will co-operate with private initiative. But beyond this no obvious case is made out for a system of State Socialism which would embrace most of the economic life of the community" (1936, 378).

Finally, how can income redistribution (Kalecki's third method) help in the pursuit of full employment? The idea is that when income is redistributed from the higher- to the lower- income earners, total consumption will increase, as the latter group has a higher propensity to consume. One possible policy would be to increase the income taxes of the rich (and use them to subsidize private consumption) and simultaneously decrease indirect taxation on necessities consumed by the poor. The problem with this type of policy is that governments have to watch out for the overall impact on private investment.

My view is that, in practice, governments should pursue a sensible combination of public and private investment, along with subsidies to consumption. The private sector should invest in all those activities that it con-

---

[11]   In general, relying on private investment for economic growth is problematic for several reasons. First, it tends to introduce inflationary pressures, since at the aggregate level prices of consumer goods must be marked up over the wage bill required to produce these goods. This means that the workers that produced them cannot consume all of them, leaving consumption goods for workers (and others) in other sectors to consume. Second, it tends to produce inequality, since wages and profits in the investment sector are higher because of greater economic power (of unions and firms). Third, it creates excessive productive capacity unless demand rises sufficiently (with capital-saving innovations, it is likely that the supply side effects of investment outstrip the demand side effects—leaving capital idle and depressing demand). Finally, modern investment goods are expensive and long-lived, requiring complex financial instruments and relations. Minsky argued that investment-fueled economic growth produces growing private debt ratios that increase financial fragility. This is why Minsky argued that government spending–led growth is more sustainable, as it allows private sector spending to grow based on income rather than on private debt. I am grateful to Randy Wray for sending me this note and making this point clear.

siders profitable;[12] the public sector should invest in all those areas that are needed for the development of the country (and that complement the private sector); and the gap to full employment should be covered, as argued above, by higher consumption. How is the government's spending program to be split? This is a matter of social priorities, and the government will have to decide whether in a given year it will, e.g., build more schools or provide more milk for children.

[12] One option being considered today is the so-called public–private partnerships as a mechanism to develop physical infrastructure. These partnerships act as an alternative to traditional public sector finance through freeing up resources and accelerating investment programs. They have the advantage that they reduce the fear of deficits and encourage private participation.

7

Why Is "Planning Development" Necessary?

Unless India initiates a well-planned program to increase GDP growth to 8–9% on a sustained basis, we believe that the expanding work force could become an increasing threat to social stability.

—Morgan Stanley (2006, 28)

One important implication of the discussion in the previous chapters is that, in general, many developing countries find it difficult to run on a *balanced development path*. Achieving structural equilibrium between investment and consumption and noninflationary economic development is vital for developing countries, although virtually impossible. For developing countries under pressure to accept the effects (good and bad) of globalization, introduce market reforms, and reduce the role of government, the political obstacles to development are phenomenal. Achieving inclusive growth in these circumstances is not easy. Amsden (2007) argues provocatively that the more freedom a developing country has to shape its own policies, the faster its economy will grow.

As Keynes (1936, 320) argued, "the duty of ordering the current volume of investment cannot safely be left in private hands." For this reason, the strategy of full employment based on stepping up investment requires "planning", a term that, unfortunately, has acquired a bad name (see, for example, Easterly 2006, 2008), although it is done everywhere. Indeed, most, if not all, medium- and long-term development plans of both developed and developing countries specify the amount of total (public) investment as well as the allocation across sectors.[1] For example, Malaysia's Ninth Five-Year Plan, 2006–2010, and the Third Industrial Master Plan, 2006–2020, contain policies to *push* its industry

---

[1]   And certainly also do the so-called "country strategy programs" prepared by the international financial institutions that lend to the developing countries. These are heavily criticized by Easterly (2006).

up the value chain and have well-defined *targets* in terms of growth rates and sectors' shares in output. Through the Malaysian Industrial Development Authority, the government executes policies and initiatives intended to shape an industrial base to face the future challenges of the country. The authority assumes the key roles of *planning, coordinating,* and *promoting* the growth of industries in the manufacturing sector (also, Pakistan Institute of Development Economics [PIDE 2006] for a development plan for Pakistan).[2]

A balanced development path requires coherent planning, not only of the forthcoming volume of investment but also of the composition of investment (sectors and types of goods), which must be directed *purposefully* toward the breaking of bottlenecks in supply.[3] However, given that resources are scarce, perhaps "planners" ought to think, and surely many do, in terms of unbalanced growth à la Hirschman (1958), i.e., by selecting the projects that contribute the most to development.

I must stress that by planning I do not mean establishing a command economy, or even a developmental state. Easterly is right when he argues (in the same vein as Hayek) that "no top–down central planner can possibly have enough information to allocate resources and make factories work" (Easterly 2008, 5). What I mean is the establishment of a partnership between public and private sectors to coordinate their activities (Hausmann and Rodrik 2006). Public–private cooperation is needed because production requires both private and public inputs. While markets provide private inputs (which have prices that convey information, resources allocated by capital markets, and firms motivated by profit), the provision of public inputs (e.g., postal system, labor market for engineers) is complex. The provision of public goods is not guided by prices that convey information; the incentives to provide these inputs are not clear (political?); and even in case incentives exist, how resources would move is not clear. It is in this sense that my words about the role of the public investment in chapter 6 must be understood.

I consider five reasons why planning the development of a country is necessary. First, because development is a long-term process. The introduction of new industries involves substantial time lags between the decisions to build new facilities and the output that they produce. Second, planning is necessary because, as discussed in chapter 6, private invest-

---

2   Planning continues being the norm among the People's Republic of China's policy makers. The Plenary Sessions of the Central Committee of the Chinese Communist Party provide important guidelines for the macroeconomic management of the country as well as for many development issues.

3   Governments in developing countries have to be imaginative and design investments and projects that are socially beneficial, such as fixing potholes, cleaning streets, upgrading roads and railroads, restoring historical sites, child and elderly care, etc.

ment may not go into all areas of the economy. The private sector will direct investment to the areas where it expects its venture will be profitable (and this is how it should be!) and not necessarily to where a developing country needs capital the most. This argument applies to private foreign investment as well. Will it go into education and health? What about the objectives of employment and job creation? Full employment is the government's responsibility. The private sector alone cannot be responsible for the achievement of full employment simply because, as already noted in chapter 3, it is not its responsibility. Private investors are not driven by the social well-being, but by a *Smithian* self-interest ("It is not from the benevolence of the butcher, the brewer, or the baker, that we expect our dinner, but from their regard to their own interest" Smith [1776, 23–24]). What we must accept with regard to the general level of employment and output is that there is no invisible hand channeling self-interest into some social optimum. Surely growth in a market economy has to be driven by a dynamic private sector. But the government cannot be reduced to a mere supporter of private sector activities, especially when achievement of full employment to reduce poverty is what is at stake. Government has two key roles in a developing economy. First, it has to allow the operation of the free-market dynamics. And second, it has to intervene actively in selected areas, the most important being the creation of physical infrastructure and the provision of a platform to enable the workforce to participate in productive activities.[4]

Third, and related to the previous point, planning is necessary because the government must coordinate with the private sector to avoid mismatches, bottlenecks, and waste of scarce resources.

Fourth, planning is necessary because only when the structure of investment across sectors and types of goods has been determined will the country be able to decide the technique of production, a key issue for economies with considerable labor surpluses. Some sectors of the economy, by their own nature, require capital-intensive techniques. These will absorb large shares of investment, but will not absorb too much labor. This is also the case of much foreign investment, i.e., it embodies techniques with relatively high capital–labor ratios. What can developing countries do? A solution could be

---

[4] Claiming, for example, that the role of government is simply to develop and maintain a business-friendly private sector environment by addressing market failures, institutional weaknesses, and policy shortcomings—as well as by investing in infrastructure and human capital, building institutions, maintaining macroeconomic stability, protecting property rights, and maintaining the rule of law—is to recognize openly that government action is key to development. The problem is that governments in many developing countries cannot execute these functions adequately (hence these countries have both weak private sectors and weak governments). This is why reforms of the public sector are necessary in many cases.

to favor labor-intensive techniques that absorb the labor surplus in areas such as public investments (infrastructure), housing construction, and agriculture as long as this is permitted by the supply of food surplus (however, these new workers would not be highly productive), and simultaneously favor capital-intensive techniques in other areas of the economy where this is unavoidable. But an additional issue must be taken into account: the sectors that will most likely lead to the largest increase in total output are those intensive in capital, while additional demand resulting from the increase in the overall wage bill would be directed to consumer necessities, whose supply would probably not increase at the same pace.

Finally, planning is needed in deciding how to finance development. Aggregate decisions are between domestic resources and foreign assistance and debt. Regarding domestic finance, the key issue is the understanding of the role of savings and investment. I have already argued that the key constraint of many developing countries is lack of productive capacity. But do savings finance investment? The classical answer is yes: savings are a prerequisite for investment, hence the need to implement policies to raise the level of savings. The Keynesian answer (chapter 6), on the other hand, is that encouraging investment will generate its own saving through increases in output and profits (when the economy is below full capacity); or through income redistribution from groups with a low propensity to save to groups with a high propensity to save (when the economy is working at full capacity). What is important is not so much incentives for saving but incentives for investment. The Keynesian view is that all that is needed to initiate additional real investment is finance provided by an increase in total bank loans, with no need for increased savings, as long as the banking system can create new finance. In chapter 12, I will argue that governments' fear of budget deficits are often unfounded. Government spending (and deficits) lead to inflation once the economy reaches full employment, but not below. I will also dismiss the idea that government deficits crowd out private investment. Developing countries should maximize the use of domestic resources for development.

What is the role of external finance? In an open economy, governments and firms can borrow from abroad to complement domestic sources. The most important problem to consider here is the debt-servicing problems. As is well known, this has led developing countries on many occasions to debt crises, as they need to generate foreign exchange to repay debt denominated in foreign currency. Kalecki (1966b) questioned the role of foreign capital for development (he was especially skeptical of government credits). While in theory foreign capital obviously contributes to capital formation, its role is not entirely clear. The importance of foreign investment, he argued, lies not so much in its contribution to increasing capital accumulation, but in easing balance-of-payments problems (i.e., finance current-account deficits). Foreign direct investment, which is undertaken by the private sector, is directed to what the investing company expects to be profitable, and not to what the developing country needs.[5] In this regard, Stiglitz (2005, 21) argues that the "obsession with attracting foreign investment" results from the observation that private capital has increased in importance relative to development assistance, although most of these flows are concentrated in a few countries. As a result, many policy makers think that for a country to be successful, private capital flows are the key. Countries that have attracted great amounts of foreign direct investment into natural resources exercise care as they are prone to the "Dutch disease" problem. For this reason, attempts must be made to attract these investments into the manufacturing sector, so as to create employment and bring in new technologies. Stiglitz (2005, 22) concludes that, "the bottom line here is that for countries to rely on foreign borrowing is a mistake," and continues, "I have increasingly come to the view that countries should not rely on foreign borrowing. They should work to attract FDI [foreign direct investment] that promotes economic development. But they should not try to attract portfolio investment" (2005, 23).

Summing up: to embark upon a large investment program without a coherent plan will mean a great deal of wasted effort, as it will surely lead to disproportional (across the different sectors of the economy) and disruptive growth.

---

[5]   That this is true is clear in the analysis of the Asian Development Bank (ADB 2007d) in its annual publication, the *Asian Development Outlook Update 2007*. In its analysis of Pakistan, it lamented that much of the recent surge in foreign direct investment went into services, and not into manufacturing. It argued that, "Unlike some other countries in the region, Pakistan attracts little FDI [foreign direct investment] into manufacturing. This feature needs to be remedied to stimulate economic and employment growth, by bringing in improved technologies, business practices, and innovation so as to raise the level of manufacturing competitiveness and to accelerate structural change" (ADB 2007d, 115).

8

What Is Industrial Policy?
Full Employment III

In this chapter, I address the question of how a country can induce structural change and diversification, and plan transitions to higher growth rates. This is a fundamental aspect of the problem of developing countries, namely, the need to increase productive capacity. Indeed, the transition from agriculture into a modern industrial and service economy, and decisions about how much to invest and where, can be viewed as problems of *self-discovery* and of understanding the externalities that lessen incentives for productive diversification. Today's developed countries directed policies to industrialize. Chang (2002) argues that today's developed countries—such as the United Kingdom, Germany, France, the United States, Sweden, and Japan—used industrial, trade, and technological policies when they were developing and catching up. They used some form of infant-industry policy or tariff protection. More recently, the Republic of Korea is the clearest case of successful economic development achieved through infant-industry protection measures.

Industrial policy has traditionally been understood as any type of selective intervention or government policy that attempts to alter the structure of production toward sectors that are expected to offer better prospects for economic growth than without such intervention. This type of intervention has its adherents—those who believe in market failures—and its detractors—those who believe in the efficient working of markets. The latter argue that industrial policy interventions have often degenerated into an exercise in "picking winners," a game played by government officials deciding what activities and sectors to promote and to spend public money on.[1]

In a series of papers, Rodrik (2004, 2006a) has argued in favor a new type of industrial policy. He acknowledges the existence of generic market failures, but argues "that the location and magnitude of these market failures is highly uncertain" (Rodrik 2004, 3). He argues that information and

---

[1] The literature evaluating the pros and cons of industrial policy is inconclusive. While some authors argue positively about it (e.g., Amsden [1989]), others are critical (e.g., Pack and Sagi [2006]).

coordination externalities are more important than technological externalities, for the former weaken the entrepreneurial drive to restructure and diversify low-income economies. Rodrik argues that industrial policy is not about addressing distortions in the traditional way (i.e., by enumerating technological and other externalities and then targeting policy interventions on these market failures), but about eliciting information from the private sector on significant externalities and about the constraints to structural transformation (hence industrial policy also encompasses activities in agriculture and services) and the opportunities available. This requires "strategic collaboration" between the public and private sectors to determine the areas in which the country has a comparative advantage. The reason is that entrepreneurs may lack information about where the comparative advantage of a country lies and governments may not even know what they do not know. And certainly most governments do not have the adequate knowledge to pick winners. Uncertainty arising from lack of communication—that is, from one decision maker having no way of finding out the concurrent decisions and plans made by others—may, if sufficiently great, inhibit investment decisions and arrest growth. In these circumstances, markets alone are likely to undersupply the incentives and demand for new activities necessary to transform the economy. These market failures are more prevalent in developing economies. As Rodrik (2004, 12) notes: "The trick for the government is not to pick winners, but to know when it has a loser." This requires the development of the appropriate institutional arrangements for industrial policy. Box 8.1 summarizes Rodrik's (2004) basic elements of the institutions for industrial policy. It is along these lines that Pau (2005), for example, analyzes Ireland's recent success attracting foreign direct investment. Against what some believe to be the key to Ireland's success, i.e., the market, the island's success in fact lay in the development of a coordinated institutionalized development strategy with proactive government policies. Jomo and Tan (1999) and Brown (1997) provide analyses of industrial policy in East and Southeast Asia, respectively.

Commenting on Rodrik's (2004) basic elements of the institutional architecture, Rodriguez (2005, 7) states: "Evidently, this design makes sense in theory, but is it likely to work in practice? I have my doubts." He argues that these principles have been applied with success in only three countries: Chile; the Republic of Korea; and Taipei,China. What is the reason? These three countries had an enormous political pressure: economic success and social stability were seen as necessary to sustain the regime. The consequence for failing was the possibility of succumbing to the communist threat. Therefore, Rodriguez (2005, 7) argues: "successful developmentalist strategies will be carried out by states that are sufficiently strong and autonomous so as to impose the social goal of development over the short-

> ## Box 8.1. Institutions for Industrial Policy
>
> The following are the basic elements of an institutional architecture for industrial policy: (i) place political leadership at the top, (ii) set up coordination and deliberation councils, and (iii) set up mechanisms of transparency and accountability. Ten design principles for the formulation of industrial policy are proposed: (i) incentives should be provided only to "new" activities; (ii) there should be clear benchmarks for success and failure; (iii) there must be a built-in sunset clause; (iv) public support must target activities, not sectors; (v) activities that are subsidized must have the clear potential of providing spillovers and demonstration effects; (vi) the authority for carrying out industrial policies must be vested in agencies with demonstrated competence; (vii) the implementing agencies must be monitored closely by a principal with a clear stake in the outcomes and who has political authority at the highest level; (viii) the agencies carrying out promotion must maintain channels of communication with the private sector; (ix) optimally, mistakes that result in "picking the losers" will occur; and (x) promotion activities need to have the capacity to renew themselves, so that the cycle of discovery becomes an ongoing one.
>
> Source: Rodrik 2004.

run interests of the private sector, yet also sufficiently oriented towards a development strategy in which the private sector plays a central role." The key issue is the threat of the disappearance of the private sector. The latter, therefore, cooperated with the regimes in power to prevent a communist takeover and the consequent expropriation of private assets. The overall system was at stake. These governments were far less transparent than Rodrik (2004) may suggest, but all of them provided a high level of public goods and services that improved the life of citizens. I have three comments about this issue. First, the experience of the Southeast Asian countries can be understood from a similar thesis. Indonesia, Malaysia, Singapore, and Thailand also had similar threats during the 1960s and 1970s during the Viet Nam War. Second, Rodriguez's argument could explain why countries like the Philippines have not been able to implement developmentalist strategies. The Philippines still today has a communist threat and a separatist Muslim threat. But the probability of the government being overthrown by these forces is minimal. Discontent in the Philippines is due to accusations of corruption and to the perception that growth is benefiting only a minority. But as long as the country achieves annual growth rates of at least 5%, the situation will not become critical. This allows the private sector elite to operate without much concern for the overall welfare of the rest of society.

Third, does this mean that only states with a significant threat can implement Rodrik's strategy? This is Rodriguez's view. I think that agents behave according to incentives, and in the three cases mentioned by Rodriguez, as well as in the Southeast Asian economies, the incentive was to avoid the communist threat. But other factors can trigger collaboration between the state and private sector for the common good. For example, the People's Republic of China and Viet Nam more recently have not had a communist "threat" and yet their governments strive to deliver goods and services to their citizens.

Industrial policy should be conceived as a joint effort of the state and the private sector to diagnose the sources of blockage in new economic activities and propose solutions to them. Industrial and technological upgrading requires purposeful effort in the form of industrial policy, in particular, effective government action and public–private collaboration. But this needs, first, a government that does not take any particular stand on the activities to be promoted or the instruments to be deployed. It only requires the government to build the private–public institutional setting from which information on profitable activities and useful instruments of intervention can be extracted. The key issue is not whether to protect, but how to protect and promote industry in order to ensure technical progress leading to higher labor productivity.[2] And second, it needs a private sector that is willing to do its part of the deal, i.e., invest.[3]

Understood this way, industrial policy is a powerful tool for successful industrialization and structural change. Perhaps a market-driven development model could not, by itself, have accelerated transitions between different patterns of specialization and delivered the high growth rates that some Asian countries experienced. This is not because market-based successes were absent, but because theory suggests exactly the opposite, that market forces are unlikely to address efficiently the coordination problems that arise in the transition across production and trade patterns. Indeed, coordination failures are likely to arise in the transition from old to new patterns of production and trade specialization. This situation is characteristic of

---

[2] Amsden (2000) and Amsden and Hikino (2000) argue that the new rules of the World Trade Organization (WTO) allow countries to promote their industries, including the manufacturing sector, in particular under the umbrella of advancing science and technology (e.g., by setting up technology parks). Subsidies in exchange for monitorable, results-oriented performance standards are acceptable. Countries can, for example, target national champions. The hurdles that developing countries face are the following: (i) informal political pressures by the developed countries in favor of market opening, (ii) the subjection of countries that make use of WTO rules to promote their industries to "reciprocal control mechanisms", and (iii) their lack of "vision."

[3] This is important in some developing countries, where a well-established elite may not see change with good eyes.

semi-industrialized countries, in which old comparative advantages in labor-intensive industries are being eroded, and new ones in capital and technology-intensive activities emerge only slowly. This view explains the successes not only of the Republic of Korea and Taipei,China, but also of Singapore. Young (1992), in a well-known paper, compared the growth record of Hong Kong, China, and Singapore, and argued that the latter's growth had been based exclusively on capital accumulation (Soviet-style, according to Krugman [1994]). Felipe (2000, 2008) and Felipe and McCombie (2001, 2003) have discussed this literature and argued that its theoretical and empirical problems make the results and implied conclusions far from correct and useful. The Government of Singapore did push the economy into new and more advanced sectors, and perhaps the effort was not a complete success, but certainly without such a push the economy would not have ventured "by itself" into many of the areas in which it is doing well now.[4] As I document in chapter 9, Singapore's manufacturing sector is the most technologically advanced in developing Asia (see Box 8.2 on Singapore's efforts to develop its biotechnology industry). Box 8.3 provides a telling example, based on two different ways of implementing industrial policy, namely, the Republic of Korea and India, in the 1970s. And Box 8.4 describes the efforts that the Korean shoe industry is making toward upgrading.[5]

---

[4]   I am thinking of the post-1979 rapid rise in real wages, partly encouraged by the Government of Singapore in an attempt to stimulate productivity growth.

[5]   Wan (2004) analyzes industrial policies in the Republic of Korea; Singapore; Hong Kong, China; and Taipei,China.

Box 8.2. Building the Biotechnology Industry in Singapore

After making significant strides in electronics, engineering, and chemicals, Singapore is now turning biotechnology into its next manufacturing pillar, and is making huge investments to nurture its development. In 2003, the government opened Biopolis, a S$500-million research park that provides facilities for biotechnology activities and provides legal and laboratory support services. This first-class facility is envisioned to create an atmosphere of inspiration and creative thinking. It features, for instance, a S$33-million high-tech air-conditioning system that cools even open-air parks. Besides providing physical infrastructure, government initiatives also include research grants and tax incentives, funding start-ups, as well as education programs and scholarships to develop the workforce.

The country's national policy of attracting foreign talent is contributing to the effort, particularly in training the workforce. Some top scientists in molecular biology, cancer research, and neurology are already based in Singapore, and the government encourages long-term assimilation into the society. The country's attractiveness to researchers is also helped by a strong intellectual property rights regime and a well-developed health care industry.

The government recognizes the risks involved, such as the long period before investment returns are realized (if at all) and the threat of workers trained in its facilities to seek better opportunities elsewhere, notably in the United States, Europe, and Australia. But it is determined to move ahead as the changing economic environment calls for it.

S$ = Singapore dollars.
Source: Wong 2003.

Box 8.3. Industrial Policy in the Republic of Korea and India

Jacobsson and Alam (1994) provide an example that shows that a successful industrial policy program requires not only a dose of creativity and experimentation but also some clear guiding principles that combine a carrot to promote investments in nontraditional areas with sticks to weed out investment projects that fail.

Both India and the Republic of Korea started producing hydraulic excavators (equipment used to remove soil and stones) in the 1970s. Both countries protected these infant industries by restricting imports of finished hydraulic excava-

continued on next page

Box 8.3 (continued)

tors. Technology was imported through licenses. Protection was supplemented by requirements for local component inputs, which became more stringent over time. Despite these initial similarities, the development of the hydraulic excavator industry differed substantially in the two countries, and the way India and the Republic of Korea promoted their infant industries contrasts sharply.

By the late 1980s, the two Korean excavator manufacturers, Samsung and Daewoo, were producing more than 10 times the annual production of Larsen and Toubro, the largest Indian excavator manufacturers. Moreover, the Korean manufacturers had designed and developed their own excavators, which were competitive enough to be exported starting in 1987. By contrast, none of the Indian manufacturers had introduced an excavator based on their own design and none was in any position to export.

Two aspects of government policy in these countries are crucial in explaining this difference in industry performance. First, although both governments guided private investment decisions in the industry, the Government of the Republic of Korea recognized the importance of economies of scale. It limited the Korean industry to two firms and allowed them to expand production capacity and exploit production economies. The Government of India, by contrast, encouraged a large number of firms to enter the industry and limited their individual production capacities in the belief that this would foster competition in an otherwise protected market. Second, the Korean government managed to instill a sense of competition and dynamism in its two producers by announcing a credible program of time-bound protection. Indian protection was not time-bound. This impending liberalization of the industry was the main factor driving the Korean firms to formulate a clear strategy for developing an internationally competitive design for excavators and an export marketing plan. The cases of India and the Republic of Korea reinforce the critical role that greater openness after a limited period of protection plays in developing competitive infant industries.

Source: Jacobsson and Alam 1994.

Box 8.4. Reviving the Republic of Korea's Shoe Industry

From all indications, the Republic of Korea's shoe industry is dying from competition, mainly from the People's Republic of China's (PRC) cheap labor. Since the early 1990s, many production lines have moved to the PRC and Southeast Asia, and, as a result, exports have dwindled. From a peak of $4.3 billion in 1990, shoe exports fell to $702 million in 2001, and continue to fall. The fortunes of the city of Pusan, the hub of the Korean shoe industry, had plummeted even before the Asian financial crisis as it failed to find new industries to replace shoemaking.

Regardless of these threats the Korean shoe industry is attempting a revival, and investing heavily to achieve it. It is, however, using a different approach, one that makes use of its current comparative advantage and is compatible with its level of development: high technology. Digital Shoes, for instance, an innovation to produce custom-made shoes, can receive made-to-measure shoes in just 3 days, from foot measurement to home delivery. The company president invested 3 billion won ($2.5 million) on equipment and employing technicians for this project.

The change is occurring industrywide. The shoe industry in Pusan plans to spend almost 400 billion won to transform its grimy shoe factories into technological powerhouses. More than 95% of the budget will be used by the end of the year [2003] to build a huge footwear industrial park to house the factories and new design facilities. This will also include educational facilities, design centers, and research and development facilities for firms unable to finance the costs of training their own designers. Meanwhile, the local government in Pusan is providing subsidies for these research and design facilities and funding courses on footwear design. The provisions for human capital upgrading are also meant to address the looming shortage of manpower in the industry, which suffers from an aging workforce and talent moving to more lucrative offers in the PRC. The industry is also taking steps to attract young designers who will lead the industry in its next phase of development.

The outcome of all these efforts will take years to be realized, and the PRC will not be far behind, but the Korean shoe industry recognizes the realities of competing in the global economy as well as the dynamic nature of competitiveness.

Source: Kim 2003.

9

Structural Transformation, Industrialization, and Technological Change in Developing Asia: What Does the Empirical Evidence Show?

Progress is impossible without change, and those who cannot change their minds cannot change anything.

—George Bernard Shaw

I argued in chapter 6 that a key policy to achieve full employment is to spend on investment to increase the investment-to-output ratio. This has been the basis for the policy of industrialization followed by a number of successful East and Southeast Asian economies, including the People's Republic of China (PRC). The result is that the expansion of the manufacturing sector has been the catalytic force underlying the economic transformation that East and Southeast Asia has undergone during the last three decades. As the Asian Development Bank (ADB 2007b), Felipe and Estrada (2008), and Felipe et al. (2007) document, the newly industrialized economies (NIEs), Malaysia, Thailand, Indonesia, and the PRC, have seen their economies transform in the direction of industrialization. And the structures of output and exports have changed in the direction of a higher sophistication, e.g., larger shares of electrical machinery and transport equipment. In this chapter, I provide an in-depth empirical analysis of the transformation of developing Asia's manufacturing sector. Box 9.1 presents the empirical regularities that recent research on the patterns of economic growth has highlighted. These regularities highlight the importance

---

Box 9.1. Regularities in Patterns of Growth and Development

The stylized facts on the patterns of growth that the recent literature has identified are summarized here:

(i)   Industrialization is the key to structural transformation and growth, which requires purposeful action, i.e., policy.
(ii) Rapidly growing countries are those with large manufacturing sectors.
(iii) Economic development requires diversification, not specialization. Specialization patterns tend to be indeterminate and possibly shaped by idiosyncratic elements, and not by factor endowments.
(iv) Growth accelerations are associated with structural changes in the direction of manufacturing.
(v)   Countries that promote exports of more "sophisticated" goods, given their level of income, grow faster.
(vi) Developing new capabilities and activities is a difficult task. Some specialization patterns are more conducive than others to industrial upgrading.
(vii) Industrial policy, viewed as an exercise in coordination between public and private sectors, can be an important development tool.

Source: Rodrik 2006a.

---

of the manufacturing sector. This has been well known since the work of the British economist Nicholas Kaldor in the 1960s labeled "Kaldor's Laws" (Box 9.2).

Figure 9.1 shows the scatter plot of the annual growth rate of output vis-à-vis the absolute change in the share of manufacturing in total output for the 1970s through 2000–2004. The figure documents the positive correlation between both variables. Among the countries in the first quadrant with the highest increases in the manufacturing share and in the output growth rate are Cambodia, Indonesia, the Republic of Korea, Lao People's Democratic Republic (Lao PDR), Malaysia, and Thailand. ADB (2007b) provides evidence that growth accelerations are associated with increases in the manufacturing sector.

Structural Transformation in Developing Asia since the 1970s

During the last three decades, most countries in developing Asia have undergone massive structural change, particularly in terms of changes in both

---

Box 9.2. Kaldor's Laws

As Rodrik (2006a) notes, development economists of the "old" school under-stood that structural transformation is key in the course of development. Among these economists, Nicholas Kaldor (1966, 1967) probably provided the most thorough explanation of why industry is the "engine of growth." Indeed, the so-called "Kaldor's Laws" provide a solid starting point for sector analyses of growth and structural change. These laws are a series of empirical regularities put forward by Kaldor to explain differences in growth rates across countries. The most important are the following:

(i) *First law* states that the faster the growth rate of manufacturing output, the faster the growth rate of GDP. This law gives to manufacturing the role of engine of economic growth, because of its strong input–output linkages, and also because capital accumulation and technical progress are strongest in industry, having important spillover effects on the rest of the economy. Kaldor viewed the high growth rates characteristic of middle-income countries as an attribute of industrialization.

(ii) *Second law* posits a strong positive relationship between the growth of manufacturing production and the growth of manufacturing productivity. This law is also known as *Verdoorn's Law* and has been interpreted as evidence in support of the existence of increasing returns in the manufacturing sector (see, for example, McCombie et al. [2002]). The expansion of output leads to macrodynamic increasing returns that derive from productivity gains. This can also be interpreted in relation to employment creation: sectors subject to scale economies have lower employment elasticities with respect to output, as productivity grows as a by-product of output expansion.

(iii) *Third law* states that when manufacturing grows, the rest of the sectors (not subject to increasing returns) will transfer labor to manufacturing, raising the overall productivity of the economy. Dynamic sectors absorb workers from the stagnant ones in which the level and growth of labor productivity are very low. This raises the overall productivity and growth rate of the economy.

Jaumotte and Spatafora (2007) and Felipe et al. (2007) discuss Asia's growth performance by studying its sectors. Felipe et al. (2007) show that both industry and services are key engines of growth in developing Asia, and find evidence of endogenous, growth-induced technological progress. And Asian Develop-ment Bank (2007b) provides evidence that growth accelerations are associated with increases in the manufacturing sector.

GDP = gross domestic product.

Figure 9.1. Output Growth vs. Change in Manufacturing Output Share (%)

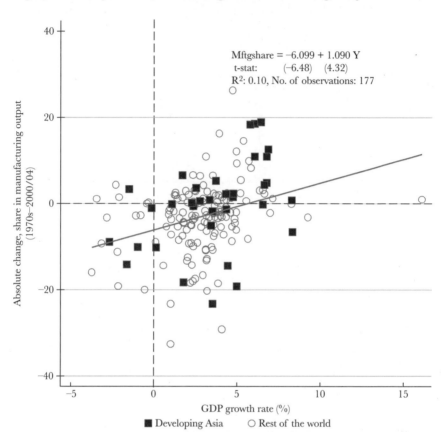

Mftgshare = −6.099 + 1.090 Y
t-stat: (−6.48)   (4.32)
R^2: 0.10, No. of observations: 177

R^2 = goodness of fit.

Note: Positive change in the share indicates that the share at the end of the period was higher.

Source: Felipe et al. 2007. Authors' estimates based on data from the World Development Indicators.

output and employment sector shares (Table A5.2). The rise in developing Asia's share in world manufacturing value-added during the last few decades has been significant (Figure 9.2). In particular, the joint share of the PRC, NIEs (Hong Kong, China; the Republic of Korea; Singapore; and Taipei,China), and the ASEAN-4 (Association of Southeast Asian Nations) countries (Indonesia, Malaysia, the Philippines, and Thailand) has more than doubled since the 1980s, representing in 2000–2004 close to 14% of the world total. This increase has been due, obviously, to a much faster growth of manufactured value-added—8%–10% per annum since the 1970s—than in the rest of the

Figure 9.2. Share of Global Manufacturing Value-Added, Developing Asia

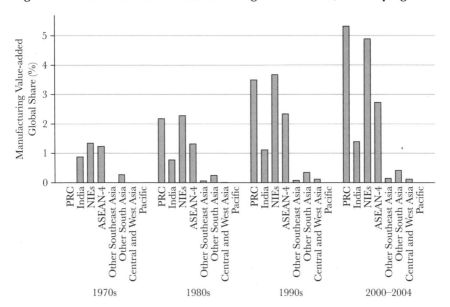

ASEAN = Association of Southeast Asian Nations, NIE = newly industrialized economy, PRC = People's Republic of China.

Note: ASEAN-4 includes Indonesia, Malaysia, the Philippines, and Thailand. Central and West Asia covers Armenia, Azerbaijan, Kazakhstan, the Kyrgyz Republic, Mongolia, Tajikistan, Turkmenistan, and Uzbekistan. NIEs consist of Hong Kong, China; the Republic of Korea; Singapore; and Taipei,China. Other Southeast Asia comprises Cambodia, the Lao People's Democratic Republic, Myanmar, and Viet Nam. Other South Asia covers Bangladesh, Bhutan, Maldives, Nepal, Pakistan, and Sri Lanka. Pacific includes Fiji Islands, Kiribati, Marshall Islands, Federated States of Micronesia, Palau, Papua New Guinea, Samoa, Timor-Leste, Tonga, and Vanuatu.

Source: Felipe and Estrada 2008. Authors' estimates based on data from the *World Development Indicators* (World Bank 2006); and the Directorate General of Budget, Accounting and Statistics (2006) for Taipei,China.

world. Nevertheless, the share of the PRC (the highest among all developing countries) is just over 5% of the world's manufacturing value-added, significantly less than the shares of Japan or the United States (US) (more than 20% each), while the share of India has barely increased during the period considered. Growth in manufacturing value-added has been substantially higher than that in GDP in many countries in developing Asia, including India, NIEs (except Hong Kong, China, which registered a shrinkage), ASEAN-4 (except the Philippines, which also registered a decrease), as well as the economies listed under Other Southeast Asia (Cambodia, Lao PDR, Myanmar, and Viet Nam) and Other South Asia (Bangladesh, Bhutan, Maldives, Nepal, Pakistan, and Sri Lanka). In the PRC, however, manufacturing growth was slightly below that of GDP. Several of the former Soviet republics (Armenia, Azerbaijan, the Kyrgyz Republic, and Tajikistan) registered contraction in manufacturing value-added after the breakup of the Soviet Union.

Developing Asia's increased share in world manufacturing value added has been accompanied by a significant degree of structural transformation within manufacturing. Table 9.1 shows the structure of manufacturing output of developing Asia by decadal averages (except the latest subperiod). In the 1970s, food and beverages; textiles; and apparel, leather, and footwear accounted for about 39% of total manufacturing output, while electrical and nonelectrical machinery and transport equipment accounted for about 17%. By 2000–2003, the former three accounted for a substantially lower 22% while the latter three accounted for about 34%. This shows a very clear change (upgrade) in the structure of manufacturing production. It also shows that the production structure has become slightly more diversified, especially compared to the 1970s. Table A9.1 at the end of the chapter provides additional information.

Table 9.2 shows regional shares of manufacturing value-added by subsector. The most salient feature of the table is the increase in developing Asia's share in every single of the 15 categories. The shares of the other regions of the world are either stagnant or have decreased. To complete the analysis, the top 10 manufacturing subsectors in terms of value-added and employment shares by country at two distant points in time are shown in Tables A9.2 and A9.3 at the end of the chapter. Overall, the shift in manufacturing value added toward higher-technology and higher-scale sectors in the NIEs, the PRC, India, and ASEAN-4 appears as a shift toward electrical machinery and industrial or other chemicals. In some countries, the shift is toward nonelectrical machinery, transport equipment, or petroleum refining.

Tables 9.3 and 9.4 show decadal averages of the manufacturing share in output and employment. The NIEs have undergone severe deindustrialization as manufacturing has lost significant weight in total output between the 1970s and 2000–2004. In terms of manufacturing employment, all four NIEs have clearly deindustrialized, especially Hong Kong, China, where the share decreased by about 25 percentage points in two decades. The declines in the other three economies are significant but smaller. These developments should not be interpreted as "failure" of these economies, but as the result of the natural and dynamic process of development, i.e., the transition to service-led economies. Rowthorn and Ramaswamy (1997, 1999) have noted that this group of economies is following a similar pattern to that of the Organisation for Economic Co-operation and Development's (OECD) countries, although this process is mostly affecting Taipei,China, and especially, Hong Kong, China, and to a much lesser extent the Republic of Korea and Singapore. This is the result of transferring production facilities (footloose

Table 9.1. Manufacturing Structure by Decade, Developing Asia
(% of total manufacturing)

Type	1970s	1980s	1990s	2000–2003
Food and beverages	19.40	14.14	12.45	12.55
Textiles	14.77	11.02	7.11	5.84
Apparel, leather, and footwear	5.27	4.89	4.74	4.20
Wood and wood products	3.01	2.10	2.01	1.82
Paper and paper products	2.20	2.10	2.09	2.28
Printing and publishing	2.11	1.95	2.58	1.89
Industrial chemicals	9.41	10.19	10.21	11.45
Petroleum and coal products	4.90	4.73	4.07	3.57
Rubber and plastic products	4.55	4.84	4.38	3.85
Nonmetal mineral products	4.46	5.42	5.34	4.60
Basic metals	5.86	7.75	7.60	7.71
Metal products	3.43	4.24	4.23	3.42
Nonelectrical machinery	3.88	8.32	8.58	8.66
Electrical machinery	8.07	9.43	13.69	16.57
Transport equipment	5.74	5.49	8.28	9.26
Others	2.94	3.39	2.62	2.33
Total	100.00	100.00	100.00	100.00

Source: Felipe and Estrada 2008. Authors' computations based on data from INDSTAT (UNIDO 2005).

industries) to the PRC.[1] In the Republic of Korea and Singapore, the share of manufacturing has remained at about 27% since the 1980s.

India's manufacturing output share has remained stable at about 15%–16% since the 1970s, while the share of manufacturing employment has been at about 11% during the period under consideration. The ASEAN-4 countries (except the Philippines), Cambodia, and the Lao PDR have seen their manufacturing shares rise significantly, in terms of both output and employment. Although Indonesia, Malaysia, and Thailand are cases of what can be labeled as "successful industrialization", this must be qualified with the following two observations. First, other than Singapore, the Republic of Korea; Taipei,China; Malaysia; and the Kyrgyz Republic, none of the other countries

---

[1]   Wan (2004, 258–260) argues that both public and private circles in Hong Kong, China, "remain interested in 're-industrialization'" after 1997. The reasons are twofold. First, deindustrialization brings hardship for the poor, worsens income distribution, and, as a consequence, threatens social stability. Second, Hong Kong, China, has specialized in services that are PRC-oriented. However, Hong Kong, China, may lose this privileged position once Shanghai flourishes as a service center. Wan goes on to argue that both private and private circles in Hong Kong, China, tried to prevent the city's deindustrialization, but could not stop it because of the lack of any industrial policy in the 1970s.

Table 9.2. Regional Shares of Manufacturing Value-Added by Subsector (%)

Sector	Group	1970s N	1970s Share of World Mftg.	1980s N	1980s Share of World Mftg.	1990s N	1990s Share of World Mftg.	2000–2004 N	2000–2004 Share of World Mftg.
1. Food and beverages	Developing Asia	14	4.44	19	8.56	17	10.03	11	10.69
	OECD	22	81.44	23	77.36	23	74.35	16	79.11
	Latin America	20	5.99	22	6.48	21	8.66	8	4.11
	Sub-Saharan Africa	31	2.07	31	2.05	23	1.06	5	0.14
	Rest of the World	20	6.06	30	5.56	33	5.90	25	5.96
2. Textiles	Developing Asia	13	8.33	17	18.83	16	21.67	10	25.44
	OECD	22	75.25	23	64.72	23	63.73	17	67.61
	Latin America	19	3.37	22	4.10	21	6.58	8	2.05
	Sub-Saharan Africa	30	1.93	30	1.77	22	1.31	5	0.14
	Rest of the World	19	11.12	29	10.57	33	6.71	24	4.76
3. Apparel, leather, and footwear	Developing Asia	14	4.12	17	11.77	17	18.18	11	21.98
	OECD	22	84.59	23	73.75	22	65.52	16	67.21
	Latin America	19	2.93	21	4.04	18	8.00	8	1.96
	Sub-Saharan Africa	25	1.44	25	1.51	19	1.18	5	0.10
	Rest of the World	20	6.92	28	8.93	31	7.12	25	8.75
4. Wood and wood products	Developing Asia	14	2.30	19	4.82	17	6.24	11	5.69
	OECD	22	90.00	23	86.33	23	86.47	16	90.04
	Latin America	20	1.41	22	1.95	20	2.83	8	0.79

continued on next page

Table 9.2 (continued)

Sector	Group	1970s N	1970s Share of World Mftg.	1980s N	1980s Share of World Mftg.	1990s N	1990s Share of World Mftg.	2000–2004 N	2000–2004 Share of World Mftg.
	Sub-Saharan Africa	30	1.08	31	1.23	22	0.80	4	0.03
	Rest of the World	20	5.22	29	5.66	33	3.65	25	3.45
5. Paper and paper products	Developing Asia	14	1.83	18	4.52	16	6.32	10	7.54
	OECD	21	92.11	23	88.84	23	85.09	16	87.13
	Latin America	20	2.28	22	2.89	20	5.43	8	2.36
	Sub-Saharan Africa	24	0.99	25	1.05	21	0.63	4	0.04
	Rest of the World	20	2.78	28	2.71	32	2.53	25	2.93
6. Printing and publishing	Developing Asia	14	1.31	18	2.99	16	6.88	10	7.21
	OECD	22	94.82	23	93.57	22	88.20	14	87.50
	Latin America	18	1.07	21	1.26	17	2.83	8	1.51
	Sub-Saharan Africa	27	0.84	25	0.61	19	0.35	4	0.05
	Rest of the World	20	1.96	28	1.57	31	1.74	21	3.73
7. Industrial chemicals	Developing Asia	14	2.81	18	7.39	17	8.81	10	10.85
	OECD	22	89.09	23	83.14	23	77.71	15	78.98
	Latin America	20	2.61	22	3.93	21	7.79	8	2.39
	Sub-Saharan Africa	30	1.03	31	1.13	23	0.63	4	0.04
	Rest of the World	20	4.46	30	4.41	33	5.07	25	7.75

continued on next page

Table 9.2 (continued)

		1970s		1980s		1990s		2000–2004	
Sector	Group	N	Share of World Mftg.	N	Share of World Mftg.	N	Share of World Mftg.	N	Share of World Mftg.
8. Petroleum and coal products	Developing Asia	10	4.67	12	12.20	15	17.91	8	20.12
	OECD	21	79.55	21	65.19	21	59.42	11	60.44
	Latin America	17	5.94	18	9.62	15	8.52	7	3.48
	Sub-Saharan Africa	16	1.53	13	2.56	11	0.70	2	0.01
	Rest of the World	18	8.31	24	10.42	26	13.46	16	15.96
9. Rubber and plastic products	Developing Asia	14	4.04	18	9.64	16	9.96	11	9.48
	OECD	21	88.69	22	83.05	22	82.20	16	85.89
	Latin America	17	2.09	19	2.93	17	4.53	8	1.48
	Sub-Saharan Africa	21	1.13	20	1.07	16	0.51	4	0.04
	Rest of the World	20	4.05	27	3.31	31	2.81	25	3.12
10. Nonmetal mineral products	Developing Asia	14	3.10	19	9.66	17	13.24	11	12.89
	OECD	22	85.70	23	78.23	23	73.23	17	77.09
	Latin America	19	2.94	22	3.76	21	5.81	7	3.20
	Sub-Saharan Africa	28	1.38	28	1.31	21	0.81	4	0.07
	Rest of the World	20	6.88	29	7.05	33	6.91	25	6.74

continued on next page

Table 9.2 (continued)

Sector	Group	1970s N	1970s Share of World Mftg.	1980s N	1980s Share of World Mftg.	1990s N	1990s Share of World Mftg.	2000–2004 N	2000–2004 Share of World Mftg.
11. Basic metals	Developing Asia	13	2.19	16	9.16	16	14.07	11	18.90
	OECD	22	87.98	23	78.68	23	68.43	16	69.14
	Latin America	16	2.78	20	4.66	18	9.39	7	2.99
	Sub-Saharan Africa	18	1.41	16	1.42	12	0.83	3	0.01
	Rest of the World	16	5.64	25	6.08	30	7.28	22	8.96
12. Metal products	Developing Asia	14	1.45	19	5.14	17	6.54	11	5.59
	OECD	22	91.61	22	87.27	22	88.54	16	90.78
	Latin America	18	1.31	20	1.78	18	1.40	8	0.70
	Sub-Saharan Africa	28	1.29	30	1.30	22	0.67	3	0.03
	Rest of the World	20	4.34	29	4.51	30	2.86	23	2.91
13. Non-electrical machinery	Developing Asia	14	1.00	15	5.47	15	8.07	11	9.22
	OECD	21	93.41	22	89.14	22	86.45	17	87.10
	Latin America	18	0.58	20	1.02	16	2.55	6	0.69
	Sub-Saharan Africa	18	0.48	16	0.43	16	0.24	3	0.00
	Rest of the World	19	4.54	24	3.94	28	2.69	25	2.99
14. Electrical machinery	Developing Asia	14	2.72	17	6.60	15	12.77	11	16.15
	OECD	22	91.89	22	88.48	22	81.85	16	80.85
	Latin America	18	0.91	21	1.22	17	2.81	7	0.47
	Sub-Saharan Africa	21	0.52	19	0.41	15	0.24	4	0.01
	Rest of the World	20	3.96	25	3.30	29	2.34	24	2.53

continued on next page

Table 9.2 (continued)

Sector	Group	1970s		1980s		1990s		2000–2004	
		N	Share of World Mftg.	N	Share of World Mftg.	N	Share of World Mftg.	N	Share of World Mftg.
15. Transport equipment	Developing Asia	14	1.64	16	4.12	15	7.77	11	9.70
	OECD	22	92.58	22	89.91	22	84.63	17	84.99
	Latin America	17	0.97	20	1.87	17	4.84	6	2.01
	Sub-Saharan Africa	20	0.60	20	0.84	14	0.32	3	0.01
	Rest of the World	19	4.21	25	3.26	29	2.44	25	3.29

Mftg = manufacturing, N = number of countries in each group, OECD = Organisation for Economic Co-operation and Development.

Source: Asian Development Bank 2007b. Computations based on data from UNIDO INDSTAT.

in Table 9.4 had in 2000–2004 a share of manufacturing employment as high as that of the OECD average. Second, in terms of labor productivity, there is still a large differential between most developing Asian countries and the OECD average (Figure 9.3). Indeed, it appears that many countries across developing Asia have industrialized at low levels of productivity. This could be because of two reasons: (i) the product mix of new employment has been toward relatively low-productivity industries, and/or (ii) the increase in employment has taken place in low-productivity techniques.

Overall, apparently only a handful of Asian developing countries have been able to upgrade their industrial performance and capabilities and, in doing so, have succeeded in catching up in productivity with the advanced industrial countries. Many others, however, have partly industrialized, but with much lower labor productivity than the advanced countries showed, probably because industrial employment in most developing countries has been in occupations which have extremely low labor productivity. These countries seem to have had both low-productivity industrialization and a high degree of polarization across sectors. In many countries, modern industry is growing at high and rising productivity levels and, simultaneously, many other backward and small-scale industries operate at low productivity. This is different from the successful industrialization that took place in the developed countries.

Table 9.3. Developing Asia Manufacturing Output Shares by Decade (%)

	1970s	1980s	1990s	2000–2004
China, People's Republic of	37.27	36.26	32.90[a]	34.50[b]
India	15.32	16.43	16.58	15.71
NIEs				
Hong Kong, China	–	21.18	9.43	4.32
Korea, Republic of	21.61	27.51	27.14	27.82
Singapore	24.84[c]	26.09	26.11	27.39
Taipei,China	32.43	34.95	27.11	22.80
ASEAN-4				
Indonesia	10.42	15.35	23.72	29.04
Malaysia	16.82	20.42	27.05	31.21
Philippines	25.72	25.03	23.29	22.94
Thailand	18.98	23.32	29.55	34.00
Other Southeast Asia				
Cambodia	–	–	11.08	19.40
Lao PDR	–	9.27[d]	14.20	18.67
Myanmar	9.64	9.07	6.90	8.49[e]
Viet Nam	–	19.69[f]	15.23	19.94
Other South Asia				
Bangladesh	–	13.76	14.87	15.73
Bhutan	–	5.29	10.39	7.79[e]
Maldives	–	–	–	–
Nepal	4.11	5.24	8.77	8.85
Pakistan	15.89	15.98	16.44	15.99
Sri Lanka	19.02	15.39	15.68	15.90
Central and West Asia				
Armenia	–	–	27.56	22.68
Azerbaijan	–	–	14.08	7.87

continued on next page

Table 9.3 (continued)

	1970s	1980s	1990s	2000–2004
Kazakhstan	–	–	13.30[g]	16.33
Kyrgyz Republic	–	–	20.04	16.19
Mongolia	–	31.04	18.70	6.37
Tajikistan	–	27.70[f]	25.43	32.35
Turkmenistan	–	–	26.30[h]	15.47[e]
Uzbekistan	–	25.06[i]	11.96[h]	9.40
Pacific				
Fiji Islands	11.79	10.59	14.44	15.02[j]
Kiribati	1.62[k]	1.16	0.98	0.89[j]
Marshall Islands	–	–	1.63	4.54[l]
Micronesia, Federated States of	–	0.40[m]	–	–
Papua New Guinea	7.26	10.06	8.89	8.50[e]
Palau	–	–	0.97	1.19[j]
Samoa	–	–	17.10[h]	15.37
Timor-Leste	–	–	2.78[n]	3.29
Tonga	6.63[c]	5.42	4.85	4.61
Vanuatu	3.90[o]	4.45	4.88	4.21[l]

– = data not available, ASEAN = Association of Southeast Asian Nations, Lao PDR = Lao People's Democratic Republic, NIEs = newly industrialized economies.

[a] Refers to 1990–1992 average.
[b] Refers to 2000.
[c] Refers to 1975–1979 average.
[d] Refers to 1989.
[e] Refers to 2000–2003 average.
[f] Refers to 1985–1989 average.
[g] Refers to 1992–1999 average.
[h] Refers to 1994–1999 average.
[i] Refers to 1987–1989 average.
[j] Refers to 2000–2002 average.
[k] Refers to 1978–1979 average.
[l] Refers to 2000–2001 average.
[m] Refers to 1983.
[n] Refers to 1999.
[o] Refers to 1979.

Source: *World Development Indicators* (Word Bank 2006); Directorate General of Budget, Accounting and Statistics, Taipei,China (various years).

Table 9.4. Developing Asia Manufacturing Employment Shares by Decade
(Manufacturing as % of total employment)

	1980s	1990s	2000–2004
China, People's Republic of	15.11[a]	13.47	11.16[b]
India	11.05[c]	10.92[c]	11.22[c]
NIEs			
Hong Kong, China	35.89	19.02	10.20[d]
Korea, Republic of	23.93	23.40	19.44
Singapore	27.91	24.53	18.31[e]
Taipei,China	33.41	28.66	27.40
ASEAN-4			
Indonesia	9.68[f]	11.73	13.15[b]
Malaysia	15.95	22.59	21.94
Philippines	9.93	10.06	9.65
Thailand	8.87	12.33	14.58
Other			
Azerbaijan	–	9.36[g]	5.44[b]
Kyrgyz Republic	–	20.11	19.19
Pakistan	13.66	10.99	12.66
Viet Nam	–	8.32[h]	10.33
OECD	21.58[i]	19.20[i]	16.89[i]

– = data not available, ASEAN = Association of Southeast Asian Nations, NIEs = newly industrialized economies, OECD = Organisation for Economic Co-operation and Development.

[a] Refers to the period 1987–1989.
[b] Refers to the period 2000–2002.
[c] The figure for each decade refers only to a single year, as follows: 1983, 1993/94, 1999/2000.
[d] Refers to the period 2000–2001.
[e] Refers to the period 2001–2003.
[f] Refers to the average for the years 1980, 1982, 1985, and 1989.
[g] Refers to the period 1992–1999.
[h] Refers to the period 1996–1999.
[i] Refers to the average for the years 1980, 1982, 1985, and 1989.

Source: LABORSTA (International Labour Statistics Organization); Directorate General of Budget, Accounting and Statistics, Taipei,China (various years); Anant et al. (2006).

Figure 9.3 Total Labor Productivity (2000 $), Logarithmic Scale

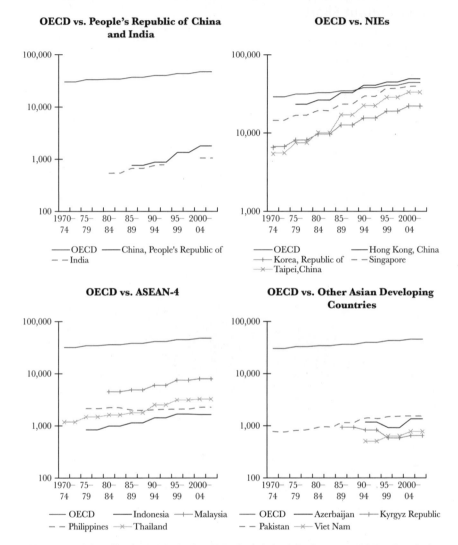

OECD vs. People's Republic of China and India

------ OECD ——— China, People's Republic of
– – India

OECD vs. NIEs

——— OECD ——— Hong Kong, China
—+— Korea, Republic of – – Singapore
—×— Taipei,China

OECD vs. ASEAN-4

——— OECD ——— Indonesia —+— Malaysia
– – Philippines —×— Thailand

OECD vs. Other Asian Developing Countries

——— OECD ——— Azerbaijan —+— Kyrgyz Republic
– – Pakistan —×— Viet Nam

ASEAN = Association of Southeast Asian Nations, NIE = newly industrialized economy, OECD = Organisation for Economic Co-operation and Development, $ = US dollars.

Note: The 1980–1985, 1986–1989, 1990–1995, and 2000–2004 data for India refer only to 1983, 1988, 1994, and 2000 figures, respectively. Similarly, the 2000–2004 data for the People's Republic of China, Indonesia, the Kyrgyz Republic, and Pakistan refer only to 2000–2002; the 1986–1989 data for Indonesia only to 1989; the 1976–1979 data for the Philippines only to 1978; and the 1970–1975 figure for Pakistan only to 1973–1975.

Source: Asian Development Bank 2007b. Calculations based on data from International Labour Organization, LABORSTA Labour Statistics Database, downloaded 9 August 2006; World Bank, World Development Indicators online database, downloaded 2 August 2006; Directorate General of Budget, Accounting and Statistics. http://eng.stat.gov.tw/public/, downloaded 13 December 2006.

A Logistic Regression of the Manufacturing Sector Output Share

Figure 9.4 shows the scatter plot of the output share of manufacturing in output vis-à-vis income per capita, pooling data since 1970 for the whole world. The figure shows that as countries' income per capita increases, so does the share of output in manufacturing, but there seems to be a point beyond which the share starts declining. The figure also shows a wide dispersion in this share for a given income per capita, from very low shares up to 50%.

Figure 9.5 graphs the logistic regression estimated for the logarithm of the share of the manufacturing sector in GDP. This regression includes

Figure 9.4. Manufacturing Output Share vs. Per Capita GDP, 1970–2004
(All countries in the world)

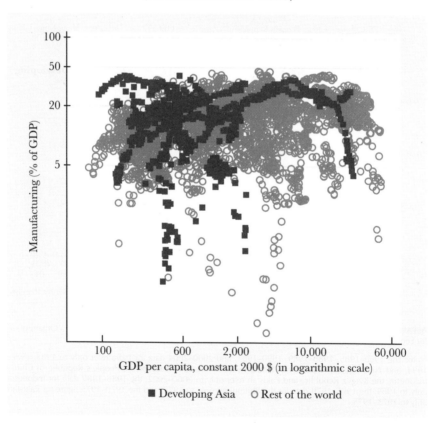

GDP = gross domestic product, $ = US dollars.

Source: World Development Indicators Online (World Bank 2006).

as regressors (also in logarithms) income per capita, income per capita squared, population (a proxy market size), and the trade ratio in GDP. As expected (given the shape of the data in Figure 9.5), the relationship between the logarithm of the manufacturing share and the logarithm of income per capita is nonlinear (a hump-shaped relationship), indicating that the actual elasticity varies with income per capita. The hump-shaped relationship implies that the elasticity of the manufacturing share is relatively high (positive, i.e., the share increases as income per capita increases) when a country is poor and then falls as the country becomes rich (becomes negative, i.e., the share decreases as income per capita increases).

Figure 9.5. Fitted Regression Line of Manufacturing Output Share vs. GDP Per Capita, 2000

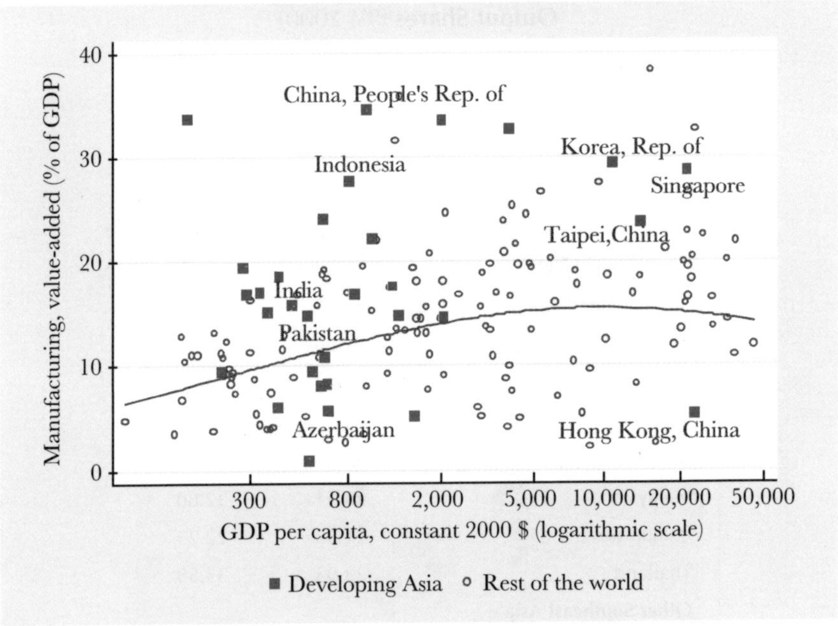

GDP = gross domestic product, Rep. = Republic, $ = US dollars.

Note:
1. The line gives the expected value for a trade openness of 30% and a population of 100 million.
2. Estimated regression:

$\ln S_i = -4.628 + 0.710 \ln y - 0.039(\ln y)^2 + 0.289 Tr + 0.180 \ln P$
t-stat: (−4.05)** (2.97)** (−2.55)** (2.76)*** (5.92)***

where S_i = manufacturing output share, y = GDP per capita, P = population, Tr = trade ratio

*** and ** mean significant at 1% and 5%, respectively.

Source: Felipe and Estrada 2008.

The regression results allow the calculation of the turning point, that is, the point at which the elasticity turns from positive into negative (at this point the manufacturing share becomes highest and the income elasticity zero). This occurs at $9,998 (2000 value).

Actual and predicted shares (where the latter is each country's expected share given its income per capita, population and trade ratio) for developing Asia are shown in Table 9.5. Countries can be divided into three groups, depending on whether (i) the actual share is higher than the predicted one, (ii) the actual share is lower than the predicted, or (iii) whether predicted and actual shares are about the same and the country is on or very close to the regression line.

Table 9.5. Predicted vs. Actual Manufacturing Output Shares (%, 2000)

	Predicted	Actual
China, People's Republic of	27.31	34.50
India	19.55	15.85
NIEs		
Hong Kong, China	21.72	5.39
Korea, Republic of	22.04	29.42
Singapore	21.68	28.73
Taipei,China	20.82	23.76
ASEAN-4		
Indonesia	21.90	27.75
Malaysia	25.51	32.60
Philippines	21.53	22.23
Thailand	23.93	33.59
Other Southeast Asia		
Cambodia	11.84	16.86
Lao People's Democratic Republic	8.95	17.00
Viet Nam	17.96	18.56
Other South Asia		
Bangladesh	13.54	15.23
Bhutan	7.75	8.06

continued on next page

Table 9.5 (continued)

	Predicted	Actual
Nepal	10.18	9.44
Pakistan	14.31	14.81
Sri Lanka	15.37	16.83
Central and West Asia		
Armenia	9.83	24.07
Azerbaijan	11.99	5.64
Kazakhstan	16.48	17.66
Kyrgyz Republic	9.29	19.46
Mongolia	9.92	6.13
Tajikistan	9.86	33.66
Turkmenistan	13.67	10.85
Uzbekistan	12.20	9.44
Pacific		
Fiji Islands	10.98	14.62
Kiribati	5.05	0.90
Papua New Guinea	13.00	8.36
Samoa	7.16	14.82
Tonga	5.99	5.16

NIEs = newly industrialized economies.

Source: Felipe and Estrada 2008.

In the first group of countries, we find the PRC; NIEs except Hong Kong, China; ASEAN-4 countries except the Philippines; Cambodia, the Lao PDR, Armenia, the Kyrgyz Republic, Tajikistan, Fiji Islands, and Samoa. The PRC's and the NIEs' high manufacturing shares are the result of explicit industrialization policies (i.e., investment) as the basis for their development (Wang and Li [1995] on the PRC). Although down from the average of the 1980s, the share of the manufacturing subsector in total output in the PRC has been traditionally much higher than anywhere else. It still accounts for about 34.5% of total output, only matched in developing Asia by Malaysia, Thailand, and Tajikistan. The share of manufacturing employment, on the other hand, has declined from about 15% in the 1980s to 11% at present.

In the second group, we find India; Hong Kong, China; Azerbaijan; Mongolia; Turkmenistan; Uzbekistan; Kiribati; and Papua New Guinea. The case of Hong Kong, China was already discussed above: this economy has undergone deindustrialization as a result of the transfer of manufacturing plants to the PRC. Today it is one of the most service-oriented economies in the world. The other interesting case in this group is India. India's manufacturing share in GDP is about 4 percentage points lower than what it *should* be (i.e., India's manufacturing base is relatively small by international standards, after controlling for income per capita, population size, and openness to trade). Economists have not been able to agree on the causes, or resolve the issue empirically (Box 9.3).[2]

Finally, the rest of the countries (i.e., the Philippines, Viet Nam, Other South Asia countries, Kazakhstan, and Tonga) are in the third group. In the case of the Philippines, although the share is well predicted (and therefore is not low when benchmarked), this country had the highest manufacturing output share among the ASEAN-4 in the 1970s, but by 2000–2004 its share had decreased by about 3 percentage points and was the lowest in the group. Its industrialization policies have been a failure, so that its actual manufacturing share is now much lower than that of Indonesia and, especially, Malaysia and Thailand. What are the reasons for the lack of industrialization? As in India, several reasons account for the poor performance of the sector (Box 9.4). Boxes 9.5 and 9.6 discuss the transition economies of the former Soviet Union and the Pacific Islands.

The Technology Level of Developing Asia's Manufactures

The different branches of the manufacturing sector can be grouped according to the level of technology. This was done by dividing all manufacturing branches into four groups according to level of technology and scale, following Ng (2002). Group 1 corresponds to the manufacturing branches with the lowest technology and scale economies, e.g., food and beverages, tobacco,

---

[2] Five decades ago, Rao (1959) noted, in the context of India, that where the labor force was growing as a consequence of rapid population growth, a proportional decline in the share of agricultural employment in total employment similar to that experienced by the developed countries over a comparable period would still imply a higher number of people employed in the sector in absolute terms. In India, while the number of people employed in agriculture was about 210 million in the early 1980s, representing close to 70% of total employment, the number of people working in the sector had increased to about 240 million by 2000, although the share had declined to 60%. And as far back as 1964, Doctor and Gallis reported that:

> In India the share of the modern sector in total employment, which was over 6 per cent in 1951, increased by barely 1 percentage point over the decade 1951–61, despite, as noted, an annual growth rate of 4 percent of modern sector employment. In the Philippines the corresponding share, which was about 22 percent in 1956, moved up by a mere 2 percentage points by 1961 (Doctor and Gallis 1964, 558).

Box 9.3. What Accounts for India's Undersized Manufacturing Sector?

India's manufacturing base is relatively small by international standards, after controlling for income per capita, population size, and openness to trade (Morgan Stanley 2004, 2006; Felipe and Estrada 2008). India has not yet succeeded in creating the kind of labor-intensive manufacturing jobs that have transformed the economy of the People's Republic of China (PRC), and are now transforming Viet Nam and other economies in the region. Its politicians had ambitious industrialization plans after independence, and the country indeed went through a period of rapid industrialization, but this stalled. Three possible explanations are widely discussed. The first centers on the negative effects of the "reservation," even today, of many products for small-scale industries (Lewis 2004, chapter 8). The number of items in the reservation peaked in 1984 at 873. The number has been progressively reduced and in January 2007 it affected 239 items. This system, it is argued, has prevented the utilization of economies of scale and affects industry more than services. This is why, it is also argued, Indian export-oriented services have done so much better than industry.

The second explanation posits that India's development strategy at the time of independence was premised on the view that the binding constraint for maximizing the economy's long-term growth potential was lack of domestic capital goods. But to meet the employment objective—a legitimate concern in a labor-surplus economy—an extended version of the model envisaged protection of traditional methods and organizations of production with fiscal and administrative measures. To implement this strategy, a large administrative machinery came into existence to grant industrial and import licenses, known as the "license-permit Raj."

The third explanation emphasizes the debilitating effects of the country's rigid labor laws. Critics point out that these three reasons obviously harm Indian manufacturers, compared with PRC counterparts, who do not face these restrictive policies. This is why the textile industry in the PRC, for example, has flourished and done much better than India's (the reservation in this sector ended in 2001).

While some authors argue that these three explanations still represent a constraint on India's growth prospects (e.g., Besley and Burgess [2004]; Kochhar et al. [2006]), others argue that their impact has been exaggerated. For example, although it lasted until 1991, the license-permit Raj was phased out gradually, while the policy of reservation has limited impact because some large companies have been exempted from some of its strictures (Bardhan 2006).

continued on next page

Box 9.3 (continued)

The labor laws (particularly chapter V-B of the Industrial Disputes Act) make it, on paper, difficult to lay off workers in large firms, even when they are inefficient or when demand declines, and to employ short-term contract labor, and this—the argument goes—discourages new hires by employers, induces capital intensity in production, and inhibits entry and exit of firms from the market. Roy (2004), however, concluded that the negative impact of the labor laws is statistically insignificant. Also, case studies by Deshpande (2004) suggest that the Indian labor market is not as inflexible as it has been claimed. This issue is clearly very contentious (Felipe and Hasan 2006, chapter 5).

If the policies that these three explanations discuss are not the sole reason for manufacturing's underachievement, what other policies could account for India's undersized manufacturing sector? India suffers from inadequate long-term finance for small firms and infrastructure deficiencies. Bardhan (2006) has argued that India suffers from three types of such deficiencies: physical (roads, power, ports, irrigation etc.), social (particularly health and education), and regulatory (in contract enforcement). India's poor physical infrastructure is well known. It affects issues as diverse as the cost of power for manufacturing, the turnaround time of ships in port, the time it takes to ship exports, the low number of telephone and internet users, and the poor state of transport in general. Many of these issues fall into the sphere of the government. In terms of social infrastructure, particularly education and health, India also falls behind many other countries (Asian Development Bank 2006b). India also falls low in the ranking of corrupt regulatory bureaucracy, as the World Bank (2006) notes in its *Doing Business in 2006* report.

Overall, a combination of factors has kept India's manufacturing back during the last two decades. The reservation policy, the "license-permit Raj," and the somewhat restrictive labor laws, combined with lack of adequate physical, social, and regulatory infrastructure, are responsible for the relative underperformance of the sector.

wearing apparel, and leather products. Group 2 consists of plastic and rubber products, and paper, among others. Group 3 consists of iron and steel, and nonmineral products, among others. Group 4 consists of products with the highest technology and scale economies, such as electrical and nonelectrical machinery, industrial chemicals, professional equipment, and transport equipment. Table 9.6 shows the results. We can see that developing Asia's shares in the four categories have increased substantially between the 1970s and 2000–2003: from 4.86% to 12.75% in low technology; from 2.51% to 8.42% in medium technology and low economies of scale; from 2.14% to 11.34% in medium technology and medium economies of scale; and from 2.19% to 11.33% in high technology. The PRC's shares have also increased in all four categories. On the other hand, the shares of the NIEs and ASEAN-4 increased until the 1990s, but then decreased in 2000–2003.

Box 9.4. Why Did Philippine Industrialization Stagnate?

Felipe and Estrada (2008) estimate that the Philippine manufacturing sector is about the right size when controlling for income per capita, population size, and openness to trade. However, Philippine and other economists have argued for years that the country's record over the last three decades has been disappointing, particularly when compared to those of countries like Malaysia or Thailand: manufacturing output has grown slowly, little structural change has occurred, and exports are highly dependent on the electronics sector.

So what are the reasons for the poor performance of the Philippines' manufacturing sector? This is a tricky question given that in the 1950s a sophisticated manufacturing sector emerged, bolstered by protection and a well-developed human capital base (Hill 2003). The problems for manufacturing began subsequently. Hill has argued that one cause alone cannot be blamed for the poor performance, but a combination of several, including costly and misguided interventions, a tendency to focus on rents rather than efficiency, poor physical infrastructure, and an uncompetitive cost structure. Indeed, a fairly recent analysis of the Philippine investment climate (Asian Development Bank 2005) notes, among others, the following constraints to doing business in the country, as identified by businesspeople themselves: cost of electricity, tax rates, cost of financing, and poor transportation infrastructure.

Ofreneo (2003) has also offered complementary reasons to explain the poor performance of the manufacturing sector. Unlike its Asian neighbors, which encouraged export orientation and at the same time continued to protect domestic and export industries, the Philippines took a purist approach and had "one-sided liberalization." Since the early 1980s, the Philippines has pursued aggressive tariff reduction and a phaseout of import restrictions, investment liberalization, privatization, and deregulation in various sectors (e.g., finance, agriculture) at a significantly faster pace than its neighbors and faster than required by international commitments. Therefore, Philippine industry found it difficult to compete. Also, the Philippines did not cultivate its own export and domestic champions, and more privileges were given to foreign investors than to domestic investors.

continued on next page

Box 9.4 (continued)

Other Philippine economists add that the country's economic stagnation and lack of industrialization are due as well to the existence of an elite group of Filipino industrialists and landowners, including their political allies, who wield enormous economic and political power. Indeed, Aldaba et al. (2005) have offered three complementary explanations for the state of the economy: a well-established oligarchy, coordination failures, and institutional failures and high transaction costs. In essence, the industrialization problem of the Philippines is a case of distributive conflict, collective action, and failure to develop the institutional prerequisites for sustained growth. The persistence of dysfunctional institutions in the Philippines is troublesome. The country developed self-reinforcing mechanisms for the persistence of socially suboptimal institutions. At some point, these institutions were chosen by some initial adopters because they suited their interests; but then the whole system became "locked in." One might wonder why these institutions have barely changed since 1986, when Ferdinand Marcos was overthrown. The reason is that powerful vested interests ensure that institutional change faces a high political wall. Vested interests act as a constraint to economic progress. Magnoli Bocchi (2008) also argues that the Philippine capital-intensive private sector does not find it convenient to expand investment at a faster pace. The politically connected corporate conglomerates, which are protected by favorable rules and regulations, enjoy barriers to competitors' entry and oligopolistic market power.

Coordination failures refer to the inability of the government and other segments of society to harmonize their decisions and actions to foster economic growth and advance public welfare. The various sectors are not advocating an integrated development agenda that will benefit the whole Philippine society. Lack of coordinated investments between the oligarchy and the other sectors results in the utilization of inappropriate technologies and in low intersector linkages. Coordination failures also discourage people from trusting the government and encourage the citizens not to pay their taxes. Within the government, this lack of coordination is reflected in a duplication of functions and in an overstaffed bureaucracy.

Finally, Prichett (2003b) has argued that institutional uncertainty has recently increased in the Philippines. The country had developed a set of institutions that served it well in a state of semi-industrialization. But the situation changed with the transition to democracy in the 1980s. As one set of institutions changed to a new and better one, uncertainty among both past and future

continued on next page

Box 9.4 (continued)

investors increased, as "investors under the old regime will be leery and under siege for having made corrupt deals and hence will be reluctant to create substantial new investments . . . w investors will be reluctant to come in until the stability of the property rights regime is fully established." In this context, five crucial areas for institutional improvements were identified by Aldaba et al. (2005): (i) corruption, as it squanders resources; (ii) property rights, vital for the implementation of the agrarian reform; (iii) regulatory institutions to foster investment and to avoid vested interest groups that control regulatory agencies; (iv) social insurance institutions to benefit disadvantaged Filipinos; and (v) conflict management institutions to solve the communist insurgency and rebellion in the southern Philippines.

Summing up, the problems underlying Philippine industrialization are varied, ranging from an uncompetitive cost structure, fast liberalization, and poor infrastructure, to distributive conflicts and dysfunctional institutions that have prevented the development of the appropriate institutional prerequisites for sustained growth. The lack of modern infrastructure is perhaps what is leading the country to shift into a services-driven economy, particularly business process outsourcing. This sector employed in 2007 about 300,000 workers, and its revenues represented about 3% of the Philippines' GDP (Magtibay-Ramos et al. 2008). However, despite the increasing importance of this sector for the Philippine economy and its positive growth prospects, it cannot be the solution to the high unemployment and underemployment that afflict the economy. While the business process outsourcing sector can continue growing and contributing to both growth and employment, the Philippines still needs to devise an industrialization strategy.

Box 9.5. Structural Transformation Patterns in the Transition Economies of the Former Soviet Union

The increase in the share of agriculture in total employment and the decline in the corresponding share of industry across the former Soviet republics of Central Asia observed since the breakup of the Soviet Union are somewhat abnormal. What are the reasons underlying this pattern of structural transformation?

Given pre-transition conditions—relatively low shares of agriculture and services and relatively high shares of industry—the observed pattern of structural change across the region can be attributed in part to transition-induced corrections for the severe distortions of central planning (Fardmanesh and Tan 2005). Observed trends, therefore, reflect corrections of pre-transition biases favoring heavy industry and large-scale agriculture, and neglect of market-oriented services (e.g., trade, communications, and finance).

Labor flows between sectors have been driven by two distinct but related mechanisms shaping the transition: restructuring and reallocation (Blanchard 1997). The former involves the downsizing and closure of existing enterprises; the latter involves resource reallocation from state firms to new private firms, and from old to new activities. Restructuring becomes inevitable as profitability and competitiveness replace specialization and interdependence as factors driving economic decision making. In practice, industrial restructuring has been protracted and is ongoing in most of these economies, caused, among other things, by asset rigidity and political considerations.

The natural resource industries have gained importance in most of these economies during the post-transition period: energy in Azerbaijan, Kazakhstan, and Uzbekistan; gold in the Kyrgyz Republic and Uzbekistan; and aluminum in Tajikistan. Increasing the intensity of natural resource exploitation has also spurred growth of new activities in services, e.g., trade and transport components of fuel exports in Azerbaijan and Kazakhstan. New industrial and service activities narrowly based on the natural resource subsectors, characterized by lower labor intensity (Mitra 2006) together with relatively stagnant manufacturing activity, account for industry's underperformance in generating new jobs. Mirroring this trend, evidence exists of a declining share of skilled labor and capital-intensive exports in these economies and of a move toward natural resource exports.

Informalization of economic activity induced by a heavy regulatory burden is another factor that helps explain industry's declining employment share. This phenomenon reflects the choice made by new enterprises not to register

continued on next page

Box 9.5 (continued)

formally, and by existing enterprises to cross over from the formal to the informal economy. The result is underreporting of formal employment. Indeed, this phenomenon fits in with survey findings that new private enterprises find the business environment more difficult than do state or privatized firms, particularly with regard to regulations, institutions, property rights, and taxation.

In agriculture, in contrast, the restructuring of collective farms and reallocation into new private and household farms and new agricultural activities have moved faster due to post-transition land reforms. These reforms have aimed to move away from the pre-transition state ownership of land, and large-scale collective farms, toward varying degrees of farm privatization, transferability of rights, and freedom in farm decision making. Responses to the improved incentive framework have been mixed. In Armenia, characterized by relatively labor-intensive production farms, decollectivization has resulted in land fragmentation, the substitution of labor for other inputs, and the growth of labor-intensive household farming (Macours and Swinnen 2005). In Kazakhstan, characterized by land-intensive mechanized farming, land fragmentation did not take place, but neither was labor laid off, allowing households to combine large-farm employment with household-plot farming. The related phenomenon of urban-to-rural migration was reinforced by the disruption of nonagricultural production in urban areas. The ascendancy of private and household farming and greater freedom in farm decision making have been accompanied by a shift to new agricultural activities focusing on higher-value-added production. The exception to the pattern (at least among the larger Central Asian republics) is Uzbekistan, where the agricultural policy, implemented through legal limits on the size of individual household plots (0.7 hectares), favors large-scale farming.

Unlike industry, where a protracted industrial restructuring phase was needed to rectify overindustrialization, market-oriented services were neglected in the Soviet era. Consequently, they did not need lengthy restructuring. At the same time, new activities, particularly in retail trade, mushroomed to cater to consumers' pent-up demand. In the pre-transition era, delivery of nonmarket-oriented service activities was largely undertaken by the state, e.g., state-owned industrial and agricultural enterprises provided health and education services to their employees. Restructuring of these enterprises during transition has resulted in the transfer and reclassification of these activities from agriculture and industry into services. This sector has become the "employer of last resort" for those without access to even subsistence agriculture, which could be the reason that services has become the dominant employment branch in several of these transition economies.

continued on next page

Box 9.5 (continued)

What effect have these structural changes had on net job creation during transition? Little or none, according to the World Bank (2005), especially in the formal sector. A still-significant number of workers hold low-productivity jobs in unrestructured and unprofitable enterprises in the informal sector and in subsistence agriculture. Labor demand, which plummeted with the breakup of the Soviet Union, remains anemic. Labor supply rendered surplus has responded by moving into agriculture and into services, with part of the labor force falling off the radar screen into the informal economy. Policy makers in the region must, then, seek to create productive employment in the formal economy by accelerating industrial restructuring of state and privatized enterprises, forging stronger linkages between sectors (e.g., private agro-industries and agro-services), and improving the business environment for new enterprises.

Summing up, the pattern of structural change in the Central Asian transition economies is the result of realignment toward the standard pattern. The pace of this realignment has been driven by the degree of distortions prevailing in the pre-transition period, which needs to be corrected during transition; and by the relative speed of restructuring and reallocation in the different sectors.

Source: Based on an essay by Padmini Desikachar.

Box 9.6. What Options Do the Pacific Islands Have?

The Pacific Islands are unique in developing Asia, given the natural disadvantages that they face, particularly their small size and remoteness (Commonwealth of Australia 2006). Moreover, growth during the last 15 years has, overall, been slow, leading to unemployment and joblessness. In addition, several countries face serious environmental problems as a consequence of climate change and rapid urbanization. The region also suffers from high population growth, poor education, weak governance, poverty, and poor infrastructure. The public sector provides a high share of total employment, although many of these people are highly underemployed; and many of the islands in the region suffer from a "dependency mentality" on transfer payments related to aid, military bases, and workers' remittances.

How can the Pacific economies generate structural change and thus growth in these circumstances? Progress in three areas is fundamental. First, most countries need more private sector investment. This requires tackling a number of problems, such as political instability, lack of law and order, and corruption. The region also needs to develop its financial systems, reform its legal and regulatory approaches, and revamp its state enterprises. Second, land reform, however sensitive an issue, is necessary in many countries. Given the importance of customary ownership, a gradualist approach must be taken. Improving both record keeping for land rights and land administration services will prove crucial. Third, strengthening political governance is required (the 2006 coup in the Fiji Islands, and civil unrest in the Solomon Islands and Timor-Leste, spring to mind), and cannot be postponed. It will involve strengthening parliaments and electoral systems as well as the development of partnerships with civil society.

How can economic transformation help deliver higher growth? As Hausmann and Rodrik (2006) indicate, policy makers have to try to identify the new activities that a country can develop, activities that exploit the existing capabilities (markers, inputs, institutions). This is especially important for relatively backward economies, because creating new activities that require factors and capabilities that an economy does not have is very difficult. For this reason, developing a wide range of competitive traditional manufacturing activities is next to impossible in most of these countries. The economies of Papua New Guinea, Solomon Islands, and Vanuatu have developed some small manufacturing sectors, but far from what is required to induce high and sustainable growth. The Fiji Islands had a garment industry, but this has been in decline

continued on next page

Box 9.6 (continued)

since the end of the Multifibre Arrangement. It also developed a small sugar industry and recently has started bottling mineral water. Samoa has a small automotive harnessing industry.

What can the Pacific economies therefore do? Agriculture is still their largest employer, and so it has to be developed. In particular, agricultural productivity has to increase. Poor infrastructure in this sector is a binding constraint, and farmers' access to the latest technologies has to be improved. Given the vast oceanic and coastal resources that the Pacific economies have, fisheries offer large opportunities, but management of coastal resources has to improve as they face environmental risks. Forestry also offers opportunities, but again, logging has to be properly managed, since at current rates of exploitation it is unsustainable. Plantations also offer opportunities, but establishing large plantations will require land reform and community plantations. Papua New Guinea and Timor-Leste have significant petroleum reserves, but they have to be managed adequately and with transparency, especially as they may generate substantial revenues. Mining also has potential but, like logging, needs to be managed to be environmentally sustainable. Finally, tourism is an activity in which the Pacific islands have a natural advantage. The geographic area is vast, and offers upmarket venture and exploration possibilities. The pre-coup Fiji Islands and Cook Islands have done well in this area. To attract a higher number of tourists, infrastructure has to improve, as well as the quality of tourism professionals.

Using the same classification of manufacturing branches, Figure 9.6 shows the technology and scale scores of manufacturing value-added against income per capita for several Asian countries. The scores are calculated by weighing the share of group 1 by a score of 1; the share of group 2 by a score of 2; the share of group 3 by a score of 3; and the share of group 4 by a score of 4. The indices of the NIEs display strong upward trends, with the exception of Hong Kong, China.[3] Singapore has the highest score. This is the result of having explicit policies to upgrade the technical sophistication of its manufacturing base. The pace of upgrading of the Republic of Korea and Taipei,China has been slower than that of Singapore. Only in the 1970s did they reach the levels that Singapore had passed in the 1970s,

---

[3] The reasons for this are complex, but two of them can be singled out. First is the relationship with the PRC. The relocation of footloose industries has prevented the upgrading of manufacturing. Second, the British knew that colonial rule would end in 1997. Hence, no attempt was made to upgrade the sector.

although in more recent times this gap has narrowed. In the case of Hong Kong, China, lack of proper industrial policy has clearly resulted in deindustrialization and a lower technology level than the other NIEs.

The PRC's and India's indices also display increasing trends, but at a slower pace than those of the NIEs. Nevertheless, the scores of these two countries are very high given their per capita income. Comparable values for the NIEs were only attained at higher levels of income per capita. The PRC has only recently achieved the Republic of Korea's 1960's per capita income level, yet its score is comparable to that of the Republic of Korea in the 1980s and early 1990s. Most likely the PRC's successful participation in global value chains has been instrumental in this upgrading. The case of India is similar.

The value-added technology and scale indices of the ASEAN-4 countries also display upward trends. The indices of Malaysia and Indonesia have increased faster than those of the Philippines (in this case there is no discernible pattern) and Thailand. The value-added technology and scale indexes of the other South Asian countries do not exhibit a steady increase. Bangladesh and Pakistan show an upward trend in the 1960s and 1970s, but the index seems to have declined somewhat in the late 1980s and early 1990s.

Figure 9.7 shows the evolution of the shares of the four groups (as in Table 9.6) for the Republic of Korea, Malaysia, Pakistan, and the Philippines; and Figure 9.8 for India; Taipei,China; the PRC; and Indonesia. The index is graphed against income per capita. For the Republic of Korea, increasing sophistication (i.e., a greater share of manufacturing subsector group 4) is more readily apparent than for Taipei,China. Nevertheless, even today, the Republic of Korea is not on the technological frontier, as Hobday et al. (2004) document (Box 9.7). Malaysia and the Philippines provide a stark contrast: while for Malaysia the increase of group 4 has been magnificent, the share of manufacturing group 4 has been stagnant in the Philippines. The share of group 4 has also increased in India, and has remained stable in the PRC and Indonesia.

Summing up, the two most significant features of the transformation of developing Asia's manufacturing sector are as follows: First, it has an increasing share in world total manufacturing output. Second, the manufacturing sectors of a number of Asian economies, especially the Republic of Korea; Malaysia; Singapore; and Taipei,China, have undergone important transformations and shifted their manufacturing output to more technology- and scale-intensive subsectors. This shift upward is an important component of structural change, as the production of more sophisticated manufactured products leads to faster growth, enlarging the potential for catch-up. In the PRC and India, the shift to more technology- and scale-intensive subsectors is taking place more slowly, while in most other Asian countries the evidence is lacking.

Table 9.6. Share of World Manufacturing by Type of Technology and Decade (%)

Group	N	1970s	N	1980s	N	1990s	N	2000–2003
1. Low Economies of Scale/Low Technology World								
Developing Asia	14	4.86	19	10.40	17	12.26	11	12.75
OECD	22	81.91	23	75.73	23	73.40	17	78.40
LAC	20	4.35	22	5.11	21	7.41	8	3.08
SSA	31	1.80	31	1.82	23	1.08	5	0.12
Rest of the World	20	7.08	30	6.94	33	5.85	25	5.66
Total	107	100.00	125	100.00	117	100.00	66	100.00
Developing Asia								
China, People's Republic of	–	–	1	3.63	1	3.78	1	6.74
India	1	0.77	1	0.69	1	0.68	1	0.91
NIEs	4	2.31	4	3.66	4	4.28	3	3.26
ASEAN-4	4	1.42	4	1.97	4	2.97	2	1.51
Other Southeast Asia	0	0.00	1	0.01	1	0.02	2	0.17
Other South Asia	3	0.32	5	0.41	4	0.51	2	0.16
Central and West Asia	–	–	–	–	1	0.02	–	–
Pacific	2	0.03	3	0.04	1	0.01	–	–
Total	14	4.86	19	10.40	17	12.26	11	12.75
2. Low Economies/Medium Technology World								
Developing Asia	14	2.51	19	6.08	17	8.23	11	8.42
OECD	22	91.58	23	88.27	23	84.97	17	86.56
LAC	20	1.88	22	2.13	21	3.81	8	1.65
SSA	30	0.97	31	0.93	23	0.51	5	0.07
Rest of the World	20	3.07	30	2.59	33	2.49	25	3.30
Total	106	100.00	125	100.00	117	100.00	66	100.00

continued on next page

Table 9.6 (continued)

Group	N	1970s	N	1980s	N	1990s	N	2000–2003
Developing Asia								
China, People's Republic of	–	–	1	1.91	1	1.87	1	3.47
India	1	0.35	1	0.31	1	0.34	1	0.53
NIEs	4	1.62	4	2.87	4	3.82	3	3.35
ASEAN-4	4	0.47	4	0.92	4	2.10	2	0.99
Other Southeast Asia	–	–	1	0.01	1	0.01	2	0.04
Other South Asia	3	0.06	5	0.06	4	0.09	2	0.04
Central and West Asia	–	–	–	–	1	0.00	–	–
Pacific	2	0.01	3	0.01	1	0.00	–	–
Total	14	2.51	19	6.08	17	8.23	11	8.42
3. Medium Economies/Medium Technology World								
Developing Asia	14	2.14	19	7.77	17	10.82	11	11.34
OECD	22	88.70	23	81.84	23	77.79	17	80.96
LAC	19	2.30	22	3.35	21	5.23	8	2.01
SSA	29	1.37	30	1.34	23	0.76	4	0.03
Rest of the World	20	5.49	29	5.70	33	5.40	25	5.66
Total	104	100.00	123	100.00	117	100.00	65	100.00
Developing Asia								
China, People's Republic of	–	–	1	3.64	1	3.95	1	6.20
India	1	0.60	1	0.69	1	0.74	1	0.90
NIEs	4	1.06	4	2.47	4	4.55	3	3.58
ASEAN-4	4	0.42	4	0.82	4	1.43	2	0.59
Other Southeast Asia	–	–	1	0.01	1	0.01	2	0.06
Other South Asia	3	0.06	5	0.13	4	0.14	2	0.02

continued on next page

Table 9.6 (continued)

Group	N	1970s	N	1980s	N	1990s	N	2000–2003
Central and West Asia	–	–	–	–	1	0.00	–	–
Pacific	2	0.01	3	0.01	1	0.00	–	–
Total	14	2.14	19	7.77	17	10.82	11	11.34
4. Medium or Strong Economies/Medium or Strong Technology								
Developing Asia	14	2.19	18	6.07	17	9.41	11	11.33
OECD	22	90.90	23	86.76	23	81.96	17	82.68
LAC	20	1.56	22	2.36	21	4.62	8	1.39
SSA	30	0.71	31	0.77	23	0.36	4	0.01
Rest of the World	20	4.64	30	4.04	33	3.64	25	4.58
Total	106	100.00	124	100.00	117	100.00	65	100.00
Developing Asia								
China, People's Republic of	–	–	1	2.51	1	2.57	1	4.89
India	1	0.55	1	0.55	1	0.59	1	0.69
NIEs	4	1.21	4	2.38	4	4.74	3	4.78
ASEAN-4	4	0.35	4	0.54	4	1.42	2	0.93
Other Southeast Asia	–	–	–	–	1	0.01	2	0.02
Other South Asia	3	0.07	5	0.09	4	0.09	2	0.01
Central and West Asia	–	–	–	–	1	0.00	–	–
Pacific	2	0.01	3	0.00	1	0.00	–	–
Total	14	2.19	18	6.07	17	9.41	11	11.33

Note: – means data are not available. N denotes number of countries. OECD is the Organisation for Economic Co-operation and Development. LAC refers to Latin America and the Caribbean. SSA is Sub-Saharan Africa. ASEAN-4 (Association of Southeast Asian Nations) includes Indonesia, Malaysia, the Philippines, and Thailand. Central and West Asia covers Armenia, Azerbaijan, Kazakhstan, the Kyrgyz Republic, Mongolia, Tajikistan, Turkmenistan, and Uzbekistan. NIEs (newly industrialized economies) consist of Hong Kong, China; the Republic of Korea; Singapore; and Taipei,China. Other Southeast Asia covers Cambodia, the Lao People's Democratic Republic, Myanmar, and Viet Nam. Other South Asia covers Bangladesh, Bhutan, Maldives, Nepal, Pakistan, and Sri Lanka. Pacific covers Fiji Islands, Kiribati, Marshall Islands, Federated States of Micronesia, Palau, Papua New Guinea, Samoa, Timor-Leste, Tonga, and Vanuatu.

Source: Felipe and Estrada 2008. Authors' computations based on data from INDSTAT (UNIDO 2005).

Figure 9.6. Technology and Scale Index

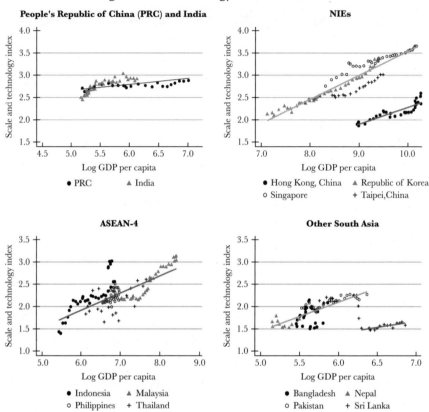

ASEAN = Association of Southeast Asian Nations, GDP = gross domestic product, NIEs = newly industrialized economies.

Source: Asian Development Bank 2007b. Calculations based on data from United Nations Industrial Development Organization's Industrial Statistics International Standard Classification Revision 2 (2005).

Figure 9.7. Shares of Manufacturing Groups in GDP based on Technology and Scale (%): Republic of Korea, Malaysia, Pakistan, and Philippines

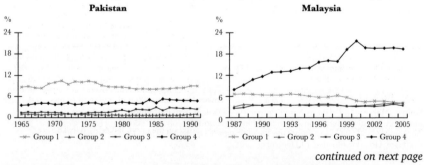

continued on next page

Figure 9.7 (continued)

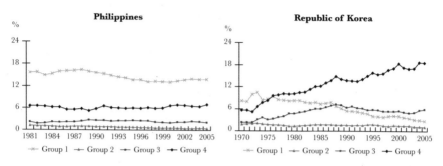

GDP = gross domestic product.

Source: Felipe 2007. Author's calculations based on data from United Nations Industrial Development
Organization's Industrial Statistics International Standard Classification Revision 2 (2005).

**Figure 9.8. Shares of Manufacturing Groups in GDP Based on Technology
and Scale (%): People's Republic of China, India, Indonesia,
and Taipei,China**

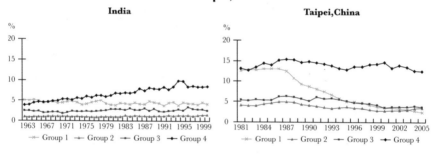

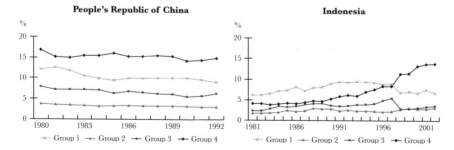

GDP = gross domestic product.

Source: Author's calculations based on data from United Nations Industrial Development Organization's
Industrial Statistics International Standard Classification Revision 2 (2005); Directorate General of Budget,
Accounting and Statistics. http://eng.stat.gov.tw/public/, downloaded 13 December 2006; CEIC Data
Company Ltd., downloaded 13 December 2006.

Box 9.7. Is the Republic of Korea Close to the Technological Frontier?

Korean companies like Samsung, LG, or Hyundai represent brands whose prestige has recently increased. Probably, if one country in Asia other than Japan could be thought of as being on the technological frontier, that is the Republic of Korea. However, recent research by Hobday et al. (2004) based on case-study analyses suggests that Korean firms are still far from the technology frontier. In-depth interviews with 25 firms in seven sectors leads the authors to conclude that although some of the leading *chaebols* are reaching the innovation frontier in some product areas, and are getting into new product design and research and development (R&D), the strength of leading Korean firms in international leadership capabilities such as new product creation and capital goods technology is questionable. The notion that the large Korean firms have reached the innovation frontier characterized by R&D and new product development is inconsistent with the fact that most large exporters offer a portfolio of products, some of which are highly advanced and others much less advanced.

Hobday et al. (2004) provide information that helps acquire an overall understanding of innovation capabilities, challenges, and strategies followed by many Korean firms, which can be referred to as latecomer innovators in transition. Many Korean firms are facing a strategic dilemma, whether to continue with their tried-and-tested formula of low-cost, catch-up competitiveness while relying on the global leaders to generate new products and new markets; or to try to compete as international leaders by deploying in-house R&D to develop their own leading products and systems. This is the *innovation dilemma* that firms like Samsung or Hyundai are facing.

Perhaps the most appropriate model to characterize innovation research by latecomers is a "general reversal process" in which the sequence of innovation is reversed, with developing countries moving from mature to early stages of innovation: first, firms acquire foreign mature technologies from developed countries, including package assembly processes that only require some limited local production engineering; in the second phase, the firm assimilates these technologies and concentrates on the development and innovation of a specific process technology; finally, in the third phase, firms apply R&D to manufacture new product lines. Evidence seems to confirm this general reversal process for electronics in the four upper-tier newly industrialized economies (Hobday 1995a). This model shows that contingency factors such as the nature of product technology, government policy, and the socioeconomic environment are central to innovation.

What are the challenges facing firms in the transition from catching up to leadership position? There are two main issues: (i) these firms face increased competition from firms in developed countries; and (ii) these firms need to develop new products backed up by R&D into new materials, processes, and future product designs.

continued on next page

Box 9.7 (continued)

The 25 firms selected represent a wide spectrum of sectors (telecommunications services, electronic goods and components, capital goods for electronics, automobiles, foodstuffs, venture firms, others); firm sizes in terms of both employment and sales; ownership (foreign and locally owned); and technology strategy (imitator, designer). All these firms were analyzed in terms of different aspects of their technological capability, including awareness of the need to improve, development of a technology strategy to support business, and the ability to assess and select the appropriate technological solutions.

Some of the specific conclusions the authors found are as follows:

(i) Some Korean firms, a minority, are indeed in the innovation dilemma summarized above, and this is a measure of the extent of their success. These are successful firms that, following the catch-up model, have managed to reach an upper bound and are thus now considering moving beyond process innovation into new product creation. Transition to full leadership requires brand development. Even the most advanced firms continue to act as subcontractors with foreign partner companies within some product lines.

(ii) Most firms interviewed believed that in several key product areas they could continue moving forward technologically and serving the international market without actually catching up with the leaders in the short term. Many of these firms thought that as long as international markets for low-cost, high-technology hardware continue to expand (e.g., as will probably happen in electronics), they could continue progressing "behind the frontier" by improving on existing designs.

(iii) Leading Korean firms argued that they offer a wide range of products, including some less advanced products. Firms do not follow one single strategy for innovation, but follow a sort of *portfolio strategy*, carefully tailored to the needs of specific products. Therefore, these firms have a hybrid of innovation strategies, including leadership, followership, and latecomer approaches, for various products.

(iv) Many firms lag even behind the Republic of Korea's leaders. These firms simply try to maintain a strategy of "copy and improve," while they contend against lower-cost competition from other Asian countries such as the People's Republic of China.

(v) The financial crisis of 1997–1998 resulted in setbacks to the broad strategy of catch up and transition, as several firms reported a retreat from basic research and increasing concentration on supporting business divisions. The financial crisis also forced some firms to rethink the old Korean reluctance to engage with foreign firms, leading to joint ventures, which can help Korean firms become leaders. Joint ventures would enable Korean companies, for example, to trade their manufacturing process advantages for access to capital goods, new markets, and fundamental research.

As I argued in chapter 6, some Asian countries made huge efforts toward increasing investment (much of it into the manufacturing sector). But these countries were initially somewhat lucky. In the late 1960s, the developed world started relocating entire industries or particular industrial processes to the Third World. One important reason was the increase in wages in the advanced economies, because the social contract established after World War II favored labor (chapter 3). At the same time, rapid technological progress led to the development of highly standardized manufacturing processes. This made it possible to transfer particular stages of production, the labor-intensive processes that required low-skilled workers. What options did companies in the developed world have? Only two: Latin America and East and Southeast Asia. However, Latin America was ruled out for being much more politically unstable. This left only Asia. Thus, in the late 1960s, a number of electronics firms, including Hewlett-Packard and Texas Instruments, built factories in Singapore to assemble components, particularly semiconductors. This process was extended to Malaysia, Thailand, and the Philippines. But what were the internal conditions that enabled capitalist Southeast Asia to respond to the opportunities created by restructuring in the industrial core? In chapter 6, I argued that the repression of labor facilitated capital accumulation. Indeed, as Brown argues, "one crucial condition . . . was the presence of a copious supply of cheap, largely unskilled, and essentially *docile labour*" (1997, 262; italics added). The success of the East Asian exporters was, to a large extent, based on shifting the costs of industrialization to the workforce, in the form of low hourly wages, long and intensive work shifts, and high industrial accident rates. Certainly this was not an inclusive way of achieving high and sustained growth.[4] To this factor, one must add the use of young female workers, whose "dexterous fingers and patient temperament fitted them for such repetitive, minutely detailed tasks as electronic components assembly or garment production" (Brown 1997, 262–63).[5]

---

[4] In retrospect, the question is whether the mechanism worked, as it may be inferred that fast growth requires labor repression and the transfer of resources to capital. This question has no simple answer and requires an in-depth analysis of the issue well beyond the scope of this book. In the Republic of Korea, the mechanism probably worked. Fast capital accumulation was no doubt a key factor in the country's development. And during the last two decades, the country has seen democratization. But probably this is not true, at least to the same extent, in other countries. The PRC is another economic success. As noted in Box 6.1, the labor share has declined significantly. So far this has not been a source of contention, because the high growth in labor productivity has led to increases in real income; but only time will tell how far this can go.

[5] Today, much foreign manufacturing in the PRC is assembly activity and the workforce is disproportionately female and recruited from rural areas. The high female literacy rate has given the PRC a crucial advantage in attracting foreign investment in manufacturing vis-à-vis India.

A second condition was that Southeast Asia was resource rich (except Singapore). This gave the region an important advantage in the production of manufactures such as wood products, processed foods, cement, chemical fertilizer, and paper, all of which involve the intensive use of local inputs. Finally, a third condition was that these countries possessed acceptable communication, commercial, and administrative infrastructure.

However, a dose of luck and these internal conditions do not explain entirely the East and Southeast Asia's success. To these, one must add the particular social contract implemented in many countries (i.e., class-biased socialization of the costs of accumulation against workers) and the political pressure derived from the communist threat. Underlying these, a series of complex structures of political, economic, and bureaucratic interests favored the accumulation of capital.

Structural Transformation: Intrasector Productivity Growth and Labor Relocation

In this section and in section *Production Structure Similarities and Catch-Up*, I discuss the results of two empirical exercises that answer the following question: what is the contribution of structural change to productivity growth and catching up? Chenery et al. (1986) have shown that the economy-wide growth rate of labor productivity can be decomposed into two parts: one, the sum of the growth rates of labor productivity *within* sectors (weighted by the sector's share in output); and two, the effect of labor relocation across sectors of different productivity, calculated as the sum of the changes in the employment shares of the sectors receiving employment moving out of agriculture (i.e., industry and services) multiplied by the differential in labor productivity with respect to agriculture.[6] The argument is that, given the low productivity in agriculture, as workers leave this sector and are absorbed in

---

[6] The formula used is: $\hat{q} = \sum_i k_i \hat{q}_i + (\lambda_I^{'} - \lambda_I^0)\dfrac{(q_I - q_A)}{q} + (\lambda_S^{'} - \lambda_S^0)\dfrac{(q_S - q_A)}{q}$, where $\hat{q}$ is the

growth rate of overall labor productivity; $\hat{q}_i$ is the growth rate of each sector's labor productivity; k represents the respective output shares; $(q_I - q_A)/q$ is the difference between the levels of labor productivity in industry and agriculture divided by the overall level of productivity; $(q_S - q_A)/q$ is the difference between the levels of labor productivity in services and agriculture divided by the overall level of productivity; and λ denotes the employment shares of each sector. The first term of the decomposition represents the component of overall growth that is due to the growth of labor productivity *within* each sector (weighted by the output shares). The remaining two terms represent the effect of the relocation of labor *across* sectors of unequal productivity (measured with respect to the productivity of the agriculture sector).

either manufacturing or services, major productivity gains ensue. Detailed calculations are provided in Table A9.4 at the end of the chapter.

Figure 9.9 shows the contributions of intrasector labor productivity growth and intersector labor productivity growth (i.e., reallocation of labor) to overall labor productivity growth in a number of Asian countries.

The intrasector or pure productivity growth effect is unaffected by changes in the employment share and thus isolates the contribution due solely to productivity improvements within sectors. In general, the output share of agriculture tends to decline over time, that of industry rises in the intermediate stage of growth, and that of services increases in the final stage. As the growth rate of labor productivity tends to be highest in industry, the rise of the output share of this sector is part of the explanation of the growth acceleration that takes place during this phase. Similarly, the rise of the output share of the tertiary sector at the expense of industry in the later stages of growth is part of the explanation for the growth deceleration in that stage of growth. In most countries in Figure 9.9, intrasector productivity growth is more important.[7]

Intrasector contributions to labor productivity growth (i.e., the subcomponents of intrasector productivity growth) are shown in Figure 9.10. Agriculture contributes the least to overall labor productivity growth.

The remainder of the overall growth in labor productivity is due to labor reallocation from agriculture into industry and services (Figure 9.11). If labor shifts from a sector with low labor productivity to a sector with higher labor productivity, this relocation contributes to overall growth, over and above the growth of labor productivity within sectors. As, in general, labor productivity is lowest in agriculture and highest in industry, part of the acceleration of growth in the early stages is due to the shift of labor out of the agriculture sector and into the other sectors. Likewise, part of the deceleration in growth during the later stages is due to the shift of labor from industry into services. One reason for the slower growth of labor productivity in agriculture and services lies in the limited possibilities of mechanization of these two sectors (especially services), while the growth of labor productivity is much higher in industry because it offers much greater possibilities for mechanization. However, not *all* services activities have productivity growth rates lower than those in all individual manufacturing industries, or even below the average for all manufacturing industries. Figure 9.11 indicates that services have, in general, absorbed much more labor transferred out of agriculture than industry.

---

[7]   Given the high level of aggregation used (the three sectors), the decomposition hides shifts within manufacturing and within services, for example.

Figure 9.9. Intrasector and Intersector Shares of Labor Productivity Growth (%)

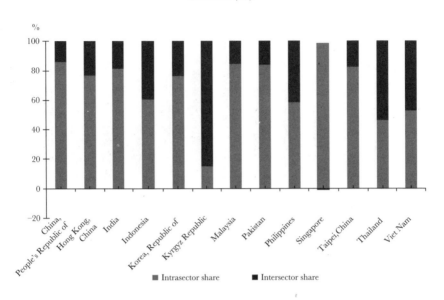

Time period: The People's Republic of China: 1987–2002; Hong Kong, China: 1978–2004; India: 1983–2000; Indonesia: 1976–2002; the Republic of Korea: 1970–2004; the Kyrgyz Republic: 1987–2002; Malaysia: 1980–2004; Pakistan: 1973–2002; the Philippines: 1971–2004; Singapore: 1970–2003; Taipei,China: 1965–2004; Thailand: 1971–2004; Viet Nam: 1991–2004.

Source: Asian Development Bank 2007b. Calculations based on data from International Labour Organization, LABORSTA Labour Statistics Database, downloaded 9 August 2006; and World Bank, World Development Indicators online database, downloaded 2 August 2006.

The effect of the transfer of labor on the level of productivity is what Baumol et al. (1985, 1989) have called the "structural bonus." Backward economies with a large pool of employment in low-productivity activities (normally agriculture) experience a bonus from structural change. This occurs because the transfer of labor from low- to high-productivity activities automatically increases the productivity *level* of the economy (i.e., a composition effect), even if this transfer of resources is mainly a shift from agriculture to services (where productivity might not be significantly higher). However, as the logistic pattern of structural change drives resources toward services, and given that productivity growth in this sector is usually slower than in industry, countries experience a "structural burden." This "burden" means that structural change hinders productivity *growth*. As the share of labor in services increases, the average growth rate of the economy decreases. In the limit, as most of the labor force has moved into the services activities, economies experience "asymptotic

Figure 9.10. Sector Contributions to Labor Productivity Growth (%)

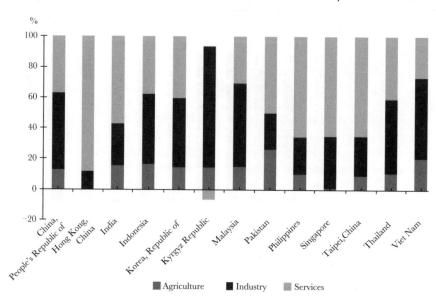

Source: Asian Development Bank 2007b. Calculations based on data from the World Development Indicators.

Figure 9.11. Baumol's Structural Bonus: Industry vs. Services

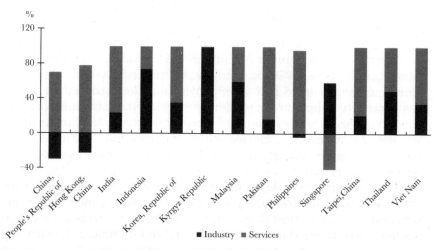

Source: Asian Development Bank 2007b. Calculations based on data from the World Development Indicators.

stagnancy" as productivity growth is mostly determined by services. This means that structural change increases the productivity of the economy but, at the same time, as the economy matures, productivity growth slows down. The decomposition used here does not consider the structural burden.

The relationship between Kaldor's third law and Baumol's asymptotic stagnancy theory is evident. The importance of a sector depends not only on how it generates scale economies but also on how it absorbs resources from other sectors, leading to "structural bonus" and "structural burden" effects. Although a sector with low productivity growth can absorb resources from agriculture leading to increased productivity *levels*, this source of economic growth is asymptotically exhausted. In the transition, Kaldor's third law will be an important source of growth but, in the limit, induced productivity growth is the key to generating growth (see, for example, Fagerberg [2000]; Timmer and Szirmai [2000]).

Production Structure Similarities and Catch-Up

For countries lagging behind the technological frontier, endogenous technological progress will be partly dependent on the acquisition and mastery of more advanced production techniques from the leader countries, which in turn will be determined by such factors as national research and development, human capital, and trade openness. If technology is (at least to a certain extent) sector specific, its diffusion from the most advanced to the less advanced countries will be more intense and faster the higher the degree of structural (or sector) similarity between them. As a result, other things being equal, technological progress will be faster for a less-advanced country the more its production structure resembles that of the technological leader. This reasoning is in line with that of Abramovitz (1986, 1993), who has argued that the extent to which developing economies can benefit from the superior technology developed in advanced countries depends on their "absorption capability." The latter is itself a composite variable, determined by social as well as economic and structural factors, such as the degree of "technological congruence" with countries on the technological frontier.

Here, I follow a simple approach to measuring the significance of the extent to which the productivity growth of the Asian countries has benefited from technological spillovers from the most advanced countries flowing via a "structural channel" (Felipe et al. 2007). First, in the spirit of the technology-gap approach to growth and convergence (Gerschenkron 1962; Nelson and Wright 1992), a measure of the potential for technology transfer from the most advanced to the less advanced countries is defined by the labor productivity ratio between the two, i.e., $GAP_i(t) = \dfrac{q_L(t)}{q_i(t)}$, where t denotes time, q_L (t) is the level of labor productivity in the technologically most advanced country and q_i (t) is its counterpart in the less-advanced country i.

Second, a measure of structural similarity is defined making use of the specialization index developed by Midelfart-Knarvik et al. (2000).[8] At each point in time, the index is constructed as the sum over the k sectors of the absolute differences between the sectors' shares of value added in country i and in the technological leader. Its value ranges between 0 and 2 and increases with the degree of specialization, i.e., it is higher the more a country's production structure differs from that of the technological leader. For instance, a K-index value of 0.5 indicates that 25% of the country i's production structure is out of line with that of the technologically most-advanced country, in the sense that one quarter of its total output does not correspond to the average sector composition in the latter.[9]

This way, one can build a structurally weighted gap variable by first designing a measure of structural weights as $W_{iL}(t) = 1 - \dfrac{K_{iL}(t)}{2}$, where $0 \le W_{iL}(t) \le 1$, which increases with the degree of structural similarity, i.e., as $K_{iL}(t)$ falls. The structurally weighted gap variable is $SWGAP_i(t) = W_{iL} \times GAP_i(t)$. This variable can then be introduced in a growth regression to capture the idea that the impact of technology spillovers on the less advanced countries' growth will be dependent not only on the size of the technology gap but also on the degree of structural similarity between technological leaders and followers. I examine this hypothesis by making use of a simple reduced-form growth equation.

Given the nature of the hypothesis under examination, finely sectorally disaggregated data are essential for estimation. Taking this into account, attention is restricted to manufacturing and structural weights $W_{iL}(t)$ are

---

[8] When applied to country-level bilateral comparisons it is constructed as follows:

$$K_{iL}(t) = \sum_k abs\left[v_i^k(t) - v_L^k(t) \right], \text{ where } v_i^k(t) \equiv \dfrac{x_i^k(t)}{\sum_k x_i^k(t)} \text{ and } x_i^k(t) \text{ denotes country } i\text{'s value}$$

added in sector k at time t and $v_L^k(t)$ refers to the technological leader. Instead of value added, Midelfart-Knarvik et al. (2000) employed the gross value of output as a measure of activity level, on the grounds that this makes the results of the analysis less likely to be biased by the effects of structural shifts in outsourcing to other sectors. This option was precluded by data unavailability in our case.

[9] The upper bound of the index equals two because, by construction, it takes into account both positive and negative deviations across sectors. Thus, when calculating the "implied-percentage deviation" the value in question must be halved: in the example, $(0.5/2)\% = 25\%$.

constructed using the United Nations Industrial Development Organization's (UNIDO) data for 28 sectors.[10] The remaining data are taken from the World Bank's World Development Indicators and the International Labour Organization (ILO).[11]

To smooth out cyclical effects, structural weights $W_{iL}(t)$ were computed as 3-year moving averages of annual values. The regression was estimated by means of panel data techniques using an unbalanced panel of annual data over 1982–2002 for nine Asian countries—Bangladesh; the PRC; Hong Kong, China; Indonesia; Malaysia; Singapore; the Republic of Korea; Sri Lanka; and Taipei,China. I estimated a regression of the growth rate of labor productivity on the gap variables, constructed taking the US and Japan as the two technological leaders with respect to the less-advanced Asian countries in our sample. Results are reported in Table 9.7.[12]

Table 9.7. Technology Gap Regression

Variables	Coefficient	Standard Error	t-value
GAP_JP	(0.008)	0.005	(1.85)
GAP_JP(–1)	0.050*	0.020	2.54
SWGAP_JP	0.050**	0.017	2.95
SWGAP_JP(–1)	(0.050)	0.037	(1.31)
GAP_US	0.016	0.008	1.95
GAP_US(–1)	(0.064)**	0.020	(3.16)
SWGAP_US	(0.070)**	0.025	(2.77)
SWGAP_US(–1)	0.074**	0.025	2.92

Note: * indicates significance at the 5% level, ** at the 1% level; _JP denotes that the leader is Japan, _US that it is the United States; and (–1) indicates the first lags.

Source: Author.

---

[10] The data are from the UNIDO Industrial Statistics Database 2006 at the 3-digit level of ISIC Code (Revision 2).

[11] The source of the manufacturing value-added series for the US is the Department of Commerce, Bureau of Economic Analysis.

[12] The regression estimated is

$$\hat{q}_{it} = \alpha_i + \sum_{j=1}^{2} \beta_i GAP_{it}^j + \sum_{j=1}^{2} \theta_j SWGAP_{it}^j$$

where $\hat{q}_{it}$ is the rate of labor productivity growth in country i and the gap variables are constructed taking both the US and Japan as the two technological leaders with respect to the less-advanced Asian countries in our sample. I used the fixed-effects Least Squares Dummy Variables estimator and, since we are dealing with annual data and a fairly short time series, I allowed for just one lag. The introduction of more lags of the independent variables did not change the results qualitatively. Moreover, estimation of a dynamic version of the growth regression using the Generalized Method of Moments resulted in an insignificant coefficient on the lagged dependent variable, leading me to favor the static-version results reported.

The R^2 of the regression is 0.49, suggesting that the gap and structurally weighted gap variables explain roughly half of the variation in labor productivity growth. GAP_JP is not statistically significant; however, it becomes highly significant and takes on the expected positive sign when it is interacted with $W_{iL}(t)$, i.e., in SWGAP_JP, to take account of structural similarities. The coefficient of GAP_JP(–1) is also significant and positive so that, overall, one can read the results in Table 9.7 as supporting the view that Japan, as the technological leader in the region, is a significant source of technological spillovers to the other Asian countries in our sample.

When the technological gap is measured with respect to the US, results are different. Both the structurally weighted gap variable SWGAP_US and its first lag SWGAP_US(–1) turn out to be significant at the 1% level, but the former takes on a negative sign so that they have negligible effect on labor productivity growth. Furthermore, the first lag of the GAP_US variable is also negative and significant.

Table A9.1. Share of Manufacturing Subsector by Decade—Developing Asia (%)

Country	Food and Beverages	Textiles	Apparel, Leather, and Footwear	Wood and Wood Products	Paper and Paper Products	Printing and Publishing	Industrial Chemicals	Petroleum and Coal Products	Rubber and Plastic Products	Nonmetal Mineral Products	Basic Metals	Metal Products	Nonelectrical Machinery	Electrical Machinery	Transport Equipment	Others	Total
1970s																	
China, People's Republic of	–	–	–	–	–	–	–	–	–	–	–	–	–	–	–	–	–
India	11.19	20.53	0.99	0.68	2.57	2.03	14.79	2.60	2.46	3.80	11.78	3.16	7.67	7.23	7.38	1.14	100.00
Newly Industrialized Economies																	
Hong Kong, China	5.18	17.96	26.60	1.93	1.27	3.70	1.66	0.00	9.22	0.94	1.15	7.50	2.19	11.41	2.60	6.68	100.00
Korea, Republic of	18.41	14.43	5.76	2.81	2.17	2.03	9.45	5.51	4.28	5.29	6.62	3.05	3.26	8.17	5.96	2.80	100.00
Singapore	6.87	2.59	3.77	4.19	1.06	3.66	5.02	16.79	3.60	2.97	2.03	4.84	7.53	19.00	12.70	3.39	100.00
Taipei,China	16.42	7.98	5.05	3.27	2.14	5.26	6.28	5.19	4.76	5.20	4.20	4.77	9.50	9.04	4.91	6.02	100.00
ASEAN-4																	
Indonesia	39.41	14.68	1.50	3.77	1.61	1.55	11.21	0.00	4.42	6.84	0.71	3.37	1.46	4.10	4.98	0.39	100.00
Malaysia	25.06	5.38	1.52	12.66	0.85	4.32	6.28	3.09	12.23	4.93	2.94	3.79	2.86	9.74	3.29	1.08	100.00
Philippines	37.22	7.56	2.69	4.46	3.85	1.46	12.30	7.65	3.26	4.39	3.47	2.51	1.35	3.11	4.08	0.65	100.00
Thailand	41.63	15.63	0.59	3.61	1.47	1.41	5.26	6.29	2.94	7.93	2.42	3.01	0.71	2.06	4.63	0.39	100.00
Other Southeast Asia																	
Myanmar	–	–	–	–	–	–	–	–	–	–	–	–	–	–	–	–	–
Viet Nam	–	–	–	–	–	–	–	–	–	–	–	–	–	–	–	–	–

continued on next page

Table A9.1 (continued)

Country	Food and Beverages	Textiles	Apparel, Leather, and Footwear	Wood and Wood Products	Paper and Paper Products	Printing and Publishing	Industrial Chemicals	Petroleum and Coal Products	Rubber and Plastic Products	Nonmetal Mineral Products	Basic Metals	Metal Products	Nonelectrical Machinery	Electrical Machinery	Transport Equipment	Others	Total
Other South Asia																	
Bangladesh	31.44	37.26	1.64	0.30	2.27	0.68	13.59	0.43	0.50	1.80	3.85	1.22	0.57	2.05	1.38	1.03	100.00
Bhutan	–	–	–	–	–	–	–	–	–	–	–	–	–	–	–	–	–
Nepal	–	–	–	–	–	–	–	–	–	–	–	–	–	–	–	–	–
Pakistan	30.45	27.78	2.04	0.26	1.61	1.22	11.20	5.27	1.80	4.43	3.06	1.62	1.84	3.31	2.99	1.11	100.00
Sri Lanka	28.06	13.86	6.66	1.78	3.59	0.84	8.80	5.36	6.31	8.48	1.59	4.01	3.29	4.29	1.83	1.24	100.00
Pacific																	
Cook Islands	–	–	–	–	–	–	–	–	–	–	–	–	–	–	–	–	–
Fiji Islands	63.14	0.00	2.03	8.64	1.74	3.25	2.57	0.00	1.98	5.26	0.00	5.68	1.44	0.89	3.01	0.37	100.00
Papua New Guinea	36.90	0.17	0.59	15.86	1.14	3.29	5.23	0.00	0.75	2.61	0.39	5.79	8.27	2.06	13.67	3.28	100.00
Tonga	–	–	–	–	–	–	–	–	–	–	–	–	–	–	–	–	–
1980s																	
China, People's Republic of	12.36	12.33	3.07	1.45	2.05	1.18	11.45	4.79	3.69	6.89	9.54	4.36	13.81	5.94	3.88	3.20	100.00
India	11.81	14.18	1.40	0.53	1.81	1.88	14.82	3.85	3.17	4.80	12.18	2.88	8.50	8.41	8.50	1.32	100.00
Newly Industrialized Economies																	
Hong Kong, China	5.52	14.77	24.59	1.29	1.67	4.93	1.61	0.02	8.46	1.01	0.69	7.02	4.05	13.74	2.36	8.26	100.00

continued on next page

Table A9.1 (continued)

Country	Food and Beverages	Textiles	Apparel, Leather, and Footwear	Wood and Wood Products	Paper and Paper Products	Printing and Publishing	Industrial Chemicals	Petroleum and Coal Products	Rubber and Plastic Products	Nonmetal Mineral Products	Basic Metals	Metal Products	Nonelectrical Machinery	Electrical Machinery	Transport Equipment	Others	Total
Korea, Republic of	13.13	10.35	5.88	1.58	2.26	2.29	8.78	3.95	5.31	4.66	7.59	4.44	5.32	12.95	8.23	3.26	100.00
Singapore	5.32	0.84	3.36	1.99	1.45	4.15	9.12	9.46	2.69	2.29	1.43	6.11	10.01	29.95	8.92	2.92	100.00
Taipei,China	10.95	7.66	6.79	2.83	2.72	3.08	7.86	6.41	7.37	3.77	5.92	4.30	5.82	12.47	6.00	6.04	100.00
ASEAN-4																	
Indonesia	26.90	11.40	2.45	10.71	1.71	1.56	11.09	0.00	5.37	5.20	7.26	4.68	1.19	3.45	6.57	0.46	100.00
Malaysia	20.23	3.67	2.48	7.81	1.28	3.67	11.72	2.76	8.68	6.40	3.60	3.38	2.80	15.81	4.12	1.59	100.00
Philippines	35.76	5.44	5.27	4.32	2.69	1.39	11.46	10.10	3.35	3.26	4.64	1.96	1.22	5.69	2.48	0.96	100.00
Thailand	33.40	10.37	3.03	1.94	1.56	7.13	5.83	5.52	6.31	7.50	3.96	2.64	0.27	4.85	4.38	1.30	100.00
Other Southeast Asia																	
Myanmar	34.13	0.00	0.00	15.65	0.00	0.00	0.00	0.00	19.13	4.68	19.64	1.89	0.00	0.00	0.00	4.88	100.00
Viet Nam	—	—	—	—	—	—	—	—	—	—	—	—	—	—	—	—	—
Other South Asia																	
Bangladesh	23.96	31.36	4.96	0.87	2.50	1.13	17.46	4.38	0.57	2.00	3.53	1.40	1.30	2.42	1.41	0.77	100.00
Bhutan	19.64	5.27	0.00	19.85	0.29	1.09	22.86	0.00	2.49	27.99	0.00	0.51	0.00	0.00	0.00	0.00	100.00
Nepal	41.30	15.96	8.10	2.48	1.13	0.94	6.05	0.00	2.21	13.00	3.02	2.83	0.00	2.24	0.00	0.75	100.00
Pakistan	30.94	18.14	2.37	0.39	1.15	1.06	14.29	6.01	1.80	7.75	6.20	1.06	2.14	3.26	2.89	0.55	100.00
Sri Lanka	49.60	7.84	9.30	1.60	1.98	1.52	4.36	5.74	5.06	6.46	0.85	1.50	0.92	1.12	0.69	1.46	100.00

continued on next page

Table A9.1 (continued)

Country	Food and Beverages	Textiles	Apparel, Leather, and Footwear	Wood and Wood Products	Paper and Paper Products	Printing and Publishing	Industrial Chemicals	Petroleum and Coal Products	Rubber and Plastic Products	Nonmetal Mineral Products	Basic Metals	Metal Products	Nonelectrical Machinery	Electrical Machinery	Transport Equipment	Others	Total
Pacific																	
Cook Islands	10.95	7.66	6.79	2.83	2.72	3.08	7.86	6.41	7.37	3.77	5.92	4.30	5.82	12.47	6.00	6.04	100.00
Fiji Islands	59.99	3.03	1.67	8.30	2.15	4.18	4.45	0.00	2.41	4.58	0.00	4.97	0.86	0.28	2.43	0.71	100.00
Papua New Guinea	52.67	0.13	0.59	17.35	1.22	2.71	3.20	0.00	0.97	3.18	0.55	7.37	5.22	0.53	4.29	0.00	100.00
Tonga	69.24	0.00	4.01	8.66	0.69	3.17	1.61	0.00	0.00	5.36	0.00	5.12	0.00	0.66	0.87	0.61	100.00
1990s																	
China, People's Republic of	14.66	8.02	4.48	1.31	1.95	1.14	11.44	3.62	3.43	7.34	10.24	3.34	9.19	10.35	6.35	3.15	100.00
India	12.08	9.97	2.79	0.39	1.80	1.58	19.14	4.49	3.28	4.66	12.17	2.52	7.39	7.30	8.69	1.75	100.00
Newly Industrialized Economies																	
Hong Kong, China	10.44	13.06	16.00	0.52	2.20	11.43	2.36	0.10	3.90	1.87	0.87	5.08	8.97	12.25	3.72	7.24	100.00
Korea, Republic of	9.34	6.01	4.52	1.86	2.29	2.52	8.89	3.58	4.78	4.73	6.89	5.00	8.93	16.85	11.68	2.11	100.00
Singapore	3.70	0.33	1.31	0.93	1.34	4.51	10.03	5.82	2.97	1.93	0.67	6.29	27.32	22.92	7.05	2.86	100.00
Taipei,China	9.22	6.43	3.89	1.96	2.20	1.32	9.04	7.21	7.11	4.53	7.06	6.74	4.79	17.35	7.61	3.54	100.00
ASEAN-4																	
Indonesia	20.05	10.29	7.11	8.77	3.92	1.81	9.83	0.13	4.48	2.91	7.60	3.74	1.55	6.09	10.64	1.08	100.00

continued on next page

Table A9.1 (continued)

Country	Food and Beverages	Textiles	Apparel, Leather, and Footwear	Wood and Wood Products	Paper and Paper Products	Printing and Publishing	Industrial Chemicals	Petroleum and Coal Products	Rubber and Plastic Products	Nonmetal Mineral Products	Basic Metals	Metal Products	Nonelectrical Machinery	Electrical Machinery	Transport Equipment	Others	Total
Malaysia	9.75	3.01	2.16	6.95	1.59	2.63	9.31	2.69	7.93	5.26	3.08	4.02	5.07	29.41	5.15	1.99	100.00
Philippines	33.25	3.39	6.30	1.92	2.01	1.54	13.09	7.58	3.39	4.40	5.07	1.72	1.34	10.06	3.68	1.26	100.00
Thailand	15.52	9.24	7.32	1.56	1.09	15.42	2.31	8.89	2.99	6.00	3.00	2.06	10.96	6.69	5.16	1.80	100.00
Other Southeast Asia																	
Myanmar	36.20	0.00	1.39	9.96	0.00	0.00	23.28	0.00	5.99	8.20	9.92	0.35	0.00	0.00	0.00	4.74	100.00
Viet Nam	–	–	–	–	–	–	–	–	–	–	–	–	–	–	–	–	–
Other South Asia																	
Bangladesh	25.08	16.72	21.60	0.76	1.75	2.11	12.81	0.51	0.54	4.92	2.86	1.20	0.33	4.04	4.27	0.50	100.00
Bhutan	–	–	–	–	–	–	–	–	–	–	–	–	–	–	–	–	–
Nepal	32.26	26.25	11.07	2.62	1.14	0.97	4.80	0.03	2.56	9.92	2.39	3.61	0.01	1.82	0.00	0.54	100.00
Pakistan	22.89	25.06	2.80	0.37	1.54	2.00	15.50	3.26	1.42	7.76	5.13	0.81	2.09	5.43	3.05	0.88	100.00
Sri Lanka	40.00	8.87	20.25	0.99	1.40	1.13	5.26	1.56	6.41	4.49	0.95	1.05	1.63	1.39	1.98	2.63	100.00
Mongolia																	
Mongolia	36.80	17.58	21.14	4.28	0.00	1.59	1.14	0.00	0.00	3.98	0.15	2.41	0.00	0.64	0.00	10.29	100.00
Pacific																	
Cook Islands	9.22	6.43	3.89	1.96	2.20	1.32	9.04	7.21	7.11	4.53	7.06	6.74	4.79	17.35	7.61	3.54	100.00
Fiji Islands	48.73	12.67	0.96	10.44	3.37	5.76	5.41	0.00	2.33	3.70	0.00	3.66	0.99	0.00	1.07	0.92	100.00
Papua New Guinea	–	–	–	–	–	–	–	–	–	–	–	–	–	–	–	–	–
Tonga	–	–	–	–	–	–	–	–	–	–	–	–	–	–	–	–	–

continued on next page

Table A9.1 (continued)

Country	Food and Beverages	Textiles	Apparel, Leather, and Footwear	Wood and Wood Products	Paper and Paper Products	Printing and Publishing	Industrial Chemicals	Petroleum and Coal Products	Rubber and Plastic Products	Nonmetal Mineral Products	Basic Metals	Metal Products	Nonelectrical Machinery	Electrical Machinery	Transport Equipment	Others	Total
2000–2003																	
China, People's Republic of	14.30	6.25	4.73	1.35	2.16	1.07	11.59	3.95	3.57	5.48	9.40	3.20	7.34	15.63	7.59	2.38	100.00
India	13.22	9.01	2.78	0.52	2.33	1.53	20.77	5.61	3.63	5.68	10.19	2.66	6.81	5.87	7.18	2.20	100.00
Newly Industrialized Economies																	
Hong Kong, China	9.31	11.19	8.89	0.19	1.29	19.87	3.68	0.00	1.78	3.00	1.09	2.62	5.57	19.54	5.36	6.63	100.00
Korea, Republic of	8.19	4.81	3.12	1.44	2.25	2.47	9.53	2.48	4.17	4.00	6.48	4.06	11.28	19.76	14.06	1.91	100.00
Singapore	2.34	0.18	0.76	0.70	0.78	3.54	17.35	4.20	2.86	1.03	0.29	5.37	21.95	26.03	8.16	4.42	100.00
Taipei,China	–	–	–	–	–	–	–	–	–	–	–	–	–	–	–	–	–
ASEAN-4																	
Indonesia	21.25	8.84	7.17	8.67	5.51	1.53	11.01	0.09	4.45	0.04	4.68	2.50	2.90	8.30	11.93	1.15	100.00
Malaysia	8.39	2.18	1.75	5.75	2.11	1.99	8.08	8.63	6.96	4.91	2.64	3.17	9.10	27.11	4.98	2.25	100.00
Philippines	–	–	–	–	–	–	–	–	–	–	–	–	–	–	–	–	–
Thailand	–	–	–	–	–	–	–	–	–	–	–	–	–	–	–	–	–
Other Southeast Asia																	
Myanmar	59.85	0.00	1.25	0.89	0.00	0.00	0.00	0.00	6.54	0.37	12.20	2.80	5.07	3.16	5.71	2.15	100.00
Viet Nam	30.19	4.55	16.42	2.36	1.75	2.21	6.26	0.41	3.42	10.57	2.17	2.62	2.37	5.81	6.92	1.97	100.00

continued on next page

Table A9.1 (continued)

Country	Food and Beverages	Textiles	Apparel, Leather, and Footwear	Wood and Wood Products	Paper and Paper Products	Printing and Publishing	Industrial Chemicals	Petroleum and Coal Products	Rubber and Plastic Products	Nonmetal Mineral Products	Basic Metals	Metal Products	Nonelectrical Machinery	Electrical Machinery	Transport Equipment	Others	Total
Other South Asia																	
Bangladesh	–	–	–	–	–	–	–	–	–	–	–	–	–	–	–	–	–
Bhutan	–	–	–	–	–	–	–	–	–	–	–	–	–	–	–	–	–
Nepal	45.42	10.48	8.78	1.50	1.46	2.12	10.40	0.00	3.98	6.43	2.26	5.23	0.07	1.57	0.07	0.21	100.00
Pakistan	–	–	–	–	–	–	–	–	–	–	–	–	–	–	–	–	–
Sri Lanka	38.57	10.48	20.81	0.64	1.95	0.68	3.76	3.11	7.12	4.30	0.21	0.75	1.71	1.64	2.29	1.96	100.00

– = data not available, ASEAN = Association of Southeast Asian Nations.

Source: Author's calculations based on data from United Nations Industrial Development Organization's Industrial Statistics 2005.

Table A9.2. Value-Added Share by Manufacturing Subsector
(% Manufacturing)
a. People's Republic of China and India

People's Republic of China	1980		2003
Machinery, except electrical	15.04	Machinery, electric	16.18
Textiles	15.03	Industrial chemicals	11.12
Industrial chemicals	7.98	Transport equipment	8.52
Iron and steel	7.33	Iron and steel	8.30
Fabricated metal products	5.45	Machinery, except electrical	7.64
Other nonmetallic mineral products	4.96	Food products	6.27
Petroleum refineries	4.73	Textiles	5.60
Food products	4.22	Tobacco	4.62
Tobacco	3.97	Other nonmetallic mineral products	3.97
Machinery, electric	3.60	Petroleum refineries	3.78
Share of top 5	50.82	Share of top 5	51.76
Share of top 10	72.31	Share of top 10	76.02
Standard deviation	3.84	Standard deviation	3.85
Specialization index	12.97	Specialization index	12.30

India	1970		2002
Textiles	20.25	Petroleum refineries	10.08
Iron and steel	9.93	Industrial chemicals	9.88
Food products	9.65	Iron and steel	9.62
Transport equipment	7.13	Other chemicals	9.36
Machinery, except electrical	6.84	Food products	8.33
Industrial chemicals	6.79	Textiles	7.90
Other chemicals	6.78	Transport equipment	7.79
Machinery, electric	6.25	Machinery, electric	5.80
Fabricated metal products	3.54	Machinery, except electrical	5.72
Other nonmetallic mineral products	3.27	Other nonmetallic mineral products	4.01
Share of top 5	53.80	Share of top 5	47.26
Share of top 10	80.43	Share of top 10	78.48
Standard deviation	4.45	Standard deviation	3.53
Specialization index	18.08	Specialization index	14.13

continued on next page

Table A9.2 (continued)

b. NIEs

Hong Kong, China	1973		2003
Textiles	26.91	Printing and publishing	25.39
Wearing apparel	19.66	Textiles	13.46
Electrical machinery	9.16	Food products	11.45
Plastic products	9.10	Machinery, electric	10.57
Fabricated metal	7.02	Wearing apparel, except footwear	10.31
Printing and publishing	3.78	Transport equipment	6.51
Transport equipment	3.35	Machinery, except electrical	4.52
Other manufactures	3.26·	Other manufactured products	4.46
Food products	2.51	Industrial chemicals	4.36
Nonelectrical machinery	1.49	Fabricated metal products	2.05
Share of top 5	71.85	Share of top 5	71.19
Share of top 10	86.23	Share of top 10	93.09
Standard deviation	6.19	Standard deviation	5.88
Specialization index	26.76	Specialization index	23.87

Republic of Korea	1970		2002
Textiles	13.82	Machinery, electric	20.05
Tobacco	9.04	Transport equipment	14.80
Food products	8.55	Machinery, except electrical	10.70
Beverages	8.07	Industrial chemicals	5.44
Petroleum refining	7.07	Iron and steel	5.36
Industrial chemicals	5.95	Food products	5.27
Transport equipment	5.04	Other chemicals	4.48
Other chemicals	4.80	Fabricated metal products	4.01
Nonmetallic minerals	4.69	Textiles	3.99
Electrical machinery	3.96	Plastic products	3.28
Share of top 5	46.55	Share of top 5	56.34
Share of top 10	70.99	Share of top 10	77.37
Standard deviation	3.31	Standard deviation	4.60
Specialization index	11.90	Specialization index	17.16

continued on next page

Table A9.2 (continued)

Singapore	1970		2003
Petroleum refining	18.43	Machinery, electric	21.98
Transport equipment	13.95	Other chemicals	21.66
Electrical machinery	11.14	Machinery, except electrical	18.81
Food products	6.67	Transport equipment	8.97
Fabricated metal	6.32	Fabricated metal products	5.03
Wood products	5.26	Petroleum refineries	4.06
Rubber products	4.91	Professional and scientific equipment	4.02
Printing and publishing	4.47	Printing and publishing	3.13
Beverages	3.07	Industrial chemicals	2.46
Other chemicals	2.98	Plastic products	2.22
Share of top 5	56.50	Share of top 5	76.45
Share of top 10	77.21	Share of top 10	92.34
Standard deviation	4.39	Standard deviation	6.44
Specialization index	16.73	Specialization index	29.53

Taipei,China	1973		1996
Electrical machinery	13.16	Electrical machinery	20.98
Textiles	12.64	Industrial chemicals	7.94
Petroleum refining	7.72	Transport equipment	7.39
Food products	6.49	Fabricated metal	7.26
Wearing apparel	5.39	Petroleum refining	6.31
Industrial chemicals	4.92	Textiles	5.85
Plastic products	4.83	Iron and steel	5.84
Iron and steel	4.82	Plastic products	5.30
Transport equipment	4.53	Food products	4.84
Wood products	4.32	Nonelectrical machinery	4.61
Share of top 5	45.39	Share of top 5	49.88
Share of top 10	68.82	Share of top 10	76.33
Standard deviation	3.32	Standard deviation	4.21
Specialization index	12.07	Specialization index	15.30

continued on next page

Table A9.2 (continued)

c. ASEAN-4

Indonesia	1970		2003
Food products	35.14	Tobacco	13.34
Tobacco	28.35	Transport equipment	11.80
Textiles	11.65	Food products	11.47
Other chemicals	4.66	Textiles	7.90
Fabricated metal	3.28	Machinery, electric	6.74
Nonmetallic minerals	3.10	Industrial chemicals	5.85
Beverages	1.86	Wood products, except furniture	5.68
Footwear	1.67	Paper and products	5.16
Industrial chemicals	1.37	Other chemicals	5.14
Rubber products	1.34	Wearing apparel, except footwear	4.27
Share of top 5	83.09	Share of top 5	51.25
Share of top 10	92.43	Share of top 10	77.35
Standard deviation	8.34	Standard deviation	3.79
Specialization index	37.27	Specialization index	14.58

Malaysia	1970		2002
Food products	15.39	Machinery, electric	22.37
Rubber products	13.90	Petroleum refineries	8.93
Wood products	12.43	Machinery, except electrical	8.55
Tobacco	6.58	Food products	7.64
Printing and publishing	6.11	Transport equipment	7.10
Nonmetallic minerals	5.89	Industrial chemicals	6.84
Other chemicals	5.80	Plastic products	5.21
Petroleum refining	4.81	Wood products, except furniture	3.29
Fabricated metal	3.82	Other nonmetallic mineral products	3.15
Beverages	3.65	Fabricated metal products	3.14
Share of top 5	54.41	Share of top 5	54.58
Share of top 10	78.39	Share of top 10	76.21
Standard deviation	4.20	Standard deviation	4.57
Specialization index	17.81	Specialization index	17.84

continued on next page

Table A9.2 (continued)

Philippines	1970		1997
Food products	23.83	Food products	18.40
Other chemicals	8.31	Electrical machinery	10.07
Beverages	7.95	Other chemicals	10.06
Petroleum refining	7.11	Beverages	9.35
Tobacco	6.81	Petroleum refining	7.58
Textiles	6.46	Wearing apparel	5.57
Industrial chemicals	4.35	Tobacco	5.03
Wood Products	4.02	Transport equipment	3.89
Electrical machinery	3.58	Iron and steel	3.75
Transport equipment	3.42	Textiles	3.19
Share of top 5	54.01	Share of top 5	55.46
Share of top 10	75.85	Share of top 10	76.87
Standard deviation	4.70	Standard deviation	4.17
Specialization index	17.86	Specialization index	16.16

Thailand	1970		1994
Other chemicals	23.74	Nonelectrical machinery	9.24
Tobacco	23.34	Petroleum refining	3.90
Textiles	13.17	Wearing apparel	2.90
Fabricated metal	8.36	Food products	7.96
Beverages	7.53	Textiles	9.33
Rubber products	5.70	Electrical machinery	0.32
Wood Products	4.60	Transport equipment	0.29
Nonmetallic minerals	4.45	Printing and publishing	1.27
Printing and publishing	3.15	Beverages	0.44
Glass products	2.89	Nonmetallic minerals	1.67
Share of top 5	76.14	Share of top 5	33.33
Share of top 10	96.93	Share of top 10	37.31
Standard deviation	6.74	Standard deviation	4.13
Specialization index	20.31	Specialization index	16.58

continued on next page

Table A9.2 (continued)

d. Other South Asia

Bangladesh	1970		1998
Textiles	45.41	Wearing apparel, except footwear	19.26
Food products	15.28	Tobacco	14.54
Tobacco	13.89	Textiles	13.02
Other chemicals	8.36	Food products	8.77
Industrial chemicals	2.65	Machinery, electric	7.27
Iron and steel	2.47	Footwear, except rubber or plastic	7.23
Other manufactures	1.92	Other chemicals	7.03
Paper products	1.82	Industrial chemicals	4.41
Transport equipment	1.08	Iron and steel	3.50
Electrical machinery	1.02	Fabricated metal products	2.91
Share of top 5	85.59	Share of top 5	62.86
Share of top 10	93.89	Share of top 10	87.94
Standard deviation	9.08	Standard deviation	5.05
Specialization index	42.49	Specialization index	24.34

Nepal	1986		2002
Food products	32.13	Food products	19.92
Tobacco	14.60	Tobacco	13.34
Textiles	13.32	Beverages	11.86
Nonmetallic minerals	12.27	Textiles	10.41
Other chemicals	4.48	Other chemicals	10.21
Wearing apparel	4.08	Wearing apparel	7.48
Beverages	2.83	Nonmetallic minerals	6.38
Fabricated metal	2.66	Fabricated metal	5.20
Iron and steel	2.26	Plastic products	3.28
Wood products	1.97	Printing and publishing	2.11
Share of top 5	76.80	Share of top 5	65.75
Share of top 10	90.61	Share of top 10	90.19
Standard deviation	6.92	Standard deviation	5.18
Specialization index	27.06	Specialization index	22.70

continued on next page

Table A9.2 (continued)

Pakistan	1970		1996
Textiles	35.94	Textiles	23.47
Food products	15.27	Food products	15.18
Tobacco	8.07	Industrial chemicals	8.52
Petroleum refining	7.93	Other chemicals	7.73
Other chemicals	5.16	Electrical machinery	7.66
Nonmetallic minerals	4.05	Nonmetallic minerals	7.15
Industrial chemicals	3.66	Tobacco	6.18
Electrical machinery	3.38	Iron and steel	4.15
Iron and steel	2.42	Transport equipment	3.50
Rubber products	2.09	Petroleum refining	3.06
Share of top 5	72.37	Share of top 5	62.57
Share of top 10	87.96	Share of top 10	86.61
Standard deviation	7.18	Standard deviation	5.31
Specialization index	31.38	Specialization index	22.58

Sri Lanka	1970		2001
Tobacco	10.88	Tobacco	15.25
Textiles	10.52	Wearing apparel, except footwear	15.22
Other chemicals	10.28	Textiles	15.21
Food products	9.55	Food products	14.17
Nonmetallic minerals	7.38	Beverages	7.21
Beverages	5.93	Other chemicals	5.37
Fabricated metal	5.56	Rubber products	4.53
Wearing apparel	5.44	Petroleum refineries	4.26
Nonelectrical machinery	5.32	Other nonmetallic mineral products	2.91
Rubber products	4.84	Transport equipment	2.17
Share of top 5	48.62	Share of top 5	67.07
Share of top 10	75.71	Share of top 10	86.31
Standard deviation	3.46	Standard deviation	5.06
Specialization index	13.22	Specialization index	22.50

continued on next page

Table A9.2 (continued)

e. Pacific

Fiji Islands	1970		1994
Food products	50.11	Food products	41.77
Fabricated metal	7.26	Textiles	13.55
Beverages	6.82	Wood products	9.56
Nonmetallic minerals	6.55	Beverages	5.96
Wood products	4.38	Printing and publishing	5.05
Printing and publishing	4.06	Paper products	3.74
Furniture	4.00	Fabricated metal	3.17
Other chemicals	2.89	Other chemicals	3.05
Transport equipment	1.96	Nonmetallic minerals	2.92
Tobacco	1.79	Plastic products	2.01
Share of top 5	75.12	Share of top 5	75.88
Share of top 10	89.81	Share of top 10	90.78
Standard deviation	9.42	Standard deviation	8.15
Specialization index	36.53	Specialization index	27.19

Papua New Guinea	1970		1989
Transport equipment	20.35	Food products	42.17
Wood products	20.20	wood products	14.21
Beverages	10.76	Fabricated metal	6.92
Nonelectrical machinery	10.28	Beverages	6.76
Professional equipment	7.46	Transport equipment	4.43
Food products	6.63	Tobacco	4.38
Tobacco	5.70	Nonelectrical machinery	4.10
Electrical machinery	3.84	Printing and publishing	2.59
Fabricated metal	3.11	Furniture	2.22
Other chemicals	2.95	Nonmetallic minerals	1.77
Share of top 5	69.05	Share of top 5	74.49
Share of top 10	91.28	Share of top 10	89.55
Standard deviation	5.67	Standard deviation	8.19
Specialization index	18.72	Specialization index	31.94

ASEAN = Association of Southeast Asian Nations, NIEs = newly industrialized economies.

Source: Author's calculations. The degree of specialization h is defined as $h = 100 \times \left(1 + \dfrac{\sum_i (s_i \ln s_i)}{h_{max}} \right)$,

where $h_{max} = \ln$(no. of sectors), s_i is the share of the i-th branch in total manufacturing value added. By construction $0 \leq h \leq 100$. If the shares of all sectors are equal, the degree of specialization is 0; and if only one sector exists, then the value of the indicator is 100.

Table A9.3. Employment Share by Manufacturing Subsector
(% Manufacturing)

a. People's Republic of China and India

People's Republic of China	1977		2003
Nonelectrical machinery	26.9	Food products	11.1
Textiles	11.3	Petroleum refineries	10.3
Iron and steel	8.5	Iron and steel	10.1
Industrial chemicals	7.8	Industrial chemicals	9.5
Electrical machinery	6.5	Textiles	6.4
Food products	6.4	Transport equipment	6.0
Nonmetallic minerals	5.8	Other chemicals	5.9
Transport equipment	5.0	Machinery, electric	5.8
Other chemicals	2.5	Machinery, except electrical	5.3
Nonferrous metal	1.9	Other nonmetallic mineral products	3.5
Share of top 5	61.0	Share of top 5	47.5
Share of top 10	82.6	Share of top 10	74.1
Standard deviation	5.4	Standard deviation	3.4
Specialization index	19.8	Specialization index	10.4

India	1970		2002
Textiles	28.5	Food products	15.9
Food products	14.0	Petroleum refineries	15.3
Transport equipment	8.1	Iron and steel	6.8
Iron and steel	7.5	Industrial chemicals	6.3
Nonelectrical machinery	6.4	Textiles	6.3
Electrical machinery	4.6	Transport equipment	5.8
Nonmetallic minerals	3.8	Other chemicals	5.7
Fabricated metals	3.6	Machinery, electric	5.5
Other chemicals	3.5	Machinery, except electrical	4.3
Printing and publishing	3.3	Other nonmetallic mineral products	4.3
Share of top 5	64.4	Share of top 5	50.5
Share of top 10	83.2	Share of top 10	76.2
Standard deviation	5.8	Standard deviation	4.0
Specialization index	23.5	Specialization index	15.0

continued on next page

Table A9.3 (continued)

b. NIEs

Hong Kong, China	1970		2003
Textiles	23.1	Printing and publishing	20.4
Wearing apparel	20.1	Wearing apparel, except footwear	13.8
Plastic products	12.8	Textiles	13.6
Electrical machinery	8.8	Food products	11.4
Fabricated metals	8.4	Machinery, electric	8.9
Other manufactures	7.2	Nonferrous metals	5.5
Printing and publishing	3.3	Transport equipment	5.2
Transport equipment	2.4	Other manufactured products	4.1
Rubber products	2.2	Industrial chemicals	3.5
Food products	2.0	Machinery, except electrical	3.0
Share of top 5	73.3	Share of top 5	68.1
Share of top 10	90.4	Share of top 10	89.3
Standard deviation	6.0	Standard deviation	5.3
Specialization index	28.3	Specialization index	24.8

Republic of Korea	1970		2002
Textiles	24.4	Machinery, electric	16.2
Food products	8.6	Transport equipment	12.2
Wearing apparel	5.8	Machinery, except electrical	11.8
Other manufactures	5.7	Industrial chemicals	7.3
Electrical machinery	4.7	Iron and steel	7.1
Transport equipment	4.3	Food products	6.1
Wood products	4.2	Petroleum refineries	5.1
Fabricated metals	4.0	Textiles	5.0
Nonmetallic minerals	3.9	Fabricated metal products	3.5
Printing and publishing	3.5	Plastic products	2.9
Share of top 5	49.2	Share of top 5	54.5
Share of top 10	69.1	Share of top 10	77.1
Standard deviation	4.6	Standard deviation	4.1
Specialization index	15.2	Specialization index	16.1

continued on next page

Table A9.3 (continued)

Singapore	1970		2003
Transport equipment	12.8	Machinery, except electrical	20.2
Electrical machinery	10.7	Machinery, electric	18.5
Wearing apparel	7.9	Other chemicals	14.5
Wood products	7.2	Petroleum refineries	10.6
Food products	7.1	Transport equipment	4.8
Fabricated metals	6.8	Fabricated metal products	4.8
Other manufactures	6.4	Industrial chemicals	4.7
Textiles	5.6	Professional and scientific equipment	4.3
Printing and publishing	5.5	Food products	2.9
Rubber products	5.1	Printing and publishing	2.4
Share of top 5	45.7	Share of top 5	68.6
Share of top 10	75.1	Share of top 10	87.7
Standard deviation	3.4	Standard deviation	5.6
Specialization index	12.6	Specialization index	24.2

Taipei,China	1973		2001
Electrical machinery	18.9	Machinery, electric	24.1
Plastic products	12.8	Industrial chemicals	11.6
Food products	7.9	Food products	7.4
Wearing apparel	7.8	Transport equipment	7.1
Wood products	6.3	Fabricated metal products	6.7
Nonelectrical machinery	5.5	Iron and steel	5.3
Fabricated metals	4.6	Textiles	3.8
Other manufactures	4.4	Machinery, except electrical	3.4
Transport equipment	4.3	Plastic products	3.1
Nonmetallic minerals	3.8	Petroleum refineries	3.0
Share of top 5	53.7	Share of top 5	56.9
Share of top 10	76.4	Share of top 10	75.5
Standard deviation	4.2	Standard deviation	4.8
Specialization index	16.5	Specialization index	17.4

continued on next page

Table A9.3 (continued)

c. ASEAN-4

Indonesia	1970		2003
Textiles	29.4	Food products	13.9
Tobacco	27.3	Textiles	12.9
Food products	19.0	Transport equipment	10.7
Other chemicals	4.2	Tobacco	7.6
Fabricated metals	2.8	Machinery, electric	6.4
Printing and publishing	2.5	Wood products, except furniture	5.2
Nonmetallic minerals	2.2	Iron and steel	4.4
Wood Products	1.4	Industrial chemicals	4.3
Other manufactures	1.3	Paper and products	4.0
Rubber products	1.2	Other chemicals	3.6
Share of top 5	82.7	Share of top 5	51.6
Share of top 10	91.3	Share of top 10	73.1
Standard deviation	7.9	Standard deviation	3.8
Specialization index	35.5	Specialization index	16.1

Malaysia	1970		2002
Wood products	19.9	Machinery, electric	22.3
Food products	12.4	Machinery, except electrical	7.8
Rubber products	12.3	Food products	7.2
Printing and publishing	7.5	Petroleum refineries	7.0
Fabricated metals	5.4	Transport equipment	6.4
Textiles	5.0	Industrial chemicals	5.1
Nonmetallic minerals	4.4	Plastic products	4.7
Nonelectrical machinery	4.1	Fabricated metal products	4.6
Other chemicals	3.2	Iron and steel	4.3
Transport equipment	3.2	Wood products, except furniture	4.3
Share of top 5	57.5	Share of top 5	50.7
Share of top 10	77.4	Share of top 10	73.7
Standard deviation	4.6	Standard deviation	4.4
Specialization index	18.9	Specialization index	18.5
Standard deviation	4.4	Standard deviation	4.4
Specialization index	17.5	Specialization index	17.5

continued on next page

Table A9.3 (continued)

Philippines	1970		1997
Food products	20.1	Food products	17.5
Textiles	13.2	Wearing apparel	16.2
Wood products	9.7	Electrical machinery	12.1
Wearing apparel	6.3	Textiles	6.7
Tobacco	5.7	Fabricated metals	3.5
Other chemicals	4.2	Other chemicals	3.4
Fabricated metals	4.0	Other manufactures	2.8
Printing and publishing	3.9	Wood products	2.8
Beverages	3.8	Beverages	2.8
Electrical machinery	3.4	Plastic products	2.7
Share of top 5	55.0	Share of top 5	56.1
Share of top 10	74.3	Share of top 10	70.6
Standard deviation	4.4	Standard deviation	4.4
Specialization index	17.5	Specialization index	17.5

Thailand	1970		1994
Textiles	20.7	Wearing apparel	28.5
Food products	16.1	Textiles	16.3
Wood products	9.8	Food products	12.3
Tobacco	7.7	Fabricated metals	5.6
Rubber products	5.4	Electrical machinery	5.2
Other chemicals	5.1	Transport equipment	3.1
Nonmetallic minerals	4.9	Nonmetallic minerals	3.1
Transport equipment	4.4	Other manufactures	2.7
Beverages	3.8	Rubber products	2.3
Fabricated metals	3.6	Plastic products	2.3
Share of top 5	59.6	Share of top 5	68.0
Share of top 10	81.4	Share of top 10	81.5
Standard deviation	4.9	Standard deviation	6.1
Specialization index	18.3	Specialization index	25.3

continued on next page

Table A9.3 (continued)

d. Other South Asia

Bangladesh	1970		1998
Textiles	63.2	Food products	46.9
Food products	12.7	Beverages	29.9
Other chemicals	6.5	Tobacco	6.6
Tobacco	2.0	Textiles	2.3
Fabricated metals	1.9	Wearing apparel, except footwear	1.8
Paper products	1.5	Leather products	1.7
Transport equipment	1.5	Footwear, except rubber or plastic	1.5
Printing and publishing	1.2	Wood products, except furniture	1.4
Nonelectrical machinery	1.2	Furniture, except metal	1.0
Industrial chemicals	1.1	Paper and products	0.8
Share of top 5	86.3	Share of top 5	87.4
Share of top 10	92.9	Share of top 10	93.8
Standard deviation	12.0	Standard deviation	10.2
Specialization index	53.3	Specialization index	50.7

Nepal	1986		2002
Nonmetallic minerals	31.9	Nonmetallic minerals	29.3
Textiles	17.4	Textiles	17.3
Food products	17.3	Food products	15.7
Tobacco	6.4	Wearing apparel	10.4
Wearing apparel	6.1	Other chemicals	3.9
Other chemicals	3.8	Fabricated metals	2.7
Fabricated metals	2.9	Plastic products	2.5
Wood products	2.6	Printing and publishing	2.2
Printing and publishing	1.9	Wood products	2.0
Furniture	1.8	Furniture	1.9
Share of top 5	79.0	Share of top 5	76.6
Share of top 10	92.0	Share of top 10	87.9
Standard deviation	7.2	Standard deviation	6.7
Specialization index	30.1	Specialization index	30.3

continued on next page

Table A9.3 (continued)

Pakistan	1970		1996
Textiles	50.0	Textiles	41.8
Food products	8.6	Food products	13.9
Fabricated metals	4.3	Iron and steel	5.9
Transport equipment	4.1	Other chemicals	5.3
Electrical machinery	3.9	Electrical machinery	3.6
Other chemicals	3.4	Industrial chemicals	3.6
Iron and steel	3.2	Nonelectrical machinery	3.1
Nonelectrical machinery	3.0	Nonmetallic minerals	2.8
Nonmetallic minerals	2.8	Transport equipment	2.5
Tobacco	2.5	Wearing apparel	2.4
Share of top 5	70.9	Share of top 5	70.5
Share of top 10	85.9	Share of top 10	84.9
Standard deviation	9.3	Standard deviation	8.0
Specialization index	37.1	Specialization index	31.0

Sri Lanka	1970		2001
Textiles	15.1	Petroleum refineries	28.5
Food products	12.1	Food products	17.3
Wearing apparel	9.6	Wearing apparel, except footwear	15.1
Nonmetallic minerals	8.6	Textiles	5.3
Nonelectrical machinery	7.3	Tobacco	4.5
Other chemicals	7.0	Rubber products	4.2
Fabricated metals	6.7	Other chemicals	2.6
Paper products	5.0	Beverages	2.2
Rubber products	4.4	Other nonmetallic mineral products	2.1
Electrical machinery	2.9	Other manufactured products	1.7
Share of top 5	52.7	Share of top 5	70.7
Share of top 10	78.6	Share of top 10	83.5
Standard deviation	3.9	Standard deviation	6.4
Specialization index	15.4	Specialization index	27.6

ASEAN = Association of Southeast Asian Nations, NIEs = newly industrialized economies.

Source: Author's calculations. The degree of specialization h is defined as $h = 100 \times \left(1 + \dfrac{\sum_i (s_i \ln s_i)}{h_{max}} \right)$,

where $h_{max} = \ln$(no. sectors), s_i is the share of the i-th branch in total manufacturing value added. By construction $0 \leq h \leq 100$. If the shares of all sectors are equal, the degree of specialization is 0; and if only one sector exists, then the value of the indicator is 100.

Table A9.4. Decomposition of the Growth Rate of Labor Productivity

		People's Republic of China	Hong Kong, China	Singapore	Taipei,China	Republic of Korea
		1987–2002	1978–2004	1970–2003	1965–2004	1970–2004
Average Annual Growth Rate of Labor Productivity	Total	0.0606	0.0326	0.0327	0.0422	0.0353
	Agriculture	0.0344	(0.0061)	0.0244	0.0361	0.0387
	Industry	0.0863	0.0327	0.0363	0.0403	0.0424
	Services	0.0176	0.0236	0.0311	0.0385	0.0155
	Manufacturing	–	0.0296	0.0387	0.0435	0.0495
Change in the Labor Share	Agriculture	(0.1593)	(0.0122)	(0.0320)	(0.3989)	(0.4236)
	Industry	(0.0452)	(0.3541)	(0.0601)	0.1292	0.0999
	Services	0.2045	0.3663	0.0921	0.2697	0.3236
	Manufacturing	–	(0.3730)	(0.0405)	0.1103	0.0584
Productivity Differential with Agriculture	Industry	2,587	9,116	24,221	11,038	14,770
	Services	1,344	30,529	11,021	19,330	8,365
	Manufacturing	–	4,256	26,193	11,950	14,624

continued on next page

Table A9.4 (continued)

	People's Republic of China 1987–2002	Hong Kong, China 1978–2004	Singapore 1970–2003	Taipei,China 1965–2004	Republic of Korea 1970–2004
Weighted Average of Sector Growth Rates (average annual) of Labor Productivity Growth (INTRA)					
Agriculture	0.0072	0.0000	0.0003	0.0043	0.0048
Industry	0.0342	0.0069	0.0126	0.0103	0.0129
Services	0.0070	0.0185	0.0199	0.0240	0.0088
Total	0.0483	0.0253	0.0328	0.0386	0.0266
Relocation Effects (average annual) (INTER)					
Industry	(0.0059)	(0.0031)	(0.0016)	0.0018	0.0029
Services	0.0138	0.0107	0.0011	0.0066	0.0053
Total	0.0080	0.0076	(0.0005)	0.0085	0.0082
Total Productivity Growth					
Total	0.0563	0.0329	0.0324	0.0471	0.0347
Average Annual Growth Rate of Labor Productivity					
Total	0.0335	0.0283	0.0327	0.0076	0.0476
Agriculture	0.0231	0.0286	0.0254	0.0040	0.0361
Industry	0.0220	0.0285	0.0132	0.0064	0.0520
Services	0.0097	0.0171	0.0250	0.0033	(0.0047)
Manufacturing	0.0265	0.0408	0.0438	0.0086	—

continued on next page

Table A9.4 (continued)

	Thailand 1971–2004	Malaysia 1980–2004	Indonesia 1976–2002	Philippines 1971–2004	Viet Nam 1991–2004
Change in the Labor Share					
Agriculture	(0.3443)	(0.2241)	(0.2164)	(0.1327)	(0.1676)
Industry	0.1365	0.0600	0.0990	(0.0031)	0.0529
Services	0.2078	0.1641	0.1174	0.1357	0.1146
Manufacturing	0.0974	0.0422	0.0655	(0.0196)	0.1170
Productivity Differential with Agriculture					
Industry	6,067	8,615	3,517	3,946	1,419
Services	4,041	2,168	1,050	2,023	1,246
Manufacturing	6,437	6,864	2,107	4,655	601
Weighted Average of Sector Growth Rates (average annual) of Labor Productivity Growth (INTRA)					
Agriculture	0.0036	0.0042	0.0056	0.0007	0.0097
Industry	0.0075	0.0127	0.0055	0.0020	0.0175
Services	0.0049	0.0069	0.0091	0.0017	(0.0019)
Total	0.0160	0.0239	0.0202	0.0044	0.0253
Relocation Effects (average annual) (INTER)					
Industry	0.0093	0.0027	0.0098	(0.0001)	0.0078
Services	0.0094	0.0019	0.0035	0.0033	0.0148
Total	0.0187	0.0046	0.0132	0.0032	0.0225
Total Productivity Growth	0.0347	0.0284	0.0334	0.0076	0.0479
Average Annual Growth Rate of Labor Productivity					
Total	0.0374	0.0255	(0.0970)		
Agriculture	0.0183	0.0221	(0.0536)		
Industry	0.0346	0.0257	(0.0170)		
Services	0.0376	0.0197	0.0286		
Manufacturing	–	0.0291	–		

continued on next page

Table A9.4 (continued)

	India 1983–2000	Pakistan 1973–2002	Kyrgyz Republic 1987–2002
Change in the Labor Share			
Agriculture	(0.0820)	(0.1523)	0.1878
Industry	0.0280	0.0406	(0.1433)
Services	0.0540	0.1116	(0.0445)
Manufacturing	0.0000	0.0136	(0.0945)
Productivity Differential with Agriculture			
Industry	825	671	1,479
Services	1,371	1,221	46
Manufacturing	–	694	485
Weighted Average of Sector Growth Rates (average annual) of Labor Productivity Growth (INTRA)			
Agriculture	0.0059	0.0068	(0.0162)
Industry	0.0087	0.0053	(0.0069)
Services	0.0160	0.0096	0.0084
Total	0.0306	0.0217	(0.0147)
Relocation Effects (average annual) (INTER)			
Industry	0.0017	0.0007	(0.0815)
Services	0.0055	0.0035	(0.0008)
Total	0.0072	0.0042	(0.0823)
Total Productivity Growth	0.0378	0.0259	(0.0970)

– = data not available.

Note: The formula used is: $\hat{q} = \sum k_i \hat{q}_i + (\lambda_I' - \lambda_I^0)\frac{(q_I - q_A)}{q} + (\lambda_S' - \lambda_S^0)\frac{(q_S - q_A)}{q}$, where $\hat{q}$ is the growth rate of overall labor productivity; $\hat{q}_i$ is the growth rate of each sector's labor productivity; $(q_I - q_A)/q$ is the difference between the levels of labor productivity in industry and agriculture divided by the overall level of productivity; $(q_S - q_A)/q$ is the difference between the levels of labor productivity in services and agriculture divided by the overall level of productivity; λ denotes the employment shares of each sector; and k denotes the respective output shares. The first term of the decomposition represents the component of overall growth that is due to the growth of labor productivity within each sector (weighted by the output shares). The remaining two terms represent the effect of the relocation of labor across sectors of unequal productivity (measured with respect to the productivity of the agriculture sector).

Source: Asian Development Bank 2007b.

10

Why Do Export Diversification and Sophistication Matter?

The way countries succeed in development is often by finding a big hit in export markets. What will be the big hit is impossible to foresee [. . .] Who would have predicted that cut flowers in Kenya would capture 40 percent of the European market for romantic men bringing flowers home to their wives? You could say the same about women's cotton suits in Fiji (42 percent of the US market), or "floating docks" in Nigeria (84 percent of the Norwegian market), or electronic integrated circuits in the Philippines (71 percent of the world market), or regional jets in Brazil (Embraer now has 22 percent of the world market). Egypt's largest single manufacturing export success, accounting for 30 percent of the total, is bathroom ceramics, of which 93 percent goes to Italy. Can you picture development experts telling Egyptians, "The secret is just export toilets to Italy!?"

—William Easterly (2008, 9)

T his chapter expands the analysis of structural transformation in developing Asia. I rely on recent work on economic diversification, the importance of export sophistication and the product space. All this body of work has very important policy implications.

Comparative Advantage and Diversification

Recent research by Imbs and Wacziarg (2003) suggests that at low levels of income per capita, economies tend to diversify and subsequently, as their income rises, they then specialize: whatever drives economic development, it is not comparative advantage. Figure 10.1 graphs the degree of specialization in the manufacturing sector in the vertical axis vis-à-vis the logarithm of income

Figure 10.1. Specialization Index of Developing Economies in Asia: Manufacturing Value-Added

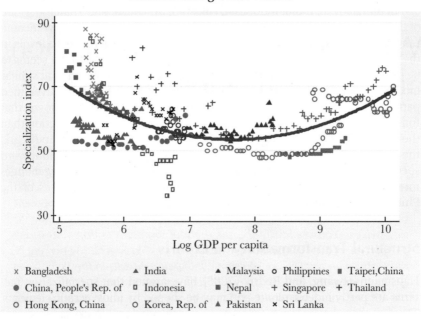

x Bangladesh	▲ India	▲ Malaysia	o Philippines	■ Taipei,China
● China, People's Rep. of	□ Indonesia	■ Nepal	+ Singapore	+ Thailand
o Hong Kong, China	o Korea, Rep. of	▲ Pakistan	× Sri Lanka	

GDP = gross domestic product, Rep. = Republic.

Note: The estimated regression line is:
Specialization = 122.80 - 28.00log GDP per capita + 1.82(log GDP per capita)^2
t-stat: (14.15)   (–11.76)   (11.50)
R^2: 0.26; No. of observations: 416

Source: Author's estimates. The calculations are based on data from UNIDO Industrial Statistics International Standard Classification Revision 2 (2006).

per capita in the horizontal axis.[1] As noted above, the new literature emphasizes the importance of diversification as opposed to traditional comparative advantage (i.e., the idea that as countries open up trade, they will specialize in those activities that use intensively those factors that are in abundant supply). Graphically, this corresponds to a U-shape relationship between specializa-

---

[1]   The degree of specialization was constructed using the United Nations Industrial Development Organization's (UNIDO) 3-digit manufacturing data. The degree of specialization h is defined as $h = 100 \times \left(1 + \dfrac{\sum_i (s_i \ln s_i)}{h_{max}}\right)$, where $h_{max} = \ln(\text{no. of sectors})$, s_i is the share of the i-th branch in total manufacturing value added. By construction $0 \le h \le 100$. If the shares of all sectors are equal, the degree of specialization is 0; and if only one sector exists, then the value of the indicator is 100.

tion and income per capita, which Figure 10.1 corroborates.[2] The figure shows increasing diversification as income per capita increases (at low levels) in Bangladesh, India, Indonesia, Pakistan, Sri Lanka, and Thailand. None of these economies become more specialized within comparable low-income ranges. Increasing specialization is only detected at higher income levels in the Republic of Korea, Malaysia, and Singapore. Hong Kong, China seems to be increasing its level of diversification. The figure also shows that, at similar income levels, the People's Republic of China (PRC) has a more diversified pattern of manufacturing output. Kochhar et al. (2006) have shown that India has a more skill-based and capital-intensive pattern of production than the PRC. The figure also shows a trend toward diversification in India and the PRC. Thailand exhibits increasing specialization. While the trend toward specialization remains in Malaysia and Singapore, the index barely changes in the Republic of Korea, the PRC, and Taipei,China. In the cases of the Philippines and Nepal, the index wiggles without any clear pattern.

Structural Transformation and Exports

Hausmann, Hwang, and Rodrik (2005) have argued that specialization patterns are partly indeterminate and may be shaped by idiosyncratic elements. These authors have shown that a very strong relationship exists between a country's income level and a measure that they construct of the sophistication of exports. This variable is a very good predictor of the country's future growth. One important implication of this relationship is that as development takes place, countries change their export package, i.e., they undergo structural transformation. Indeed, structural change appears reflected in the improvements in quality and diversification of a country's exports, which has two further implications. First, the range of goods that an economy ends up producing and exporting changes in time. Second, and more important, while for the standard theory of comparative costs the transition from the production and export of one type of goods into a different one is a function of the changing factor endowments with no role for active policy, the range of goods in Hausmann, Hwang, and Rodrik's model is determined not just by factor endowments, but by the number of entrepreneurs that can be stimulated to engage in "cost discovery" in the modern sectors of the economy. The key and primary source of international gains is international learning, leading to technical progress and increased labor productivity. However, upgrading and diversification will not occur automatically, as they require proactive measures. The cost of discovery is the uncertainty that an entrepreneur

---

[2]   The figure shows that individual country experiences in developing Asia do not fit the U-shaped pattern of specialization for value added or employment suggested by Imbs and Wacziarg (2003). This, on the other hand, is not surprising as data cover a short period.

faces when producing a good for the first time in a developing economy. Even when the good is produced with a standard technology, the institutional reality of many developing countries requires a substantial degree of adaptation. Therefore, an entrepreneur will have to explore the underlying cost structure of the economy. This entails considerable positive externalities for other entrepreneurs since, if the investment is successful, other entrepreneurs will follow and emulate the forerunner. This way, the private returns to the first entrepreneur arc socialized. If the first entrepreneur fails, however, his cost remains private. Therefore, the "knowledge externality" implies that investment levels in cost discovery are suboptimal unless the industry or the government finds some way in which the externality can be internalized.

This implies that the mix of goods that a country produces and exports powerfully affects its economic growth. Not all goods have the same consequences for economic performance: specializing in some products will bring higher growth than specializing in others. In other words, exports can be seen both as a tool of development and as a test of a country's success. In this framework, the authors argue, government policy can positively shape the production structure. The authors show that countries that latch on to a set of goods that are placed higher on the quality spectrum tend to perform better.

Figure 10.2 graphs the country scores of export sophistication for a selected group of Asian countries, following Hausmann, Hwang, and Rodrik's (2005) method. The method consists in calculating first an index of the per capita GDPs of each exported product (denoted PRODY); and then, in the second step the income level of a country's export basket is calculated (denoted EXPY).[3] The results show that the newly industrialized

---

[3] To construct Hausmann, Hwang, and Rodrik's (2005) index of sophistication or complexity of exports, I used data from the United Nations' Commodity Trade Statistics Database at the 5-digit level. First, I constructed the proxy for the income level of a commodity PRODY, as the weighted average of the per capita GDPs of the countries exporting a given product (i.e., each product has an associated PRODY) as $PRODY_k = \sum_j Y_j \times \dfrac{(x_{jk}/X_j)}{\sum_j (x_{jk}/X_j)}$, where Y_j is the per capita GDP of country j; x_{jk} denotes exports of country j of product k; X_j denotes total exports of country j, that is, $X_j = \sum_j x_{jk}$. Note that the weight of income per capita (Y_j) is the revealed comparative advantage of each country in each good it exports. The advantage of using this weighted average is as follows: a country may export less of a given product than another country in absolute terms. This may, however, be more in relative terms (i.e., revealed comparative advantage). This way, the first country's income per capita will be weighted more heavily in calculating the productivity level associated with the given product. The second step consists of constructing the productivity level associated with a country's export basket, EXPY, as the weighted average of the PRODY associated with each product, that is, $EXPY_i = \sum_k PRODY_k \times \dfrac{x_{jk}}{X_j}$. Certainly, there is, by construction, a relationship between EXPY and income per capita. However, this is not a mechanical outcome. Hausmann, Hwang, and Rodrik note that

Figure 10.2. Export Sophistication Score (EXPY)

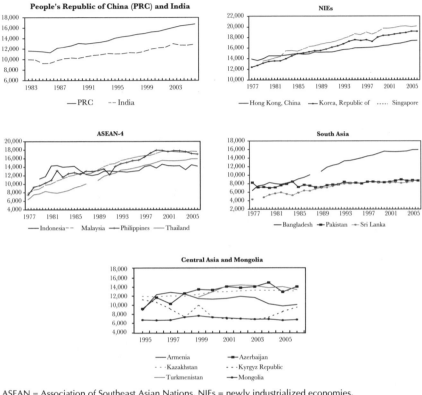

ASEAN = Association of Southeast Asian Nations, NIEs = newly industrialized economies.

Source: Asian Development Bank 2007b. Calculations based on data from the United Nations Commodity Trade Statistics Database (UN Comtrade).

economies (NIEs) have the highest scores, followed by the countries of the Association of Southeast Asian Nations (ASEAN-4). The PRC and India have relatively high indexes both displaying a rising trend. These two countries have succeeded in exporting more sophisticated products than is usual in countries with similar income per capita. For the South Asian countries, the index is much lower and has increased at a slow pace (in the case of Pakistan, the value in 2006 was the same as in 1986).

I also analyzed the top 10 exports for a group of countries with available data in 1986 and 2006. Table 10.1 summarizes the PRODY and EXPY scores for these 2 years. The most important conclusions are as follows:

"calculating country specific PRODYs by excluding own exports from the calculation of these measures does not change the results much."

Table 10.1. Percentage Share of Top 10 Exports, PRODY and EXPY Scores (1986 and 2006)

1986		2006*	
China, People's Republic of			
% share of top 10 exports	31.1%	% share of top 10 Exports	31.7%
Average PRODY score of the top 10 exports	9,324	Average PRODY score of the top 10 exports	18,444
EXPY score	11,294	EXPY score	16,757
India			
% share of top 10 exports	44.0%	% share of top 10 exports	30.8%
Average PRODY score of the top 10 exports	6,738	Average PRODY score of the top 10 exports	11,127
EXPY score	9,278	EXPY score	12,944
Hong Kong, China			
% share of top 10 exports	30.0%	% share of top 10 exports	41.7%
Average PRODY score of the top 10 exports	13,753	Average PRODY score of the top 10 exports	18,192
EXPY score	14,823	EXPY score	17,432
Korea, Republic of			
% share of top 10 exports	32.1%	% share of top 10 exports	51.2%
Average PRODY score of the top 10 exports	16,079	Average PRODY score of the top 10 exports	20,119
EXPY score	15,054	EXPY score	19,131
Singapore			
% share of top 10 exports	42.1%	% share of top 10 exports	60.8%
Average PRODY score of the top 10 exports	16,087	Average PRODY score of the top 10 exports	19,966
EXPY score	15,812	EXPY score	20,130
Indonesia			
% share of top 10 exports	77.6%	% share of top 10 exports	40.5%
Average PRODY score of the top 10 exports	9,725	Average PRODY score of the top 10 exports	13,869
EXPY score	13,188	EXPY score	14,222
Malaysia			
% share of top 10 exports	67.4%	% share of top 10 exports	46.9%
Average PRODY score of the top 10 exports	12,549	Average PRODY score of the top 10 exports	18,602
EXPY score	12,605	EXPY score	7,640
Philippines			
% share of top 10 exports	57.3%	% share of top 10 exports	65.0%
Average PRODY score of the top 10 exports	8,185	Average PRODY score of the top 10 exports	17,776
EXPY score	12,332	EXPY score	17,027

continued on next page

Table 10.1 (continued)

1986		2006*	
Thailand			
% share of top 10 exports	47.7%	% share of top 10 exports	31.8%
Average PRODY score of the top 10 exports	7,512	Average PRODY score of the top 10 exports	16,287
EXPY score	9,510	EXPY score	15,955
Bangladesh			
% share of top 10 exports	81.2%	% share of top 10 exports	74.4%
Average PRODY score of the top 10 exports	6,651	Average PRODY score of the top 10 exports	7,653
EXPY score	6,687	EXPY score	7,996
Pakistan			
% share of top 10 exports	58.5%	% share of top 10 exports	56.5%
Average PRODY score of the top 10 exports	7,942	Average PRODY score of the top 10 exports	7,288
EXPY score	7,742	EXPY score	8,717
Sri Lanka			
% share of top 10 exports	62.0%	% share of top 10 exports	49.7%
Average PRODY score of the top 10 exports	6,405	Average PRODY score of the top 10 exports	7,816
EXPY score	6,385	EXPY score	8,503
Fiji Islands			
% share of top 10 exports	81.6%	% share of top 10 exports	58.7%
Average PRODY score of the top 10 exports	9,470	Average PRODY score of the top 10 exports	7,299
EXPY score	8,013	EXPY score	8,517

* Bangladesh (2004); Sri Lanka (2005).

EXPY = index of export sophistication of the country, PRODY = index of export sophistication of the product.

Source: Author's calculations based on data from UN Comtrade (SITC Revision 4; 4-digit level).

(i)   The average PRODY scores of the top 10 exports of the PRC; Hong Kong, China; India; Indonesia; the Republic of Korea; Malaysia; the Philippines; Singapore; and Thailand show marked increases. This is also the case of Bangladesh and Sri Lanka. Pakistan and the Fiji Islands' average PRODY deteriorated.

(ii)   The table displays a trend for some countries to diversify their export basket: India, Indonesia, Malaysia, Thailand, Bangladesh, Sri Lanka, and the Fiji Islands. On the other hand, in the cases of Hong Kong, China; the Republic of Korea; Singapore; and the Philippines, the share of the top 10 exports increased; while in the cases of the PRC and Pakistan the shares hardly changed.

Since there is evidence that a higher export sophistication (EXPY) score is associated with more diversified exports, I derived the Gini coefficient using the shares of exports at the 2-, 3-, 4-, and 5-digit levels according to the Standard International Trade Classification (SITC) Revision 2. Figure 10.3 shows both variables. A significant correlation appears between the degree of diversification of exports (measured by the Gini coefficient of the shares of exports) and export sophistication (EXPY). The more diversified the export structure is (a lower Gini score), the higher the EXPY score.

The correlation coefficients of the two variables for developing Asia and for the world for 1977–2004, for 1977–1990, and for 1990–2004, are shown in Table 10.2. All correlation coefficients are statistically significant at the 1% level. The correlation coefficients of the two variables are higher using 2-, 3-, and 4-digit SITC Revision 2 codes (with the strongest correlation achieved using the 3-digit codes) than with the 5-digit codes. This may be because when the disaggregation level is too fine, the number of commodities increases to several thousand, and many of them have zero export values, which makes the Gini coefficient look more concentrated for all countries. As the Gini coefficients increase for all countries, the range they take becomes smaller. The level of dispersion declines and the calculated

Figure 10.3. Correlation between EXPY and Gini Coefficient

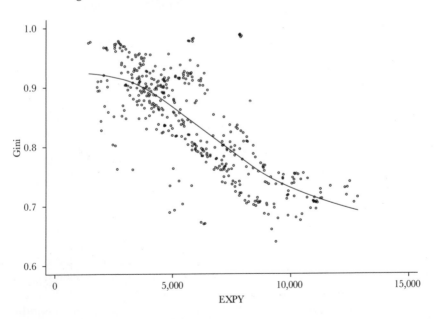

EXPY = index of export sophistication of the country.

Source: Author's calculations.

Table 10.2. Correlation Coefficients between EXPY and Gini Coefficient

SITC level	World			Developing Asia		
	1977–2004	1977–1990	1990–2004	1977–2004	1977–1990	1990–2004
2-digit	0.6753	0.6394	0.6947	0.6394	0.5092	0.6749
3-digit	0.6683	0.6057	0.6993	0.6887	0.5936	0.7057
4-digit	0.6400	0.5767	0.6728	0.6394	0.5760	0.6450
5-digit	0.5078	0.4355	0.5544	0.4493	0.3426	0.4602

EXPY = index of export sophistication of the country, SITC = Standard International Trade Classification.

Note: All coefficients are negative.

Source: Author's calculations.

correlation coefficient is smaller. The correlations for the world and for developing Asia at all digit levels are higher in 1990–2004 than for 1977–1990, most likely the result of the faster pace of trade liberalization since the 1990s.

The strong correlation between export diversification and EXPY is due to two reasons. First, higher-performing economies develop bigger capacities and become more competitive in the production of an increasingly wide array of products for the international market. Second, diversification of exports is a good coping mechanism to deal with the vagaries of the international market, which is beyond the control of any country. Successful diversification leads to better export performance and growth sustainability. Products with high PRODY (i.e., products that, overall, embody more advanced technologies, knowledge intensity, and economies of scale) produce spillovers on the rest of the economy. Countries can "jump" from one product to another whose specific inputs (physical, social, and legal infrastructure; technology) are similar or related. This is more prevalent with products reflecting high technology and economies of scale.

I also undertook an analysis of the scores for technology and economies of scale of the different manufacturing sectors (as calculated in *The Technology Level of Developing Asia's Manufacturing* in chapter 9), and the scores of the exported products corresponding to these sectors. This required matching the product codes in the United Nations' Commodity Trade Statistics Database with the industry codes. Table 10.3 shows the PRODY scores of the four groups of products. The result indicates that the exported products corresponding to the high-technology and high-economies-of-scale sectors get higher scores than those in the low-technology and low-economies-of-scale sectors. For groups 2 and 3, the average PRODY scores are similar, with group 3 actually having a slightly lower score than group 2. This is most likely because paper products and printing and publishing, as well as plastic

Table 10.3. PRODY Scores for Sectors Classified by Technology and Economies of Scale

Industry	ISIC	PRODY Score
Group 1: Low Economies of Scale, Low Technology		
Food products	311	10,993
Footwear	324	7,739
Furniture	332	14,998
Leather products	323	10,396
Textiles	321	11,327
Tobacco	314	13,514
Wearing apparel	322	8,393
Wood products	331	12,067
Average score		10,765
Group 2: Low Economies of Scale, Medium Technology		
Other manufactured products	390	15,207
Paper products	341	19,139
Plastic products	356	17,239
Printing and publishing	342	15,872
Rubber products	355	17,888
Average score		17,190
Group 3: Medium Economies of Scale, Medium Technology		
Fabricated metal products	381	15,816
Glass products	362	17,879
Iron and steel	371	16,212
Nonmetallic mineral products	369	16,044
Pottery and china	361	12,917
Average score		16,095
Group 4: Medium or Strong Economies of Scale, Medium or Strong Technology		
Electrical machinery	383	18,637
Industrial chemicals	351	18,223
Nonelectrical machinery	382	20,433
Nonferrous metal	372	13,146
Other chemicals	352	18,522
Petroleum and coal products	354	11,057

continued on next page

Table 10.3 (continued)

Industry	ISIC	PRODY Score
Petroleum refining	353	13,069
Professional equipment	385	21,349
Transport equipment	384	16,967
Average score		18,460

ISIC = International Standard Industrial Classification, PRODY = index of export sophistication of the product.

Source: Author's estimates.

(and other manufactured) products, in group 2, include knowledge-intensive products (e.g., books) and design-intensive products. Thus, knowledge intensity is one dimension probably not measured in the technology and scale classification. However, as the previous analysis on the technology and scale sectors showed, groups 1 and 4 are the ones that critically determine a country's score in terms of its technology and scale index.

Regression analysis confirmed the predictive power of EXPY. Output growth was regressed on the logarithm of initial GDP per capita, the logarithm of initial EXPY, and the change in industry's share in total output. The regressions include only countries in developing Asia. Results are shown in Table 10.4. Ordinary least squares (OLS) and instrumental variable (IV) regressions are shown. For the latter, the instruments used were the logarithm of population and the logarithm of land area. Two types of regressions were run, cross-sectional and 5-year panel. In all regressions, coefficients have the correct sign and are statistically significant.

The upper half of the table shows the estimates without controlling for industrialization and the lower half shows the estimates controlling for it. The estimates in both halves of the table are similar.

Taking the midpoint of the range of estimates of the coefficients of the logarithm of EXPY, the results imply that a 10% increase in EXPY (i.e., a more sophisticated export package at the beginning of the period) raises growth by about a half percentage point, an estimate very similar to that of Hausmann, Hwang, and Rodrik (2005).

Overall, the empirical evidence presented in this section corroborates Hausmann, Hwang, and Rodrik's conclusion that countries that latch on to a set of goods that are placed higher on the quality spectrum tend to perform better. As these authors argue, "the implication is that the gains from globalization depend on the ability of countries to appropriately position themselves along this spectrum." What matters for future growth is not the volume of exports, but the capacity to continue latching on to higher-

Table 10.4. EXPY and Growth (Dependent variable is output growth)

	Cross-Sectional		5-Year Panel	
	OLS	IV[a]	OLS	IV[a]
Initial GDP per capita (log)	–0.010	–0.014	–0.010	–0.010
	[2.0]*	[1.72]**	[2.42]**	[1.79]*
Initial EXPY (log)	0.040	0.055	0.050	0.051
	[3.53]***	[2.05]*	[3.79]***	[2.21]**
Observations	20	20	83	83
R^2	0.36	—	0.24	—
Controlling for the Change in Industry Output Shares				
Initial GDP per capita (log)	–0.009	–0.014	–0.007	–0.010
	[1.50]	[1.41]	[1.80]*	[1.8]*
Initial EXPY (log)	0.038	0.055	0.048	0.060
	[3.09]***	[1.91]*	[3.72]***	[2.75]***
Change in industry output shares	0.009	0.001	0.051	0.050
	[0.48]	[0.02]	[2.57]**	[2.51]**
Observations	20	20	81	81
R^2	0.43	—	0.31	—

— = data not available, EXPY = index of export sophistication of the country, GDP = gross domestic product, IV = instrumental variable, OLS = ordinary least squares, R^2 = goodness of fit.

[a] Instruments are the logarithms of population and land area.

Note: 1. Absolute value of t-statistics in brackets.
  2. * significant at 10%; ** significant at 5%; *** significant at 1%.
  3. Panel results correspond to an unbalanced panel. Time periods range, depending on data availability. The earliest period is 1965 and the latest is 2005.

Source: Author's estimates.

income products over time. Industrial policies geared toward upgrading the production and export structure therefore seem to matter and have a positive impact on future growth.

The Product Space and Its Implications for Development

Box 10.1 summarizes the ideas underlying a novel procedure to analyze structural change based on network theory. It leads to a graphical representation of all products being exported in the world, called the product space, shown in Figure 10.4. This is a very useful tool that can help policy makers understand the options that their country has to succeed in exporting.

Box 10.1. The Product Space: On Forests, Trees, Monkeys...and Structural Change

Developing new activities and products is not easy for most developing countries. Lack of markets and coordination problems can create insurmountable difficulties. For this reason, new activities are rarely created in a vacuum, as their development has to take place in the context of the existing capabilities, which are useful to the extent that they are similar to those of the new products and activities. However, the similarity of capabilities might vary between any pair of activities. For example, a country that has developed capability, infrastructure, a regulatory framework, a trained labor force, and knowledge in the production of garments might be able to develop a shoe industry. However, these capabilities are unlikely to be very useful in developing a new steel industry. Capabilities are specific to each activity.

For this reason, one can think of products as trees in the forest—i.e., the product space—and being at some distance from each other in terms of capabilities. Firms are monkeys that live on trees. The distance between the trees reflects the similarity of the required capabilities. In general, new activities more easily develop close to the areas where monkeys already live, since they will require similar capabilities. Producing very different new products—i.e., at larger distances—requires capabilities that the monkeys—i.e., firms—do not possess.

Hausmann and Klinger (2006) and Hidalgo et al. (2007) have proposed a measure of the distance between products. If similar capabilities, infrastructure, and technology, for example, are needed to produce two different products, countries that are good at one will also be good at producing the other. This idea of "proximity"—the ability of a country to manufacture a product depends on its ability to manufacture similar products—allows the authors to "map the

continued on next page

The product space is not a tool to be used to "pick winners" but to reduce uncertainty in deciding what to do, given that public resources are scarce. It is a tool to set the basis for a dialogue with the private sector.

The technical details of its construction can be found in Hidalgo et al. (2007). The circles with different colors represent all the products exported (at the SITC 4-digit level).[4]

---

[4]   I am grateful to Ricardo Hausmann, Bailey Klinger, and Cesar Hidalgo for providing me with these figures.

Box 10.1 (continued)

space" of products in the world.[a] What are some characteristics of the forest, or product space? First, it is heterogeneous, with a core and a periphery. Second, some parts of the forest have trees (products) with many monkeys (firms), while other parts contain few. This implies that the development of comparative advantage in new products is strongly affected by the distance between the products being currently produced—i.e., is a function of the existing comparative advantage—and the potential new ones. In the authors' words, "monkeys tend to jump short distances." The key to progressing in terms of sophistication is to position the country in a well-connected part of the forest where it is easier to move to other products.

This research shows that the ways countries develop their comparative advantage are far from random. Some developing countries produce on the periphery of the product space, with few opportunities for diversification; others have developed capabilities that are easy to deploy in a wide range of products, creating a path to convergence. Progress is slow in the area of the forest with few trees or firms. The probability of jumping to a new tree depends on how far it is from the ones now occupied. Also, the average distance to the trees eventually occupied is much smaller than the distance to a randomly chosen tree. Moreover, the position of a country in the forest at a point in time is a good predictor of how quickly the country upgrades. Evidence indicates that economic upgrading is not easy and that using the existing capabilities to develop new products is not automatic. In fact, when monkeys jump to new trees—or firms jump to new products—they land on the lower branches of the tree. Then, they move up the tree more easily. This means that once a firm can start developing a new activity, it can more easily tackle coordination failures and gain the specific knowledge required. Still, whenever a firm moves toward new products, it has to start producing without the required capabilities, and this can be done only at lower qualities. For this reason, moving within products is easier and more feasible than moving between products.

---

[a]   Strictly speaking, the proximity between two products is the minimum of the pairwise conditional probability of a country exporting a good, given that it exports another one.

The size of the circles is proportional to the world trade volume, and the lines joining them represent proximity, not as physical distance, but as the conditional probability of exporting a product given that another product is exported. The rationale is that if two goods need the same capabilities, a country should show a high probability of having comparative advantage in both. A light blue line indicates a proximity of under 0.40; a beige link a proximity between 0.40 and 0.55; a dark blue line a proximity between 0.55 and 0.65; and a red link a proximity greater than 0.65. We can see in Figure 10.4 that the product space is highly heterogeneous. Some peripheral products are only weakly connected to other products. Some groupings appear among these peripheral goods, such as petroleum products, seafood products, garments, and raw materials. Furthermore, in the center of the network is a core of closely connected products, mainly machinery and other capital-intensive goods. The heterogeneous structure of the product space has important implications for structural change. If a country produces goods in a dense part of the product space, then structural transformation is much easier because the set of acquired capabilities can be easily redeployed to other nearby products. However, if a country specializes in the peripheral products, this redeployment is more challenging as no set of products requires similar capabilities. A country's position in the space can impede its structural transformation.

Figure 10.5 shows the products in which Malaysia had revealed comparative advantage greater than or equal to one (i.e., the country's world market share in that good is greater than its world market share in all exports) in 1975 and then in 2000 by placing a black square over them. According to Figure 10.5, in 1975, Malaysia had comparative advantage on a few products that were mostly in the periphery: oil, forest products, and garments. It also had a slight presence in electronics. The most important change in the 25-year period until 2000 was the development of a solid and wide presence in electronics. Malaysia has undergone deep structural change and it is very well positioned in the product space, as it has developed capabilities in a dense area of the forest, where it can easily redeploy its capabilities.

If we look now at Figure 10.6 for Pakistan, the situation is very different. First, Pakistan's overall orientation in the product space as far back as 1975 can be described as peripheral. Like many other developing countries, it had little production in the tightly packed industrial core of the product space, in which structural transformation is rather easy. Instead, the country's productive capabilities were spread in the periphery of the space, particularly in garments and textiles. Second, we can see that between 1975 and 2000, Pakistan consolidated its presence in the tightly packed garments and textiles clusters. While these clusters are tightly connected within themselves (i.e., once a country knows how to make trousers, moving into the production of shorts and skirts is probably easy), they are weakly connected to the rest of the space (i.e., it is difficult to move from trousers into automobiles). Pakistan has almost fully occupied the tight garment cluster and seems to be left with few nearby options for structural transformation around these sectors. Finally, between 1975 and 2000, Pakistan did not make any substantial jumps and occupy new areas of the product space.

Figure 10.4. The Product Space

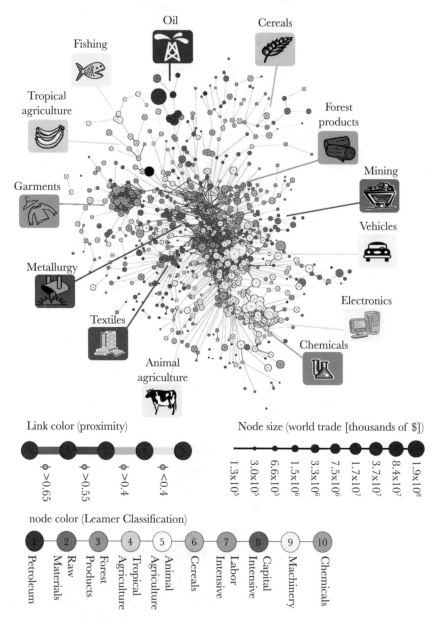

Link color (proximity)

$\phi > 0.65$ $\phi > 0.55$ $\phi > 0.4$ $\phi < 0.4$

Node size (world trade [thousands of $])

1.3×10^5 3.0×10^5 6.6×10^5 1.5×10^6 3.3×10^6 7.5×10^6 1.7×10^7 3.7×10^7 8.4×10^7 1.9×10^8

node color (Leamer Classification)

1 Petroleum   2 Raw Materials   3 Forest Products   4 Tropical Agriculture   5 Animal Agriculture   6 Cereals   7 Labor Intensive   8 Capital Intensive   9 Machinery   10 Chemicals

$ = US dollars.

Source: Hidalgo et al. 2007.

Figure 10.5. Malaysia in the Product Space, 1975 and 2000

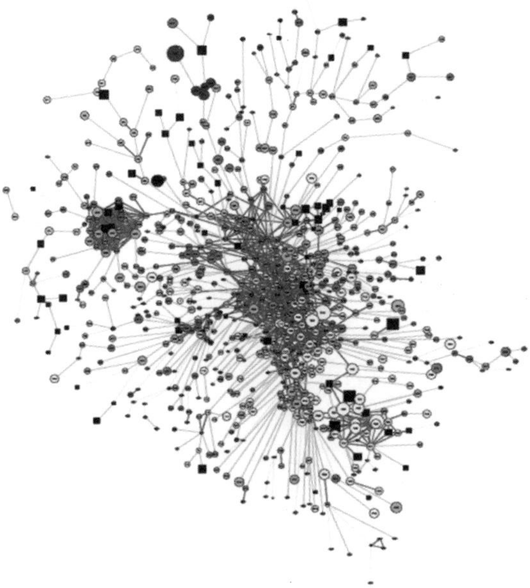

Malaysia 1975

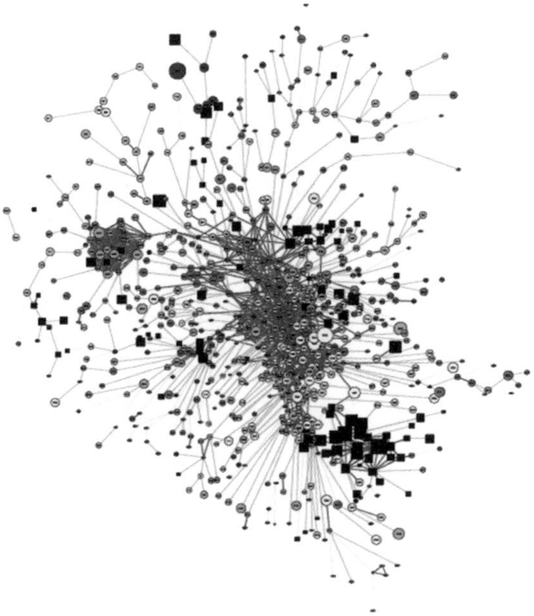

Malaysia 2000

Source: Author.

Figure 10.6. Pakistan in the Product Space, 1975 and 2000

Pakistan 1975

Pakistan 2000

Source: Author.

Hausmann and Klinger (2006) have also developed a summary measure of a country's unexploited export opportunities, called open forest, which is shown in Figure 10.7.[5] A high open forest value indicates that the country is located in a dense part of the product space. This measure should predict well how a country's productive structure will shift over time. Figure 10.7 graphs open forest versus GDP per capita in 2005. The figure indicates, for example, that, given its income per capita, Pakistan (marked with the arrow) has some options. However, Pakistan is not as well positioned as competitors such as Indonesia, India, or the PRC. Its activities are peripheral, meaning that it faces much more difficulty in transforming the structure of production and moving to new products, as these seem to require capabilities completely unlike those that presently exist in the economy.

I close this chapter with a reference to the recent work by Hwang (2006) on convergence because it is related to the questions of diversification and export sophistication. Hwang delves into the failure of developing countries to converge unconditionally in per capita income to the

Figure 10.7. The Open Forest (2006)

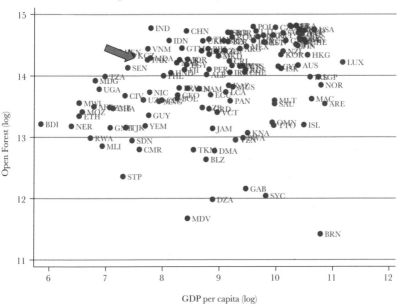

Source: Author's calculations.

---

5   Open Forest is a measure of the distance between a country's export basket and the products not exported with comparative advantage.

developed countries. He offers a novel angle to this important issue: that poor countries appear to converge to the rich countries' income unconditionally (i.e., the result does not depend on holding constant variables that are supposed to affect growth) within the set of goods that they produce. The implication is that many developing countries fail to grow because the range of goods in which convergence can occur is rather limited.

Hwang argues that countries can expand output either by improving the quality of a given range of goods (vertical dimension), or by entering new sectors and increasing the number of products (horizontal dimension). He shows empirically that significant and rapid unconditional convergence occurs along the vertical dimension. To show this, he calculated unit values (a proxy for quality) at a disaggregated level and estimated different regressions that lead to the conclusion that the larger the distance between the average quality of the Organisation for Economic Co-operation and Development (OECD) and a country's own quality, the faster the country moves up vertically. The estimated speed of convergence ranges from 4% to 6% per annum. This indicates that it takes about 14 years (for the mid-point of 5% convergence rate) to reduce the gap to the steady-state value by half.

Why don't *all* developing countries take advantage of this possibility? Hwang shows that developing countries differ greatly in how much room they have to catch up vertically. The laggard countries are stuck in the production and export of products that have little room for catch-up, while the fast-growing countries manage to get into sectors where the frontier is far. The result is that countries with the greatest vertical distance with respect to the OECD grow the fastest unconditionally. On the other hand, the poorest nongrowing countries are in sectors with little room to catch up. The result, in the words of Hwang, is that "there is a strong convergence force that allows a country to learn and catch up to the frontier rapidly but not all countries benefit from this force equally, because some have moved into sectors with a higher frontier and others have not."

Therefore, what is peculiar about the countries that have managed to open large vertical distances? Hwang postulates that what matters is the rate at which countries enter new sectors. If a country produces goods where the frontier is not far ahead, then diversification, or the attempt to produce goods where the frontier is farther ahead, would be an important mechanism for growth through imitation. In other words, countries differ in the rate at which new goods are added to their production and export structure. The key lies in getting into the production of new goods where the frontier is far and firms start at the bottom of the quality ladder. This explanation provides a rationale for Hausmann, Hwang, and Rodrik's (2005) result that countries with a higher level of export sophistication level grow faster. What this new research indicates is that while it is true that "you always have a comparative advantage in *something*" (Krugman 1996; italics added), not all products are the same and therefore, they carry consequences for an explanation of why countries trade (Box 15.1) and for development in general.

11

Unemployment Versus Inflation: Which One Should Be *the* Public Enemy Number One?

I n chapters 5 and 6, I argued that inflation can potentially damage developing countries because it erodes the purchasing power of wages and shifts the burden of financing development to workers. This is unethical and conflicts with the idea of inclusive growth. In this chapter, I address the following three questions: (i) Can full employment be achieved without inflation? (ii) How high does inflation have to be to represent a serious problem? (iii) What causes inflation? This discussion serves as prologue to the discussion of monetary and fiscal policies in the next chapter. As the discussion in chapter 6 made clear, price increases that lead to real wage reductions (especially for the workers at the bottom of the wage distribution, for whom low inflation is a public good of special importance) are inconsistent with the notion of inclusive growth, and measures should be taken to combat it.

Unemployment and Inflation

Many economists have long accepted that a trade-off exists between unemployment and inflation (rate of change of money wages). This trade-off is summarized statistically in the Phillips curve. The degree of trade-off and the interpretation varies depending on the theory. Perhaps with the exception of the New Classicals (who think that the trade-off is an illusion), most economists believe in some sort of Phillips curve, namely, that unemployment will fall if demand expands faster than the economy's long-run productive capacity, and that if demand keeps on expanding faster than the economy's long-run productive capacity then, in the long run, inflation will rise.[1] Why does this happen? Mainstream economists argue that this is the result of scarcity and the free market: as labor becomes more scarce because of increasing activity, pressures on wages increase. Nonmainstream economists provide a different explanation: higher activity reduces unemployment. During low unemployment, workers manage to bid up wages, and profits need not be reduced. Firms might pass on the higher labor costs to customers through price increases, setting off a wage-price spiral.

As noted in chapter 3, between the end of World War II and the early 1970s unemployment was the true test of economic performance in the developed countries. But by the 1970s, the full-employment policies (plus the creation of social security nets) that many governments had followed in the developed world could not be sustained. Today, controlling inflation and keeping prices stable is the dominant objective of central banks and of economic policy in general across the globe; and countries have tended to reduce safety nets. The argument is that price stability will ensure a better allocation of resources and improved planning for the private sector, which will lead to strong growth.[2] The underlying rationale is that markets function efficiently so that the prices of factors of production and goods adjust quickly to their equilibrium level.

---

[1] In chapter 3, I made a reference to NAIRU, the so-called natural rate of unemployment, where the Phillips curve is vertical and there is no trade-off between unemployment and wage inflation. This implies that an increased rate of monetary expansion can reduce unemployment below the natural rate only if the resulting inflation is unexpected. But as soon as inflation is anticipated, unemployment will return to the natural rate because it will be incorporated into wage bargaining. The natural rate of unemployment can only be reduced by pursuing supply-management policies designed to improve the structure and functioning of the labor market and industry, rather than demand-management policies. Stiglitz et al. (2006, 15–16) argue that while research has studied the question of how low the unemployment rate can be pushed without setting off inflationary pressures, a similar question could be asked in relation to underemployment. Nevertheless, the meaning of a trade-off between inflation and unemployment is unclear when, in developing countries, underemployment in the agricultural and urban informal sectors coexists with the formal economy, but without a clear boundary. Empirically, researchers have failed to estimate the NAIRU properly in the United States (US). See the Winter 1997 issue of the *Journal of Economic Perspectives*. I believe the NAIRU is an ambiguous and unimplementable concept that has failed to provide useful policy prescriptions. Moreover, empirical evidence shows that changes in capacity utilization need only be inflationary when capacity is near full utilization. Before this, inflation will not increase. Only with high capacity utilization might a trade-off arise between inflation and unemployment. See Eisner (1995) for the US and Chaudhry and Choudhary (2006) for Pakistan.

[2] This is the reason for advocating (supply-side) reforms in trade, financial markets, and labor, i.e., to make a more dynamic and flexible economy that can adjust better and faster to shocks. The empirical evidence for these alleged benefits, however, is scant, especially regarding capital market liberalization as it may lead to increased risk.

Stiglitz et al. (2006, 17–26), however, argue that there is considerable confusion about the role of price stability. Inflation is interpreted by many as an indicator of economic *malperformance*. The problem with this view is that the indicator is interpreted by many as a policy objective, when in reality it is only an *intermediate* variable (Stiglitz et al. 2006, 32). Unemployment, meanwhile, argues Galbraith (1996, 45), "has become a price-stabilizing instrument . . . [because] . . . those who have political voice and influence are more damaged by inflation than by unemployment." And further, "prominent among those preferring price stability over unemployment is the financial community" (Galbraith 1996, 46).[3] The key lies in understanding the causes of inflation, for these have different implications for economic policy.

Can unemployment and inflation be reconciled? Here there are differing views. Galbraith has argued that it is not possible: "the good and achievable society cannot hope to reconcile full employment with fully stable prices." That is, full employment (in the sense of job opportunities for all willing workers) and stable prices cannot exist at the same time. If the state is committed to a high-employment policy (through appropriate monetary and fiscal policies), price stability will be very difficult to maintain. Under the current system, the government has to force unemployment to fight inflation, so that full employment and price stability are inconsistent and the choice between the two cannot be evaded. Given this, the objective of policy making has to be to minimize the conflict.

But William Vickrey argued for years that policy choice need not be made between inflation and unemployment and, specifically, that unemployment is not needed to control inflation (Vickrey 1997). Vickrey proposed a "market in rights to raise prices" (1992) as an anti-inflationary program, and the use of what he called "savings-recycling public employment" (1996), also known as Public Employment Services (PES) programs (discussed in chapter 14), to achieve full employment.

In my view, successful policy making cannot relegate large segments of the labor force to be unemployed and underemployed to achieve price stability, especially during episodes of moderate inflation, or when the unemployment required to get rid of inflation is equivalent to "arson."[4] Unemployment is simply an immoral way of holding down inflation that violates society's collective normative judgment and prevents the achievement of inclusive growth. Surely inflation is bad, but

---

[3]   This is because they are lenders. However, inflation also affects the poor, as the distributional effects of inflation are more serious than the efficiency effects. Inflation transfers income to the rich and those with financial assets and away from fixed-income earners and the poor, who are less able to protect themselves against inflation. Hence the characterization of inflation as a tax on the poor.

[4]   This is a term used by William Vickrey.

unless it gets out of hand or affects severely the lower-income groups, its negative repercussions are much smaller than those derived from unemployment.[5] In the words of William Vickrey, while inflation is a "redistribution of the given total output . . . analogous to embezzlement . . . unemployment involves a reduction in the total product to be distributed, analogous to vandalism" (1992, 341). And "an economy with 10 percent inflation and 2 percent unemployment would be far healthier in human terms than one with 1 percent inflation and 8 percent unemployment" (1997, 505). Stiglitz et al. (2006, 26) also agree that unemployment and underemployment have larger social costs than inflation. In the final analysis, one could argue that this is simply a question of "asking people." This is indeed what the International Social Survey Program did in 1996 (Jayadev 2006), asking the question, "if the government had to choose between keeping down inflation and keeping down unemployment, to which do you think it should give highest priority?" Survey results indicated that in only 5 countries out of 20 did more than half the respondents consider controlling inflation the highest priority. In the other 15 countries, the majority of respondents preferred the government to keep unemployment down.

How High Does Inflation Have to Be to Become a Problem?

One may ask if a clearly negative relationship has been established between inflation and growth (i.e., higher inflation is associated with lower growth). Much to the surprise of some, this is not the case. The empirical evidence available indicates that high inflation undermines growth and social stability. There is no evidence that inflation, at the moderate rates that have prevailed in recent times, significantly harms output, employment, growth, or the distribution of income. Bruno (1995) found that inflation and growth are positively related up to an inflation rate of about 5% per annum, and then diminishing returns to inflation set in. Both variables are negatively related once inflation rises above 30%. Barro (1997) found that these two variables are unrelated when inflation is below 20%–30%. Bruno and Easterly (1998) found that inflation rates below 40% do not damage growth. They argued that the negative inflation-growth correlation is only present with high-frequency data, and that there is no cross-sectional correlation between these two variables using (averages) long-run data. Dornbusch (2000) cites a study by the World Bank according to which truly damaging inflation does not start until about 40%, and argues that "countries with 15 percent inflation per month must stabilize with urgent priority: nothing

---

[5]   Of course, people have different views. Ronald Reagan once described inflation as being as violent as a mugger, as frightening as an armed robber, and as deadly as a hit man.

is likely to be more important. On the other hand, countries with 15 percent inflation per year certainly should not belittle inflation. They definitely should attempt, on average, to bring inflation down. But they must see this as one of a number of priorities, and they should view it as a process of five or even more years." Dornbusch (2000, 52) cites the example of Chile: "Chile's policymakers recognize that strong growth, modernization, and integration in the world economy are not held back by 6, 10, or even 15 percent inflation, but could be seriously hampered if overambitious disinflation created a macroeconomic problem" (2000, 53).[6] These results have been corroborated recently by Pollin and Zhu (2006), who find that higher inflation is associated with moderate gains in GDP growth up to an inflation threshold of about 15%–18%. Stiglitz et al. (2006, Table 2.1) have examined growth in several countries (Argentina, Brazil, Chile, Israel, Poland, and Turkey) that have experienced episodes of low inflation (below 10%), moderate inflation (up to 70%), and hyperinflation (in the hundreds or thousands). Their data show that (i) low inflation is not associated in general with high growth; (ii) hyperinflation is associated in general with low growth; and (ii) moderate rates of inflation, 20%–30% per year, have been associated with rapid growth quite often.

What about the welfare losses derived from inflation? Shiller (1997) reports that a 10% rate of inflation is associated with welfare losses of 0.30%–0.45% of national income due to the impact of inflation on the demand for money. Certainly inflation may pose some problems for the private sector to operate efficiently, but does the magnitude of this welfare loss justify the current degree of concern with inflation? This does not mean that inflation in every Asian country running at 20%, for example, will not be a problem. And of course it does not deny that *high* inflation has brought huge costs to some countries. It means, instead, the following: (i) that, "given the uncharacteristically unified view among economists and policy analysts that countries with high inflation rates should adopt policies that lower inflation in order to promote economic prosperity, the inability to find simple cross-country regressions supporting this contention is both surprising and troubling" (Levine and Zervos 1993). Overall, no scientific evidence suggests that a necessary condition for faster growth is that inflation should be as low as possible; (ii) that neither theoretical nor statistical support exists for the popular notion that inflation has a built-in self-perpetuating tendency to accelerate (an assumption underlying the nonaccelerating inflation rate of unemployment [NAIRU] model). Moreover, no

---

[6] Dornbusch (2000) also refers to another study by the International Monetary Fund where the threshold is set at a much lower level, 8%. And Khan and Senhadji (2001) estimated the threshold after which inflation hurts growth at 1%–3% for the developed countries and at about 7%–11% for the developing countries.

empirical evidence exists that inflation, should it increase slightly, cannot be reversed at a relatively minor cost (Blinder 1987, Eisner 1995, Stiglitz et al. 2006); and that (iii) probably many countries can afford slightly higher inflation rates, possibly permitting higher growth and employment (the so-called Okun's Law), without derailing the economy.

Two aspects are important in this regard. The first concerns the effort necessary to keep inflation down. In recent econometric work on Pakistan, Akbari and Rankaduwa (2006) estimate an output–inflation trade-off model and find out that "a one percent decline in inflation rate caused by a permanent reduction in monetary growth rate would result in a cumulative output (GDP) decline of 0.87 percent below its potential level . . . if monetary policy were to target the inflation rate of 3.4 percent, the resulting cumulative decline in output below its potential level (trend) would be about 5.1 percent" (Akbari and Rankaduwa 2006, 185).

Second, what is truly damaging for an economy is unpredictable, unexpected, and volatile inflation, but not steady and predictable inflation (Blinder 1987, chapter 2). We must, therefore, be concerned with the likely sacrifices being made by many developing countries across Asia in terms of output losses (and, consequently, employment) as a result of trying to maintain very low inflation rates. This is even more obvious when moderate inflation around the world is clearly not the result of central banks' policies, but the result of the increased competition that derives from globalization.[7]

What Causes Inflation?

To understand the problems that inflation poses (and, as a consequence, the type of policies required to tackle it), we must first understand what causes it. Inflation can be caused by supply shocks such as natural disasters or wars; or it can be imported through increases in oil prices (or of other

---

[7] See Rogoff (2006). He addressed the "[the People's Republic of] China [PRC] is exporting deflation" theory and argued that competitive PRC exports only affect relative prices: cheap PRC goods simply imply that other goods must become more expensive. Why is this? Think of inflation as a weighted average of increases in PRC prices and in the rest (domestic prices), that is, $\hat{P} = \alpha \hat{P}_{PRC} + (1-\alpha)\hat{P}_{other}$. In a context where the central bank targets inflation in the overall price level (e.g., $\hat{P} = 5\%$), if the growth of the price of PRC goods is negative (e.g., $\hat{P}_{PRC} = -2\%$), this forces $\hat{P}_{other}$ to be higher. This implies that, if anything, the PRC exports inflation. But the argument (i.e., the PRC exports deflation) is true from a different point of view: cheap PRC exports represent terms-of-trade gains, and a favorable terms-of-trade shock will allow inflation to drift below target. But if growth rates in the developing world slow significantly, the result may be a transitory upward pressure on inflation. And a crash in the PRC's growth, Rogoff argues, would resemble an oil shock.

materials) or currency depreciations, or by supply-side bottlenecks on the real side of the economy, as discussed in chapter 5. In the first case, production declines drastically and, faced with a given demand, sellers increase the price. In the second case, a higher new bill feeds directly into higher domestic prices. And in the third case, the authorities in the Ministry of Agriculture must look into the issue. (I noted in the preface that supply bottlenecks happened in early 2008 in some Asian countries.) Capital inflows that expand the monetary base—i.e., not sterilized by the central bank, excessive bank lending, or increases in government deficit spending when the economy is operating at full employment—also lead to inflation if they stimulate demand. All these causes often interact and their effects are difficult to disentangle.

Some economists argue that inflation is (always) a demand-led phenomenon, ultimately the consequence of excessive growth in the money supply, with excess demand in the market for goods as well as an excess demand in the market for labor, due to scarcity.[8] The cause of this is that the money supply is growing faster than real output, i.e., there is excess supply of money, and people will try to get rid of it. Given that the economy's capacity to supply goods has not changed, a greater demand will cause prices to increase.[9]

However, an appropriate theory must explain why the money supply would grow faster than real output. Without this explanation, justifying why an excess supply of money would drive inflation is difficult, because no exogenous flow of money fuels inflation. Put in different words: the supply of money only responds to the demand for money; the money stock must grow for reasons that logically precede this growth. Such a theory must take into account that it is firms that increase prices. Therefore, a connection or transition mechanism must exist between increase in the money supply and firms' decisions to increase prices.

What causes firms to increase prices? In my view, inflationary pressures arise, ultimately, whenever the recipients of money income (wages, profits, rents) seek to increase their own share of real income at the expense of others. That is, inflation is a symptom of social conflict. This struggle for income distribution is never neutral, as it always affects relative prices. Inflation is not the result of an objective scarcity. Rather, it arises from conflicting views about the proper distribution of income and, therefore, is a phenomenon with economic, social, and political roots. Pretending that inflation is strictly an economic phenomenon runs into the risk of

---

[8] This is the so-called quantity theory of money, which assumes the economy is at full employment.

[9] De Grauwe and Polan (2005) show that the standard relationships embedded in the quantity theory of money are hard to identify in countries with inflation rates below 10%.

falling into dangerous abstractions as the basis for the formulation of economic policy.[10]

Two such causes for why firms would increase prices are wage inflation and increases in markups (Weintraub 1958).[11] Wage inflation will drive up inflation when the increase in nominal wages is above that of labor productivity. Increases in nominal wages can lead to inflation before full employment or full capacity is reached. Markup or profit inflation is associated with an increase in profit margins, often as a result of market power due to monopolistic or oligopolistic situations, rather pervasive in developing countries. These are the two essential components of bargaining between firms and workers. On the one hand, workers try to get an increasing share of the product through wage increases above labor productivity (i.e., wage setting). Certainly the scarcity of labor can trigger wage increases, but these tend to be restricted to specific sectors rather than the economy in general. In most developing countries, millions of people are unemployed or underemployed. But in a situation approaching full employment, nominal wages will tend to spontaneously increase, which will lead to an increase in prices, and to a secondary rise in wages, and so on. As long as the increase in wages is less than or equal to the increase in labor productivity, the wage–price spiral will not occur. Problems will occur if nominal wages increase above the productivity of labor. The irony of this, however, is that this differential would be reflected in higher prices so that the increase in money wages would be offset.

On the other hand, firms try to appropriate a higher share of the overall product by increasing their markups (i.e., price setting). Profit inflation need not be the result of excess demand, as in a monetarist explanation. Indeed, firms may decide at one point to increase their markups in an attempt to adjust the standard rate of return to the historically observed rate of profit, which may have been high due to high growth. Certainly profit inflation is caused by high demand, but not necessarily by excess

---

[10] Recall that in the preface I argued that inflation in 2007 and 2008 (at the time of writing this book) was mostly caused by rising commodity prices for energy, food, and industrial metals, and by soaring demand from countries like the PRC. This is not the type of inflation that I describe here and the policy measures are radically different. I discuss in some detail the conflict theory because I believe it is ultimately what drives inflation, even in case it is triggered by rising commodity prices. Sooner or later, it will turn into a problem of income distribution.

[11] This can be best seen in the context of a price model based on a markup on unit labor costs: $\hat{P} = \hat{\mu} + (\hat{w}_n - \hat{q})$, where $\hat{P}$ denotes the growth rate of the overall price level, $\hat{\mu}$ is the growth rate of the markup, and $(\hat{w}_n - \hat{q})$ is the differential between the growth rates of the nominal wage rate and labor productivity. In the long run, one would not expect the markup to increase forever (this would imply that the share of profits in total output would approach 1). Therefore, the proximate determinant of inflation is the differential between the growth rates of nominal wages and labor productivity.

demand, since utilization rates may be below unity. Also, firms may decide to increase markups as a result of higher interest costs, or as a result of changes in the perception of competitive pressures from abroad. Again, this is not caused by excess demand.

This means that oligopolistic pricing can set off an inflationary cycle independent of the monetary policy. In general, and this is the crucial aspect, the monetary authorities *validate* this process through the monetary expansion. This is why the money supply increases. In this case, monetary policy to curb inflation by, for example, increasing interest rates, is not only ineffective but may also have perverse effects if increases in interest rates raise the cost of capital, which, as noted above, would justify an increase in prices thereafter, i.e., interest rates and prices can move together (Keynes 1930).

Can the effects of wage and profit inflation be tamed? This is difficult because often the real wage target of workers and the profit margin that firms seek are in conflict. Nevertheless, the conflict may be addressed in two ways. The first one is to develop mechanisms for cooperation between workers and firms, as exist in countries like Sweden, to prevent an institutional power struggle for higher incomes.[12] The key is restraint on both sides. Both parties can walk to the negotiating table with a clear understanding of what is at stake—that the income distribution struggle leads to temporary winners, yet to a no-win game in the aggregate—and, therefore, work together.[13] This way, the effects of profit and wage inflation can be minimized, if not neutralized.[14] The second mechanism, an incomes policy, is discussed in the next chapter.

---

[12]   Japan provides also an example. Workers in many sectors are not expected to oppose innovation, even of the labor-saving type. See Landes (1998), last section of chapter 27, titled "'They can have any color they want': The American and Japanese automobile industries."

[13]   This, of course, is not so simple. As far back as 1776, none other than Adam Smith, in *The Wealth of Nations*, indicated that the property relations developed under capitalism gave the manufacturing class a decisive advantage in the conflict over wage rates: "It is not, however, difficult, to foresee which of the two parties must, upon all ordinary occasions, have the advantage in the dispute, and force the other into a compliance with their terms. The masters, being fewer in number, can combine much more easily; and the law, besides, authorizes, or at least does not prohibit their combinations, while it prohibits those of the workmen. We have no acts of parliament against combining the price of work; but many against combining to raise it. In all such disputes the masters can hold out much longer. A landlord, a farmer, a master manufacturer, or merchant, though they did not employ a single workman, could generally live a year or two upon the stocks which they have already acquired. Many workmen could not subsist a week, few could subsist a month, and scarce any a year without employment" (Smith 1776, 94). The situation in many developing countries today is well depicted by this unequal power relation.

[14]   The key is the increase in labor productivity. The higher it is, the more willing will workers be to accept nominal wage increases below it, thus making $(\hat{w}_n - \hat{q})$ negative.

Finally, another source of inflation is worth mentioning. This takes us again to the inflationary role of investment (discussed in chapter 6). Theoretically, the maximum sustainable growth rate of an economy occurs when all profits are reinvested as productive inputs (Kaldor 1937, Neumann 1945–1946, Leontief 1953). This occurs when the growth rate of capital equals the rate of profit. An implication of this relationship is that, in the long run, the highest possible investment will be achieved when all available enterprise profits are plowed back as productive inputs, when all profits are saved. This implies that the maximum rate of capital accumulation cannot exceed the profit rate, without affecting the rate of inflation (Shaikh 1999).[15] If at some point excess demand occurs along with unemployed labor, this will accelerate the rate of output and capital and reduce unemployment as long as the economy has not reached the maximum growth rate. But as the gap between actual and maximum growth rates narrows, less room will exist for output growth and, therefore, pressure on prices will develop. The ratio of the actual growth rate of capital accumulation to the profit rate (or, equivalently the ratio of investment to the level of profits) can serve to indicate the degree of utilization of the economy's growth potential (Shaikh 1999). A ratio below 1 indicates that the country's capacity for investment is not fully utilized. As this ratio approaches 1, the probability increases that excess demand will end up accelerating inflation rather than boosting growth. This implies that while investment is necessary for development, it can induce inflationary pressures, and therefore developing countries have to watch it carefully.

This approach contrasts with most standard theories of inflation, which anticipate that excess demand stimulates inflation in the vicinity of full employment (however defined). Shaikh's insight is that inflation will tend to rise as the economy's accumulation rate approaches the profit rate. This may be a significant source of inflation in developing countries that are trying to increase the rate of investment.

---

[15] This result can be derived from a Harrodian warranted growth (i.e., the rate of growth necessary to absorb society's saving in investment projects) path with a Kaldorian classical savings function, which implies that $I = s_c \Pi$, where I is investment, and s_c is the propensity to save out of profits (Π). Dividing both sides by K, it follows that $(I/K) = \hat{K} = s_c(\Pi/K) = s_c r$. When all profits are saved $s_c = 1$ and the maximum $\hat{K}$ equals r.

12

What Should Be the Role of Fiscal and Monetary Policies for Development? Full Employment IV

None of the post war expansions died of old age. They were all murdered by the Fed.

—R. Dornbusch, late Massachusetts Institute of Technology professor (quoted in *The Economist* [2007, 76]).

In this chapter, I discuss the roles of fiscal and monetary policies in achieving full employment. These two are the main tools that governments have at hand to achieve this objective. I start with a discussion of fiscal policy and budget deficits and address the widely held belief that budget deficits cause inflation, lead to increases in interest rates, and crowd out private investment. I move in the following section to a discussion of monetary policy and the evidence of the role of interest rates in stimulating investment and averting inflation. In this chapter, I argue that governments and central banks have powerful tools to contribute to full employment. In fact, failure to understand how these tools operate in modern economies is an important reason for pervasive involuntary unemployment.

For a long time, economists have distinguished between policies for stabilization (short- and medium-term issues) and policies for growth (long-term issues). The tools to stabilize the economy (i.e., to counteract economic fluctuations) are monetary and fiscal policies that focus on aggregate demand. Some economists think that these have no impact on long-run growth (i.e., the neutrality-of-money proposition). Growth policy, on the other hand, concentrates on aggregate supply. This artificial division of areas (and policies), however, is not shared by other economists. In the words of Stiglitz et al. (2006, 245): "Stabilization policy cannot be separated from growth policy. Failure to stabilize may hurt growth, but stabilization, in the traditional sense of the term (price stability and fiscal adjustment), does not necessarily lead to economic growth." Indeed, after the financial crises of the 1990s, many developing countries sacrificed their long-run growth potential to show fiscal discipline. Ball (1999) and Blanchard (2002) have argued that monetary and fiscal policies affect both short- and long-run trends in unemployment. And most likely, changes in aggregate demand permanently affect potential output. In a world where prices adjust slowly to equilibrium following a shock, the argument that economic policy is ineffective need not be true, especially in the presence of unemployment. This slow-adjustment scenario is particularly realistic in the labor market because of the conflict between firms and workers over the distribution of income. Monetary policy can be used to speed up adjustment by causing nominal demand to grow (Akerlof 2002).[1] Maintaining strong aggregate demand appears to be particularly effective if tax, spending, and monetary policies are appropriately coordinated with both wage bargaining and social policy. Monetary and fiscal policies can, therefore, help increase countries' productive capacity and thus help achieve full employment, if their role is correctly understood.

The reader will realize that the views I express especially regarding deficit spending are heterodox and, therefore, differ significantly from those that usually appear in the press and in standard textbooks. This obeys my conviction that many standard arguments are a mix of fallacies, politically driven claims, and misunderstandings about how modern economies work. *Facts* about how central banks and governments operate in real modern economies (for example, on "financing budget deficits") are different from how they are often explained and conceptualized in widely used economic models. For example, the treatment in both modern neoclassical and neo-Keynesian models that study the impact of government spending on private consumption and private investment (the crowding-out debate) relies on assumptions that completely disregard facts about what central banks and treasuries actually do. See, for example, the recent survey by Perotti (2007).

---

[1] Although, as I shall argue later in the discussion, any impact of monetary policy on money, prices, unemployment, or growth rates is very indirect.

This leads me to an explanation of the role of fiscal and monetary policies significantly different from the standard ones. The arguments I develop do not intend to describe how central banks and treasuries operate in every country across developing Asia. They are valid, however, for countries with flexible exchange rates, which implies that monetary policy is not constrained by the need to defend foreign exchange reserves; and for countries where a government has the monopoly to create money that cannot be converted (by the government itself or anybody else) into anything else, such as gold, and also has the power to ensure that citizens use it to pay taxes. This is enforced by law in modern economies. Since citizens must obtain this currency to pay taxes, they offer either their services or goods for sale to the government (and certainly to the market). This has two important implications: (i) the government can buy anything that is for sale in the currency that it produces by simply issuing it; and (ii) the government does not need its citizens' money to pay for its expenditures; rather, the public needs the government's money in order to pay taxes (and other goods and services).

How Can Policy Makers in Developing Countries Use Fiscal Policy to Achieve Full Employment?

Fiscal policy is one area in academic macroeconomics where economists do not agree. While Keynesian economists accept that fiscal policy is useful (many would probably argue that fiscal policy is effective in the short run. However, the effects of fiscal policy in the long run are probably more contentious), the new classical school doubts its usefulness, both theoretically and practically. During the 1990s, the developments of new classical economics, as well as work on rational expectations and the Ricardian equivalence (that there is no significant macroeconomic difference between tax finance and debt finance of public spending), wiped out any possible role for fiscal policy. Some debates in the profession seem to indicate that only one policy goal exists, the control of inflation, which is the task of monetary policy. "Fiscal policy is either impossible or undesirable" (Solow 2004, 23). Indeed, intertemporal dynamic general equilibrium models with infinitely lived rational individuals conclude that deficits have no impact on the economy: rational agents simply reallocate their intertemporal spending decisions to offset any government change.

However, fiscal policy is a key tool for policy makers in all countries (probably because of commonsense reasoning) and as Solow (2004, 23) notes, 40 years ago no one would have bothered to ask "is fiscal policy possible? Is it desirable?" The dilemma for policy makers is how to balance the short-run stabilization needs of the economy and the long-run aspect of budgets. The key problem is the long-run sustainability of government finances. This is an even more acute problem in developing countries, many of which suffer from a shortage in revenue collection. Hence financing expenditures for development is a problem. In most developing countries, the ratio of tax revenues to GDP is very low as a result of a low tax base, often the result of corruption. A solution is to implement a progressive tax system and, simultaneously, try to eliminate corruption and tax evasion (pervasive in customs and in direct taxation, for example).[2] Banerjee (1996), for example, proposes the privatization of tax collection through auctions of the right to collect taxes to private individuals. Disagreements between the tax collector and the taxpayer would be resolved by a tax court, which would evaluate the taxpayer's claim and award him/her compensation if he/she is correct. If this additional revenue were used for much-needed public investment (chapter 6), the externalities gained from public spending would have a large payoff. Indeed, spending on public infrastructure is widely recognized as likely to increase private sector productivity and reduce private sector costs, which might encourage private investment. As long as tax revenues are not increased, the argument goes, achieving a level of public investment consistent with full employment will be very difficult. Foreign investment can contribute a great deal to supplying the funds that developing countries need. But this (private) investment is not guaranteed to go into the areas that developing countries need. Such private investment requires liberalization of the country's capital account. And while this can bring in enormous benefits, many developing countries are wary that opening their capital accounts may destabilize their economies, especially through the impact of portfolio investment.[3] Moreover, as the case of the People's Republic of China (PRC) proves, a country can attract huge amounts of foreign investment without liberalizing its capital

---

[2] Haque and Sahay (1996) argue that increasing tax rates without considering civil servants' wages may not increase tax collection due to lack of incentives. In their view, civil servants' low salaries are the cause of low tax collection and corruption. Other measures are better technologies for record keeping, more careful procedures for selecting bureaucrats, and limiting bureaucratic discretion. Corruption in some countries is pervasive. For example, at the end of 2007, another scandal tainted the already-low reputation of the Philippine administration (*The Philippine Star* 2008). While contracts with the Government of the Philippines are known to be overpriced by about 20% to facilitate kickbacks, allegations that a high government official asked for $130 million as his commission in a $329 million broadband deal with the PRC's ZTE (this was twice the normal cut) came to light and caused uproar. In countries like the Philippines, corruption is also a mechanism used by the elites of the private sector to maintain the oligopolistic structure of some sectors.

[3] Foreign investment can complement domestic investment. The problem is that today much foreign investment in many developing countries is portfolio investment used for speculation.

account. The other option is for countries to finance their own investment plans incurring budget deficits. Ideally, a combination of both foreign and domestic capital (both private and public) should be, in most cases, the proper way to finance a country's development plans.

Functional Finance Doctrine

As I argued in chapter 6, government spending on public investment is probably the best mechanism to achieve full employment. However, can the case for a budget deficit be made? This is a politically difficult option in modern times, given the widespread fears against running budget deficits. The case for a budget deficit depends, however, on what the deficit is for, and not on what may appear to be *sound* or *unsound* according to "any established traditional doctrine" (Lerner 1943, 39). Judging fiscal measures by the way they work or function in the economy is known as the doctrine of "Functional Finance" (Lerner 1943). As with all macro policies, budget deficits should be judged in relation to the results. Moreover, budget deficits have different impacts depending on whether the economy is at full employment or far from it. In the former case, deficits are likely to have adverse effects, e.g., may crowd out private investment by increasing interest rates and lead to inflation (because of excessive aggregate demand), although the empirical evidence linking cause and effect is scant. If the economy is not at full employment, a deficit need not crowd out private investment. Therefore, a budget deficit incurred to achieve full employment should, at least, be considered. Lerner (1943, 42) maintained that "there is no reason for supposing that the spending and taxation policy which maintains full employment and prevents inflation must necessarily balance the budget over a decade any more than during a year or at the end of each fortnight."

Kalecki (1944, 40) made it clear that "a budget deficit always finances itself—that is to say, its rise always causes such an increase in incomes and changes in their distribution that there accrue just enough savings to finance it." From the national income accounts, it follows that the budget deficit plus gross private investment equals gross savings. And likewise, net savings are always equal to the budget deficit plus net investment. This means that, "whatever is the general economic situation, whatever the level of prices, wages or the rate of interest, any level of private investment and Budget deficit will always produce an equal amount of saving to finance these two items" (Kalecki 1944, 41). This is always true and it implies that government expenditure will induce an increase in incomes that will create an increase in savings equal to the increase in the budget deficit.

One can therefore rationalize (the need for) a budget deficit as follows (Vickrey 1993, 1997). Firms' savings out of profits represent income not spent. These savings cause the income of others to fall (through the multiplier effect). This is because savings not immediately transformed into capital simply "vanish" and lead to reduced income. Therefore, private sector investment is the mechanism through which the sector's profits are recycled into the income stream (i.e., the mechanism through which non-spending is transformed into spending). If a country's total surplus were reinvested (as it has happened for decades in some Asian countries—recall the discussion in chapter 6), the economy would get closer to the achievement of full employment. But when the total *full-employment level of firms' savings* is not recycled into spending by private investment (in fact, Vickrey believed that the private sector would not recycle the full-employment level of its savings), some of the *full-employment level of output* will not be justified by actual sales, i.e., part of the product will not be sold and goods will accumulate in stock. This will lead to reductions in production and employment. Unemployment is, therefore, the evidence of this gap (i.e., savings that are "kept idle" and not transformed into productive investment). Income (the equilibrating variable, and not interest rates) will fall and consequently savings will also decline until they are brought back to match the *below full-employment level of private investment*. Contrary to Kalecki (1943: see chapter 6 above on why the achievement of full employment through a large volume of public investment faces political obstacles; see also chapter 13), for Vickrey there is only one solution to closing this gap and bringing the economy to full employment: government deficits.[4] It should not be inferred from these arguments that I am proposing budget deficits without limits. The size of the deficit is market-determined by the desired net saving of the private sector. Full employment is the limit. For this reason, functional finance is not about spending without limit. Functional finance is compatible with, for example, changing governments' budgeting procedures from annual to a 3- to 5-year moving average budget. Colander and Matthews define a moving average budget (2006, 61) as a "budget in which revenue flows are smoothed out so that spending depends on a moving average of revenues rather than yearly revenues. Thus, the spending and tax cut limit determined by the budget is only partially determined by revenues in the current year, and are instead determined by revenues in past years . . . if the economy is in a boom, spendable revenues will not rise as fast as they otherwise would, and if the economy is in a recession, spendable revenues will not fall as fast as they otherwise would."

---

[4]   Vickrey argued that export-led growth is not the solution, as exporting unemployment through "export surpluses . . . is essentially a beggar-my-neighbor policy not available as a general policy" (Vickrey 1997, 499). See chapter 16. To this it must be added that improving a country's trade balance either by forcing down nominal wages by reducing labor production costs, and/or by a devaluation of the exchange rate, will only foster global stagnation and recession as one trading partner's attempt to regain its competitive edge will induce similar policies in others.

The discussion above indicates that government expenditure and fiscal policy in general should be seen from the point of view of how to keep the total spending in the economy at the rate that would buy all the goods that is possible to produce. Fiscal policy should be conceived as a mechanism that balances the system, exogenously increasing aggregate demand (e.g., by injecting expenditures) whenever private sector spending falls short of a full-employment level of effective demand, and reducing aggregate demand (by taxing) if this exceeds the full-employment level. This also means, as I shall further argue, that the purpose of taxation is not to finance or allow government spending, but to remove spending power from the private sector so as to reduce current aggregate demand, and maintain the (government-created) demand for the government's money. The key is to ensure that government spending is at the right level to induce neither inflationary nor deflationary forces. However, given the usual private sector preferences regarding net saving, economic growth will most often require government deficits.[5] Until full employment is reached, deficits can be increased to allow incomes to rise. Once full employment is reached, additional deficit spending will generate additional income that most likely will induce inflation.[6] This also means that, in general, unemployment is the evidence that the government's deficit is too low. Deficit spending increases incomes and generates additional spending, and thus additional employment. This additional spending will most likely stimulate the private sector, create more jobs, and reduce unemployment.[7]

---

[5] Recall that $(I_p - S_p) + (G - T) + (X - M) \equiv 0$, where $(I_p - S_p)$ is the private sector's net injection into the system; $(G - T)$ is the government's budget deficit–surplus; and $(X - M)$ is net exports. Note that $(I_p - S_p)$ also represents the net change in financial claims against the private sector; $(G - T)$ is the net change in government debt (i.e., financial claims on the government); and $(X - M)$ is the net change in foreign assets of the country (i.e., net financial claims on foreigners). This expression shows that the sum of net injections in the private, government, and foreign sectors should sum to zero. It implies that an expansionary demand contribution (where injections exceed leakages) from any given demand component increases its financial liabilities and will require some other sector to increase its financial claims (which are assets) on this sector. This identity implies that a country can have an aggregate flow of saving over any time of period that exceeds its aggregate flow of investment. This follows from the fact that $S_p \equiv I_p + (G - T) + (X - M)$. That is, saving can exceed investment as long as $(G - T) + (X - M)$ covers the difference.

[6] Budget deficits can generate inflation before they reach full employment. This will happen when there are bottlenecks that lead to supply constraints and cost-push inflation. Likewise, inflation will happen if the tax system collapses, in which case the government's money (debt) becomes worthless. This would degenerate in hyperinflation.

[7] I want to reinforce that I am not advocating budget deficits without limits. Rather, I argue that what seems to happen to many developing countries (i.e., their low level of productive capacity) is the failure to recycle a significant amount of savings out of profits of the private sector into the system as productive and useful investment. Hence, budget deficits have to fill in the gap, given that the private sector's investment is often below the level of full employment.

In what follows, I dispel the myths that deficits cause higher interest rates and inflation (the conservative "deficit fetishism", as Stiglitz et al. [2006, 238] refer to it), and that they crowd out private investment. If these result, they need not be directly related to the budget deficit itself. William Vickrey once claimed that misconceptions about budget deficits are the result of "unreasoned ideological obsession . . . [by the] . . . apostles of austerity" (1996, 217).

The "Loanable Funds" Model versus Keynesian Theory

Two main points must be made in regard to budget deficits. The first one is that, empirically, budget deficits have little effect on interest rates (Mitchell 2003). This lack of empirical evidence supporting the claim that budget deficits lead to higher interest rates could result from the fact that the theory that leads to this claim does not describe adequately the real world. The theory underlying the link between higher budget deficits and higher interest rates (with causality running from the former to the latter), reduced national saving, and crowding out of investment is the "loanable funds" framework. In this model, the interest rate (the reward for abstinence or thrift, that is, postponed consumption) is determined by the intersection of savings (supply of loanable funds) and investment (demand for loanable funds). Budget deficits in this framework are a reduction in the supply of funds, and therefore result in an increase in the equilibrium rate of interest. The government has to sell bonds to finance the deficit at a rate dictated by the market. There is fear that a continuous deficit could expose the government to a financial crisis if nobody wants to buy and hold its bonds. Permanent deficits must be avoided because governments cannot permanently roll over the debt. At some point, depending on a number of factors, markets lose trust in the government and therefore cannot issue further debt. A government may be forced to borrow in a foreign currency if its citizens do not take up all the domestic debt, in which case it will be subject to the dictates of the international community and, for example, may need to impose austerity measures on its population to make sure that bonds are sold internationally.

Moreover, when the government borrows to finance its deficit, the argument goes, it crowds out households and firms that otherwise would borrow. As a result of the decline in capital formation, productivity growth slows, hindering the performance of the economy. The increase in interest rates attracts portfolio investment, which drives the currency up and increases the current-account deficit. Therefore, reducing the deficit should enhance confidence in the economy. However, as Stiglitz et al. (2006, 239) note: "We know of no instance in which this confidence 'trick' has worked in a developing economy."[8] For policy makers and academics who think in terms of this model, budget deficits are, except in special circumstances (e.g., recessions), to be avoided. A balanced budget is seen as desirable, and a surplus is even better for it reflects sound management.

Unfortunately, this explanation reflects neither how interest rates are set in actual economies nor the role of debt issuance. The mainstream explanation has several problems. The first one is the theory of the determination of interest rates. The belief that interest rates automatically equate planned saving and investment (like the price of oranges) is an illusion. The reality is that a gap tends to exist between the amounts for which the private sector can find profitable investments and the amounts individuals save. Only deliberate intervention by the monetary authorities can close this gap.

Moreover, Keynes' (1936) theory of interest rates differs from that embedded in the loanable funds approach. Keynes rejected the notion that the interest rate is determined by thrift and productivity. He argued that interest rates are purely a monetary phenomenon. The short-term interest rate is set exogenously by the central bank, taking into account certain economic indicators, such as the rate of inflation (actual or expected), unemployment, or the value of the domestic currency.[9] Therefore, according to this view, the rate of interest is not determined by the supply and demand for loanable funds.

Second, savings do not increase the amount of loanable funds. Therefore, providing incentives for individuals to induce more saving will most likely not stimulate investment and growth. Many people mistakenly believe that income that is not used for consumption will be devoted to capital formation. For most individuals, higher saving means lower consumption. This, however, represents lower income for somebody else. In the aggregate, saving does not increase, and it will possibly decline, as potential sellers (i.e., those who would have received the income not spent) will in turn reduce their purchases. In the simple case of a service such as a haircut, this chain of events is obvious and instantaneous. In the case of a commodity, e.g., a car, inventories will temporarily increase, but this increase will be

---

[8]   Recent evidence on the Philippines (between 2006 and 2008) shows that, at least in the short run, balancing the budget is increasing the country's "confidence." Nevertheless, time will tell.

[9]   Two points are important. First, in modern economies today, the central bank sets the short-term interest rate; the market sets the investment rate. Second, and as an implication, central banks can choose an interest rate of zero. If they do not do it, it is because they operate within a framework that says that the nominal interest rate needs to be higher than the rate of inflation (i.e., the real interest rate must be positive) for monetary policy to be neutral.

eliminated as the car company reduces production (thus affecting its suppliers of parts) and employment. In other words, saving does not create "loanable funds", unless one can prove the thesis that the increased bank balance of the saver raises the ability of his or her bank to extend credit by more than the credit-supplying ability of the seller's bank is reduced. Most likely this is not true: the seller's capacity to boost the economy (e.g., through investment) is higher than the saver's (e.g., by depositing money in a savings account). It is important to understand that while saving *funds* investment, it does not *finance* it. The latter is done by the banking system and the provision of credit (Thirlwall 2007, 450). Saving with a corresponding reduction in spending does not increase the willingness of banks to finance investment projects (Vickrey 1997). The corollary is that savings do not determine investment. Since money is a flow responding to the needs of trade, i.e., a result of credit, it is investment that determines savings. Since modern economies are credit economies, banks are able to create money without the prior existence of bank deposits. This suggests that deposits do not create loans, but that loans (assets) create deposits (liabilities).

The second important point about budget deficits is that the source of the deficit matters for assessing its future economic impact (Brunner 1986, Tatom 2006). Studies for the countries of the Organisation for Economic Co-operation and Development (OECD) show that fiscal tightening achieved by increasing taxes and by cutting public investment tends to be contractionary and unsustainable (Baldacci et al. 2003). In the case of developing countries, the empirical evidence indicates that expenditure composition is critical. Baldacci et al. (2003, 29) report that a study concluded that "an increase in spending on government wages and salaries had a negative impact on growth, while expenditures on other goods and services and capital projects tended to raise the growth rate significantly."[10] Therefore, these authors conclude: "fiscal policy has to be tailored to country-specific conditions to foster growth. That is, a uniform approach to fiscal policy—in which all countries are counseled to reduce their deficits under all circumstances—is not appropriate" (2003, 31). In other words, the "quality" of the fiscal deficit (i.e., the use of expenditures) is a key issue. As Berglund and Vernengo argue (2004, 5): "Fiscal responsibility is not about permanent balanced budgets but about the quality of the deficits, and whether the public debt accumulated is sustainable."

---

[10]   As noted earlier, Haque and Sahay (1996) argue that paying salaries to ensure an efficient public administration system is important, and that reductions in the real wages of civil servants are not conducive to the establishment of an efficient public sector. Cutting wages could lead to an increase in the budget deficit. They recommend a wage policy that enables the public administration to attract human capital of high quality.

Whether government expenditure results from wage payments, from payments to suppliers of tables, or from payments to a construction company makes no difference in the injection of net financial assets into aggregate demand. It will make a difference, however, for purposes of expanding the productive capacity of the economy. In other words, the question of what activities are sensible for the government to carry on is independent of that of the government's contribution to the flow of disposable income to bring the economy closer to full employment.

Since real investments (e.g., public works) contribute to increasing future well-being, spending for this purpose, and thus incurring debt, should be socially and economically desirable. Future generations will enjoy the fruits of today's investment, and thus such debt should not be seen as a burden on them. Therefore, debt should be viewed as an investment in the future. Moreover, debt incurred today is the means to provide for the current generation in the future, so that future generations are relieved from the burden of providing for the earlier generations. Of course, even these investments should not be carried out without considering the inflationary consequences. Empirical estimates showing high returns to public infrastructure and education spending have been used extensively to motivate the call for more "fiscal space" (i.e., the idea that a government should have budgetary room to provide resources for a desired purpose, especially spending on goods and services with significant externalities) and more spending on infrastructure and education—even more so after the financial crises of the 1990s, when a debate started on the perceived constraints on fiscal policy. But as I shall argue, while the spending structure of many developing countries may be inefficient, which calls for reforms, such inefficiency does not imply that balancing the budget, or achieving a surplus, is the right solution. Indeed, some argue that "fiscal consolidation" can be expansionary if cuts in government spending lead to a perception of permanently lower taxes. The argument is that if the government decided to spend less, then taxpayers would have to pay less in the future, and, being aware of this, they would increase consumption and investment in the present. Consequently, if the increase in consumption and investment were large enough to outweigh the decrease in government spending, then higher levels of current activity and income would result.[11]

---

[11] Indeed, during the Clinton administration in the US, some were led to believe that the fiscal adjustment caused the economic expansion. The reality is that the increase in the revenue was caused by the economic expansion of the late 1990s, and the reduction in the deficit was in large part a consequence of the economic boom.

The Functioning of Modern Economies

The third problem with the loanable funds approach is that it conflicts with how modern economies operate. The following points should be noted:[12] (i) modern monetary economies use *fiat* currencies issued by the government (today, this consists of currency or cash, and bank reserves, i.e., currency held by banks in vaults and in the central bank). This means that the unit of account is convertible only into itself and not legally convertible by the government into gold as it was under the gold standard, or into any real good or service. Moreover, the currency of issue is the only unit that is acceptable for payment of taxes and other financial demands of the government; (ii) governments spend by crediting accounts and tax by debiting them. These transactions are electronic adjustments to banking system accounts (that have a reflection in the central bank's books). The final settlement of accounts among banks takes place in the government's currency; (iii) as indicated above, the government does not need its citizens' money to pay for its expenditures; rather, the public needs the government's money to pay taxes (and other goods and services); as a consequence, (iv) governments can spend before they tax. In fact, they must spend first so that people obtain their currency; (v) only the government can be a "net" supplier of money. Every private creation of money held by someone ("bank money") is offset by creation of an equal private liability.[13] However, when government creates fiat money to purchase goods and services, it shows up in the books of the public as a credit of fiat money and a debit of goods and services sold to the government. This is "money creation" because it is not offset by a private sector liability; and (vi) with a floating exchange rate system, the central bank has to set an interest rate as it is the sole supplier of net balances for the payments clearing system with the member banks.[14]

Over any period of time, the government can incur a deficit, a balanced budget, or a surplus. None of these situations makes any difference to the government's ability to credit a bank account to pay for a good or service it has purchased, or to pay a civil servant's wage. When a government spends, it issues a check drawn on the treasury. The recipient of

---

[12] These arguments draw largely on Lerner (1943), Wray (1998), and Mitchell and Muysken (2008). I am deeply grateful to Randall Wray and William Mitchell for patiently and thoroughly answering my many questions. I have also learned a great deal through conversations with officials of the Philippine treasury and central bank.

[13] Money created by the banks is an asset of the holder (i.e., the depositor) that is offset by the bank liability. This means that it is never an asset of the private sector.

[14] Of course, not all countries operate under the same monetary system. Some, like Hong Kong, China, have currency boards; and other countries do not have convertible currencies.

this check will cash it or most likely deposit it in his or her account.[15] In this latter case, the bank's reserves are credited by the central bank in the amount of the deposit. This implies that when the government runs a deficit, it is, in overall terms, *net* crediting bank accounts. And assuming the injection resulting from government spending is higher than the increased private demand for loans, this situation implies that overall bank reserves increase. In general, an increase in bank reserves (i.e., excess reserves in the form of cash supplies in the clearing balances of the commercial banks at the central bank) will put downward pressure on the central bank's overnight interest rate (the so-called support rate). This is the rate that the central bank offers to commercial banks for keeping their excess reserves overnight, which in some countries is zero (e.g., Japan, United States [US], the Philippines). This rate is determined by the central bank, and it is the reference for other interest rates in the economy, in the sense that it represents the floor rate for the economy.[16] The short-run or operational interest rate of the central bank is set between the lending, or discount, rate and the support rate. It is this difference (spread) that the central bank manages in its operations. Commercial banks that are in deficit can borrow funds from the central bank (to maintain required reserves at the central bank) at the lending rate. Those banks that have excess reserves have two options. They can either place these excess reserves in the central bank at the support rate, or lend them at market rates to the other commercial banks in deficit. But eliminating excess reserves takes time (weeks, months, or even years). The process induces competition on short-term interest rates (overnight funds) among banks with excess reserves. But certainly, an aggregate reserve surplus in the system (as interbank lending cannot eliminate the excess) will put immediate pressure on the overnight rate (unless the central bank wants to change it).[17] Where interest rates will finally settle down depends on the overall liquidity of the system. In the long run, banks can adjust to this situation through normal growth of their loan portfolio. But in the short run and particularly if excess liquidity is very high, this competition may drive

---

[15] If people instead cash these checks, they would spend the money. This cash would end up in the reserves of the commercial banks one way or another. Giving people cash merely exchanges one very liquid financial asset (a bank deposit) for another, cash. Net financial assets of the private sector are unchanged. The other possibility is that people decide to hoard the cash. In this case, the central bank would act to sustain the interbank rate at its target. None of this changes the net financial assets of the private sector.

[16] The central bank does certainly take into account different issues in determining this rate (e.g., protect currency, fight inflation, budget deficit, etc.) that it believes are important. But the rate is not determined by the market in the sense of the loanable funds approach, i.e., supply and demand.

[17] And an aggregate reserve deficit puts upward pressure on the rate.

the interbank rate even below the central bank's operational interest rate. Clearly, all else equal, a budget deficit should, if anything, drive interest rates down. This is why we fail to see an unambiguous causal relationship between budget deficits and increases in interest rates. If the positive relationship between the two variables were so obvious, then interest rates in Japan should have skyrocketed and collapsed the economy. Instead, the government issues debt at a virtually zero interest rate. India is another country that is able to run a large public sector deficit without driving up inflation and interest rates.[18]

When the central bank realizes that there is downward pressure on the overnight rate, it will intervene to maintain its target.[19] The central bank (and treasury; whether one of the two or both act will vary across countries) will intervene by selling bonds to drain excess reserves from the system and thus keep its overnight rate on target. How the treasury and central bank coordinate their operations can be quite complex, varying across countries.[20] At some point the treasury itself sells its own bonds. But in general, the treasury and central bank coordinate to ensure that some combination of sales of bonds by both drains excess reserves from the system. Interestingly, central bank bond sales are referred to as monetary policy, while treasury sales are categorized as fiscal policy. Most likely, the treasury sees these operations as "borrowing" to finance the deficit. But in reality, these bond sales drain reserves from the banking system to support a desired interest rate structure.[21] When the government sells securities in its own currency, it debits the reserve account of the member bank at the central bank and credits a securities account at the central bank. When the security matures, the central bank debits the account and credits the reserve account of the same bank. None of this has any operational connection to revenue collection. Bond issuance, therefore, is a process whereby the government offers alternative interest-bearing assets to noninterest-bearing reserves accounts at the central

---

[18] India has a well-developed local bond market that allows the government to issue long-dated fixed-rate securities in its own currency. This, coupled with a high savings rate and external capital controls, has meant that large fiscal deficits have been comfortably financed from what are in effect captive private savings. Virtually all India's public debt is denominated in local currency and held by residents. Most public external debt is owed to multilateral and bilateral institutions.

[19] Central bank operations aim to manage the liquidity in the banking system such that short-term interest rates match the official targets, which define the current monetary policy stance. This is mostly done by intervening in the interbank money market.

[20] See Wray (1998, chapter 5) for the case of the US.

[21] As argued above, the central bank determines the overnight interest rate. The rate on short-term government bills is arbitraged in line with overnight rates; and longer-term bond rates are mostly determined by expectations of future overnight targets.

bank. This means that bond issuance functions not to finance government spending, but to enable the central bank to maintain some target short-term interest rate.

Two important questions in this regard are as follows: first, does the market (i.e., demand and supply) determine the interest rate at which these bonds are issued? Given that bond issuance is an interest rate maintenance operation, the government will decide the interest rate as long as bonds are issued in domestic currency, because when there are excess reserves, the market will demand bonds at any positive interest rate, since the alternative is zero. At some point the government may offer bonds at a relatively high interest rate not because it needs to finance the deficit or because the market desires a high interest rate, but because the government wants to mop up liquidity from the system. These operations do not signal that the government is forced to pay higher interest rates to finance the deficit.[22]

If the central bank and treasury did not intervene and sold no securities (i.e., if they did not pay interest on reserves), the interest rate would fall as excess reserves remain in the banking system.[23] This may also be the case if private agents refused to hold additional government securities. In either case, there would be no debt issues to drain reserves. At this point, the private sector could only dispense with unwanted cash balances by increasing consumption. This reduced desire to net save would generate a private expansion and reduce the deficit, restoring the portfolio balance, although it would lead to inflation if the economy could not expand real output.

The second question is, what is the role of taxes if not to finance government expenditures? As noted above, taxes reduce current aggregate demand by removing spending power from the private sector, and maintain demand for the government's money. But they are also crucial for redistribution purposes. The problem developing countries face is that their governments cannot enforce the tax collection system. Governments in developed countries can impose a high tax liability and a penalty for failure to pay taxes. This way they transfer to themselves a significant portion of the nation's output. This happens not because these governments need

---

[22] In some developing countries, capital may "fly" abroad because domestic investors prefer to send their money to another country perceived by them as less risky (or to evade taxes). In this case, the government (central bank) may find that there are no buyers for its bonds and then it may be forced to offer them at a higher interest rate. Also, the government may at some point sell, for example, long-term debt that is not desired by the private sector. This will lead to high interest rates for that debt.

[23] This would potentially lead to a Japan-like zero-interest-rate economy. Indeed, Japan maintains a zero-interest-rate policy in the face of huge budget deficits simply by spending more than it borrows.

tax payments to purchase goods and services from the private sector, but because the tax liability is necessary to force the citizens to provide things to the government to obtain currency.[24] The key in this system is the trust that the state will impose and enforce a tax liability payable in the fiat currency that it issues. Many developing countries' governments do not have this power to enforce the tax liability on its citizens.

I also stress that a government can spend whatever it wants as long as real goods and services are being offered for sale, although it should not necessarily do so.[25] Would this be inflationary? It would surely be if all the government did was to constantly issue currency and the private sector did not want to sell goods and services to the government, at which point the private sector would not want to accept the latter's currency. If this happens, then the government cannot enforce the tax liability, because its citizens would not have currency to pay their taxes and this would surely lead to inflation.[26] But as long as the government issues currency, the private sector sells its goods and services in exchange for this currency, and the government can enforce the tax liability, then inflation need not result. For this, government spending has to be at the right level, i.e., not pushing the economy beyond full employment.

I also said above that governments can spend before they tax. In fact, they do not need taxes to spend because the money that modern economies use is the one whose production the government controls. The central bank has the exclusive legal right to issue the particular country's fiat currency. This means that the treasury issues the currency and simply credits accounts when it spends; in other words, governments are never revenue-constrained.[27] Moreover, unlike private citizens, who must finance their

---

[24] Certainly, even individuals with no tax obligations demand money. This does not change the argument. Indeed, as long as the government imposes a tax liability on a percentage of its citizens, even those with no tax liability will accept the government's money because the rest of the citizens will be willing to provide goods and services for those without the tax liability to obtain currency. Therefore, the tax liability need not be imposed on all the citizens to create a widespread demand for money.

[25] An interesting case to consider is if the private sector refused to sell goods and services to the government in return for government checks. Then, certainly limits on government spending would occur. But it is unlikely that a profit-seeking firm would turn down sales because the source of spending is the government, unless, as noted above, the tax system has collapsed and then government checks are worthless.

[26] If the government starts printing more and more money, but does not increase the tax liability and announces that it will pay more for the goods and services it buys, its money will become less valuable; in other words, prices would increase.

[27] And to stress the point made above, the treasury may want to support the central bank in its ambition to keep a positive overnight interest rate. In that case, it will issue debt to drain liquidity. But a tax rise will do the same. And both would have nothing to do with the treasury's capacity to spend.

spending in advance, a sovereign government's spending is facilitated by its capacity to issue checks drawn on the central bank.[28] In other words: the government must spend first (i.e., credit accounts) before it can subsequently collect taxes (i.e., debit private accounts). The government is the source of the funds the private sector requires to pay taxes and to net save.[29] This is a key point worth elaborating upon.

When the recipients of government checks deposit them in their banks, they are cleared through the central bank's clearing balances (reserves); and credit entries appear in thousands of accounts in the commercial banking system. This means that in modern actual economies, governments spend by crediting private sector bank accounts at the central bank. This process is practically independent of any prior revenue, including taxing and borrowing. By the same token, when taxes are paid by the private sector, checks (or bank transfers) are drawn on private accounts, and the central bank debits a private sector bank account. This means the following: first, that no real resources (i.e., actual dollars) are transferred to the government so that it can spend them (i.e., finance the deficit); second, that the government's ability to spend does not increase when taxes are paid; third, that the only financial constraints that a government has, e.g., to balance the budget, are self-imposed, perhaps for political reasons, as they are not inherent in the monetary system—government spending is constrained only by the private sector's willingness to provide goods and services to the government in exchange for fiat money; and fourth, that the argument that governments have to raise taxes or sell

---

28 The analogy with borrowing by individuals is false. It could be argued that private citizens can also use their credit cards. However, in contrast to the government, private citizens are users of currency and thus have a budget constraint. This implies, first, that they must finance spending in advance; and second, that credit cards have limits, determined by the cardholders' ability to repay. Moreover, in case the cardholders do not pay the balances, their banks will act upon it. A private citizen has to repay all debt over time because the transaction that led to the debt had an equal and offsetting asset attached to it (the loan). This is not the case of the government, which must spend first before it debits private accounts. Why would the issuer of currency have to "pay back" in case its expenditures are above its tax revenues? What is the operational meaning of "paying back"? Recall that the government issues debt to maintain a desired interest rate structure. The debt instruments it issues will have some repayment schedule. But this is not the same operation as a person borrowing to spend, and then having to pay back with interest. Finally, the analogy between government and individual is false because deficits add to the net disposable income of individuals, and this provides markets for private production, inducing producers to invest in additional plant capacity.

29 The fact that a government is not financially constrained does not mean that it should exercise that privilege to infinity. As argued above, the penalty for spending above full employment is inflation and undesired allocation of resources, but not insolvency or bounced government checks. But operationally, an unlimited number of checks can be drawn to pay for the government expenditures.

bonds in order to spend unless they "print money" (and therefore cause inflation, i.e., the monetarist excess money supply argument) is a fallacy.[30]

Budget Surpluses? No, Thank You

In this context, it is important to understand that a government deficit equals the nongovernment sector's surplus. In other words, a deficit adds to the nongovernment sector's savings. This is simply a matter of accounting between sectors. And it implies that, in the aggregate, the nongovernment sector cannot show net savings of financial assets without cumulative government deficit spending. Therefore, budget deficits must increase private demand. They are a passive reflection of the private sector's desire to save. Any worries about the size of the deficit have to be considered in relation to the private sector saving plans. Certainly, a budget deficit out of proportion to the flow plans of the private sector can cause unemployment (if it is too low) or inflation (if it is too high). But given the private sector's usual desire to net save, as noted above, then a budget deficit would be essential for maintaining full capacity and full employment. If the government increased the deficit (i.e., if it increased the supply of fiat money), actual household net saving would rise, and the additional spending would create new income and employment. Why most economies do not do this is strictly a political decision. As argued in chapter 3, perhaps unemployment serves a purpose. As it happens, the desires of the private sector to net save tend to fluctuate, so the "right" size of the budget deficit varies constantly and countercyclically.

---

[30] Standard expositions of these issues use the Government Budget Constraint (GBC) framework. See, for example, Perotti (2007), who argues that this constraint "is certainly always there" (Perotti 2007, 12). This constraint is written as $G + iB \equiv T + \Delta B + \Delta M^D$, where G denotes noninterest expenditures, iB denotes interest expenditures, T denotes taxes, ΔB denotes new borrowing (bonds), and ΔM^D denotes the government's net position with respect to the banking sector. Note that this expression can be rewritten as $(G - T) + iB - \Delta M^D \equiv \Delta B$, and the argument is made that to sustain G the government must issue securities. The problem is that the GBC is used as an *ex-ante* financial constraint, when in reality it is an *ex-post* accounting identity (hence the symbol $\equiv$). By voluntarily constraining themselves, national governments have acted as if the GBC were truly an *ex-ante* financial constraint. One can further write the last expression as $(G - T) + iB - \Delta M^D \equiv \Delta B + \Delta M^U$, where ΔM^U denotes the unwarranted cash balances that appear as excess reserves in the banking system, clearly showing the possibility of excess liquidity in the banking system. If the government issues securities and these are not purchased by the private sector, the central bank's overnight interest rate will fall. In this case, one would have to ask why the private sector would prefer to keep excess reserves (at zero interest rate) rather than interest-bearing government securities. I am thankful to Randall Wray for making this point clear.

The other side of the coin is that a balanced budget implies that the non-government sector has no net financial wealth; and a budget surplus manifests as a decline, dollar for dollar, in private sector savings. That is, when a government runs a surplus, the private sector owes the government (in the sense that the latter will be extracting more from the private income stream in taxes than it will be putting back as expenditure), which harms the private sector in two ways: (i) the stock of financial assets held by the private sector (i.e., its wealth) falls; and (ii) private disposable income also falls, in line with the taxes that it has to pay. All this means that the private sector is dependent on the government to provide funds for its desired net savings. This is, once again, a matter of accounting. And in the face of persistent budget surpluses, private sector savings would decline and households would run out of net money hoards. Therefore, the idea that budget surpluses add to national savings is flawed.[31] And this also implies that budget surpluses cannot lower interest rates by increasing national savings, simply because they do not increase national savings. The only thing they do is to substitute for private sector surpluses. Recall that when a government runs a budget surplus, it is net debiting the private sector, and this is simply a contraction in private liquidity (i.e., destruction of net wealth) that does not increase the capacity of the government to inject liquidity into the system in the future. In other words, a surplus, or net receipts, cannot be stored for the future, because it only represents net debits to accounts. Therefore, the argument that a budget surplus today represents resources for the government to finance projects in the future is odd, to say the least. A government will always be able to finance these projects in the future by simply spending in its own currency.

Summing up, the pursuit of budget surpluses is a contractionary policy, for it amounts to the pursuit of nongovernment deficits. However, fiscal discipline does help maintain low inflation, acting as a deflationary mechanism

---

[31] In simple terms, a claim such as "the government's fiscal surplus has increased by 10 billion" is tantamount to the claim that "financial assets savings of the private sector recorded a decline of 10 billion." The Government of Singapore, for example, has been running budget surpluses, but the central bank has been injecting net financial assets into the system through its operations and foreign exchange deals. Therefore, it is important to consider the liquidity position of the consolidated government sector, i.e., the treasury plus the monetary authority. In general, in countries that *appear* to run budget surpluses, the central bank either purchases foreign currency from the public, and therefore injects domestic fiat money into the system, or buys domestic financial assets, including domestic goods and services. This is necessary so that the citizens of the country have the fiat money to pay taxes. In sum, these countries run a budget deficit on the treasury's accounts and a surplus on the central bank's. These are accounting issues. In general, purchases by the treasury and the central banks are treated differently, the former as an expenditure, and the latter as an asset. Since purchases of the central bank are not called "expenditures," central banks cannot have deficits.

by forcing the economy to have excess capacity and unemployment. Budget surpluses to keep the level of debt low will ensure a deterioration of nongovernment savings until aggregate demand decreases sufficiently to slow down the economy (i.e., a reduction in consumer demand).[32] Quite often, contractionary policies resulting from excessive austerity simply add misery in developing countries and have long-run costs.

Monetization and Inflation

As I noted above, it is widely believed that governments have to raise taxes or sell bonds to spend unless they print money, which causes inflation. In some countries, governments can finance themselves by appealing to the central bank through money creation (i.e., printing money). The government can issue bonds and ask the central bank to buy them. The central bank then pays the government with money it creates. This is the money the government uses to finance the deficit. And since this process increases the money supply, all else equal, it leads to inflation. This idea, however, is a misconception in a floating exchange regime. As already argued, government expenditures are reflected as credits to bank accounts that lead to excess reserves in the banking system. These are immediately drained by central bank intervention (e.g., through open-market sales of bonds), thus preventing unwanted cash balances left in the system to cause inflation. The central bank does not have the option to monetize any of the outstanding government debt or newly issued debt, because the central bank has to maintain a target short-term interest rate. This implies that the size of its purchases and sales of government debt are not discretionary. Once a short-term interest rate is decided, the portfolio of government securities changes exclusively due to the transactions required to support the target interest rate. Unless forced to do so, the central bank cannot monetize the debt by purchasing government securities because doing so would cause the short-term interest rate to fall to zero, in which case it would be pointless to claim that the central bank has a short-term interest rate to defend. In other words, if the central bank purchased securities from the treasury and the latter spent the money it received in return, these expenditures would be excess reserves in the banking system. As argued above, this

---

[32] To further elaborate, budget surpluses arise because the government destroys net financial assets held in the private sector. These "surplus funds" are not stored anywhere, as it would not make sense for the government to save coins and bills that it can issue at will whenever it wants. Moreover, the current budget balance position in no way improves or detracts from the ability of the government to spend tomorrow. The reason is that the government is not financially constrained, so tax revenue is not required for spending to occur.

would put pressure on the overnight interest rate, and the central bank would be forced to sell an equal amount of securities to offset the funds added to member banks by the government spending, and to defend its target interest rate. The result is that the central bank would buy securities from the treasury and sell them to the public, and hence monetization would not occur.[33]

Debt

I have argued in this chapter that budget deficits should not be an issue (in the sense of, for example, being inflationary) up to full employment. Therefore, the same applies to any level of cumulated debt as long as its purpose is to maintain the proper level of total demand for current output. Kalecki (1944, 44–46) indicated there are two serious misconceptions regarding debt. The first one is that debt cannot be a burden to society as a whole, as it is an internal transfer. And the second one is that, in a growing economy, this transfer need not rise out of proportion with the tax revenue at the existing tax rates.

Debt denominated in domestic currency should not be a problem. With an economy running at full employment, tax revenues would increase, and expenditures on some social safety nets like unemployment insurance would decline. Interest would be paid by borrowing still more. As long as the public is willing to keep on lending to the government, the latter has no difficulty in paying debt. Most economists today would argue that future generations have to bear the burden resulting from today's public spending financed by public debt. The burden is the reduced private consumption supposedly required by the withdrawal of resources from the private sector. Indeed, at the time government spending occurs, private sector consumption is reduced to buy bonds. But the deficit spending represents a flow of income that creates the same amount of aggregate saving: the public will hold bonds instead of currency. The supposed burden imposed on the future generations (i.e., taxes to retire the outstanding debt) is simply the result of the government's decision to run a budget surplus. Therefore, debt will not burden the future generations by compelling them to reduce their

---

[33] Strictly speaking, monetization means "to convert to money." Therefore, deficit spending is the process of monetizing government purchases. Monetization occurs, for example, when the central bank buys foreign currency. When this occurs, the central bank converts (i.e., monetizes) the foreign currency into domestic currency, adding funds into the banking system. Often central banks will then issue securities that the private sector will buy. These securities withdraw liquidity from the banking system and allow the latter to earn interest (i.e., sterilization).

consumption to pay taxes to retire the outstanding debt (Lerner 1961).[34] This was also Tobin's (1965) view. If the public does not wish to lend to the government (i.e., buy government bonds), the former must either save the money or spend it.[35] In the first case, the government could print the money necessary to pay interest. The public would hold fiat money instead of more government bonds, and thus interest payments would not increase in the future. In the second case, the public would spend its own money, and therefore the rate of total spending would increase so that the government would not have to borrow for this purpose. If at any point the public's rate of spending becomes too high, then the government would have to tax to prevent inflation. Certainly countries should pay attention to the problems of debt sustainability and default. My argument, based on the notion of functional finance, is that government deficits and the consequent accumulation of debt should be instruments to maintain full employment. But debt should not grow without limit. The debt-to-GDP ratio tends to increase at explosive rates when the rate of interest exceeds the rate of growth. When this happens, the burden of debt will rise faster than the ability to pay and the proportion of debt to GDP must rise. At some point, the government may be unable to sell its bonds, leading to default.

Debt problems in developing countries may arise when debt is denominated in foreign currency, as this, unlike debt denominated in domestic currency, requires servicing and repayment in terms of exports. A government will issue debt denominated in foreign currency when it cannot buy goods and services in the domestic fiat money (because they are not for sale). Interest payments, in this case, cannot be financed through the creation of fiat money. If the market believes that default is possible, then the government will be forced to impose an austerity program to achieve a trade surplus to obtain the foreign currency (Box 12.1 on the Philippines and Box 12.2 on

---

[34] Lerner's (1961) arguments should be compared with those of Perotti (2007). The latter argues that: "We certainly know that in order to increase some type of government spending now we need either to reduce other types of spending now or in the future, or increase current and future revenues (including seigniorage or foreign aid)—or inflate away existing nominal debt" (Perotti 2007, 17). But Lerner, over four decades previously, had already dismissed this line of reasoning: "The 'red herring' nature of having the Lowells lend the money now (so that we can call them the present generation) and having the Thomases pay the taxes in the future (so that they can be called the future generation) jumps to the eye if we note that the shifting of the real burden of the project from the Lowells to the Thomases (or indeed of any other burden) could take place just as well at the time of the project (or at any other time) by simply taxing the Thomases instead of the Lowells" (Lerner 1961, 139). Galbraith et al. (2009) make clear the fallacies that underpin the notion of "intergenerational accounting," that is, the idea that there is a debt burden that our generation will leave for future generations.

[35] And recall that a decline in government debt is equivalent to a decline in nongovernment holdings of government debt. In other words, private sector wealth is destroyed.

Box 12.1. The Philippines: A Case of Self-Imposed Constraints

Some analysts argued a few years ago that the Philippines was on the verge of a financial crisis. In 2002, the budget deficit reached 5.3% of GDP, debt of the national government was over 70% of GDP, and consolidated public sector debt (debt of the general government plus debt of nonfinancial public corporations and financial public corporations) was over 100% of GDP. In the case of the national government, debt was evenly split between domestic and foreign, while after adding the nonfinancial public corporations and financial public corporations (i.e., the consolidated public sector), the largest share was foreign.

Republic Act No. 7653, or the New Central Bank Act (June 1993), prohibits the Central Bank of the Philippines (or Bangko Sentral ng Pilipinas [BSP]) from engaging in development financing. Although the act refers to growth and employment objectives, the act requires BSP to focus on purely central banking functions, i.e., ensuring price stability. Moreover, in 2002 BSP adopted inflation targeting as its monetary regime. Before 1993, BSP performed monetary, development, and quasi-fiscal operations (e.g., it could buy bonds issued by the treasury). Problems relating to foreign exchange covers led to the New Central Bank Act that today separates the activities of BSP and those of the national government. The New Central Bank Act establishes that the national government can spend only if it has resources in the so-called general fund (the treasury's account at BSP). If not, it has to issue securities in the primary market. The national government cannot borrow from BSP and the latter cannot issue its own debt for the purpose of open-market operations. If BSP desires to mop up liquidity from the system, it has to sell treasury bills in its hands, and/or engage in reverse repurchase instruments (overnight operations).

In the institutional structure established, the Government of the Philippines appears to be financially constrained, i.e., it needs to consider tax payments and available cash balances when it makes expenditures. However, these are self-imposed constraints.

Interest payments in the Philippines appear to be "unreasonably" large as a share of total expenditures (about one-third). Why is it a problem? Even though policy makers may argue that every peso spent by the government may create several pesos of income in the near future, the effects will disappear. If a high national income is to be maintained, the argument goes, the government will have to continue spending (as long as private sector spending is insufficient to provide full employment). Unless the situation is redressed, the government

continued on next page

Box 12.1 (continued)

will have to keep on borrowing and debt will grow to unreasonable levels. Then, if interest payments on debt must be raised out of taxes, these will take a large share of the budget, as is indeed the case of the Philippines. However, Philippine policy makers could borrow further or even print money to pay interest. This will not bring about inflation, because the economy is below full employment. Once this state is reached (or about to be reached), then authorities should increase tax collection to curtail spending power.

The above also means that the Philippine Congress could approve a substantially larger budget, consistent with full employment, and therefore interest payments would represent a smaller percentage. What prevents Philippine policy makers from approving a significantly larger budget? It is the belief that without taxes the government cannot spend and that deficits have to be "financed", that deficits lead to inflation and increases in interest rates, and that deficits crowd out private investment. These are misconceptions. The country does have a tax collection problem, but this does not constrain spending. The Philippines needs to approve a full-employment budget that allows the country to employ productively all its labor force and expand productive capacity. As argued in the main text, domestic-currency debt can always be repaid, because a sovereign nation can always issue its own fiat currency. The absolute size of the national debt (when this is in domestic currency) does not matter at all. The assumption that current interest on debt must be collected out of taxes stems from the idea that debt must be kept at a "reasonable" level. This misconception forgets that debt naturally tends to stop growing before it becomes an astronomical figure. The country needs a fiscal policy that, while sensible and prudent, is not paralyzed by dogmas about balancing the budget (supposedly to be achieved in 2008, although it was decided to postpone it due to the financial crisis). And it also requires a monetary policy guided not by dogma but by pragmatic regard for the state of the economy.

Many developing countries rely too much on debt denominated in foreign currency. Policy makers must understand that self-imposed and needless monetary and fiscal rules constrain the country's policies. A full-employment economy would do much to help solve many of the problems that afflict the Philippines.

GDP = gross domestic product.

Source: Author.

Box 12.2. Pakistan Has to Go to the International Monetary Fund Again

In November 2008, the Government of Pakistan and the International Monetary Fund (IMF) reached an agreement according to which the latter would make available a 23-month "Stand-by Arrangement" amounting to $7.6 billion to support the country's "economic stabilization program," and, in this way, prevent a balance-of-payments crisis. The arrangement releases around $3.1 billion immediately and then quarterly reviews will determine the availability of the remaining tranche. The arrangement is five times the special drawing rights (SDR) quota available to Pakistan as a member of the IMF. The agreement emphasizes that the two key objectives of the program are to

- restore macroeconomic stability and confidence through a tightening of macroeconomic policies, and
- ensure social stability and adequate support for the poor and vulnerable in Pakistan.

The specific areas being targeted to meet these key objectives are the following:

- External balance—to be targeted via a fiscal tightening.
- Fiscal balance—the program requires a fiscal tightening from 7.4% of GDP for fiscal year (FY) 2008 to 4.2% in FY 2009 and then 3.3% in FY 2010. The tightening will come principally by "phasing out energy subsidies, better prioritizing development spending and implementing strong tax policy and administration measures."
- Monetary tightening—reflecting an inflation-targeting approach to monetary policy, the IMF considers further interest (discount) rate rises are necessary but did not specify a preferred trajectory.
- Financial institution reform—structural changes to deal with risk contingencies, insolvent banks and to "strengthen the central bank's resolution capacity."
- Some foreign exchange intervention by the State Bank of Pakistan (SBP) but only "geared toward achieving the program's reserve targets and smoothing excessive exchange rate volatility."
- Social assistance to be strengthened but better targeted such that "spending on the social safety net will be increased . . . to 0.9% of GDP in 2008–2009," an increase of 0.6 percentage points of GDP.

The problem with the IMF's approach is that it is less than clear on (i) the nature of currency sovereignty, (ii) the nature and financing of budget deficits, and (iii) the nature and financing of trade deficits. This matters because while it is true that Pakistan's problems are largely the result of misguided policies, it does not

continued on next page

Box 12.2 (continued)

mean that the only solution available is to subject the economy to an austerity program. Further, I believe that the IMF program does not portray correctly the source of the inflation pressures, or the constraints on economic development.

In retrospect, there were no surprises with the conditionalities attached to the loan. Much of what is offered is based on standard prescriptions applied for more than 60 years: tightened fiscal and monetary policies, through lower expenditures, and higher taxes and interest rates. Government financing from SBP is also to be eliminated. The stated goal of the program is to restore confidence while protecting the poor. What will be the impact of these adjustments? In the short-run they will depress demand. Will they revive the economy in the medium to long term?

It all depends on how one views the IMF analysis. This rests on the fact that a domestic spending boom financed by foreign inflows is the cause of Pakistan's problems. Then, the prescriptions do make sense and, in due time, budget restraints and current account surpluses will put the economy back on track.

There are four important questions with the IMF analysis and prescriptions. First, in Pakistan, stabilization policy cannot be separated from growth policy. A failure to reduce imbalances will hurt growth. But stabilization, based only on price stability and fiscal adjustment, will cut economic growth. Fiscal discipline will lead to low inflation. However, it will also become a deflationary force, since it creates excess capacity and unemployment.

Second, prior to the signature of the agreement, Pakistan's central bank increased the commercial discount rate by 2 percentage points to 15%. The aim was to contain inflation, which was running at about 25%. Interestingly, practically at the time all other central banks around the globe were reducing rates to deal with the economic crisis. On their own, at least in this case, interest rate adjustments may not have much impact on inflation. In Pakistan, the transmission mechanism from interest rates to the broad economy is not clear. It is not unlikely that higher rates will damp investment. In Pakistan, it is the profitability outlook, not the price of investment that influences the latter. This means direct credit control might have been a more effective instrument of monetary policy.

Third, Pakistan needs a "good" fiscal deficit. Its private sector does not spend enough. The result is that the economy is far from its potential output. Pakistan needs public housing, roads, airports, ports, railways, power and energy; and investments in health and education. This spending needs to be in areas where production can meet the combined demand of government and other sectors. Right now, the public sector has to lead this investment. Defense expenditures ought to decrease and many subsidies—especially those that keep rent-seek-

continued on next page

Box 12.2 (continued)

ing sectors alive—must disappear. But deficit spending is going to be unavoidable. It can be done judiciously, and it need not be inflationary, as Pakistan is very far from full employment.

Fourth, financing the fiscal deficit through SBP (monetization) is not in itself inflationary. When SBP buys securities from the Treasury and the latter spends the funds on projects, these expenditures appear as excess reserves in the banking system. This puts pressure on the overnight interest rate and SBP is forced to sell an equal amount of securities to defend its target interest rate. The result is that SBP buys securities from the Treasury and sells them to the public with the consequence that monetization hardly occurs.

While curtailing growth in Pakistan may cushion the crisis in the short term, it is also possible that it will worsen the unemployment and investment outlook, two of Pakistan's biggest problems. Pakistan's goal has to be job creation, and wage and price stability. To achieve this, the country needs to transform and diversify the economy.

Econometric estimates indicate that when Pakistan's GDP growth exceeds 5% for a number of years, the country falls prey to balance-of-payments crises. Higher growth rates have often triggered import expansion unmatched by export growth. This happens because Pakistan largely exports products that the rest of the world does not value highly—mostly unsophisticated, low-end-of-the-range garments and textiles. The solution is not to cut growth to below 5%.

The solution is to achieve faster growth by removing the balance-of-payments constraint. To get there, Pakistan needs to implement forward-looking reforms aimed at resolving the energy gap, and at transforming and upgrading the economy, with particular emphasis on industry, services, and exports. The IMF program is silent on this.

Pakistan needs to produce and export products the rest of the world wants. Demand can then be expanded without running into balance-of-payments difficulties. This demand will generate its own supply by encouraging investment, absorbing underemployment, and raising productivity. Export growth will make adjustments less painful.

For strategic and security reasons, Pakistan is of vital importance to the entire world. Helping the government define and implement a growth model that transforms the economy into a modern state and, simultaneously, generates employment is the best way to deliver prosperity and stability.

GDP = gross domestic product.

Source: Felipe, McCombie, and Naqvi 2009; Felipe, Mitchell, and Wray 2009.

Pakistan). But if debt is denominated in domestic currency, a government will certainly be able to make payments.[36] Those who argue that the harm caused by the increased debt burden cancels the stimulating effect of the deficit think in terms of the Ricardian equivalence (Barro 1974). However, the validity of this thesis depends on the tax system.[37]

Crowding Out

Finally, what about the belief that budget deficits crowd out the private sector? If the (private) funds that purchase (government) bonds are the result of government spending (as the accounting relationships indicate), then the notion that budget deficits reduce savings that could potentially be used for private-sector investment is fallacious. Government expenditure on goods and services provided by the private-sector funds will generate added disposable income, increase the demand for the products of the private sector, and make private investment more profitable. Fears of rising interest rates in the face of a budget deficit are unfounded, since the supply of treasury securities is always equal to the newly created funds. Along similar lines, Kalecki (1944, 42) also made it clear that, "the rate of interest may be maintained at a stable level however large the budget deficit, given a proper banking policy." He argued that interest rates may increase if the public does not absorb the government securities that the treasury issues, and instead keeps its savings in bank deposits. In this case, these securities would be bought by the private banks, which would then not increase their deposits. If this happens, then interest rates will indeed increase. The solution to this would be for the central bank to expand the cash basis of the banks so that they can expand deposits, while maintaining the cash ratio.

---

[36] Mainstream analyses of fiscal policy write GBC in dynamic terms and then discuss solvency and sustainability (see Perotti 2007). A government is said to be solvent if the present discounted value of the flow of all revenues is enough to cover the value of outstanding debt plus the present discounted value of all spending. And fiscal policy is said to be sustainable when, given the historical data-generating process for spending and revenues, the solvency condition is satisfied. These definitions fail to recognize (i) that the GBC is an identity; (ii) that a difference exists between domestic and foreign currency–denominated debt; (iii) that governments do not need taxes to spend; and (iv) that the state of the economy (i.e., whether it is below full employment or not) matters.

[37] In terms of an example, the Ricardian equivalence of borrowing $1 billion from households and using the proceeds to lower taxes by $1 billion does not have an expansionary effect on the economy. It is neutral. However, the Ricardian equivalence will be complete in case the debt service is financed exclusively with a tax on land value (Vickrey 1997). But financing it out of a value-added tax will result in no Ricardian equivalence. And if income taxes are the main source of government revenue, possibly there will still be no Ricardian equivalence, as few individuals will know the taxes likely to be imposed in the future as a result of the larger debt.

Under these circumstances, interest rates need not increase whatever the size of the budget deficit, and private investment will not be crowded out. Kalecki (1944, 43–44) also emphasized that with a constant interest rate, a budget deficit need not be inflationary, provided the deficit is not pushed beyond the full utilization of labor and equipment.

Summing up, fiscal policy should be conceived as a mechanism that balances the system, exogenously increasing aggregate demand whenever private sector spending falls short of a full employment level of effective demand. The size of the budget deficit is, therefore, market-determined by desired net saving of the private sector, and with the objective of achieving full employment. A balanced budget is the theoretical minimum possibility for an economy; and given the amount of underutilized resources in developing countries and the level of private sector spending in these countries, they have to run budget deficits to achieve full employment.[38] Second, the standard notion that budget deficits increase interest rates, lead to inflation, and crowd out investment does not follow from an analysis of how modern economies operate (in the presence of underutilized resources).

What many developing countries certainly need is fiscal reforms intended to increase the efficiency of the public sector so that more resources can be allocated for investment and other meritorious government spending. But this is a different issue. While the notion of fiscal space makes sense when spending is being restructured to allocate a higher share to investment (and other desirable categories), it does not imply that a balanced budget (much less a surplus) is needed. Understanding what central banks and treasuries do in modern economies is an imperative. This implies that active fiscal policies in developing countries can be crucial in achieving full employment and, therefore, inclusive growth.

Bank Money

The government may not be the only source of money to make payments. I referred earlier to the difference between government-created money (or fiat money) and bank money. However, they are not the same. Bank money is a bank liability denominated in the country's unit of account (e.g., dollars in the US, pesos in the Philippines); fiat money, on the other hand, is a government liability issued to purchase goods, services, or assets. It is debt. When one writes a bank check, the operation results in a clearing drain among commercial banks recorded in the books of the central bank.

---

[38] As I noted above, balances must balance. That is, $(I_p - S_p) + (G - T) + (X - M) \equiv 0$. This implies that all three sectors of the economy might run surpluses, that is, $S_p > I_p$, $T > G$ and $X > M$. That is, only nations that run trade surpluses can avoid a deterioration of the private sector balance in the face of fiscal austerity.

The use of, for example, bank deposits for private transactions (instead of directly using the country's unit of account) does not change the argument. Once bank liabilities (denominated in the country's unit of account) are used in private transactions, then currency has additional uses, i.e., other than paying taxes.

What about the (related) argument that the central bank can control the quantity of money in circulation (i.e., the money supply) by injecting reserves into the system? Box 12.3 analyzes the relationship between money supply and monetary base.

Box 12.3. The Money Multiplier

In the standard textbook argument, changes in the monetary base cause changes in the money supply via the so-called money supply multiplier. One important implication is that the central bank can, via the multiplier, *influence* the money supply by injecting reserves through an open market purchase. In the standard explanation, the money supply is a multiple (the money multiplier) of the monetary base, and the direction of causality goes from the monetary base to the money supply. Algebraically, $M^s \equiv \mu H$, where M^s is the money supply (by definition, currency in the hands of the public plus demand and other checking deposits), H is the monetary base or high-powered money (by definition, currency plus bank reserves), and μ is the money multiplier (the ratio of the currency–demand deposit ratio plus 1, to the currency–demand deposit ratio plus the reserves–demand deposit ratio). H is government-issued liability denominated in the country's unit of account. This is government money, not convertible into anything else. The government is liable to accept H in payment of taxes. The government (which has the monopoly on its sovereign currency) is not committed to convert (its) H on demand at any fixed exchange rate. The standard interpretation is that the equation indicates by how much the money supply would increase if the monetary base were to increase by 1 unit of currency and/or reserves. However, this relationship is an *accounting identity*, derived directly as an algebraic transformation of the definitions of money supply and monetary base.

What is the transmission mechanism between money and the real economy underlying the money multiplier? When commercial banks accept deposits, their reserves increase by a corresponding amount. Since banks have to hold only a fraction of their deposits (the reserves–demand deposit ratio) they will lend the rest. Part of these funds will be spent and part of them deposited back into the banking system (depending on the currency–demand deposit

continued on next page

Box 12.3 (continued)

ratio). These deposits give banks the possibility of further loans, and so on. In other words, bank money "increases" the monetary base as it is convertible on demand (or, in the case of time deposits, after a specified time). Standard expositions call this a "multiplier". Under this view, the money supply is exogenous in the sense that the central bank creates money independently of the real economy (the needs of trade). This view, however, is misleading.

What happens in actual (banking) practice? First of all, commercial banks lend to their customers without paying attention to their reserve positions. Lending depends on expected returns, not on reserves. Banks evaluate proposals against their creditworthiness criteria. As long as a firm's rating passes the minimum, a loan will be made. If for this the bank needs reserves, it will borrow them to meet requirements, i.e., reserves are supplied on demand. And if banks become pessimistic about the future, they will raise the required creditworthiness threshold. But this implies that the money supply causes changes in reserves and in the monetary base, and not vice versa. In other words, in reality, $H \equiv M^s / \mu$, although this ratio and the reversed causality have no theoretical substance. This has a number of additional implications: (i) the central bank has no autonomous control over the amount of bank reserves, and thus it cannot use the money multiplier to hit a monetary aggregate target (i.e., the monetary base is not discretionary to the central bank); (ii) bank money shifts pockets and, as argued above, leaves intact the private sector (as it is both a credit and a liability), except when it is used to make payments to the government. If the private sector uses bank money to pay taxes, and assuming the banking system has no undesired excess reserves, a clearing drain results so that banks cannot meet reserve requirements. In this case, the overnight interest rate is driven up as banks try to meet the legal requirement. The central bank will have to step in by providing fiat money, most likely by purchasing government bonds (maybe also foreign currency); (iii) the standard explanation of the money multiplier—according to which the central bank can increase the money supply by injecting reserves through an open market purchase—does not acknowledge that these added reserves over required reserves would, once again, put downward pressure on the overnight interest rate. And if the central bank wants to reduce the money supply by taking reserves out of the system when there are no excess reserves, then some banks would not be able to meet their reserve requirements. Then, the central bank would have to provide these reserves to prevent the overnight rate from increasing. The central bank would have to sell securities to drain the excess reserves injected. This means that the money supply does not change.

Source: Wray 1998.

What Is the Role of Monetary Policy?

Monetary policy can not be formulated and implemented in isolation of government policies no matter how independent a central bank is whether of an advanced or a developing economy.

—Ishrat Husain (2005, 3), governor of Pakistan's
central bank, 1999–2005

The conclusion of the previous section is that it is fiscal policy, rather than monetary policy, that determines the amount of new money directly created by the government. Central banks have little influence over the quantity of bank money, which is determined by the quantity of bank loans. Monetary policy has to do with interest rate management. The objective of today's central banks is to stabilize the growth of prices. In the days of monetarism (some central banks still target monetary aggregates), central banks tried to control inflation by controlling the growth of the money supply. During this time, central banks set the money supply or its rate of expansion (usually at a constant rate), letting the market determine the interest rate. However, it became clear that the velocity of money was unstable and difficult to predict. The constant rate of increase in the money supply led to high interest rates and economic volatility. At that point the money supply rule lost favor.

Today, monetary authorities in many countries more often set interest rate targets, engaging in open-market operations to allow the expansion of the money supply to whatever it needs to be to generate the desired interest rate. This way, central banks use (short-term) interest rates to fine-tune demand. Indeed, interest rates are the main tool of monetary policy today, particularly in those countries that target inflation, and monetary authorities tend to use them to avert demand-pull inflation, that is, inflation caused by the pressure of (actual) demand exceeding supply (potential output).[39]

There are two important questions regarding the role of monetary policy. First, how sensitive is the real economy to interest rate movements? During a depression, this option has little proven effect in activating an economy. In bad times, lower interest rates do not inspire consumer expenditure. And likewise, lower interest rates do not induce more investment (by making borrowing cheaper), as during these periods there tends to be excess capacity and output is not being sold.[40] It is the quantity of credit

---

[39] As of now, four central banks in Asia use inflation targeting explicitly. These are Indonesia (since 2005), the Republic of Korea (since 2001), the Philippines (since 2002), and Thailand (since 2001). Others, like Pakistan, are considering introducing it.

[40] Empirical evidence suggests that the interest elasticity of investment is nonlinear and asymmetric. While an increase in interest rates is likely to reduce investment during

rather than its price that influences investment.[41] What is true is that tight monetary policy resulting from an increase in interest rates will also be associated with increased credit tightening. Under these circumstances, some effect on aggregate demand may reasonably be assumed.[42]

Second, what is the impact of interest rates on inflation? The problem with this tool is that it *might be* effective when inflation is caused by demand pressures.[43] However, monetary authorities today use it (or threaten to use it) at the smallest sign of a price increase (often even just a one-off increase, not likely to give rise to an inflationary episode). Monetary policy is designed today to raise interest rates and reduce aggregate demand as soon as there is any indication that unemployment might drift "too low." Plenty of examples in recent history demonstrate how policy makers react (especially in developed countries): as soon as the country grows for a few quarters and unemployment declines, the monetary authorities increase interest rates to avert inflation. Many ordinary people wonder why.

Inflation caused by supply shocks (e.g., an increase in oil prices, bad crops due to adverse weather conditions), for example, cannot be averted by increases in interest rates. On the contrary, such increases will most likely aggravate the problem. Often, keeping inflation down comes at a price. In the words of Stiglitz et al. (2006, 29): "If policy makers rely too much on higher interest rates to stabilize prices, firms become reluctant to use debt financing and will rely more heavily on self-financing. Capital, which is so scarce in developing countries, will be allocated less efficiently in the short-run, and growth will be hampered in the long-run."[44] Restrictive monetary policies may have been appropriate for combating

---

economic booms (the economy is on or above capacity), the reverse is not true: that is, during a depression, a decrease in interest rates will not lead to an increase in investment.

[41] Stiglitz et al. (2006, 61; italics in the original) claim that "some economists believe that the *volume* of credit in developing countries is a more effective instrument of monetary policy than the price or credit . . . deregulation of domestic financial sectors . . . should have made interest rates a more potent instrument, but, ironically, it hasn't."

[42] Arestis and Sawyer (2006) summarize the results of simulations for the US and the United Kingdom and conclude that interest rates have an effect on aggregate demand via investment.

[43] And even in this case the impact is not entirely clear. Consumer borrowing is not very sensitive to interest rate increases. The home mortgage market is probably somewhat more elastic. But evidence indicates that what people care about when taking a mortgage is the total monthly payments and not interest payments. And, as indicated above, the effects of interest rates on investment are nonlinear and asymmetric.

[44] Interest rate policies have both allocative and distributional effects. Sometimes the latter can be substantially larger. Indeed, a significant increase in interest rates may not induce a decrease in speculative investment in real estate, but may hurt small and medium firms trying to obtain working capital.

hyperinflation episodes in some developing countries (e.g., in Latin America in the 1980s). But this is much less the case today, and countries in Asia have rarely experienced hyperinflation. Unless interest rates are changed drastically, monetary policy takes a long time to impact the economy, especially inflation. A better option is to use fiscal policy (Setterfield 2007). The government should try to identify and eliminate government programs that induce an inflationary bias to the economy.[45]

Other options should be considered. As noted in chapter 11, to tame the effects of income inflation, Davidson (2006a) has advocated the implementation of policies that constrain changes in the gross profit margins (markups) and in nominal wages relative to labor productivity. What is the rationale? Davidson (2006a, 699–700) argues that "as long as government guarantees that it will pursue a full employment policy, then each self-interested worker, union, and business entrepreneur has little fear that their demand for higher prices and money income will result in lost sales and unemployment . . . As long as the government accepts the responsibility for creating sufficient aggregate effective demand to maintain the economy close to full employment, there was no market incentive to stop this recurring struggle over the distribution of income." In other words, Davidson argues that a policy of full employment that is not backed by an incomes policy will potentially eliminate unemployment, but will generate (incomes) inflation.

What role do central banks play in Davidson's argument? As also noted in chapter 11, the monetary authorities validate the claims of firms and workers through the expansion of the money supply. Therefore, inflationary income demands (i.e., as discussed in chapter 11, firms' claims via increases in markups and workers' claims through nominal wage increases above labor productivity growth) surface *if and when* central banks decide to finance them. Today, some central banks avoid inflationary wage and profit demands by not financing these claims. How is this done? By preventing the demand-determined actual level of output from getting too close to the supply-determined level of potential output (i.e., by ensuring a lack of effective demand). This is achieved by targeting inflation through the manipulation of short-term interest rates. The result is the preclusion of full employment, i.e., a policy of stability at the cost of growth. Therefore, inflation targeting, and, in general, the pursuit of restrictive monetary

---

[45] As Stiglitz et al. (2006, 241) argue, "reducing aggregate demand when the economy faces inflation by reducing government expenditures is often alleged to be better for growth than doing so by increasing interest rates, since the latter leads to reduced investment. But whether this is the case depends on which government expenditures are cut back: if it's high return investments in infrastructure, growth would have been enhanced by using monetary policy rather than a contraction in government investment."

policies, are largely inconsistent with the pursuit of inclusive growth.[46] Inflation targeting requires fiscal discipline. Its proponents argue that the conduct of monetary policy should not be constrained by fiscal deficits due to an inefficient tax system or to an underdeveloped secondary market for domestic bonds. This requires that fiscal deficits be reduced by using revenue-based measures.

For these reasons, Davidson has advocated (2006a, 700) a "deliberately announced incomes policy," that is, a policy that constrains workers and firms from demanding increases in nominal wages that exceed labor productivity, based on penalizing the largest domestic firms in the economy when they agree to wage rate increases in excess of some national productivity improvement standard (2006a, 702). This policy has to be permanent and it has to be only a penalty for those firms that infringe on the system and not a reward for those that comply with it. In the successful East Asian countries, monetary policy was a tool used to maintain low interest rates, and not to fight inflation. The latter was contained through appropriate incomes and employment policies to ensure wage increases below productivity increases.[47]

A different but related proposal is that of Vickrey (1992). He proposed to establish a market in rights to raise prices (and obligations to lower them). Each firm is given a certain number of warrants to gross markups,

---

[46] Certainly, I do not want to portray inflation targeting as an evil for placing employment considerations secondary, if at all, to inflation. The overall idea of reducing inflation when it is high by "targeting" it is not bad. In fact, inflation targeting is a better monetary regime than monetary targeting. Although the literature concludes that the effect of inflation targeting is small and insignificant (e.g., Willard [2006])—and inflation targets have been often missed by significant margins (Rogers and Stone 2006)—the introduction of inflation targeting in the 1990s probably has contributed to the reduction of inflation by creating awareness of its costs and has helped anchor the expectations of workers and employers. Moreover, some scholars agree that inflation targeting imposes discipline on the central bank by introducing transparency and accountability. This is important in developing countries, where monetary policy has often muddled among conflicting objectives. However, inflation targeting is not a panacea as a monetary regime. Monetary authorities may be forced to increase interest rates when inflation increases, even if price increases are widely perceived as a one-off event, not an inflationary episode. Likewise, the proper adjustment to disturbances to the economy associated with higher aggregate demand is not an increase in interest rates. Inflation targeting may be highly inefficient. Also, often inflation is largely a cost-push phenomenon and/or imported, in which case inflation targeting is questionable. Finally, when the central bank manipulates interest rates to adjust current relative to potential output, its actions affect both actual and potential output. What does this mean? If potential output is not independent of actual demand, an increase in interest rates may have a long-lasting (if not permanent) impact on the economy (by, for example, affecting investment). Moreover, changes in aggregate demand affect equilibrium real interest rate so that an increase in the latter results in a rise in the long-run real rate of interest.

[47] I should add here policies such as Hong Kong, China's provision of cheap housing.

based on past performance. These allow firms to raise prices, in an analogous way to the markets in rights to emit air pollution. The initial allocation of the warrants ensures a predictable rate of inflation, and adjustments in warrants issued in subsequent periods result from changes in investment and hiring in the previous period. If a firm wishes to increase its price above what is allowed, it has to buy the rights from another firm (these transactions are conducted freely) that is seeking and willing to lower its price by a similar amount. This system ensures a stable overall price level. If a firm fails to abide by the system (i.e., if a firm's gross markup exceeds its warrants) it will have to pay a penalty.

The moral of this discussion is, first, that direct anti-inflationary policies that do not rely on forfeiting output and employment have been thought of. What is lacking is political will to implement them; and second, and related, that slightly higher inflation rates may be an acceptable side effect of substantially higher domestic spending, higher employment, and higher growth rates.

One option for central banks is not to focus exclusively on fighting inflation but, for example, to consider setting an employment target subject to an inflation constraint (Berg et al. 2006). After all, monetary authorities need not focus exclusively on inflation (this is one of the legacies of monetarism). Historically, central banks developed to secure the stability of credit. Also, central banks in developing Asia may consider a multi-objective function, e.g., having exports, inflation, and investment as ultimate targets, and focus on a competitive and stable exchange rate and real interest rates as intermediate variables.[48] If correctly done, this policy need not confuse market participants. And in any case, since uncertainty is a given, perhaps some inflation is a small cost to pay for pursuing more than one objective.

Only a change or an expansion in central banks' policy matrix and policy tools (beyond the short-term interest rate) will contribute to the achievement of inclusive growth. As Berg et al. (2006, 62–63) indicate, this proposed policy (i.e., employment target subject to an inflation constraint) can be implemented in different ways, which should be country specific. For example, if the central bank believes that a competitive exchange rate is needed to increase employment, then it must be willing to control the money supply through credit allocation mechanisms (e.g., interest rate ceilings, quantitative credit controls). The central bank could also specify credit allocation quotas for employment generation purposes that financial institutions would have to achieve by, for example, allocating credit to specific programs (e.g., employment in small and medium-sized enterprises).

[48] Some central banks in the region already follow a monetary policy that considers several objectives, e.g., India. See Jha (2006).

These policies are not inconsistent with simultaneously setting an inflation target (indeed, an explicit commitment to inflation control will serve to coordinate expectations and more likely will lead to more stable inflation), and should be designed and implemented in coordination with, and as part of, the industrial policy program (chapter 8). Stiglitz et al. (2006, 61) also advocate such measures and argue that in developing counties, where finance is less developed, they should be more effective than in developed countries.

13

Is It Possible to Achieve Full Employment in the Presence of Structural Transformation?

In chapter 4, we saw (with the Harrod–Domar model) that full employment of the labor force and full utilization of productive capacity will take place only if natural and warranted growth rates coincide. Achieving this is very difficult, and discrepancies between these two rates would take the economy further away from equilibrium. In chapter 3, I discussed developing Asia's employment record: while some countries have done well and industrialization has led to the creation of employment (e.g., the newly industrialized economies), this is not the case in other countries (e.g., India, the Philippines). In Box 5.1, I argued that growth and structural transformation are related in a circular way: in general, countries become different as they grow, as they produce a different bundle of goods and services, using different inputs and new methods of production. And Marx and Keynes, despite coinciding in various aspects in their analyses of capitalist economies, reached different conclusions about the possibility of achieving full employment (Mattick [1969] provides an excellent comparative analysis of Marx and Keynes).

In this chapter, I will discuss further obstacles, both political and technical, to the attainment of full employment. Today's developing countries must consider the impact of fast structural transformation—which includes industrialization, substantial reallocation of labor, imbalances across sectors, and technological change (e.g., introduction of new products and services)—if they are to devise sensible policies aimed at eliminating unemployment and underemployment, reducing poverty, and generating more prosperous and inclusive societies (Asian Development Bank 2007b).

I argued in chapter 6 that investment is essential in achieving the full employment of labor, and discussed three obstacles to the increase in investment.

I argued that a large volume of public investment is needed. However, this solution faces serious political obstacles. Kalecki (1943, 138) asked, "[W]hy do not they [businessmen] accept gladly the 'synthetic' boom which the Government is able to offer them?"[1] He argued that "the assumption that a Government will maintain full employment in a capitalist economy if only knows how to do it is fallacious" (1943, 138). Kalecki gave three "reasons for the opposition of the 'industrial leaders' to full employment achieved by Government spending" (1943, 139): (i) the opposition against government spending based on a budget deficit and the dislike of government interference in the problems of employment; (ii) the opposition against this spending being directed toward public investment (or toward subsidizing consumption, for example, through subsidies to keep down the prices of necessities), except when it is confined to objectives that do not compete with private investment, that is, for construction of hospitals, schools, or highways;[2] and (iii) the opposition against *maintaining* full employment as this may give workers a strong and dangerous position at the bargaining table (on this, also Shapiro and Stiglitz 1984).

What are the technical obstacles to the achievement of full employment? Often, standard analyses rely on the assumptions of perfect mobility and substitution of factors. Under these circumstances, the system "instantaneously" and easily adjusts to changes in technology. Structural change, however, is path-dependent, takes place in historical time, and leads to disproportional growth across sectors. Moreover, capital goods tend to be highly specific, which means that they cannot be shifted easily across lines of production and there is significant uncertainty regarding the future.

Pasinetti (1981; also Taylor 1995) worked out the conditions to achieve full employment in a system undergoing structural and technological change. Suppose an economy is growing, with some sectors expanding faster than others. Also assume productivity is increasing across sectors with unit labor requirements (i.e., labor per unit of output, or the inverse of labor productivity) declining at different rates. Are these trends compatible with full employment? Pasinetti's general answer

---

[1]   The grounds underlying these arguments should be considered, given that higher output and employment benefit both workers and firms, as profits rise. Moreover, a policy of full employment based on loan-financed government spending does not affect profits as it does not require additional taxes. Although Kalecki wrote this article more than six decades ago, the argument is still valid and relevant today. One just has to read some newspapers or listen to the business segment of the news.

[2]   Even these areas are contested today as domains of the private sector, and some argue that public investment crowds out private investment on the grounds that the former lowers the real rate of return of the latter (e.g., Tatom [2006]; also chapter 12, section on How Can Policy Makers in Developing Countries Use Fiscal Policy to Achieve Full Employment?).

is no. The reason is that the condition Pasinetti derived is stringent, one that actual economies most likely do not satisfy: that labor per unit of output and demand per unit of labor must be in balance if demand is to support a full-employment output level.[3] This condition obviously runs into difficulties in a dynamic context. First, labor per unit of output tends to decrease in time (since the 1950s, labor productivity has increased at a rate between 0% and 5% per annum, depending on the country). Second, per capita demand for many commodities or services may rise (e.g., iPods today) for some time, but ultimately tends to slow and even decline (demand saturation). If on one hand both unit labor requirements and demand per unit of labor are decreasing in a sector, the sector will lose employment. On the other hand, a rising demand per unit of labor in one sector may compensate a declining unit labor requirement in another sector, thus leading to employment growth. But this is not guaranteed to happen and, in general, the system will not be in balance. This means that to support employment growth, a market economy must constantly introduce new commodities and services as it eliminates the old ones.[4] Therefore, some of the major obstacles to full employment lie in the technological conditions of production. In advanced market economies, the main mechanism to enable real per capita demand to increase has been growth in real wages at a rate close to that of labor productivity. In other words, an increase in real wage rates can offset reductions in unit labor requirements by supporting a growing aggregate demand per capita. But, once again, this process is not guaranteed to go on, that is, even if wages go up to offset the decreasing unit labor requirements, higher productivity may not lead to higher output and employment (Felipe and Hasan 2006, chapter 3).

---

[3]   Algebraically, this condition is $\sum_i \lambda_i d_i = 1$, where the subscript i indexes the different sectors of the economy; λ is the labor–output ratio ($\lambda = \dfrac{\pi \sigma P}{Q}$, where π is the labor force participation rate, σ is the share of a person's time devoted to work, P is population, and Q is output); and d is demand for output per person (total demand D divided by population P). The intuition behind this representation is that the λ_i coefficients stand for the direct and indirect labor inputs required to support private and public consumption and net exports by sector, and the d_i coefficients should sum up these different sources of demand per capita.

[4]   Also, the labor force participation rate may be declining (in countries where unemployment is increasing) as well as the share of time devoted to work. The economy may have mechanisms to counteract these forces. In developed countries, female participation rates have risen steadily. This has permitted households to buy all the new commodities that have entered the market during the last few decades (e.g., computers, new TVs, VCRs, tourism). In some developing countries, labor force participation rates are not increasing (at least when measured in terms of the formal labor market). Nobody knows what other factors may bite in the future to make the attainment of full employment an even more complex problem (e.g., environmental constraints).

The different situations of disproportional demand and productivity trends that arise across sectors may require substantial labor force reallocation in order to maintain full employment. Most developing countries are not able to deal with the social consequences of labor reallocation (e.g., think of the People's Republic of China. See chapter 8 in Felipe and Hasan [2006]).

The conclusion of this discussion is that the dynamics of structural change imply that, if left to its own devices (i.e., the vagaries of the market), a developing economy will not achieve full employment. For this reason, the country's institutions, the government particularly as well as the central bank and the business class, must understand the importance of placing full employment at the top of the economic and political agendas.

14

Should the Government (Public Sector) Intervene Directly and Become the Employer of Last Resort? Full Employment V

The Conservative belief that there is some law of nature which prevents men from being employed, that it is "rash" to employ men, and that it is financially "sound" to maintain a tenth of the population in idleness for an indefinite period, is crazily improbable—the sort of thing which no man could believe who had not had his head fuddled with nonsense for years and years. . . . Our main task, therefore, will be to confirm the reader's instinct that what seems sensible is sensible, and what seems nonsense is nonsense. We shall try to show that . . . to set unemployed men to work on useful tasks does what it appears to do, namely, increases the national wealth.

—John Maynard Keynes (1972, 90–92)

Given that it is very difficult for the market to achieve full employment due to the political and technical problems discussed in chapters 4, 6, and 13, and assuming national policies have shifted toward the achievement of full employment, one could ask if governments in developing countries could and should act as employers of last resort and contribute to this objective directly. Suppose, for example, that due to the use of efficiency wages (Stiglitz 1976), during downturns firms lay off the least skilled workers. What can society do? As noted in chapter 11, William Vickrey (1996) proposed a program of "savings-recycling public employment" to achieve full employment. Here, I briefly describe a similar proposal known as Public Employment Services (PES) that falls into the broader category of active labor market policies.

Forstater (1998, 1999), Mitchell and Wray (2005), Mitchell and Muysken (2008), and Wray (1998, 2007a, 2007b) have argued that the government should promote full employment through direct job creation and have proposed the implementation of PES programs. Why? Long-term unemployment and underemployment may be due to skills mismatch or to problems with the individuals who are unemployed, in which case the solution is job brokerage or training (chapter 17). But if the problem is job shortage, then improving the match between job seekers and vacancies, as well as training, will not do much. In this case, only direct job creation by an employer of last resort that can offer an infinitely elastic demand for labor can ensure full employment. This is the only way to ensure that everyone who wants to work will be able to obtain a job. Only the government can do this. PES is a theoretically solid proposal that provides a mechanism to ensure full employment with price stability.

PES is essentially a fixed price (the public sector wage)/floating quantity (public sector employment) system that acts as a countercyclical mechanism and as a buffer stock program: when the private sector downsizes in recessions, workers who lose their jobs can find a job in PES. And when aggregate demand increases, these workers are hired again by the private sector. The system can be implemented in a variety of ways, depending on circumstances. Under this scheme, the government pledges to hire anyone willing to work at a basic public sector living (i.e., decent) salary, and the wage bill is paid for by deficit expenditure. But the program does not replace either private sector or other public sector employment.

Authors who propose a PES program argue that this service does not replace unemployment with underemployment and that it is not inflationary.[1] PES programs contribute to maintaining full employment with inflation control. When private sector demand is high enough to cause wage–price pressures, governments can manipulate fiscal and monetary policies (preferably the former, as argued in chapter 12) to reduce them. The resulting increase in PES employment indicates the degree of private

---

[1]   Some have argued that PES programs cannot be implemented because they would become unmanageable; that corruption would make them fail; that useful (i.e., productive) jobs for all workers would be impossible to find; and that they are too expensive. Mitchell and Wray (2005) address these criticisms. A properly designed PES system would mitigate or eliminate these problems. The success of a PES program depends on how it is designed and implemented, especially the mechanisms for accountability.

sector slack that is necessary to solve the distributional struggle that causes inflationary pressures.

PES programs are not inflationary, because public employment may be directed toward public works such as infrastructure revitalization that might lead to higher productivity growth in the private sector. This system can help diminish inflationary bottlenecks, as workers in it are available to the private sector. Therefore, in the view of its proponents, an economy can both have stable prices and eliminate unemployment. They also argue that workers' productivity will increase because workers taking part in the PES program will gain skills and knowledge. Workers engaged in the PES program can provide goods and services that markets do not provide, or that are too expensive for poor households (e.g., child and elderly care, tutoring, public safety); small-scale public infrastructure provision or repair (e.g., clean water and sewage projects, roads); or low-income housing.[2] Many of these activities would contribute to the decline of the informal sector as workers get integrated into formal employment, gaining protection by the labor laws. Jobs created in these programs are labor intensive, requiring little capital equipment. Finally, and somewhat ironically, PES can be viewed as a mechanism that contributes to enhancing the flexibility of the labor market: it is a *reserve army of the employed*, not of the unemployed!

---

[2]   India's National Rural Employment Guarantee Act, which guarantees 100 days of employment a year for at least one adult in every rural household, is an example of a scheme designed to help the poorest and most vulnerable (Felipe and Hasan 2006, chapter 5). The program is countercyclical with the agricultural season. One possible problem in very large countries is that, if they are net food importers, upward pressure might arise on domestic prices (people would eat more and probably better). Argentina's *Plan Jefes y Jefas* is another example. In the aftermath of the economic crisis, Argentina created a program that guarantees a job for poor heads of households. The program successfully created 2 million new jobs for poor families, and provided needed services and free goods to poor neighborhoods. Under this program, workers produce, among other things, clothing and furniture sold in formal markets (Wray 2007b). See Kaboub (2007) for a PES plan for Tunisia.

15

Can *Competitiveness* and *Globalization* Deliver Inclusiveness and Full Employment?

A s I noted in the preface, globalization has thrown development economics into a quagmire. Often arguments in recent growth debates are framed in the context of *competitiveness* (especially when the speaker or writer wants to appeal to policy makers). This is very problematic because while in the business world the term "competitiveness" has a clear meaning—a firm that is not competitive will lose market share and eventually will go out of business—its counterpart at the aggregate level (a nation) might be a "can of worms." In this chapter, I will elaborate on some of the implications of competitiveness and globalization, particularly on the policy prescription that developing countries should adopt a liberal policy stance.

At the level of the firm, competitiveness is a question of competition among individual companies, that is, about the mechanisms that help more productive and efficient companies expand and take market share from the less productive ones, which then go out of business or become more efficient. The most effective way for policy makers to help individual firms to increase productivity is to create the conditions in each sector for fierce but fair competition among all participating firms. This means that policy makers in an economy can help speed up growth by enacting regulations that support more competition in each sector and by removing factors that obstruct competition. When government actions stand in the way of competition through policies that distort it and render it less intense, then inefficient companies are not pressured to change. Poor countries, in general, have in place much more severe market-distorting measures than developed countries have.

This usage of the term "competitiveness" is meaningful and legitimate. It requires, however, that one believe that the end result of competition, namely that uncompetitive firms will end up going out of business while the competitive ones will flourish, indeed happens and improves the welfare of society, resulting in not only a bigger national income but also higher employment. Although individual firms may become more productive by adopting less labor-intensive processes and shedding staff, the combined impact of reinvesting their larger surpluses back into the economy will be higher aggregate demand.

However, competitiveness must have a very different meaning at the aggregate or national level, simply because a country cannot go out of business (Krugman 1996). Competitiveness is often a term politically loaded with a negative element of nationalism, conveying the message that nations are in competition with each other in a globalized world. The "competitiveness objective" is achieved by assembling workers and employers as a "national team" with the objective of increasing profits because workers will also benefit from it. Thus, if employers demand concessions from workers (in the form of, for example, labor market flexibility), these ought to be endorsed. This objective often translates into policies that amount to reductions in wage costs and greater flexibility in production. The heralded normative goal of competitiveness, at times being pursued with an ideological zeal, has put enormous pressure on workers. In the words of Barbara Bergman "the world labor market is not a very cheery place to compete in" (Berglund and Vernengo 2004, 8). The consequence is that a great deal of anxiety is being felt all over the world because the situation is possibly leading to a "race to the bottom", in which globalization is forcing workers to compete to attract capital by accepting lower wages.[1] For example, the switch away from the old quota system under World Trade Organization (WTO) rules has allowed buyers to move to what has become known as "reverse bidding," where factories in different countries compete for orders by offering the lowest price. The emphasis on costs, productivity, and labor market reform toward achieving greater flexibility in the labor market seems to be driving economic policy in many countries.[2] Wage restraint and limitations on social expenditures (e.g., reduction and even elimination of workers' benefits, such as unemployment

---

[1]   Rodrik (1999) discusses the impact of globalization on labor, in particular: (i) how globalization affects unskilled labor as it becomes more substitutable; (ii) how labor standards (e.g., compliance with the International Labour Organization standards) affect labor costs, comparative advantage, and foreign direct investment; and (iii) the role of national governments in developed countries in sheltering domestic society from external risks.

[2]   As I noted in chapter 6, unit labor costs are often used as a measure of competitiveness. It is easy to show (Felipe 2007) that unit labor costs are simply the labor share in value added; hence, increases/decreases in unit labor costs are not just technical issues. Unit labor costs embody the "social relations" of production that affect the distribution of income between the social classes. Under this view, a more competitive economy is that with a lower labor share or where the latter does not grow or even declines.

subsidies or minimum wages) are seen as necessary conditions for improved economic performance. Once again, this is inconsistent with the pursuit of inclusive growth. Felipe and Hasan (2006) analyzed the labor markets of five Asian countries—the People's Republic of China (PRC), India, Indonesia, the Philippines, and Viet Nam—and concluded that the seemingly rigid labor codes of these countries are not the culprit for their relatively high unemployment and underemployment. No matter how rigid these codes may seem on paper, the reality of these countries is that labor laws are systematically violated. Unemployment and underemployment in Asia have a variety of causes; labor market rigidity may only be one, perhaps small, reason.[3]

Advocates of globalization and of national competitiveness as a way to understand today's world and policy making often appeal to the principle of comparative advantage to rationalize the need to restructure labor markets with a view to making them more flexible, and to adopt a liberal policy stance. For example, Sachs and Warner (1995) and World Bank (2002) present empirical evidence that indicates that countries that liberalize more (i.e., the globalizers) grow faster, despite Chang's (2002) arguments that today's developed countries used industrial, trade, and technology policies extensively. The policies that these countries used "are almost the opposite of what the present orthodoxy says they employed 'and currently recommends that the currently developing countries should also use'" (Chang 2002, 19). "When they were in catching-up positions, the NDCs [Now Developed Countries] protected infant industries, poached skilled workers and smuggled contraband machines from more developed countries, engaged in industrial espionage, and willfully violated patents and trademarks. However, once they joined the league of the most developed nations, they began to advocate free trade and prevent the outflow of skilled workers and technologies; they also became strong protectors of patents and trademarks. In this way, the poachers appear to have turned game-keepers with disturbing regularity" (Chang 2002, 64; also Reinert 2007). And likewise, Thirlwall and Pacheco-López (2008) show that the statistical evidence does not support the view that trade liberalization unambiguously benefits countries. In related previous work, these authors studied the effect of trade liberalization on 17 Latin American countries during the period 1977–2002. They found that "in the aftermath of trade liberalisation, growth performance did improve in the majority of countries, but at the expense of trade balance deterioration. For some countries, the growth was not sustainable; for others it was sustainable only by financing larger trade or current account deficits. In the vast majority of cases, the trade-off

---

[3] In an analysis of Taipei,China's labor market, Lee (2007) also argues that the increasing labor market legislation in the country does not alone necessarily create unemployment. What matters is the way employers respond to this increasing legislation.

between growth and the trade balance did not improve as a result of liberalization, but deteriorated" (Pacheco-López and Thirlwall 2007, 481).

The global experience with trade liberalization over the last 50 years is that the most successful globalizers among developing countries (e.g., the Republic of Korea; Taipei,China; Malaysia; Thailand; the PRC) adopted institutional arrangements that did not conform to the standard recommendations, i.e., to eliminate quantitative restrictions and other administrative measures on trade and lower import tariffs. Rodriguez and Rodrik (2001) have analyzed the studies that supposedly support the argument that reduced tariff barriers lead to economic growth and find that it is not compelling. See also Felipe and Vernengo (2002), and Samuelson (2004, 135), who criticizes those who use standard trade theory to "educate and correct warm-hearted protesters who are against globalization."[4] Neither these authors nor I advocate that developing countries erect trade barriers and declare that protection is necessary to industrialize. Our argument is that history shows that today's developed countries, as well as the countries that have succeeded in the last couple of decades, did not pursue the path that developing countries are asked to follow.

Indeed, the principle of comparative advantage is probably inadequate to explain what we observe in the real world. In the words of Cohen (1998, 34): "History has shown itself to be cruel in this respect. The idea that trade is a factor of self-fulfillment in all places and at all times is theoretically naïve and historically false." What is the problem? While I believe that nobody would disagree with the general principle (to which I subscribe) that *trade is good*, the root of many economists' quasi-obsession with the principle of comparative advantage (and its modern versions) is the underlying idea that the market mechanism will balance trade and that the gains from trade outweigh the adjustment costs (e.g., unemployment). If, however, international trade were based, for example, on having an absolute advantage (rather than a comparative advantage), the conclusion would be that trade does not make all nations equally competitive, and, perhaps, some sort of managed trade, selective protection, tariffs, or export subsidies could be considered. Skarstein (2007), for example, argues that developing countries do not have a comparative advantage in the trade of agricultural goods, and that they have an *absolute disadvantage* in the trade of both agricultural and industrial goods. Therefore, further liberalization of agricultural trade will harm rather than help the poorest countries (Box 15.1).

---

[4]   As Rodrik (2008) points out, the outward orientation measures that the successful countries implemented generated supply incentives for new tradable activities without removing the protection for the existing ones. A huge advantage of the Asian model of liberalization, Rodrik argues, is that it protects employment in the transition to a new long-run equilibrium.

Box 15.1. Globalization and the Myth of Free Trade

Many observers are skeptical that financial globalization has benefited growth in developing countries (e.g., Rodrik and Subramanian [2008]). This is because it is not clear how the levels of production and employment are affected once a country opens to international competition. Hence the following question arises: Is laissez-faire the best way to participate in international trade, or is some degree of state support and management preferable?

Conventional theory concludes that neither technological backwardness nor high costs are ultimately a disadvantage in international trade. The reason is that real exchange rates will always move in such a way as to make all trading partners equally competitive, so that no country will suffer persistent trade deficits or enjoy persistent trade surpluses. However, this conclusion does not fit the reality. Where does the problem lie? Shaikh (1996) argues that the problem is the theory upon which these results are based, namely, the principle of comparative cost, which is inadequate to explain the real world. The reality is that globalization has worked as would be expected from the point of view of the classical theory of competitive advantage, according to which it should favor in general, the developed nations.

Conventional economic theory concludes that trade and financial liberalization bring in benefits such as growth and technical change. Initial dislocations are temporary. From a policy point of view, the best path to economic development is to open a country to the world market. These claims, however, are based on two important premises underlying the model: (i) that free trade is regulated by the principle of comparative costs, and (ii) that free competition leads to full employment in every nation.

The principle of comparative costs states that a nation always gains from trade if it exports the goods that it produces relatively more cheaply at home in exchange for those that it can get more cheaply abroad. To support this *normative* claim, the premise of comparative costs is supplemented by a *positive* claim: in free trade, a nation's terms of trade will always move in such a way as to eventually make the values of exports and imports equal. This follows from the following two propositions: (i) the terms of trade fall when a nation runs a trade deficit, and (ii) the trade balance improves when the terms of trade fall. The argument also assumes that no overall job loss is generated by any of these adjustments. This is important because even automatically self-balancing trade would not necessarily lead to gains for the nation as a whole. These claims apply equally to developed and developing nations. Therefore,

continued on next page

Box 15.1 (continued)

no nation needs to fear trade for lack of competitiveness: free trade will make each nation equally competitive in the world market. The problem with these propositions is that they do not seem to be supported by the empirical evidence. The reality is that persistent imbalances are the norm across the world, and there is no automatic tendency toward full employment.

The theory of comparative advantage upon which the Hecksher-Ohlin (H-O) model is based differs from the model explained above, but takes it for granted, along with the notion that full employment prevails. This theory locates differences in national comparative costs in differences in factor endowments. The theory has two important conclusions. First, in free trade, nations with capital-intensive factor endowments will have lower comparative costs in capital-intensive goods. And second, international trade will tend to equalize real wages and profit rates across countries.

Two standard approaches have tried to deal with the deficiencies of these theories. The first one is to argue that the basic predictions of the theory are supposed to hold over the long run. However, Rogoff (1996) estimated that this long run is about 75 years or longer. The second major reaction to the deficiencies of standard trade theory has been to modify some of its assumptions. Particularly, the new trade theories introduce increasing returns to scale and imperfect competition in the H-O framework. This way, the new theories can reach the conclusion that trade openness is not always good. What modifies the results of the standard models? It is the introduction of intra-industry trade, economies of scale, the composition of trade, or differences in knowledge or technology. All of these give rise to exceptions to the standard results, which in turn provide some room for state intervention in certain strategic sectors and certain strategic activities, such as research and development. The problem, however, is that even those who have developed the new trade theories are "cynical about the likelihood that subtle arguments for intervention can be translated into productive policies in the real world" (Krugman 1996, 20). Hence, for practical purposes, even those who know well the deficiencies of the standard theory end up advocating its results.

The standard theory of international trade emphasizes mutual gains from trade under the hypothesis that constant returns to scale lead to a convergence of growth rates. However, the introduction of increasing returns to scale, standard in models of cumulative causation à la Myrdal (1957), changes the perspective of adjustment by introducing the possibility of increasing divergence in comparative costs and in growth rates.

Myrdal (1957) argued that if two countries open to international trade, the one with a more developed manufacturing industry will capture cumulative advantages deriving from the expansion of the market for its products and from the resulting reduction of its production costs, inhibiting the development of the same manufacturing activities in the less advanced country. This idea goes back to the works of the classical economists, Adam Smith and David Ricardo particularly (Box 15.2).

Box 15.2. The Classical Theory of Competitive Advantage

Shaikh (1996) argues that the problem with the standard theory and the new trade models is that they are wrong in their own terms: the principle of comparative costs is flawed even under competitive conditions. Against this, Shaikh argues that the classical theory of competitive advantage does a much better job at explaining the reality, namely, that the world economy has significant and permanent imbalances, and that not all countries benefit equally from trade. The classical theory of competition of Smith and Ricardo argues that relative prices of international goods, and hence a nation's terms of trade, are regulated in the same way as relative national prices. In both cases, high-cost producers lose out to low-cost ones, and high-cost regions (nations) tend to suffer trade deficits that will tend to be covered by corresponding capital inflows (borrowing). In this theory, no mechanism exists that will automatically make all regions (nations) equal. Persistent imbalances are a normal state of affairs, and trade does not make all nations equal.

The classical theory of competitive advantage is based on the classical theory of competition, where firms utilize different strategies and tactics (including price cutting and cost reduction) to hold market shares. Classical theory argues that this real competition regulates trade between nations and regulates trade within a nation in the same way, that is, through the law of absolute costs (firms with higher unit costs of production suffer an absolute competitive disadvantage). This means that the regions with higher costs will have trade deficits that have to be financed.

How does this theory extend these results to trade between nations? A country's international terms of trade are simply international common-currency relative prices. Therefore, they will be regulated as any other relative price, by relative real costs, and the terms of trade will not adjust to eliminate trade imbalances unless relative real costs adjust. These depend on real wages and productivity (which are affected by international trade) as well as by other social and

continued on next page

Box 15.2 (continued)

historical determinants. The corollary is that under *unregulated trade* countries that have a competitive disadvantage will suffer trade deficits.

The above implies that trade liberalization will mostly benefit firms of the developed countries since they are the most technologically advanced. If firms in developing countries are not given time to prepare themselves for trade liberalization they will succumb, and developing countries will remain stuck as providers of cheap labor and cheap natural resources. The policy implication of the classical approach is that there is significantly more room for government regulation of trade and industrial policy than is contained in the new endogenous growth models.

The win–win theory of globalization—workers in poor countries getting rich through trade and then buying products from rich countries—just isn't working. This indicates that at least part of the failure to achieve inclusive growth may be attributed to the liberalization embraced by many countries recently. Of particular significance in this regard is trade liberalization, involving the reduction of tariff and nontariff barriers. For example, in preparing for WTO membership, the PRC lost about 50 million jobs from public and collective enterprises in an effort to raise the efficiency of such entities. Fortunately, some of these ideas have been formalized in the new O-ring theory of development (Kremer 1993), which has implications for trade theory and the pattern of specialization (Box 15.3).

Under the circumstances described in Box 15.3, the rich and skilled nations will produce "advanced" and "high-value" goods (or the final stages of a process in a global value chain), while the poor nations will produce raw materials (primary production in general) and "low-value" goods. This is also consistent with Lall's (2000) claim that export structures tend to be *path-dependent* and difficult to change (and with the Product Space, chapter 10), which has important implications for growth and development. Indeed, trade patterns are much less responsive to changing factor prices than is commonly assumed. Export structures and trade patterns in general are the outcome of a long, cumulative process of learning, agglomeration, increasing returns, institution building, and business culture. This means that the world's pattern of specialization and trade is, fundamentally, *arbitrary*: what each country produces is the result of history, accidents, and past government policies, and it is not dictated by comparative advantage given by tastes, resources, and technology (also, Thirlwall and Pacheco-López [2008]).

Box 15.3. The O-Ring Theory of Development

Why are wage and productivity differentials between the industrialized nations and developing countries so large? Michael Kremer (1993) put forward a theory to answer this and other related questions. An O-ring is a donut-shaped rubber seal. The malfunctioning of one such seal caused the explosion of the Challenger space shuttle in 1986. The shuttle had cost billions of dollars, required the cooperation of hundreds of teams, and combined a considerable number of components. All this joint effort was lost because one seal failed to function properly. Kremer applied the O-ring metaphor to explain the large differences in income between developed and developing countries. The implications of his theory seem to contradict a great deal of conventional wisdom, especially regarding the theory of comparative advantage.

Kremer argued that production is often the result of a series of tasks, for example, on an assembly line. These tasks can be performed at different levels of "skills," which refers to the probability of completing successfully the task. For the final product or service to be successfully made or delivered, every single task must be completed correctly. This implies that the value of each worker's efforts depends on the quality of all other workers' efforts. Kremer's theory explains why workers of similar skills have strong incentives to *match* together, i.e., highly skilled workers will attempt to work with other highly skilled workers, and low-skilled workers with other low-skilled workers. Highly skilled workers complement each other, giving rise to increasing returns to skills and even higher productivity; and unskilled workers, when they match together, lower each others' productivity even more.

The model has important implications for both economic development and labor economics. It explains, for example, why highly skilled workers, such as surgeons from India or the Philippines, want to migrate to the advanced countries, giving rise to brain drain. They will be much more productive after they have migrated, even though their individual skills remain the same. Migration allows them to match up with the skilled labor force of the developed country. Conventional economic theory would suggest that as surgeons are a scarce factor of production in India, compared with, say, the United States (US), their marginal products and pay would be commensurately higher than those of their US counterparts. In fact, their wage rates are much lower.[a] I will elaborate upon this issue in chapter 17.

---

[a] Olson (1996) argues that newly arrived immigrants have approximately the same level of human capital they had before they migrated. The difference is the new institutions and public policies in the new host country, which determine the opportunities that the newly arrived workers confront. The empirical evidence shows that these new migrants receive salaries in the US that are 55% of the salary of native-born Americans of the same age, sex, and years of schooling. This implies that new immigrants from countries where per capita incomes are only one-tenth or one-fifth as large as in the US have a wage more than half as large as comparable American workers. He concludes: "profit-maximizing firms would not have hired these migrants if they did not have a marginal product at least as large as their wage" (Olson 1996, 17).

continued on next page

Box 15.3 (continued)

Financial capital will also flow toward the richest countries since increasing returns imply that the rate of return is higher where it is already abundant. The model is also consistent with the evidence that rich countries specialize in the production of complicated products; that firms are larger in industrial countries; and that firm size and wages are positively correlated.

Differences in product quality are associated with differences in workers' skills. This explains why Italian bicycle manufacturers can compete with their counterparts from the People's Republic of China despite the difference in labor costs. The matching story also offers an explanation of income differences among countries. A small difference in workers' skills leads to a proportionally larger difference in wages and output, so wages and productivity differentials between countries with different skill levels are enormous.

Arguably, O-ring effects also exist across firms. Suppose one firm builds roads and another one automobiles. The additional value to drivers of an improvement in the quality of cars most likely will be smaller if the roads happen to be of poor quality, and vice versa. When tasks are performed sequentially (as in global value chains), highly skilled workers will perform the tasks at the later, more complex stages of production—which explains why poor countries have higher shares of primary output in GDP—and workers will be paid more in industries with high-value inputs. Also, under sequential production, countries with highly skilled workers specialize in products that require expensive intermediate goods, and countries with low-skill workers specialize in primary production. In other words, nothing is natural about the international pattern of specialization: comparative advantage in primary goods, manufactures, and services is itself endogenously determined, or, in the words of Easterly (2002, 161): "Comparative advantage in agriculture and manufactures is itself manufactured."

Finally, the problem with investing in education in a developing country can be phrased in terms of the question, "How much will my earnings increase after I become a doctor?" According to the old neoclassical model, poor countries have low levels of human capital. If this were the key problem, the educated in developing countries should receive higher incomes than the educated in the developed world. This is not the case and, in fact, well-educated people from developing countries often migrate. Why? According to the O-ring theory, the increase will depend on how successful I am at matching up with other doctors as well as with other skilled professionals such as pharmacists and nurses. The probability of a successful match is a function of how much education everyone else is getting. All this will work well in a country where

continued on next page

Box 15.3 (continued)

a lot of people are highly educated, in which case the probability of matching up with other people with high skills is high. In other words, from a personal point of view, investing in school is worthwhile in a developed country; but the incentives to do so are not present in developing countries where there are not so many skilled workers. Naturally, for the developing country, this individual decision has devastating effects: no single individual will find it valuable to attend school. And as Easterly (2002, 160) remarks, "the situation is even worse if skills are complementary to the general state of knowledge in that nation . . . Even if knowledge leaks, the value of being educated is much less if there is not much knowledge to leak." The result is that "even if the workers do go to school in a low-knowledge society, the nation will stay impoverished" (Easterly 2002, 160).

This view, therefore, may appear to place a question mark on the chances that developing countries have for development by hooking on to so-called international global value chains (GVCs; Box 15.4 on the theory of GVCs). Indeed, it may be argued that GVCs force developing countries to specialize in the low-value-added production activities (e.g., assembly) based on low wages (as part of an export-led growth strategy, chapter 16). However, in Box 15.5 on the PRC's GVCs and Box 15.6 on India's GVCs, I argue that these two countries have benefited enormously from these arrangements. Perhaps the success of these two large economies lies in their ability to link many of their firms to a large number of international GVCs so that, at some point, a virtuous cycle develops between participating in GVCs and economic diversification. Evidence is still scant, but it points toward a significant increase in vertical intra-industry trade in Asia, fostered by foreign direct investment. This has created a sophisticated production network in developing Asia, which is enabling these economies to catch up through technology transfer.[5] Intra-industry trade in emerging Asia primarily reflects greater vertical specialization that exploits the fact that different countries contribute to different stages of production (Ito and Shibata 1996). This is contributing to the building of a production network targeting foreign markets.[6]

---

[5]   For reference, in 2006 intraregional trade represented about 41% of total trade in Asia.

[6]   How much do PRC workers earn from their participation in GVCs? It has been estimated that when an iPod is sold in the US for $299, only $4 remain in the PRC in the hands of the assemblers, and about $160 goes to the American companies that design, transport, and retail iPods (*The Economist* 2008d).

Box 15.4. Global Value Chain Theory

Global value chain (GVC) theory, developed in the 1990s (see, for example, Gereffi [1996]), addresses the increasing diversification among developing countries based on geographic specialization. One of the key drivers of structural transformation in recent decades has been the globalization of foreign direct investment, trade, manufacturing, and, increasingly, innovation. Within this context, the fast-growing economies of East and Southeast Asia, along with the People's Republic of China, have developed their manufacturing exports considerably, leading to a structural shift from agriculture and simple commodity production to high-technology manufactured exports. Much of this development has occurred within so-called GVCs, sometimes called international production networks, which link advanced buyers in the developed economies to manufacturing suppliers in Asian countries.

GVC analysis is a way of looking at interfirm, buyer–supplier relations that cross international boundaries and allow developing countries to participate in producing goods and services that are then supplied to the more advanced countries. GVCs enable firms in developing nations to engage in structural transformation by accessing international export markets for manufactured goods, increasing domestic economies of scale in production, and climbing the technology ladder. Within a typical GVC, leading firms located in the developed countries convert an idea (or a research output) into a new product design with an associated manufacturing process. This manufacturing process is then located across several tiers of countries, with cost advantages to the end customer who, more often than not, is located in the advanced industrialized countries. Firms in lower-income countries typically carry out the basic assembly processes using cheap labor, while middle-income countries carry out manufacturing and process innovation (and increasingly product improvement and incremental design), and firms in the advanced countries carry out marketing, research, and new product design. Firms from developing countries initially plug in to the chain according to their particular level of skill and capability. However, successful firms move up the chain and sometimes across to other chains, depending on their performance, strategy, and capability.

In theory, GVCs offer a way for local enterprises in developing countries to engage in international markets at their own level of capability. In practice, securing an initial order is often extremely difficult and only firms with proven experience are likely to win major contracts. Entry into GVCs is easiest when an agglomeration of local buyers and manufacturers already exists, so that newcomers can learn from others through imitation. Sometimes, new entrants

continued on next page

Box 15.4 (continued)

emerge as spin-offs from existing local firms or from subsidiaries of multinational corporations with which they establish new GVC linkages. For countries and firms outside successful clusters, accessing GVCs can be difficult. For firms in very poor countries with little engagement or prior experience in GVCs, especially those based on high technology, entry is particularly difficult. Potential newcomers confront highly organized systems capable of continuous cost reduction, quality improvements, and new product generation.

GVC theory identifies three key factors in development: (i) the spread of industrialization across large areas of the Third World, (ii) export-oriented industrialization, and (iii) the increasing geographic specialization and the search for export niches by different countries. This theory is the modern version of the New International Division of Labor theories that flourished in the 1980s, according to which core capital relocates low-wage phases of manufacturing to developing countries. This has led to the creation of a myriad of networks of labor and production processes around the world whose end result is a finished commodity (e.g., a shirt, a pair of jeans).

From the point of view of the analysis in this book, the key question is, what are the implications of GVCs for development? The idea underlying this "model" of development is that countries have to acquire a niche in the global economy as part of a GVC. According to this view, countries specialize in the different phases of production: low-skilled labor-intensive, high-skilled labor-intensive, capital-intensive, technology, marketing and design, etc. The key aspect is that each of these steps yields a different contribution to the final product. Countries interested in belonging to a GVC should be able to attract those phases of the chain where they could succeed. For the developing countries, these tend to be the low-skilled labor-intensive phases. Often developing countries find themselves competing for these phases by offering tax breaks and a variety of perks to the multinational companies (the agents of development in this model) that own the chain. The bottom line is that, "development strategies should focus on creating a local institutional and infrastructural environment conducive to 'technological upgrading and integrated industrial production', e.g., increasing the level of labour's skills, providing adequate transportation and communications infrastructure, developing appropriate supporting industries, finding the right balance of government regulations, and so on" (Robinson 2002, 1053).

Does integration into a GVC offer realistic prospects for development, or simply perpetuate a hierarchy under which it is very difficult for companies in

continued on next page

Box 15.4 (continued)

developing countries to move up? To start, recall that GVCs lead to specialization based on comparative advantage. However, as noted in the section on *Comparative Advantage and Diversification* in chapter 10, recent research by Imbs and Wacziarg (2003) suggests that at low levels of income per capita, economies tend to diversify and subsequently, as their income rises, they then specialize. This means that if GVCs are a tool for development, then policy makers have to monitor where their countries are in the chain and induce the shift higher up in the global chain.

The empirical evidence is unclear, and probably experiences vary among countries. Research by Michael Hobday (1995a, 1995b) on the "Asian tigers" indicates that a key component of the success of these economies was their integration in GVCs, especially in electronics. The process, though, was not easy and involved progressive and slow learning. Hobday (1995a, 1188) has described in detail how East Asian firms climbed the ladder by slowly learning:

> East Asian latecomers did not leapfrog from one vintage of technology to another. On the contrary, the evidence shows that firms engaged in a painstaking and cumulative process of technological learning: a hard slog rather than a leapfrog. The route to advanced electronics and information technology was through a long difficult learning process, driven by the manufacture of goods for export.

Kim (1997, 129) described Hyundai's efforts to produce a car after it had purchased the foreign equipment, hired expatriate consultants, and signed licensing agreements with foreign firms as follows:

> Despite the training and consulting services of experts, Hyundai engineers repeated trials and errors for fourteen months before creating the first prototype. But the engine block broke into pieces at its first test. New prototype engines appeared almost every week, only to break in testing. No one on the team could figure out why the prototypes kept breaking down, casting serious doubts even among Hyundai management, on its capability to develop a competitive engine. The team had to scrap eleven more broken prototypes before one survived the test. There were 2,888 engine design changes . . . Ninety seven test engines were made before Hyundai refined its natural aspiration and turbocharger engines . . . In addition, more than 200 transmissions and 150 test vehicles were created before Hyundai perfected them in 1992.

Box 15.5. Technological Catching Up in the People's Republic of China's Global Value Chains

In 1992, about 20% of the PRC's exports occurred through global value chains (GVCs) via subsidiaries of multinational companies (MNCs) located in the People's Republic of China (PRC). For imports, the share was 35%. By 2003, the corresponding figure was 55% for exports and 39% for imports. Other exports from the PRC occur within GVCs through subcontracting links between overseas buyers and locally owned PRC subcontractors. The evidence suggests the PRC has done a great deal of impressive catching up, but has a long way to go.

Technological upgrading in the PRC's GVCs is considerable, and has occurred with great speed and through a wider variety of channels than hitherto seen within other Asian countries. Unlike the newly industrialized economies (and the Southeast Asian countries), the PRC boasts an enormous internal market that foreign firms are keen to enter and exploit. MNCs need to transfer their manufacturing and, increasingly, technical operations to the PRC to lower their costs and compete with other MNCs that have already entered. Upgrading has not only occurred *via* traditional original equipment manufacturer (OEM) and foreign direct investment–led technological development routes but also through foreign investment to serve the local market, the development of local firms servicing the local market, and through some major MNCs investing in research and development (R&D) centers to gain credibility with the PRC authorities to ensure their long-term future in the market.

As McDougall (2006) notes, the growth of electronics exports, the PRC's largest export sector, began when manufacturing plants from Taipei,China, and their suppliers moved plants to the PRC in the 1990s. First, assembly was relocated in the PRC, then the component input industries, and more recently design work. Today, most of the PRC's electronics export industries are supported by local firms making plastic molding and machine tools for manufacturing. For example, Flextronics, a large MNC manufacturer, employs about 41,000 people in the PRC and has hired large numbers of engineers to design the products it assembles. The Flextronics campus in the Pearl River Delta employs about 18,000 people, making cell phones, X-Box games consoles, personal computers, and other hardware in 13 factories covering 149 acres. Another 720,000-square-meter factory is nearing completion. Most essential inputs (e.g., chemicals, components, plastics, and packaging material) are available from thousands of suppliers located within a 2-hour radius of the factory site. Other examples also show that PRC companies vow to transform

continued on next page

Box 15.5 (continued)

the world's most populous nation from an electronics manufacturing center into an innovation center.[a]

Roberts (2006) reports that by 2006 the PRC had about 450 integrated circuit design companies, up from 400 in 2005, 20% of which employed United States (US) "returnees" to the PRC. These are mostly small, homegrown firms and few have annual revenues of more than $50 million. However, they testify to the growing influence of the PRC's design on the electronics industry, reminiscent of design developments in Taipei,China, in the early 1990s. An example is provided by John Yu and David Hu, who began Chipnuts Technology in Shanghai, a spin-off from Apple Corporation. These two individuals accumulated their engineering skills and management knowledge in the US in a leading firm and are now capable of supplying the growing market for chips. In 2005, the PRC consumed about $49 billion of semiconductors, 23% of the world's total. However, today, more than 90% of this supply is imported. The huge scope for local production of semiconductor designs explains the large numbers of design houses now emerging in the country.

McDougall (2006) reports that IBM opened a new software development center and a venture capital fund in 2006. The software center employs about 500 staff to create service-oriented software architectures for IBM customers around the world (e.g., for the insurance and health care industries). The venture capital fund has about $180 million allocated to invest in PRC businesses in the areas of high technology, financial services, biotechnology, and communications.

Virtually all leading US electronics makers are developing strategies to cope with "the PRC factor," which basically means taking advantage of the PRC's low labor, engineering, and design costs in order to compete with other MNCs within the US market—and to gain entry into the PRC domestic market. Engardio and Roberts (2004) examine the case of the US market for telecom networking gear, which until recently was dominated by Cisco. However, 3Com from Massachusetts, a US rival, aims to undermine Cisco's position by selling similar products at very low costs *via* a new joint venture in the PRC. The venture employs about 1,200 engineers and many thousands of manufacturing staff. Its partner, Huawei Technologies, is a telecom giant in the PRC, which gives the 3Com joint venture access to the PRC market as well as to the US market. In telecommunications networking, the PRC's engineering costs are currently about 25% of the US's.

---

a   Data Microelectronics, Vimicro, Spreadtrum Communications Inc., Analogue, SMIC, and Lenovo, are examples of PRC companies developing electronic products with the latest technologies.

continued on next page

Box 15.5 (continued)

Local firms are also rapidly entering the market, imitating the operations of MNCs in the PRC. For example, Semiconductor Manufacturing International Corp., a local chipmaker, now processes 12-inch silicon wafers, only about two generations (or 5 years) behind Intel Corporation, the US leader in the field. Semiconductor Manufacturing International produces chips on a contract basis similar to OEM, mostly for US companies, taking care not to compete directly with its US customers. Roberts (2006) argues that the PRC is only one or two generations behind on chip processes vis-à-vis US and Japanese leaders. These firms are emerging as a result of the PRC's manufacturing strength in semiconductors, much the same way as occurred in Taipei,China, in the late 1980s and early 1990s, with chip designers helping the PRC move up the technology ladder to circuit and systems design, intellectual property, and more-software-intensive activities.

The PRC's local firms are also supplying auto parts to MNCs within the PRC. The Wanxian Group in Hangzhou began as a tiny farm machinery shop in 1969. Today, it is a vast $2.4 billion conglomerate that supplies car manufacturers such as General Motors, Ford, and Volkswagen in the PRC. The Wanxian Group is now opening a $42 million plant with up-to-date American and European testing equipment to keep up with the new models being produced in the PRC. Since 1995, the firm has purchased 10 US auto part makers, acquiring skills, technology, management, and access to overseas markets.

Sleigh and von Lewinski (2006) describe efforts by local firms to go beyond OEM- and original design manufacturer (ODM)–type activities to original brand manufacturer (OBM) and service-led production. The authors stress the growth in the local market in the PRC, where retail sales have grown to more than $827 billion in 2005, a 13% increase on 2004. On the MNC front, R&D centers located in the PRC grew from just one in the early 1990s to more than 750 in 2005. The PRC's overall spending on R&D rose from 1% of GDP in the late 1990s to about 1.5% in 2005 and was forecast to reach 2.5% by 2020 (i.e., $115 billion per annum). Einhorn (2006) shows that foreign firms as diverse as Intel, Google, and Dow Chemicals are increasing their R&D in the PRC. Firms based in the PRC applied for about 130,000 patents in 2004, six times more than in 1995, making the PRC number five globally (Japan applied for 450,000 in 2004 whereas the US applied for 403,000).

As McGregor (2004) illustrates, the largest electronics producer in the PRC is in fact a European firm, Philips of Holland. Philips generated an estimated $2.5 billion in local revenues (i.e., the PRC) in 2004, plus $4.5 billion in

continued on next page

Box 15.5 (continued)

export sales, making it the largest manufacturing exporter in the PRC. Like other electronics giants, it has increasingly outsourced its manufacturing to the PRC (including 100% of its audio products). Philips has 35 joint ventures or wholly owned subsidiaries and more than 60 offices nationwide. The firm has begun integrating some common functions at its ventures into unified platforms under the One Philips principle. The consolidation covers the information technology support unit, a unified human resources management system, financing, training, marketing, and public and government relations.

Like Philips, 35% of MNCs are consolidating operations in the PRC, according to a survey by the Chinese Academy of International Trade and Economic Cooperation completed in early 2006. The survey shows that multinationals have been fine-tuning their management structure. But their methods are somewhat different. Some, such as Japan's Matsushita, put previously independent business units under the umbrella of the company's head office in the PRC. Others, like the Finnish company Nokia, have merged their manufacturing bases.

Globalization and "national competitiveness" have put workers across countries in competition with each other, resulting in employment insecurity, reduced or stagnant wages, and very destructive social pressures. The biggest threat comes, not surprisingly, from Asia, India and the PRC particularly. These countries have an unlimited supply of underemployed workers willing to work for extremely low wages and, at times, under working conditions that violate basic human rights.[7] This is putting tremendous pressure not only on workers from developed countries but also on workers of many other developing countries, especially unskilled workers occupied in the tradable sectors.

But globalization, the increasing integration of the world, is not responsible in itself for this situation. The problem with globalization is the overall context in which it takes place, the policies pursued by many countries, particularly macroeconomic policies, especially those aimed at controlling inflation through restrictive monetary policies (chapters 11 and 12). In many developing countries, external liberalization has caused revenues to fall (this is associated with lower tariff revenues and higher spending on debt service) at a time when globalization calls for increasing social spending. That is, while globalization is forcing some countries to spend more on social services, it is undermining their ability to obtain higher revenues

---

[7] Oxfam (2005) provides a vivid description of the penuries that migrant workers endure in the PRC province of Shenzhen.

Box 15.6. Global Value Chains in India

India is a more recent entrant and has had far less success overall than the People's Republic of China (PRC) in exploiting manufacturing-based global value chains (GVCs) to its advantage. However, in the business process outsourcing (BPO) cluster, India has had considerable success. While this success may not yet be sufficient to absorb a great deal of employment, the country's experience in GVCs has already had major indirect demonstration effects that could alter the entire future path of economic growth and structural transformation in India.

Ramaswamy (2006) provides insights into India's textile and apparel industry, and the ways in which some GVCs in this industry have upgraded technologically in recent years. He provides a series of case studies to show how these GVCs operate from the perspective of the supplier, and shows their attempts to upgrade their production by various means. What is particularly interesting is the use of high-technology facilities in seemingly low-technology industries. For example, the Shirt Company, a large entrepreneurial Indian firm, began in 1984 as a small-scale unit. Today, the firm boasts a turnover of more than $20 million, delivering up to 300,000 pieces per month of various kinds of woven garment. The Shirt Company deploys both Indian and imported fabrics to produce cotton, synthetic, and blended garments. To meet the quality and delivery requirements of its buyers, the company invested in state-of-the-art computer-aided design (CAD) and other high-technology equipment, including a house washing plant, modern steam press, and embroidery units. In Coimbatore in south India, the Shirt Company has built an integrated factory incorporating yarn dyeing, fabric weaving, processing, and garment manufacturing. Buyers include Otto-Versand Group and Esprit in Germany, Nautica Jeans in the United States (US), and Freeman and Pepe Jean in the United Kingdom (UK).

Kaytee Corporation Limited is a knitwear exporter with a turnover of about $15 million. Kaytee supplies buyers in the US such as Wal-Mart and Sears, and in the European Union (EU) companies such as Woolworth, Energie, and Tom Tailor. Kaytee has made efforts to improve the quality, which tends to be poor in India. Vertical integration includes knitting, embroidery, dyeing, and fabric weaving. Kaytee set up a dedicated factory that concentrates solely on producing samples to present to foreign buyers. Kaytee has invested in state-of-the-art CAD/computer-aided manufacturing (CAM) facilities and boasts an in-house lab for fabric testing, and for testing garments for color fastness and shrinkage. Upgrading also includes investments in modern garment-making machinery

continued on next page

Box 15.6 (continued)

and capacity expansion. However, as Ramaswamy (2006) notes from his field interviews: "Labor productivity in India is low relative to [the People's Republic of] China. Indian workers produce 8 shirts per day compared to 24 shirts by a Chinese worker (interview with Premal Udhani, Chairman)."

Arvind Mills Limited (AML) is the world's third-largest manufacturer of denim, with an in-house capacity of 100 million meters a year. AML produces denim cloth, shirting fabric, knit fabric and garments to GVC leaders such as Levi Strauss, Wrangler, and Tommy Hilfiger. The company responded to heavy losses sustained in the 1990s due to oversupply in the world denim market by introducing new specialty products to its denim portfolio (from just 10 in 1998 to 175 in 2003) and by moving up the value chain via forward integration, investing in a modern shirting fabric–making unit in India and an integrated plant in Mauritius. The latter includes a denim and spinning unit and a garment unit plant. Forward integration into garments allows AML to exploit its position in the fabric supplier network within the GVC. In fact, Reebok has begun outsourcing its activities to AML because of its capacity to supply a full package of production activities.

Ramaswamy (2006) points to the many challenges to the further development of GVCs in India. If India wishes to become a major exporter via GVCs, as the PRC is, then local firms will need to acquire the capability to supply lead firms with full packages based on up-to-date technology, and according to strict quality and social and environmental standards. India's poor infrastructure raises costs and restricts contractors' abilities to meet the demands of GVC leaders. Managers of firms in India point to delays in the ports and severe inland road transport problems, which increases the lead time for production and raises costs. Customs clearance difficulties are prevalent and prevent even the most flexible firms from meeting tough delivery schedules: "Meeting delivery dates is like walking on tight rope. Give us good roads and power then we can achieve more exports" (Chairman, The Shirt Company, Personal Interview by Ramaswamy, 2006).

India's BPO sector, despite its small size relative to India's GDP, is important, as its $36 billion in revenues in 2005 represented about 50% of India's total exports. Some examples serve to illustrate the routes toward upgrading from basic call centers and from simple to more complex software. Indian BPO suppliers include OfficeTiger, an outsourcing firm with most of its operations in Chennai. OfficeTiger's employment grew from 1,500 in 2004 to 6,000 in

continued on next page

Box 15.6 (continued)

2006. The firm has grown by broadening its range of services and clients and by establishing operations in the Philippines, the UK, and the US. Recently, OfficeTiger was bought by RR Donnelley, a large US printing firm. OfficeTiger's software is used to change the colors of clothes worn by models in glossy US retailing catalogues (which is much less expensive than paying models and photographers in the US). It designs display advertisements for shops and pizza vendors to place in local yellow pages in the US. One department scrutinizes legal documents. Litigation support for US MNCs such as DuPont is a major product line. This involves analyzing thousands of documents and e-mails for relevance for any particular case. A research and analysis division caters to the US commercial property market, including the generation of hugely complex cash-flow projections to support mortgage applications.

ICICI OneSource has about 7,500 staff. They work on services such as dealing with store-based credit card systems for British retailers and mobile phone service billing systems, again for British customers. The largest Indian BPO firm, Genpact, is also involved in BPO service innovation, offering new kinds of service that go beyond what the client originally outsourced. Some of these services offer profit margins of 25%–30%. Genpact has a joint venture with NDTV, a TV channel, supplying digitization, video editing, and captioning services. Major business opportunities are developing in banking and insurance, which are among the largest clients for the leading Indian firms. Potential also exists in areas such as law and pharmaceuticals. Worldwide spending on legal services is estimated at $250 billion per annum (two-thirds of the market is in the US). So far, only a minuscule amount is outsourced. But because of rising fees, legal firms are exploring outsourcing possibilities (e.g., for drafting patent filings and loan documentation). Forrester, a research firm, estimates that this market alone could employ 35,000 jobs by 2010.

In pharmaceuticals, outsourced clinical trials are increasing (forecast to reach $1 billion per annum by 2010). IGATE Clinical Research offers hospital facilities, large numbers of patients, and Western-trained doctors to encourage foreign firms to conduct their research and trials in India.

These experiences hint at a growing shift from basic call centers and voice-based services to the outsourcing of more and more sophisticated processes. This involves more professional analysis and judgment than standard call center work, and needs to be supported by more highly trained professionals and dedicated computer systems, themselves often developed by the supplier firm in India. Upgrading requires purposeful strategies of corporate leaders,

continued on next page

Box 15.6 (continued)

supported by an increasing skill base of employees and the active development of new overseas outsourcing markets. The most capable and dynamic firms stand to gain the most in this difficult upgrading.

The success of India's software and BPO sector owes to the low use of infrastructure and financial capital as well as low-cost labor, along with the lack of state intervention (Kaka et al. 2006, Schaaf 2005). Widespread use of the English language has been important, as English is India's official language. IBM's departure in the 1950s and the protection of the hardware market led to the development of software skills via "induced innovation" with many local software development programs. For this reason, India learned about information technology (IT) fairly early on. Moreover, India's IT/software/BPO clusters are located near public sector R&D institutes, defense establishments, and software technology parks. This probably helped overcome the infrastructural constraints imposed by ports, roads, power, and airports. Finally, the role of the National Association of Software and Services Companies (NASSCOM) was also important, allowing collective action. NASSCOM already had 850 private sector members in 2002 (accounting for 95% of IT/BPO/software revenues) and worked closely with state governments to represent its members' interests.:

to pay for these services. In chapter 5, I referred to Asia's "food crisis," created by the increase in demand from countries such as the PRC and India, the diversion of corn land in the US for ethanol production, or more structural factors like the neglect of investment in agriculture for decades. But these factors also show that in a globalized world, as countries' policies and trade exchanges have become more intertwined, countries have also become more vulnerable to external shortages and price spikes as they flow around the world. In early 2008, India sharply curbed exports of rice. This disrupted supply chains and led to more inflation and rice hoarding. But did India suffer from a production shortage? No, quite the opposite, production exceeds consumption in India. As a result of India's economic reforms during the past 15 years, the government has eased its control over the rice trade and the country is much more open to the rest of the world. Now farmers and traders are selling to the highest bidder, and rice that before would have been sold domestically is now sold abroad at a much higher price. This then created a shortage in India, which had to import rice at the higher ongoing world price, driving domestic prices up. Therefore, although India's export ban should have eased domestic prices, it did not, because the benchmark price was the international price and Indian traders were not willing to sell in the domestic market at a lower price.

Globalization through trade, investment, migration, dissemination of technologies such as the internet, and regional cooperation can be a powerful force *if* its benefits are widely shared. Today, technology is spreading to emerging markets faster than ever before. However, the empirical evidence does not vindicate, for example, the thesis that financial globalization (essentially understood as increasing liberalization in capital movements) has resulted in higher growth or other benefits. On paper, the appeal of capital mobility is obvious: in the absence of market imperfections, freedom to trade enhances inefficiency, and that is as true of trade in paper assets as it is of trade in wine and textiles. Capital mobility serves, for example, a disciplining function for government policy. And also on paper, the global pooling of financial resources has made it possible for companies in African countries, for farmers in Viet Nam, and for entrepreneurial women in Bangladesh to increase their living standards and to participate in the world in a way that was impossible to people one generation earlier. However, there is very little evidence that higher rates of economic growth follow capital account liberalization. Moreover, the evidence shows that open capital accounts can create very costly problems for developing countries. Rodrik and Subramanian (2008) have looked at the evidence during the last two to three decades and concluded that, "it seems increasingly clear that the benefits of financial globalization are hard to find. Financial globalization has not generated increased investment or higher growth in emerging markets. Countries that have grown most rapidly have been those that rely less on capital inflows." This study corroborates the findings of previous empirical work analyzing the impact of financial liberalization on saving and investment growth (see, for example, Gupta [1987]; Cho and Khatkhate [1990]; Bandiera et al. [2000]; Fry [1997]). This literature questions the alleged benefits of financial liberalization.

Developed and developing countries also have important differences. While today both have similar capacity to access modern technologies, the diffusion of these technologies among developing countries is much slower, and it is much more concentrated among certain groups or geographical regions (e.g., almost three-quarters of the PRC's high-tech trade is concentrated in four regions on the coast; over 50% of India's urban households subscribe to either fixed or mobile telephone services, but only about 6% of the rural households). This is because of intangibles that affect a country's capacity to absorb technology, such as education or the quality of its government.

I close this chapter with Box 15.7, which discusses some myths on the PRC and India and how globalization explains their fast growth.[8]

---

[8] See Morgan Stanley's (2004, 2006) surveys on the PRC and India.

Box 15.7. Some Myths about the People's Republic of China and India

Bardhan (2008) has argued that there are three important myths about how globalization has stimulated the People's Republic of China's (PRC) and India's recent rapid growth. The standard argument, he claims, is that, "decades of socialist controls and regulations stifled enterprise in India and [the People's Republic of] China and led them to a dead end. A mix of market reforms and global integration finally unleashed their entrepreneurial energies. As these giants shook off their 'socialist slumber', they entered the 'flattened' playing field of global capitalism. The result has been high economic growth in both countries and correspondingly large declines in poverty."

Bardhan argues that while this argument has some truth, deeper analysis questions its foundations:

Global integration. In the case of the PRC, the country had already achieved growth rates of about 9% per annum between 1978 and 1993, higher than those achieved by the successful East Asian countries between 1960 and 1980. Regarding poverty, about two-thirds of the decline in extremely poor people between 1981 and 2004 had taken place by the mid-1980s. This large decline was probably related to domestic factors, and not to global competition. What were these factors? (i) a significant increase in agricultural productivity following decollectivization, (ii) a land reform program, and (iii) increased farm procurement prices. In India, market reforms have made the corporate sector more vibrant and competitive, but most of India's economy, and more than 90% of the labor force, lies outside this sector. Likewise, while the business process outsourcing (BPO) industry is doing well in India, it employs no more than 1 million people (Magtibay-Ramos et al. 2008). Regarding poverty, the latest Indian household survey data suggest that the rate of decline slowed somewhat between 1993 and 2005, compared with the 1970s and 1980s. And the percentage of underweight children in India is larger than in sub-Saharan Africa.

The socialist slumber. India's and the PRC's policies have departed significantly from the free-market orthodoxy. For example, both countries practiced protection of "local content" of components in automobiles. One positive result was that workers in the auto parts industry acquired significant skills. While socialist control and regulations inhibited private enterprise, especially in the PRC, the positive legacy of reforms in state-controlled capitalist system has been rather successful. Moreover, the PRC's socialist period provided a

continued on next page

Box 15.7 (continued)

solid foundation for the recent high growth, e.g., wide access to education and health, highly egalitarian land distribution, increased female labor participation, and a system of economic regional decentralization. In both the PRC and India, the state was active in technological development. As we saw above, both the PRC and India have succeeded in exporting more sophisticated products than is usual in countries with similar income per capita.

The role of democracy. The PRC's superior growth vis-à-vis India is not enough to prove that authoritarian regimes are necessary (and/or sufficient) for development. Democratic states have done well (e.g., Costa Rica) and not so well (e.g., the Philippines). The relationship between democracy and development is complex, and testing statistically its relationship with growth is difficult. In any case, democracy has four clear advantages: (i) it is able to prevent catastrophic mistakes such as the PRC's Great Leap Forward; (ii) it puts pressures to share the benefits of development; (iii) it is better able to mitigate social inequalities; and (iv) it provides a better environment for nurturing the development of information technology and related technologies. However, democracy can also hinder development if it turns into populism. This may lead to low investment, particularly in infrastructure. This can also make it difficult to charge user fees for roads, electricity, and irrigation. In the Philippines, a clear case of populist democracy, a new airport in Manila was completed in the early 2000s, but opened to operations partially only recently. In the meantime, passengers have to continue using the old Ninoy Aquino International Airport, arguably the worst airport in the region. At the other extreme is the PRC, where new airports across the country are being opened constantly. The latest is Beijing's state-of-the-art new terminal 3, opened in February 2008. It took 4 years to complete, cost $2.4 billion, and employed the work of 50,000 people. This shows the capacity of the Government of the PRC to formulate and implement policies. Of course, not everything is rosy in the PRC, where complaints about pollution, consumer-product safety, and land acquisitions are abundant.

16

Export-Led Growth or Domestic Demand–Led Growth?

I had to break, once and for all, the vicious cycle of poverty and economic stagnation.

—Park Chung Hee, Republic of Korea's President, 1961–1979

As I noted in chapter 6, countries like the People's Republic of China (PRC), Thailand, or Malaysia have been advised to shift their growth model from one based on export-led growth (ELG) to one based on domestic demand–led growth (DDLG). In this chapter, I elaborate upon this issue by analyzing both growth models and their policy implications, and discuss the possible dilemmas that policy makers face.

How Is Export-Led Growth Usually Understood?

In general, the ELG strategy consists of the encouragement and support of production for exports. The rationale, going back to the classical economists, is that trade is the engine of growth, which can contribute to a more efficient allocation of resources within countries as well as transmit growth across countries and regions. Exports, and export policies in particular, are regarded as crucial growth stimulators. Exporting is an efficient means of introducing new technologies both to the exporting firms in particular and to the rest of the economy, and exports are a channel for learning and technological advancement.[1] In the

---

[1]   In their reassessment of the evidence of the relationship between trade and growth, and in the context of the East Asian miracle, Lawrence and Weinstein (2001) do not find that exporting was a particularly beneficial conduit for fast productivity growth in Japan. On the other hand, they find that imports and lower tariffs did stimulate productivity and argue that the Japanese economy would have grown even faster than it did if it had reduced domestic protection and imported more.

words of Thirlwall (1994, 365): "the growth of exports plays a major part in the growth process by stimulating demand and encouraging savings and capital accumulation, and, because exports increase the supply potential of the economy, by raising the capacity to import."[2] In developing Asia, the Republic of Korea's President Park Chung Hee in the 1960s was probably the first one to try the ELG strategy as a mechanism to break the vicious cycle of poverty and stagnation. The country took advantage of its cheap labor to manufacture shoes and clothes and sold them to consumers in the rich countries. The strategy proved successful. Whether or not it can be emulated by other countries today is a different matter.

Indeed, as a development strategy, the classical belief was that development could be transmitted through trade. This has been confirmed by the experience of some countries that today are among the richest in the world. Traditionally, ELG has been presented as the opposite of import substitution policies, based on closing the economy to imports and encouraging domestic production, which many developing countries followed for years, and which ended up in a dead end. Starting in the 1950s, and for about three decades, many saw import substitution as a crucial element for development, and protectionist policies were adopted in much of the developing world. These policies typically favored the protection of infant industries. Although supporters recognized that import substitution most likely would result in efficiency losses because of protection, they argued that the gains from increasing domestic production and moving down the cost curve would more than offset these inefficiencies. Today, import substitution is associated with government intervention and inefficiency.[3]

In mainstream circles (e.g., Krueger [1997]), ELG is presented as the desirable growth strategy, for it appears to be pursued in a context of laissez-faire. Hence, export promotion strategies are seen as optimal in the sense that they yield an outcome such that the international marginal rate of transformation equals the domestic marginal rate of transformation

---

[2] At the theoretical level, ELG models can be classified into two categories. The first category emphasizes the possibility that export growth may set up a virtuous circle of growth, that is, once a country begins encouraging exports, it is able to maintain its competitive position in world trade and perform continually better relative to other countries. The second category stresses that export growth relieves a country of a balance-of-payments (BOP) constraint on demand (Thirlwall 1994, 365).

[3] Authors like Amsdem (1989) and Wade (1988) have argued that, in the case of Asia, and perhaps with the exception of Hong Kong, China, this is far from the truth: the export-oriented economies of the region were, to a large degree, planned economies with governments exercising enormous control over investment and industrial policy. Most East Asian governments suppressed consumption, restricted foreign access to their markets, and encouraged (and provided tremendous support for) manufacturers to target international markets. The Republic of Korea and Taipei,China, implemented highly protectionist policies, often preventing competition from foreign-produced goods in local markets.

(Meier 1995, 480). Empirically, studies have found that export growth and export levels are highly correlated with output growth.

According to mainstream literature, the potential benefits associated with the ELG strategy vis-à-vis the import substitution strategy are as follows (Meier 1995, 361–63, 479–83):

(i)   the domestic resource cost of earning a unit of foreign exchange tends to be less than the domestic resource cost of saving a unit of foreign exchange;

(ii)   as ELG rests on exogenous world demand, a developing economy can overcome diseconomies of small size. And in general, technology-economic factors (e.g., minimum efficient size of plant, increasing returns to scale, indivisibilities in the production process) imply a superiority of development through export promotion;

(iii)   for being exposed to world competition, firms in the country can increase X-efficiency (i.e., the forces that intensify motivation and result in lower cost curves for the firm);

(iv)   a pro-trade strategy may attract foreign direct investment; and

(v)   ELG contributes more than import substitution to employment creation and improvement in the distribution of income.

What Do Countries Gain by Following an Export-Led Growth Strategy?

Besides the benefits of the ELG strategy discussed in the previous section, another reason, purely macroeconomic, explains countries' desires to pursue an ELG strategy. This is that the authorities of most nations see a surplus on their current-account balance of payments as a sign of success. Therefore, despite the potential problems that an ELG strategy might lead to (e.g., that not all countries can succeed), policy makers in many countries pursue it.

Nations find that by pursuing an ELG policy, rather than policies that stimulate internal effective demand, they can move toward higher employment without inducing domestic inflationary wage demands. With ELG, any latent inflationary (or deflationary) forces can be exported to one's trading partners. This implies that for every successful economy that pursues a mercantilist trade surplus policy there must be other nations that must incur trade deficits and import inflation (or deflation). History is full of episodes where nations scramble for trade, trying to export their own unemployment (e.g., the Great Depression).

After World War II, Germany and Japan, and during the 1980s, Hong Kong, China; the Republic of Korea; Singapore; and Taipei,China, were labeled "economic miracles" because they were able to expand output and employment through ELG. This policy leads to an increase in foreign reserves and increases international creditor status without causing domestic inflation. Today, probably the PRC represents the best example of a successful country following ELG policies. On the other side of the equation, successful ELG economies force trade deficits, possible loss of international reserves, and indebtedness on their trading partners.

Why do many nations see export surpluses as a more powerful tool to stimulate income rather than home investment? An explanation in terms of stylized facts goes as follows: A trade surplus is advantageous, first, because it solves the problem of effective demand and, second, because from a simple accounting viewpoint, a trade surplus represents "foreign investment." This has employment and multiplier effects. Any increase in activity at home most likely induces an increase in imports, so that an increase in income and employment derived from an increase in home investment must be partly offset by a reduction in foreign investment. On the other hand, an increase in the trade surplus due to increasing exports does not reduce home investment, and creates conditions favorable to raising it, as the experience of many Asian countries shows. This means that the two growth models, ELG and DDLG, operate through different channels and lead to different outcomes (Felipe 2003).

The ELG model depends on the willingness of a trading partner to expand its demand so that the country in question can sell its exports. When this happens, the improved export–import relationship of the economy (trade surplus and increase in reserves) leads to the appreciation of the exchange rate. Then, imported goods become cheaper in terms of domestic money, and consequently the real-wage curve will shift upward in the wage–employment space. Note, however, that the real wage rate need not decrease as employment increases. Even though the price of domestic output increases, domestic consumers do not experience inflation in the market basket of goods they purchase, as the cost of living is also affected by lower import prices (because of the exchange rate appreciation). Under these circumstances, there is less pressure to increase money wages as the domestic economy expands, and previously employed workers do not experience a decline in real wages as additional workers are employed, thus promoting social stability.

If, however, the government stimulates domestic spending to increase employment, then the real wage rate will fall as the average price level increases. Although the economy is at less than full employment, it will experience inflation with successive government attempts at increasing employment. And as workers push for cost-of-living adjustments to compensate for the increase in prices, the resulting inflation will exacerbate the problem.

The conclusion is that ELG policies can be expansionary without inducing inflationary pressures for the countries that pursue them. Politically, ELG weakens labor unions' ability and legitimacy to demand higher nominal wages. Domestic demand–led policies can result in expansion but with inflation, and the resulting lower real wages of the previously employed workers may induce further wage–price inflation if workers try to recover their previous real wage rates.

The global effects of the ELG strategy are different: unemployment and inflation are simply being passed on to the trading partners, whose rising trade deficits lead to depreciating exchange rates. For these countries, the resulting higher domestic prices for imports translate into a reduction in the purchasing power of the domestic money–wage rate. Unless they are threatened by unemployment, workers in these nations will demand increases in nominal wages, at least to offset the loss due to the depreciation of the currency. But this will create inflationary pressures. If these nations implement policies to maintain employment while workers demand that their real wages be protected, inflationary tendencies will be exacerbated. This leads to a global situation that could be labeled "competitive growth."

Keynes' (1936) analysis in *The General Theory* (chapter 23 on mercantilism) already warned about the dangers of the view of "competitiveness" as competition among countries[4] (although he did not use such a term). In a world where governments are wary of stimulating domestic spending for fear of unleashing inflationary pressures, many countries see in ELG (certainly in Asia) a desirable alternative path for expanding domestic employment. As Keynes recognized (1936, 338), a "favorable balance [of trade], provided it is not too large, will prove extremely stimulating" to domestic employment, even if it occurs at the expense of damaging employment opportunities abroad. Indeed, Keynes was aware that the domestic employment advantage obtained through ELG "is liable to involve an equal disadvantage to some other country" (1936, 338). When surplus countries pursue an "immoderate policy" (Keynes 1936, 338) of ELG, the unemployment problem of their trading partners becomes worse. These trading partners are then forced to engage in a "senseless *international competition* for a favorable balance which injures all alike" (Keynes 1936, 338–39; italics added). The standard approach for improving a country's trade balance consists in making domestic industries more competitive by either forcing down nominal wages (including fringe benefits) by reducing labor costs, or by devaluating the value of the currency. However, competitive gains obtained by manipulating these nominal variables can only foster further global stagnation and recession as trading partners attempt to regain their competitive edge by inducing similar retaliatory and depressive policies in others (Davidson 2006b).

---

4   This and the next paragraph follow closely Davidson (2006b).

Keynes realized that unless every nation actively undertook public domestic investment to generate full employment, the resulting laissez-faire system of prudent fiscal finance in tandem with a system of free international monetary flows would enable each nation to independently benefit from a policy of ELG even though pursuit of these policies simultaneously by many nations would hurt them all.[5]

Summing up, the ELG strategy encourages nations to settle problems of unemployment and inflation by pushing them off to their trading partners. If all nations act this way, the end result might be a global recession and stagnation. If one nation acts as the engine of growth and continues expanding (despite running trade deficits, e.g., the United States [US]), the trading partners that pursue ELG will experience an economic miracle that may be attributed to their excellent economic policies.

Is a New Development Paradigm Needed?

Since the East Asian financial crisis of the late 1990s erupted, most countries in the region have tried to identify what went wrong that ultimately led to the slowdown in GDP growth rates (Felipe 2003, Felipe and Lim 2005). The issue at stake was, and still is for some countries, what sort of policies and institutional reforms they should implement to resume high and sustained growth.[6] Since the beginning of the crisis, the official view has been that the financial crisis was the consequence of a fundamental flaw in the Asian financial system, in the form of "crony capitalism." During the last few years, a group of economists have been working on a different hypothesis. Thomas Palley (2002) has argued that after several decades of being presented as the optimal growth strategy, the ELG model that the East Asian countries followed has ultimately been found wanting and even harmed the growth prospects of developing countries. Blecker (2002, 2003) also contends that the adoption of a development strategy that relied on high rates of growth of

---

5   It is important to understand Keynes' arguments. During the Great Depression of the 1930s, Keynes discovered important elements of truth in the mercantilist doctrine. The gold standard of the 1930s was responsible for the existence of unemployment, as the only option for countries to counter unemployment was to try to achieve an export surplus, which would lead to an accumulation of gold at the expense of the neighbors. It was in this context, and with the aim of achieving full employment, that he argued that international competition was harmful.

6   According to the Asian Development Bank (2007c, 46), growth declined by an average of 2.5% per year between the two periods 1990–1996 and 2000–2006 in Indonesia, the Republic of Korea, Malaysia, the Philippines, and Thailand, the five countries most directly affected by the 1997–1998 crisis.

manufactured exports was the root cause of the problems, for it led to growing excess capacity, intensifying competitive pressures, and disappointing growth. Kaplinsky (2000) and Ertuk (2001–2002) suggest the possibility of immiserizing growth as a result of the creation of excess capacity in export-oriented manufacturing industries. During the 1990s, too many developing countries entered the more advanced product categories, thus creating excess capacity and fostering falling prices.[7]

These authors argue that the reliance on export growth suffers from a "fallacy of composition." The reason is that if too many countries try, simultaneously, to rely on ELG policies to stimulate growth, the market for developing countries' exports is limited by the capacity of the industrialized nations (Blecker 2002, 2003). If demand in the developed countries stagnates, it translates into overinvestment and excess capacity in the developing countries. As East and Southeast Asian countries became immersed in the financial crisis, the first policy option considered by all of them to resume growth was the ELG strategy. However, the question with this strategy is that the fallacy-of-composition problem has gotten compounded, since during the last decade, the PRC and India have been added into the equation. ELG operates hierarchically with less developed newcomers replacing more maturing export economies as their wages grow. The PRC poses an entirely different problem, for it has a fairly large supply of labor so that it can keep wages very low and, seemingly, for a long time. The argument of these authors is that the effort is doomed to fail because of global demand constraints. In the words of Blecker (2003): "the current emphasis on export-led growth in developing countries is not a viable basis on which all countries can grow together under present structural conditions and macroeconomic policies."[8] Palley (2002) goes further and contends that the ELG model followed by many developing countries during the last few decades was part of the so-called "Washington consensus"

---

[7]   In the early 1980s, Cline (1982) had already asked whether the East Asian growth model could be generalized, taking into account the constraints on international market demand. He concluded that the generalization of the ELG strategy across all developing countries would result in untenable market penetration into industrial countries. Balassa (1989) refuted this view by arguing that competition among the developing countries would be ameliorated by a progressive shift into more capital-intensive exports. Likewise, successful developing-country exporters would tend to increase their imports of skill-intensive manufactures.

[8]   If demand in the developed countries is growing at, let's say, 6% per annum, not *all* developing countries can have their exports grow at 15%. If all simultaneously try, excess industrial capacity will result. Or, put in different terms: "total exports of manufactures from the developing countries can grow faster than domestic demand in the industrialized countries, provided that the former countries take away market share from the domestic producers in the latter" (Blecker 2002, 71).

emphasis on trade liberalization.[9] As a solution, Palley proposes a new development paradigm based on DDLG.

Therefore, the discussion must be taken up whether the Asian countries can still rely on the ELG strategy, or whether, as some other authors have argued, they should start shifting from ELG to DDLG. This discussion has come to the fore again during the financial crisis that started in 2007. By the end of 2008, many voices argued that ELG could be a trap for many Asian countries, as external demand in the US and Europe will decline. The policy prescription, therefore, is for these countries to stimulate domestic consumption and help the global economy as they help themselves. Domestic demand can be stimulated by cutting taxes and/or increasing government spending. Likewise, investment in health care can boost consumption, as consumers would have to worry less about paying for medical expenses. And many countries in the region have rules and taxes that favor investment at the expense of consumption. Are these policy prescriptions meaningful?

Palley (2002) has indicated that the emphasis on ELG has damaged the economies of developing countries in several ways. First, it has prevented the development of domestic market growth. Second, it has put developing countries in a "race to the bottom" among themselves. Third, it has put workers in developing countries in conflict with workers in developed countries. Fourth, it has stoked a relationship between ELG and financial instability by creating overinvestment booms. Fifth, as a consequence of the emphasis placed on global goods and commodity markets, this model has aggravated the long-trend deterioration in developing-country terms of trade. And finally, and most importantly, ELG has reinforced the dependency of developing countries on the developed world, thus making them vulnerable to slowdowns in the latter's markets. Export-oriented economies are dependent on foreign (mostly Western) demand. The problem is that recessions in Europe, Japan, or the US translate into slow growth in the developing world.

---

[9]   The term "Washington consensus" was coined by Williamson (1990). In its original formulation, the idea encompassed fiscal discipline, reorientation of public expenditures, tax reform, interest rate liberalization, unified and competitive exchange rates, trade liberalization, openness to foreign direct investment, privatization, deregulation, and securing property rights. Therefore, Palley is not quite correct in his enumeration of what the "Washington consensus" emphasizes (see endnote 1 in his paper). What is true is that toward the end of the 1990s, the list was augmented with a series of so-called second-generation reforms that were more institutional and targeted at problems of "good governance" (Rodrik 2003). The extended list includes corporate governance, anticorruption, flexible labor markets, adherence to WTO disciplines, adherence to international financial codes and standards, "prudent" capital account opening, nonintermediate exchange rate regimes, independent central banks and inflation targeting, social safety nets, and targeted poverty reduction (Rodrik 2003, Table 1). Lin and Liu (2003) question the usefulness of policy advice for developing countries from neoclassical economics, as embedded in the Washington consensus.

The critics of ELG argue that this model suffers from a fallacy-of-composition problem in as much as it assumes that *all* countries can grow by relying on the growth of their exports, which, ultimately, depends on how fast demand grows in other countries. Countries following this model are in danger of ending up with *beggar-thy-neighbor* policies, with the result that, "export-led development may work when adopted by one or even a few countries, but it takes a *zero-sum* dimension when adopted by all" (Palley [2002], 3; italics in the original). Developing countries have ended up competing with each other to sell in developed countries, in what Palley (2002, 3) refers to as "export displacement." Blecker (2002, 2003), however, places three important qualifications on the fallacy-of-composition hypothesis. First, Asian nations and their ELG policies are diverse. Second, not all of Asia's export growth was targeted to the industrialized countries. Intraregional trade has increased. Third, and most important, the constraints on ELG in terms of the growth of global markets for manufactured imports are not fixed and given. This has two implications. The first is that these constraints can be relaxed if the industrialized countries stimulate their economies and open them to the exports of developing countries. The second is that a simultaneous export growth will be successful provided the countries that use ELG also open their own markets to imports and maintain high domestic demand. In the words of Blecker (2002, 72): "What is not feasible is for all countries to attempt to achieve trade surpluses by promoting their exports while simultaneously restricting their imports or repressing consumer demand."

Ertuk (2001–2002) and Palley (2002) have argued that the East Asian financial crisis had an underlying cause located in the real economy and was not just the result of financial speculation. The pursuit of the ELG strategy has left the region with an industrialization strategy that is excessively dependent on external demand for mass manufacturing goods and foreign capital, as well as with poorly developed internal markets and domestic firms. The consequence of the first problem is that the region has mortgaged its economic future, for it is tied excessively to the volatile global business and trade cycles. The second set of problems, i.e., poorly developed domestic economies, lies in the region's domestic economic structures and rent-based culture (Lian 2003). Most countries in the region groomed a privileged rent-seeking class mostly composed of domestic corporate owners. During the 1970s and 1980s and up until the early 1990s, this was not a problem as, because of social and political stability, multinational corporations came to the region and helped develop the export sector. Today, this problem is reflected in the recommendations to improve corporate governance in the region.

It is in this context that Palley (2002) argues that developing countries need a new model of development based on internal market growth (e.g., domestic consumption). The push for DDLG can serve two useful purposes. First, it will reduce overdependence on exports. And second, given the present cyclical difficulties and competition from the PRC in foreign markets, domestic demand can provide an important cushion.

Palley (2002) certainly acknowledges that developing countries need to export. What he argues is that, "the global trading system must be made the servant of domestic development, and domestic development must not be forgone for the sake of international competitive advantage" (Palley 2002, 4). Domestic demand growth rests on four pillars: (i) improved income distribution, (ii) good governance, (iii) financial stability, and (iv) a fairly priced supply of development finance. And the policies needed to put these pillars in place are (i) labor and democratic rights, (ii) financial reform, and (iii) a combination of debt relief, increased foreign aid, and increased development assistance through the expansion of special drawing rights.

In principle, ELG should not be a more desirable way to generate employment than internally generated demand growth (pace the arguments in the previous section). Achieving sustained growth does not depend solely on investment, technology, and other supply factors, but also on a steady expansion of expenditures for personal consumption. Countries in the region understand this and have begun working in this direction. For example, many of the measures implemented by Thailand in the early 2000s under then Prime Minister Thaksin (e.g., the local enterprise initiatives) were intended to alter the country's production structure to reduce the country's dependence on exports. During the years he was prime minister, Thaksin was determined to move the country from mass manufacturing for exports into DDLG (Box 16.1). This was an attempt at creating demand among households and businesses without creating another bubble. This is certainly not an easy road because it calls for an in-depth restructuring of the economy. Also, it has to be done in a way that avoids the problems inherent in import substitution, industrial policies, and "picking the winners."[10] These policies ended up failing in many cases partly because export capability is essential for firms to retain competitiveness.

My view is that the discussion of ELG versus DDLG is somewhat misleading, first, because Asian countries need some form of ELG to attain economies of scale, especially the smaller countries; and second, because both strategies need not be mutually exclusive. Moreover, Felipe and Lim (2005) show empirically that both domestic demand and (net) trade have contributed to overall growth in five Asian countries, although their respective contributions vary depending on the period. In the final analysis,

---

[10] Thailand's government-promoted "Competitiveness Plan" identifies five sectors where the country can develop niches. These sectors and the objectives are (i) software (world center of graphic design), (ii) auto industry (the Detroit of Asia), (iii) fashion (world center of tropical fashion), (iv) food (kitchen of the world), and (v) tourism (tourism capital of Asia).

Box 16.1. What Was *Thaksinomics*?

In August 2004, the Thai government published a white paper titled *Facing the Challenge: Economic Policy and Strategy*, explaining the economic agenda that then Prime Minister Thaksin Shinawatra had been trying to put into effect since he took office in January 2001. These policies tried to balance past excessive dependence on external demand, urban-based mass manufacturing, and unproductive asset building on one hand; with structural development in domestic demand, traditional sectors (e.g., agriculture, small and medium-sized enterprises [SMEs], and rural households) and entrepreneurs, and improvement in the pricing power of Thai goods and services on the other hand. Thus, Thaksin intended to revive domestic demand (by boosting private consumption and by developing the traditional sectors) in addition to exports, following a *dual-track strategy*, as opposed to the single-track model followed by many countries in the region, namely, producing for exports. Thaksin's dual-track strategy was five-pronged:

(i) Revitalize grassroots growth. The key policy initiatives are embodied in the following programs: one *tambon* (village in the Thai system), one product; SME and entrepreneur promotion; farmers' debt suspension; village and urban community revolving fund; The People's Bank of the Government Savings Bank; SME loans; venture capital; and asset capitalization.

(ii) Jump-start key economic sectors. For example, the white paper argues that for agriculture, new demand for Thai agricultural products must be identified both domestically and abroad. For manufacturing, the government has instituted a new Entrepreneurs Promotion Board set up to create 50,000 new SME businesses. In tourism, the policy has set out to promote Thailand aggressively and to capture the attention of upper-middle-class Chinese, Indians, and Europeans. Regarding real estate, the government has disregarded the standard prescriptions of "fire sales" (i.e., selling off assets at low prices) and driving asset prices to their true bottom. Instead, it has promoted asset reflation. Finally, in finance, Thaksin's government put in place a master plan to create a more efficient and competitive financial system.

(iii) Enhance economic efficiency and long-term competitiveness. The government has identified a series of industries to promote: automotive production, tourism, software, food, fashion, health care services, hospitality, rubber, and furniture.

continued on next page

Box 16.1 (continued)

> (iv) Provide a stable and supportive macroeconomic environment to foster growth while maintaining overall policy discipline. The government has raised tax revenue, consolidated spending, balanced the budget, and retired public foreign debt.
>
> (v) Promote exports by expanding markets, and foster financial stability through regional and global cooperation. Under the dual-track strategy, the external sector is as important as the domestic. Thus, exports have remained a cornerstone of the strategy.
>
> Source: Author.

development will manifest in increases in private consumption. But unfortunately, income levels are still low in many cases. While the possibility of developing further internal markets for growth (which presupposes a decrease in savings and an increase in consumption), as Palley (2002) recommends, must be considered, still the ELG strategy, properly understood, represents an advisable policy option for many developing countries, including the Asian countries. A radical shift toward domestic orientation would require significant internal changes and reforms that will take time. This will require the development of different sectors of the economy, something difficult to induce because in most cases it requires a complex and slow shift in resources. In the end, the magic recipe is a golden combination of ELG and DDLG.[11]

For policy purposes, and this is the key, ELG should not be simply about exporting more, but about exporting in the context of a development strategy based on upgrading and diversifying the economy (along the lines of the arguments in chapter 10 and in section *Export-Led Growth and the Balance-of-Payments Constraint* in this chapter) and producing high-value goods that others want.[12] The message of this discussion is that growing by exporting the right products and services (i.e., the ones for which world demand is elastic) is a powerful strategy. This is very different from

---

[11] We have yet to see how far Thailand's efforts, in what has been described as a "dual track" strategy (Lian 2003) by relying on external demand (first track) and simultaneously developing domestic demand and supporting domestic enterprises (second track), can go.

[12] Germany's and Japan's successes during the post-World War II period can be largely attributed to an export growth model whose objective was to increase the sophistication of the goods exported.

thinking of the ELG strategy as merely an exercise in exporting (based on low wages), which of course depends on expanding global exports markets and on an optimistic scenario of growth in Europe, Japan, and the US. The problem of the dependency of developing countries on the developed world appears different, since developed countries also depend on the other developed countries because most of their trade is intra-industry. What matters, once again, is the type of products exported. The above should not be interpreted as implying that the rate of growth of a country is the result of subjective decisions of foreign consumers. This also implies that a fallacy of composition need not exist, since firms in different countries can search and specialize in different niches to accomplish this objective. Certainly, if all Asian developing countries specialize in the same product, then overcapacity will occur and growth rates will fall. As indicated above, each country (rather, each firm) needs to find a niche where not all produce, e.g., semiconductors. The success of the East Asian economies means, in fact, that these countries are facing pressures to vacate the markets in which they succeeded (e.g., textiles, clothing, electronics) and shift to higher-value-added exports as the PRC and others enter those sectors. Their success also implies that their markets for low-skilled manufactures are expanding, thus providing export opportunities for the next generation of industrializing countries (Akyüz et al. 1998).

Globalization has made it very clear that a successful market economy must have loser firms. These are the firms that have not been capable of delivering the goods and services that consumers want. In a globalizing and intensely competitive world, the pressures on firms to deliver have increased because now they have to compete not only against other domestic firms but also against foreign firms. Firms must exert big efforts to compete by reducing costs as well as by creating new products, finding new niches, and opening new markets. One response to globalization is to acknowledge that today's world is tough. Another, quite different, response is to blame globalization for the failure of some firms. Palley's (2002) proposals for a new development paradigm based on DDLG are compatible with the message that to survive in the current world economy, firms must try to enhance their entrepreneurial and technological capabilities to deliver the products and services that consumers demand.

How Does the People's Republic of China Change the Argument?

The above arguments concerning the ELG strategy remain valid today. The only important additional point to the argument is the flood of cheap manufacturing exports from the PRC (and some other countries), which, as long as the exchange rate vis-à-vis the US dollar is kept (artificially) relatively constant, is allowing it to expand export markets and absorb the huge surplus of labor from the countryside. Many countries (both developing and developed) fear that many of their firms may be forced to lay off workers due to lack of competitiveness vis-à-vis firms from the PRC. Interestingly, the PRC government is also worried about rising unemployment as jobs are lost in unprofitable state companies and deflation remains an issue. This has weakened workers' bargaining power in some sectors in some other nations.

So far, the PRC is perceived as a successful nation and inflows of capital continue arriving, thereby putting pressure on the exchange rate to rise. Of course, the ELG strategy still has the advantage that it creates jobs, but, through double-entry bookkeeping at the international level, it forces trade deficits, loss of reserves, and increases in international indebtedness on the trading partners. And, as a consequence, this strategy also exports a country's unemployment, so that it becomes a deflationary force that, in a global economy, can feed back on all ELG nations. The short-term gain for the successful ELG nations is that they can accumulate significant sums of foreign reserves—and therefore attract more foreign capital inflows. However, unless they also have some form of capital controls, the initial buildup of foreign reserves can later on lead to a hot-money outflow and a currency crisis.

The issues of the PRC's undervalued currency, its trade surplus, and the huge amount of foreign reserves that it has accumulated have created a heated debate not only across Asia but also in the US, where some voices blame the PRC for the loss of American jobs in manufacturing. Hence, these voices are asking the Government of the United States to push the PRC to float the yuan. But this proposal is problematic for several reasons. First, since the PRC is a key engine of growth in the world economy today, putting a brake to the country's growth could pose more problems than it solves (e.g., unemployment). Second, an increase in the yuan might lead to price hikes on a wide range of products (e.g., clothes, appliances) in the US. Third, the PRC's banking system is in serious trouble. If the PRC were allowed to hold foreign currencies, this might lead not to an increase in the value of the yuan but to a bank run, leading to a collapse of the currency similar to what other East Asian countries experienced in 1997–1998. Fourth, exchange rate appreciation will not strongly affect the PRC's trade surplus, as the experience of Japan proves. Moreover, the market is focused on the nominal bilateral exchange rate of the US dollar and the yuan. However, the yuan's real effective exchange rate has appreciated. In the medium term, the PRC will probably need a more flexible exchange rate. This would give it a more independent monetary policy (as the capital account is being liberalized), especially from the US Federal Reserve. As of now, continued intervention and inadequate sterilization have resulted in excessive investment. Greater integration into today's world economy requires flexible exchange rates, which are better able to handle the flows of global capital.

Many of the arguments about the PRC are based on rhetoric, reminiscent of the focus on Japan during the 1980s. Since the PRC joined the World Trade Organization (WTO), its trade barriers have come down and imports have increased. In this respect, it is important to stress that financing of the US federal government deficits does not require a continual flow of global savings, as the rest of the world dollar savings cannot preexist the US current account deficits. Rather, it is the purchase of imports by Americans that provides the dollar savings accumulated by the foreigners. This implies that if the rest of the world did not want to exchange its output for US dollars, the US would not enjoy a trade deficit. In other words: if no one outside the US wanted to accumulate additional dollars, the US would not be able to continue running an external deficit. The problem will not be that the rest of the world refuses to lend dollars to the US, but that the rest of the world will not accumulate additional dollar claims on the US (Wray 2008b).

Two different views exist about the accumulation of massive reserves by developing Asia since 2000 (a total of almost $2.7 trillion as of 30 June 2007 [Park 2007, Table 1]). Standard ratios to measure the size of reserves indicate that the accumulated reserves exceed estimates of what the region needs for traditional liquidity purposes. This has led to the argument that the region should reallocate its surplus reserves away from safe but low-yielding assets (e.g., US government bonds) toward higher-yielding investments. Park (2007) also argues that countries should consider using these reserves to finance infrastructure projects, although he admits that this may have some macroeconomic costs (e.g., monetary expansion). India, for example, is considering such a proposal. Government estimates put at $320 billion the country's needs in infrastructure investment (ports, roads, airports, power utilities) between 2008 and 2012 (corresponding to the 11th Five-Year Plan), representing an increase in infrastructure spending from about 4%–5% of GDP to about 8%. Two means of financing this spending are on the table. The first one is to borrow funds from the central bank and lend to Indian companies implementing infrastructure projects in India, or to cofinance their external commercial borrowings from such projects, solely for capital expenditures outside India. The second one is to borrow funds from the central bank and invest them in highly rated collateral securities, to improve the credit ratings of Indian companies that raise funds in international markets for infrastructure projects in India (Park 2007, Box 5).

However, Rodrik (2006b) takes a slightly different view. He argues that an important reason underlying the increase in reserves during the last few years is as a precaution against the possibility of another crisis. Indeed, the painful memory of the 1997–1998 East Asian crisis has led some countries in the region to accumulate reserves well above what may seem reasonable for traditional liquidity purposes. Taking precaution into account, Rodrik estimates that reserves are not excessive.

The "Uncoupling" Thesis

The possibility of developing Asia's transition to a DDLG model is linked to the notion that the region is uncoupling from events in the rest of the world. What is the empirical evidence? A recent analysis by Asian Development Bank (2007c) indicates that although intraregional trade is increasing, in a globalizing world links among economies are becoming an even more powerful driver. Hence, the idea of developing Asia's uncoupling is more myth than reality. The truth is that the rise in intra-Asian economic interdependence through investment and trade is being driven by globalization. Much intra-Asian trade is conducted by multinational corporations and their affiliates in the form of intrafirm and intra-industry trade that involves fragmentation of production. More than 70% of intra-Asian trade consists of intermediate goods used in production; and of this, half is driven by final demand outside Asia. Nearly 80% of all exports from East and Southeast Asia are eventually bound for external markets. Of the total, about 60% is eventually consumed in the US, the European Union (EU), and Japan. These three areas are still the main markets for East and Southeast Asia's exports after taking into account the share of the intermediate goods trade that is assembled and produced within the region but that is eventually shipped outside the region.

Export-Led Growth and the Balance-of-Payments Constraint

As noted above, critics of ELG argue that this model suffers from a fallacy-of-composition problem because this strategy assumes that *all* countries can grow by relying on the growth of their exports, which ultimately depends on how fast demand grows in other countries. This is because under a given set of global demand conditions, the market for developing countries' exports is limited by the capacity of the industrialized nations. The result, the argument goes, is that export-led development may work when adopted by one or even a few countries, but it takes a *zero-sum* dimension when adopted by all.

However, ELG can be thought of through the role export growth plays in relieving a country's balance-of-payments (BOP) *constraint on demand*. The key aspect is that exports are the one component of demand whose growth simultaneously relaxes the BOP constraint. And likewise, exports do matter in the context explained in chapter 10, namely, that the sophistication a country's export basket is a very good predictor of its future growth.

Developing countries suffer from supply bottlenecks such as poor infrastructure, but this does not mean that demand is not also important in determining the growth performance of a country. In chapter 2, I argued that effective demand problems can become the binding constraint on production in developing countries at a fairly advanced stage of industrialization (e.g., Malaysia, Thailand, the PRC) when they are "balance-of-payments constrained." What is this BOP constraint? The BOP constrains the overall growth rate because in the long run countries aim at having a balanced current account. No country can grow faster in the long run than the rate consistent with BOP equilibrium on current account unless it can finance ever-growing deficits. What developing countries need to do, therefore, is to develop the ability to export in order to pay for full-employment imports (i.e., the value of imports that would occur if resources were fully utilized). In other words, exports relieve the BOP constraint imposed by the import requirements of rapid growth. If a country is below its growth of productive potential (i.e., the supply constraints are not binding), then its growth rate will be determined by the growth of demand. Thus, growth rates across countries, in this framework, must differ *because* the growth of demand differs among countries (also, Thirlwall and Pacheco-López [2008]).

McCombie and Thirlwall (1994) have shown that the long-run BOP equilibrium growth rate can be calculated as the product of the growth rate of world income times the ratio of the income elasticity of demand for exports to the income elasticity of demand for imports.[13] This relationship emphasizes the joint negative effect of excessive openness to imports, as reflected in a high income elasticity of import demand, and the positive effect of exports via a high income elasticity of export demand and/or rapid world income growth.

Why does the BOP equilibrium growth rate differ across countries? This is tantamount to asking why countries should differ in the values of their income elasticities of demand for exports and imports. The answer lies in the types of goods and services, and their *characteristics*, that a country exports: are they the ones for which world demand is rapidly growing,

---

[13] Algebraically: $y_b = z(\varepsilon/\pi)$, where y_b is the BOP equilibrium growth rate, z is the growth rate of world income, ε is the income elasticity of demand for exports, and π is the income elasticity of demand for imports. The income elasticity of demand for exports (ε) is a measure of how much country A's exports increase when the rest of the world's (importer) income grows by 1%. The income elasticity of demand for imports (π) is a measure of how much country A's imports increase when country A's own income increases by 1%.

such as manufactures or financial services (which generally have a high income elasticity of demand for exports); or are they primary commodities (which generally have a low income elasticity of demand for exports)? McCombie and Thirlwall (1994) argue that disparities between countries in the income elasticities of demand for exports and imports largely reflect differences in *nonprice competitiveness*, broadly defined. *The message for a country whose export growth rate is relatively slow, and has a rather high import elasticity, is that the goods it produces are relatively unattractive.*

What is meant by the "characteristics" of the goods produced? Many manufacturing industries engage quite often in nonprice rather than *price* competition (McCombie and Thirlwall 1994). Nonprice competitiveness encompasses all those factors other than price that affect consumers' choices, such as quality, reliability, speed of delivery, and extent and efficacy of the distribution network. The importance of nonprice competitiveness is that as per capita income grows, so increasingly does the demand for more sophisticated goods. For example, it is dubious that ex-Eastern bloc automobiles such as Skodas and Ladas would have ever made inroads into the markets of the advanced countries despite their exceptionally low prices. In the long run, in a world characterized by rapid product and process innovation, and where the rapid growth of demand is for increasingly sophisticated products, companies should not rely exclusively on price competition to maintain market share.

Since disparities in the income elasticities reflect differences in nonprice competitiveness, the *supply-side* factors (e.g., investment in new technology, research and development effort, education and training in skills) determine the income elasticity of demand for exports and therefore are crucial in explaining the growth of exports and, hence, income.

17

Is Education a Key Ingredient of Inclusive Growth?

In the ultimate analysis, people judge economic performance of governments in terms of employment possibilities, educational opportunities, or health care facilities for themselves and their families. The size of the budget deficit, the internal debt of the nation, the balance of payments situation or the expansion of money supply are economic abstractions that are somewhat distant from the daily lives of ordinary people.

—Deepak Nayyar (2008, 20)

This final chapter (before the conclusions) deals with the role of education, in particular with issues: (i) knowledge as a public good that produces externalities; (ii) the "low-skill, low-tech map"; and (iii) education, unemployment, and structural change.

In Solow's (1956) neoclassical model, saving rates do not affect long-run growth. The latter is determined by the exogenously given rate of technological progress. Diminishing returns to capital in this model mean that higher savings lead to a decrease in interest rates to the point where the economy saves to keep up with technological progress. Therefore, no matter what the incentives to save are, long-run growth will be at the rate of technological progress. The key issue here is whether diminishing returns to capital do set in. The so-called *new theories of growth* developed since the 1980s claim that this is not the case if one considers capital in a broader sense. One possible cause is that people have incentives to accumulate *human capital*, e.g., knowledge of new technologies that economize on labor. This way, diminishing returns may not accrue to physical and human capital together. Diminishing returns require one factor to be in fixed supply (e.g., labor), but profit-seeking entrepreneurs might find out ways to get around the constraint of the fixed factor. For example, they will seek out new technologies that economize on labor. This way, technology responds to incentives.

But technology has two peculiar features. First, technological knowledge is likely to leak from one individual to another, akin to the Keynesian multiplier. This is what economists refer to as externalities. Second, technology delivers the most when high-skilled individuals match with each other. The negative implication is that low-skilled people can be left out of the process and be stuck in a trap (discussed in Box 15.3).

An externality is a good or service resulting from a private transaction that has spillovers, that is, that affects more people than the parties directly involved in the transaction. Another example is knowledge passed on to somebody else. Easterly (2002, chapter 8) describes how Daewoo of the Republic of Korea trained workers from Desh Garments in Bangladesh in the textile business between 1979 and 1981. Before this, the garment industry in Bangladesh consisted of no more than 40 producers. According to the agreement, Desh would pay royalties and sales commissions to Daewoo, amounting to 8% of sales value. Bangladeshi workers were quickly trained (much faster than initially agreed and expected) and the agreement was canceled, after the two parties agreed on a price for the services that Daewoo had provided. But the benefits of the initial investment in knowledge went well beyond what Daewoo, and even Desh, intended. Most of the workers trained by Daewoo left Desh in a matter of years and set up their own garment firms. Moreover, they diversified (Desh produced shirts only) into gloves, coats, and trousers. The moral of the example is that investment in knowledge does not remain with the original investor. Knowledge leaks and is subject to increasing returns. All this lies at the heart of the much-discussed issue of technology transfer.

Today, economists believe that knowledge grows through conscious investment because it has a big payoff. People will respond to this incentive by investing in the accumulation of knowledge. In the example above, the real story begins with Daewoo, founded in 1967. Daewoo created new knowledge about garment production and transmitted it years later. As Easterly indicates, "creating knowledge does not necessarily mean inventing new technologies from scratch. Some aspects of garment manufacturing technology were probably several centuries old. The relevant technological ideas might be floating out there in the ether, *but only those who apply them can really learn them and can teach them to others*" (2002, 149; italics added).

Moreover, transmitted knowledge and methods have to be adapted to local conditions. This is something Desh and Daewoo did. Daewoo also helped in setting up bonded warehouse systems in Bangladesh to deal with the protectionist trading system. Also, Bangladeshi banks were advised how to open back-to-back import letters of credit.

The above example shows that knowledge is a public good because it can be used simultaneously by a large number of people. Knowledge displays increasing returns because it complements already existing knowledge. This means that increases in knowledge about textile production lead to proportionally higher increases in output. In other words, the return to capital is high where capital is already abundant. This is the opposite of the diminishing-returns-to-capital argument in the standard neoclassical model, where returns to capital are high where capital is scarce.

The previous reflections derive from the broader consideration of capital that the new endogenous growth models provide. While physical capital continues displaying decreasing returns, knowledge (human capital) is different. As soon as this type of investment leaks (e.g., in the form of how to better operate a computer or software package), it raises the overall productivity. If this effect is large, it can overcome the diminishing returns to physical capital. The higher the level of human capital, the higher the return to every new addition to this stock. And the higher the return, the higher the incentive to continue investing. All this appears to be consistent with the empirical observation that physical and human capital flow to the developed countries, where the rates of return to these investments are higher (discussed in Box 15.3).

Another important aspect should be added. This is that Desh (much less Daewoo!) was not fully rewarded for the benefits it brought back to Bangladesh. By 1985, Bangladesh had over 700 garment companies. All these companies were using the technology that Desh brought from the Republic of Korea and adapted during the next few years. The return to Desh's initial investment was appropriated as a return to society, and not as a private return. Without any leaks (e.g., because Desh workers did not leave to set up other companies), Desh would have been the only one to benefit from its own investment. Hence its returns would have become higher and higher as it continued investing in its own human capital, and the company would have become more and more successful, would have attracted more investment, and would have grown indefinitely. But no other company would have done it. This does not seem to actually occur, and as a theory of development it does not take us very far: essentially, we would be describing monopolization. The existence of leaks in the acquisition of knowledge, in the sense that a single person does not appropriate all the benefits, creates the important distinction between private and social returns. Knowledge acquisition leads to increasing social returns, which is good for society.

For single individuals who invest in the acquisition and accumulation of capital, the argument is the opposite: they do not appropriate the *full* benefit of their investments. Therefore, in a free market economy, their incentive to invest and accumulate capital will be lower than what is optimal for society, if they know that they will not be rewarded for spillovers.

This takes me to the next point, the idea that knowledge that produces spillovers leads to virtuous and vicious circles through cumulative causation.

Understanding how virtuous circles occur is easy; in fact, such a circle happened in the example described above. Knowledge called for more knowledge accumulation, and high returns led to even higher returns. Why the first wave of investment in physical and human capital took place is immaterial for the argument. What matters is simply that it happened. But countries sometimes (more often than desired) get stuck in vicious circles that lead to poverty traps. This happens because investors require a minimum rate of return, a threshold, to undertake the investment. And if a country already has a certain critical mass of human and physical capital to start with, growth will take place through a virtuous circle of capital accumulation, attracting yet more capital. If a country is just barely above the threshold, a shock (i.e., political instability because of a coup d'état, or worse, a civil war; or an oil shock) might send the country from positive to negative growth. A similar shock in a country well above the threshold will cause much less harm to growth.

As I have argued above, the rate of return on new knowledge depends on the existing level of knowledge, and the latter depends on the incentives to acquire it. The question is, what happens if at the initial stage, and for whatever reason, the level of accumulated capital (both physical and human) is low? Then, the return to capital accumulation will be low (again, it must be stressed that this runs opposite to the traditional argument that if capital is a scarce factor, its accumulation will yield a high return. Discussed in Box 15.3). If this rate of return is below the minimum required by the prospective investor, then no investment will be made. But if no investment is made today, the stock of capital will be low tomorrow (even lower than today's, taking into account depreciation and obsolescence) and the corresponding rate of return will be also low. The consequence is that no new investment will be made, creating a vicious circle. Countries where vicious circles occur end up immersed in a low-level equilibrium trap (Nelson 1956) which are not easy to escape.

The lack of investment in the argument above occurs because everybody has the same expectations, i.e., I won't invest because no one else will invest. This is akin to a coordination failure (Easterly 2002, 168; Rodrik 2004; Hausmann and Rodrik 2006). Suppose, however, that one expects that many other members of society will invest in acquiring skills. This might motivate one to invest and be enough to break the vicious circle. And naturally, the rate of return to an investment will be higher if investors expect that everyone else is investing too. Computer companies come to Bangalore because they expect other companies to locate there and invest.

What are some implications of the arguments above? For example, countries that try to progress by exploiting low labor costs (e.g., by restricting wages or through devaluations) may end up stuck in a vicious circle of low productivity, deficient training, and a lack of skilled jobs, therefore preventing key sectors from competing effectively in the markets for skill-intensive products. This situation is referred to as a "low-skill, bad-job trap" (Snower 1996). "Bad jobs" are associated with low wages and few opportunities to accumulate human capital. "Good jobs" demand higher skills and command higher wages. A second trap derives from the complementarities between capital and labor. The problem is referred to as a "low-skill, low-tech trap." If workers have insufficient skills to operate modern machines, the latter will be underutilized. Consequently, firms will have little incentive to invest in the latest technologies, which will reduce workers' productivity even more. A third problem emerges from the interaction between innovation and skills. Innovating is crucial for developing technological capabilities, but it requires well-trained workers. Economies can get caught in a vicious circle in which firms do not innovate because the labor force is insufficiently skilled, and workers do not have incentives to invest in knowledge because there is no demand for these skills. For example, Amante (2003, 275) documents the problems of the Filipino educational system and argues as follows: "The low level of benefits derived from the Philippine education, especially at the secondary and tertiary levels, is traceable to the unemployability and low productivity of Philippine labor. In turn, these could be attributed to inadequate investments and low levels of technology utilized by business establishments and the very thin economic base of the country."

Snower (1996) argues that the relatively low demand for and supply of skills in a country derives from rational decisions made by both firms and individuals within the particular legal and institutional framework in which they operate. Countries with a less-skilled workforce have greater incentives to produce nontraded services rather than tradables such as manufactured goods because the former are relatively protected from foreign competition. This pattern of specialization creates and perpetuates the demand for less skilled labor. For example, the *Philippines Presidential Commission on Educational Reform 2000 Report* lamented that "the country has too long suffered the imbalance of an overly credential-conscious society, which puts a premium more on diplomas than knowledge or skills, and values prestige institutions granting degrees more than the competence that the degree itself embodies." The report echoed the observation that, "education obtained in a typical Philippine college or university may only be equivalent to a secondary education from the better high schools in the country, or from a typical high school in Japan or Europe." Filipinos prefer white-collar professions and look down upon vocational and technical education.[1]

---

[1] These quotations from the *Philippines Presidential Commission on Educational Reform* are taken from Amante (2003, 272).

Amante argues that the Philippine labor market suffers from a substantial mismatch between the expectations of the competencies of the workforce arising from industry restructuring and the spread of information technology. In particular, "in an environment of global competition, organizations must focus upon skills and competencies" (Amante 2003, 282). Today's globalizing world demands organizations designed on skill-based systems that realize that the nature and content of jobs and their skill requirements are changing fast and adapt quickly to the new circumstances. This mismatch between the skills that firms demand and the practical knowledge that workers bring to the workplace has led to a cycle of lack of skills–unemployment and underemployment–poverty.

Where do mismatches come from? On the one hand, the type of business, level of investment, and scale of operations determine the competencies expected from employees. The prevailing global competition, and the spread of new technologies such as the internet, affect those expectations. On the other hand, the knowledge, skills, and attitudes of the workforce are shaped by existing social institutions, including the quality of education, support services, and government policy.

One of the most important consequences of the deficiency in training is that a lack of skilled workers leads to the manufacture and export of relatively poor quality and low value products. The manufacture of high-quality products requires highly trained workers. But if the country does not generate enough of these workers, firms will be forced to produce low-quality goods; and likewise, workers will acquire little training because few high-quality goods are produced, leading to a vicious circle. The choices made by employers reflect the availability of a skilled workforce. Different outputs require different types of training. Businesspeople aware that their workers are not highly skilled (and thus are more likely to make mistakes) will tend to specialize in the production of low-value products. Thus, the labor force will be more suited to the production of low-value than high-value products.

Why can this happen? The reason is that the market does not lead to the best possible outcome because, as explained above, private and social returns to knowledge are different. Individuals are not fully rewarded for the social contribution they make when they invest in knowledge by increasing the stock of knowledge available to everyone. They get no reward for this spillover, and so contributions to social knowledge will be underprovided. In the end, firms' decisions about what type of products to manufacture depend on the availability of skilled labor. The result is that "in countries that offer little support for education and training and that contain a large proportion of unskilled workers, the market mechanism may reinforce the existing lack of skills by providing little incentive to acquire more; whereas in countries with well-functioning educational and training institutions and large bodies of skilled labor, the free market may do much more to induce people to become skilled" (Snower 1996, 112).

Finally, three related issues on education should be considered. The first is that, while I believe that a type of unemployment and underemployment is caused by the mismatches and traps discussed in this chapter, amid a severe shortage of employment (as it happens in many developing countries), training and other similar solutions will not eliminate the problem, but switch some individuals between unemployment and employment. The idea of "transforming workers" by educating them so that they become high-skilled laborers is simply not true. Lack of work is not solved with microeconomic policies (i.e., policies to help workers move from one job to the next). This problem is macroeconomic. Hence policies should be devised to generate employment, ideally full employment.

The second point is that, perhaps, education matters more for political reasons than for its contribution to productivity and growth. The public debate on education is oversimplified and probably many assumptions about the relevance of education have no basis. William Lewis (2004) has pointed out that education is not the current constraint on development. The public policy debate should center on the ability of the current workforces to be trained on the job to work in high-productivity operations. He refers to this quality as "trainability," and argues that workers around the developing world can be trained to achieve much higher productivity levels. Trainability is not a constraint. On the other hand, he defines education as "the means through which societies acquire political philosophies based on individual rights" (2004, 243). And like Galbraith (1997), Lewis (2004, 243) also argues that, "these rights are necessary for political and social developments that overcome the privileges of 'special interests' and satisfy individual and consumer desires better." Education is necessary to understand the complex political systems necessary for advanced economic performance: "It's possible that poor countries today will not get out of poverty traps without political changes. Those political changes may only be possible with broader education" (Lewis 2004, 247). While this is an important issue, it differs from the emphasis on education in the public debate. This also implies that subsidies to education may not lead to increases in productivity. As Galbraith (1997, 24) argues (referring to the US), "people train themselves when they have an incentive (such as good conditions and decent pay) to stay on the job. At present, the economy is short of jobs, not of skills."

The final point comes in the form of a question: where does the almost universal emphasis on education come from? Education has always been mentioned by development economists as an ingredient for development (see, for example, Hayami [1997]). An important strand of the endogenous growth literature takes education as a key input to production (Lucas 1988).

However, the policy implications of this literature are so general that they are almost useless for real-world policy, as they miss the issues that policy makers are interested in: where? At what level? Through better teacher training or greater parental involvement?

The public debate has been misled for decades by what Braverman (1998, chapter 20) has called the "upgrading thesis." This is the idea that the changing conditions of work require a better-trained, better-educated, and therefore upgraded working population. However, Braverman argues, this is a myth resulting from three observed trends. One is that the increasing average level of skills that statistics show (in terms of average years of education) is misleading. Since with the development of technology the labor processes of society embody a greater amount of scientific knowledge, the "average" scientific content, and in some sense the "skill content," of many jobs is much greater now than in the past.[2] But this increasing skill content has affected only some jobs. Many of the jobs modern societies create, and certainly developing countries, do not require high skills. Indeed, as Mehta et al. (2007) document, many of the jobs created in India, Indonesia, the Philippines, and Thailand between the 1990s and the early 2000s (e.g., maids, drivers) did not require more skills, although workers had more years of schooling (Box 17.1).

A second trend is the shift of workers from some major occupation groups into others, that is, structural transformation. Workers classified by the statistics in the secondary sector are believed to need and have more skills than those classified as working in the primary sector, and those working in services are believed to need and have even a higher level of skills. This is not necessarily true. As Braverman argues (1998, 298), "It is only in the world of census statistics, and not in terms of direct assessment, that an assembly line worker is presumed to have greater skills than a fisherman

---

[2]   The concepts of specialization, comparative advantage, and skills are linked through another standard concept, division of labor, which goes back to Adam Smith (1776). In Book I (especially chapters I, II, and III) of *The Wealth of Nations*, Smith regarded the division of labor as the driving force of economic development; however, in Book V (chapter I, part III, article 2d), he warned about the harm caused by the division of labor. The passage is reproduced here, as it is much less well known than the references in Book I: "In the progress of the division of labour, the employment of the far greater part of those who live by labour, that is, of the great body of the people, comes to be confined to a very few simple operations, frequently to one or two. But the understandings of the greater part of men are necessarily formed by their ordinary employments. The man whose whole life is spent performing a few simple operations, of which the effects too are, perhaps, always the same, or very nearly the same, has no occasion to exert his understanding, or to exercise his invention in finding out expedients for removing difficulties which never occur. He naturally loses, therefore, the habit of such exertion, and generally becomes as stupid and ignorant as it is possible for a human creature to become" (Smith 1776, 987).

Box 17.1. Education and Structural Transformation: What Does the Microeconomic Evidence Say?

Are the numbers of workers trained at schools and colleges adequate to meet the demands of a changing economy? Can rising education levels be linked to the changing structure of employment, trade liberalization, and technological changes? Have countries with more educated workers transformed their employment structures faster? Using microeconomic evidence (for the early 1990s and 10 years later) on India, the Philippines, and Thailand, Mehta et al. (2007) show that these countries are creating educated workers faster than they are creating jobs in the sectors that historically hired them. This is leading to rising education levels across the board, including in some sectors and jobs that do not pay a premium for education, that cannot be required to compete with foreign workers, or that have not seen big changes in technology. These results suggest that in many situations, education is being acquired for reasons independent of the "requirements" of the jobs currently available. Secondary- and tertiary-education attainment rose during the period analyzed. At the same time, returns to secondary education fell, while returns to tertiary education were much more buoyant. Returns to college rose for older workers, but fell for recent Thai and Filipino entrants to the labor force. The shift in returns to education can be decomposed into and attributed to the evolving structure of employment and to inter- and intra-industry wage patterns. Secondary returns fell sharply in every sector as secondary-educated workers rapidly became available, while employment structures shifted slowly to absorb them. Conversely, modern services were instrumental in lifting the returns to tertiary education. The exercise reveals that the Philippines will need to industrialize to leverage higher growth from its human-capital stock, while returns to secondary education in India have come to depend less on manufacturing. The intercohort divergence in returns to college arises in the Philippines and Thailand because excess young college-educated workers are pushed into low-wage or low-return jobs, while older college graduates are more likely to work in modern services. The largest and growing share of services employment has been in low-wage traditional services. "Services-led development," therefore, appears to be a red herring for employment. Falling returns to education indicate that if a lack of educated workers constrained productivity initially, then this constraint has loosened, and it has loosened most obviously in agriculture, industry, and lower-status services. Also, the results show quite clearly that as the supply of basic education expanded, jobs did not grow organically to absorb the educated. Moreover, employment structures have clearly transformed fastest in the less-educated countries—India and Thailand. Of course, the reasons for this could be legion, and cannot be ascertained with a sample of only four countries. But whatever the reasons, these four examples show little evidence that higher basic education levels bring structural change.

or oysterman." He continues, "Even pick and shovel work takes more learning before it can be done to required standards than many assembly or machine-feeding jobs" (1998, 299).

The third observed trend is the prolongation of the period of education. Better and more educated workforces are assumed to be necessary today. Hence a longer period at school is required. However, we do not spend so many years at school today because the jobs that the marketplace creates require 10–12 years of formal schooling. The lengthening of the school period, Braverman (1998, 303) argues, has more to do with the need to reduce unemployment. Many of the jobs created today in most developing countries in services do not require more than basic literacy, that is, reading, writing, and performing basic arithmetical operations. These qualifications are demanded by the urban environment in which many people now live, so that they learn how to conform with the rules of society and to obey the law. Braverman goes on to point out that, "beyond this need for basic literacy there is also the function of the schools in providing an attempted socialization to city life, which now replaces the socialization through farm, family, community, and church which once took place in a predominantly rural setting" (1998, 302).

18

Conclusions: How Can Developing Countries Implement an Inclusive-Growth and Full-Employment Strategy?

For, as a matter of fact, the overcoming of all the obstacles to economic development . . . amounts to more than the upheaval created in the eighteenth century by the French Revolution.

—Michal Kalecki (1966a, 19)

I start these conclusions with a reflection about the present crisis. As I write these final pages in July 2009, the crisis that started in the housing market of the United States (US) during the summer of 2007 has spread and now is a full-blown depression that affects all spheres of economic activity in both developed and developing countries. Policy makers and economists show great concern with the future of the world economy, and some even question the viability of capitalism as a model for the future (if Karl Marx could see it…). No matter what happens, it is clear that capitalism, in all "mixed-economy" forms into which it developed during the 19th and 20th centuries, is subject to crises and depressions. To solve the crisis, economists are advocating different Keynesian-type policies. In my view, this must be a period of reflection that demands thinking outside the box. Given the severity of the crisis, I do believe that we need to return to the analyses of Keynes, Marx, and Minsky to understand its genesis and the consequences it will have. It is still too early to see where all this will lead to. But in terms of short-term consequences, it is obvious that one of the most significant will be higher unemployment.[1]

---

[1] Hausmann et al. (2006) show that the most robust predictor of the severity of output collapses is a country's location in the product space (chapter 10).

A report by the World Bank notes that "the economic crisis is projected to increase poverty by around 46 million people in 2009. The principal transmission channels will be via employment and wage effects as well as declining remittance flows . . . The latest estimates for the Ministry of Labor in [the People's Republic of] China [PRC] show 20 million people out of work . . . The garment industry has laid off 300,000 workers in Cambodia (10% of workforce) . . . In India, over 500,000 jobs have been lost over the last 3 months of 2008 in export-oriented sectors . . . ILO [International Labour Organization] forecasts suggest that global job losses could hit 51 million, and up to 30 million workers could become unemployed" (World Bank 2009, 9). It is difficult to predict the consequences of these job losses. But clearly, this state of affairs has to change. The analysis and proposals in this book can guide this transformation.

In the previous pages, I have discussed the implications for macroeconomic policy of the term inclusive growth, defined as "growth with equal opportunities." I have argued that the focus of inclusive growth must be to increase a country's productive capacity to achieve the full employment of the labor force. Societies should not tolerate unemployment (as well as underemployment) on the basis of bogus reasons, and must urge their governments to change priorities and strategies. However difficult achieving full employment may be, policies to improve upon the *status quo* exist. What is needed is political will to implement them.

Current policies are clearly not pro inclusive growth. During the last decades, the wave of free market and the emphasis on privatization led to significant wealth creation for some. During this time, employment creation was thought to be an automatic by-product of growth. The reality, however, is very different: the evidence shows that employment elasticities are not high and, consequently, many developing countries do not generate employment for all the entrants into the labor market. Full employment has not been a top priority of policy making for decades; agriculture has been neglected; and fiscal and monetary policies have been geared toward price stability under the nonaccelerating inflation rate of unemployment (NAIRU) theory.

Today, about 500 million people are unemployed and/or underemployed in developing Asia. *If* inclusive growth is a useful concept for policy purposes, it requires, above all, proactive governments and policy makers that put employment creation and the achievement of full employment at the top of their agendas. This imperative became very clear during 2008 and the first few months of 2009, as the problems that had started in the US in the summer of 2007 unfolded and became an international crisis. Unemployment rates are increasing in many countries and threaten social stability. This crisis, as all deep crises in the past, will have significant implications for future growth. We know from the 1997–1998 Asian crisis that growth settled down on a lower trajectory in the most-affected countries. The persistence of this gap implies large permanent losses of income compared with pre-crisis trends.

Pursuing inclusive growth as an objective of policy making requires a clear and open commitment by the government because the responsibility of achieving this objective rests on its shoulders.[2] While the private sector creates jobs in a market economy (as it should be!), its main objective is not employment maximization. Private firms only hire the quantity of labor needed to produce the level of output that is expected to be sold profitably. This may leave many people unemployed. Government commitment to inclusive growth, and specifically to full employment, implies (i) having explicit employment goals, as well as pro-employment fiscal, monetary, exchange rate, trade, and industrial policies; and (ii) accepting that it will be evaluated for its efforts and commitment toward bringing the economy closer to full employment. Moreover, employment objectives must consider underemployment and informal employment, which requires close coordination between private and public sectors.

Failing to maintain the economy at full employment entails high costs, while maintaining an economy as close as possible to full employment will lead to higher tax revenues, and will require lower safety-net expenditures. Although achieving and maintaining full employment is very difficult (because of both political and technical constraints), governments should not be dissuaded. How each country puts in practice the analysis and the policy recommendations in this book depends on particular circumstances. For example, Felipe and Hasan (2006, chapter 7, Box 7.7) propose a checklist of policies for the Philippines according to priority. The policies with immediate priority are population to control fertility and the implementation of a job creation program funded by the government along the lines explained in chapter 14 (i.e., a Public Employment Service).

Governments' commitment to full employment and inclusive growth requires a series of well-coordinated and coherent policies in many fronts: the expansion of agricultural production, a coherent public investment plan, an industrial policy program, fiscal and monetary policies geared toward full employment, and a public sector willing to act as employer of last resort when necessary. This commitment also requires awareness of

---

[2]   Many of the conservative criticisms to any kind of government intervention in the economy as well as the use of monetary and/or fiscal policy derive, as noted in chapter 3, from models that assume full employment. They also ignore price and wage rigidities and assume that agents are rational. Of course, under these circumstances a government-led full-employment policy is indeed ineffective and even counterproductive. The central argument of the book is that these assumptions do not hold in the developing countries. Also, conservative thinking tends to ignore distributional issues and concentrate on efficiency aspects. Distributional problems are crucial, however, in a discussion of inclusive growth.

trade-offs that they may have to face resulting from political constraints. Inclusive growth is a complex concept, and those countries embracing it (or analogous concepts) should understand the overall policy implications.

Implementing policies to achieve full employment will require a change of mind-set as well as social dialogue with the different groups of society. Employment creation must be a target of the country's overall economic policy, requiring, for example, a broadening in the mandate of central banks (one option to consider is to set a realistic employment target subject to an inflation constraint to ensure responsible policy making). Making employment creation an explicit goal acknowledges (much more than through a growth target) that the government cares about the livelihoods of workers and citizens in general. The policy tools used to put this new objective into operation can complement other government macroeconomic policies aimed at stimulating growth (e.g., fiscal policies).

Given that a large portion of the labor force in many developing countries is still in agriculture, inclusive growth demands policies that develop this sector by absorbing more workers per acre and that allow the smooth transfer of labor into industry and services. This will also require a well-coordinated investment package and fiscal and monetary policies geared toward full employment.

Policy makers must also strive to stimulate domestic investment. Interest rates will be key, because interest rate increases raise uncertainty. The objective of policy has to be to keep them as low as possible. Low interest rates may activate the economy by stimulating consumption (debtors tend to have a higher marginal propensity to consume than creditors) and through balance sheet effects (as the value of assets increases with lower interest rates). In addition, access to credit by small and medium-sized enterprises has to improve. Credit matters for the level of economic activity. The financial system and the banking sector particularly are essential (Rajan and Zingales 2003). However, in many developing countries, banking is underdeveloped and lending is not as important as it should be. For this reason, monetary authorities need to induce banks to increase lending by modifying some banking regulations (e.g., capital adequacy requirements). Governments and monetary authorities can also encourage banks to lend by (i) taxing excess reserves;[3] (ii) imposing taxes on capital gains from currency changes to dissuade them (i.e., banks) from engaging in currency speculation; (iii) not allowing them to hold foreign exchange assets (loans or bonds); and (iv) discouraging them from purchasing government bonds (Stiglitz et al. 2006, 83).[4]

---

[3] Of course, reserves are a tax as long as they pay an interest rate below the market rate.

[4] Or, perhaps, rather than discouraging banks from holding bonds, which are reserves that pay interest, instead, pay zero interest on bonds, and banks will not want to hold them.

Countercyclical fiscal policies must also be maintained. This requires increasing the tax base as well as improving the administration and enforcement of the tax code. As discussed above, taxes serve not to finance the budget deficit but to remove spending power from the private sector and to ensure demand for the government's money. Also, those countries with significant debt denominated in foreign currency should have a debt repayment schedule that does not aggravate cyclicality.

In addition, governments must be aware of the effects of globalization, competitiveness, and fast technical progress and structural change in today's world. Diversifying the economy and producing and exporting more sophisticated goods and services will lead to faster growth.

Finally, other suggestions, part of the range of tools available to policy makers to achieve full employment and inclusive growth, are as follows:

(i)   Foster regional integration, as it creates bigger domestic markets, which through cooperation and economies of scale can bolster the development of higher-value-added industries. This includes the regional coordination of exchange rate policy.[5]

(ii) Ensure a stable and competitive real exchange rate. Before the financial crisis of 1997–1998, monetary authority intervention in many countries sought to maintain a specific value or peg. Since then, the objective has been a deliberate undervaluation, accomplished through nominal intervention and targeting the real exchange rate through sterilization. Recent empirical evidence by Rodrik (2007) indicates that real exchange rate overvaluation is bad for growth, while undervaluation is good. Moreover, a competitive real exchange rate generates employment through a number of channels (Frenkel and Ros 2006).[6] The first is through its impact on the level of aggregate demand (the macroeconomic channel). The second channel is through its impact on the cost of labor relative to other goods, which thereby affects the amount of labor hired per unit of output (the labor intensity channel). And the third channel is through its impact on investment and growth (the development channel). In a full-employment economy, a competitive exchange

---

[5]   In general, monetary and financial cooperation may bring other benefits such as preventing the recurrence of a crisis (and managing it better should it occur), providing a higher leverage in shaping the financial environment affecting the region in question, or facilitating economic integration. See Chin (2005).

[6]   Certainly competitive exchange rates (especially if they follow devaluations) can lead to inflation, and this is something to watch for. However, it seems that, "when there is sufficient slack in the economy (when unemployment, for instance, is high enough), devaluations have generally not given rise to sustained inflation, at least in recent years" (Stiglitz et al. 2006, 90).

rate leads to a reallocation of the country's resources away from goods and services produced for the domestic market toward tradables, both exports and goods that compete with imports. And in an economy characterized by vastly underutilized resources, growth-related externalities are derived from a policy of maintaining a competitive exchange rate, as the higher demand for exports, as well as the increasing production of import-competitive goods, can spill over into demand for nontradables because of higher income in sectors that produce tradables. For this policy to be successful, it is necessary that countries be willing to impose capital requirements (in general, capital management techniques) if needed to fight speculative flows, as Malaysia did in 1998, which allowed the country to stabilize its economy without raising interest rates.[7] Thailand also experimented with these requirements in 2007.

(iii) Promote decent employment in services. As argued early on in the book, the objective of full employment must be complemented with that of decent employment, that is, employment that provides living wages, benefits, reasonable job security, and a healthy work environment. Services have become the employer of last resort in many developing countries. Often, jobs generated in this sector are not decent. For this reason, the creation of high-quality employment in this sector is important. In many Asian countries, labor reallocated out of agriculture tends to be absorbed by low-productivity and unskilled service activities (e.g., retail trade, restaurants, domestic service). This requires the development of a "service policy" akin to industrial policy.

(iv) Promote efficiency in labor market institutions through an established and enforced set of labor regulations and policies. If, for example, reforms intended to induce structural change are an objective, a safety and employment protection net for affected workers should be established, but where full employment is the main objective. Well-funded and comprehensive labor market policies help individual workers cope with economic shocks. The important aspect is to make sure that these policies are enforced. As an extension of active labor market policies, countries should consider the public sector as employer of last resort.

---

[7] To be unbiased, I acknowledge new research by Johnson et al. (2006) and Prasad and Rajan (2007), who find no evidence that capital controls had macroeconomic benefits for Malaysia.

I sincerely hope that policy makers in developing Asia and in other developing regions of the world see the relevance of the messages of the book and refocus policy priorities in their countries. As I argued in the preface, my objective is to challenge them and to compel them to think outside the box. I hope I have achieved this to some degree. I also hope that these pages contribute minimally to helping map a new road toward development. A serious debate will only come as a result of a deep understanding of the main obstacles that many countries face. This debate should lead to the implementation of policies that improve the lives of millions in developing Asia and in the rest of the developing world. The term "inclusive growth" might not appear in standard textbooks, and even a precise definition might slip through our fingers. This is not important. What matters is the message behind it. Grasping the key elements of the nexus *inclusive growth–full employment* will lead to better and more just societies.

References

Abramovitz, M. 1986. Catching-Up, Forging Ahead and Falling Behind. *Journal of Economic History*. 46. pp. 386–406.

———. 1993. The Origins of the Post-War Catch-Up and Convergence Boom. In Fagerberg, J., B. Verspagen, and N. von Tunzelmann, eds. *The Dynamics of Technology, Trade and Growth*. Aldershot, United Kingdom (UK): Edward Elgar.

Akbari, Ather H., and Wimai Rankaduwa. 2006. Inflation Targeting in a Small Emerging Market Economy: The Case of Pakistan. *SBP-Research Bulletin*. 2 (1). pp. 169–90.

Akerlof, George A. 1982. Labor Contracts As Partial Gift Exchange. *Quarterly Journal of Economics*. 97 (November). pp. 543–69.

———. 2002. Behavioral Macroeconomics and Macroeconomic Behavior. *American Economic Review*. 92 (3). pp. 411–33.

Akyüz, Y., H.J. Chang, and R. Kozul-Wright. 1998. New Perspectives on East Asian Development. *Journal of Development Studies*. 34 (6). pp. 4–36.

Akyüz, Y., and C. Gore. 1996. The Investment–Profits Nexus in East Asian Industrialization. *World Development*. 24. pp. 461–70.

Aldaba, Fernando, et al. (30 members of the Economics and Political Science Department) 2005. *Beneath the Fiscal Crisis: Uneven Development Weakens the Republic*. Research report, Ateneo de Manila University.

Ali, Ifzal, and Hyun H. Son. 2007. Defining and Measuring Inclusive Growth: Application to the Philippines. *ERD Working Paper Series 98*. July. Economics and Research Department (ERD). Manila: Asian Development Bank (ADB).

Ali, Ifzal, and Juzhong Zhuang. 2007. Inclusive Growth Toward a Prosperous Asia: Policy Implications. *ERD Working Paper Series 97*. July. Economics and Research Department (ERD). Manila: ADB.

Amante, Maragtas S.V. 2003. Philippines. In *Mismatch in the Labor Market. Asian Experience*. Tokyo: Asian Productivity Organization.

Amsden, Alice. 1989. *Asia's Next Giant: South Korea and Late Industrialization*. New York: Oxford University Press.

———. 2000. Industrialization under WTO Law. United Nations Conference on Trade and Development (UNCTAD). www.unctad-10.org/pdfs/ux_tdxrt1d7.en.pdf

———. 2007. *Escape from the Empire*. Cambridge, MA: MIT Press.

Amsden, Alice, and Takashi Hikino. 2000. The Bark Is Worse Than the Bite: New WTO Law and Late Industrialization. *American Academy of Political and Social Science*. 570 (July). pp. 104–14.

Anant, T. C. A., R. Hasan, P. Mohapatra, R. Nagaraj, and S. K. Sasikumar. 2006. Labor Markets in India: Issues and Perspectives. In Felipe, Jesus, and Rana Hasan, eds. *Labor Markets in Asia. Issues and Perspectives*. Basingstoke, UK: Palgrave Macmillan.

Arestis, Philip, and Malcolm Sawyer. 2006. Interest Rates and the Real Economy. In Gnos, Claude, and Louis-Philippe Rochon, eds. *Post-Keynesian Principles of Economic Policy*. Cheltenham, UK: Edward Elgar.

Asian Development Bank (ADB). 2005. *Philippines: Moving Toward a Better Investment Climate*. Manila.

———. 2006a. *Asian Development Outlook 2006*. Manila.

———. 2006b. *Key Indicators 2006*. Special chapter *Measuring Policy Effectiveness in Health and Education*. Manila.

———. 2007a. *Key Indicators 2007*. Special chapter *Inequality in Asia*. Manila.

———. 2007b. *Asian Development Outlook 2007*. Special chapter *Growth amid change* and special volume *Growth amid Change in Developing Asia*. Manila.

———. 2007c. *Asian Development Outlook 2007*. Special chapter *Uncoupling Asia: Myth and Reality*. Manila.

———. 2007d. *Asian Development Outlook Update 2007*. Manila.

Balassa, B. A. 1989. *New Directions in the World Economy*. New York: New York University Press.

Baldacci, Emanuele, Benedict Clements, and Sanjeev Gupta. 2003. Using Fiscal Policy to Spur Growth. *Finance and Development*. December. pp. 28–31.

Ball, Lawrence. 1999. Aggregate Demand and Long-Run Unemployment. *Brookings Papers on Economic Activity*. 2. pp. 189–236.

Bandiera, O., G. Caprio, P. Honohan, and F. Schiantarelli. 2000. Does Financial Reform Raise or Reduce Saving? *Review of Economics and Statistics*. 82 (2). pp. 239–63.

Banerjee, Abhijit. 1996. Can Anything Be Done About Corruption? In Quibria, M. G., and J. Malcolm Dowling, eds. *Current Issues in Economic Development: An Asian Perspective*. Hong Kong, China, and Oxford: Oxford University Press.

Bardhan, Pranab. 2001. Distributive Conflicts, Collective Action, and Institutional Economics. In Meier, Gerald M., and Joseph E. Stiglitz, eds. *Frontiers of Development Economics*. New York: Oxford University Press for the World Bank.

———. 2006. Awakening Giants, Feet of Clay: A Comparative Assessment of the Rise of China and India. Paper presented at the International Conference on the Dragon and the Elephant: China and India's Economic Reforms. Shanghai, 1–2 July.

———. 2008. What Makes a Miracle. Some Myths About the Rise of China and India. *Boston Review*. January–February.

Barro, Robert. 1974. Are Government Bonds Net Wealth? *Journal of Political Economy*. 82 (6). pp. 1095–1117.

———. 1997. *Determinants of Economic Growth: A Cross-Country Empirical Study*. Cambridge, MA: MIT Press.

Basu, Kaushik. 1995. Rural Credit and Interlinkage: Implications for Rural Poverty, Agrarian Efficiency, and Public Policy. In Quibria, M.G., ed. *Critical Issues in Asian Development: An Asian Perspective*. Hong Kong, China, and Oxford: Oxford University Press.

Basu, Santonu, and Sushanta Mallick. 2007. When does Growth Trickle Down to the Poor? The Indian Case. *Cambridge Journal of Economics*. Vol. 32. pp. 461–477.

Baumol, William J., Sue Ann Batey Blackman, and Edward Wolff. 1985. Unbalanced Growth Revisited: Asymptotic Stagnancy and New Evidence. *American Economic Review*. 75 (4). pp. 806–17.

———. 1989. *Productivity and American Leadership: The Long View*. Cambridge, MA: MIT Press.

Berg, Janine, Christopher Ernst, and Peter Auer. 2006. *Meeting the Employment Challenge. Argentina, Brazil and Mexico in the Global Economy*. Boulder, CO: Lynne Rienner.

Berglund, Per Gunnar, and Matias Vernengo. 2004. A Debate on the Deficit. *Challenge*. 47 (6). pp. 1–42.

Besley, Timothy, and Robin Burgess. 2004. Can Labor Regulation Hinder Economic Performance? Evidence from India. *The Quarterly Journal of Economics*. 119 (1). pp. 91–134.

Beveridge, W.H. 1944. *Full Employment in a Free Society*. London: Allen and Unwin.

Blanchard, Olivier. 1997. *The Economics of Post-Communist Transition*. Oxford: Clarendon Press.

———. 2002. Monetary Policy and Unemployment. Remarks at the conference on Monetary Policy and the Labor Market, New School University. New York. November.

Blecker, Robert. 2002. The Balance of Payments–Constrained Growth Model and the Limits to Export-Led Growth. In Davidson, P., ed. *A Post Keynesian Perspective on Twenty-First Century Economic Problems*. Northampton, MA: Edward Elgar.

———. 2003. The Diminishing Returns to Export-Led Growth. In Mead, W. Russell, and S.R. Schwenninger, eds. *The Bridge to a Global Middle Class: Development, Trade, and International Finance in the 21st Century*. Norwell, MA: Kluwer Academic Publishers for the Milken Institute.

Blinder, Alan. 1987. *Hard Heads Soft Hearts*. Reading, MA: Addison-Wesley.

———. 1988. The Challenge of High Unemployment. *NBER Working Paper* 2489. National Bureau of Economic Research (NBER), Cambridge, MA.

Blomstrom M., R. Lipsey, and M. Zejan. 1996. Is Fixed Investment the Key to Economic Growth? *Quarterly Journal of Economics*. Vol. 111. pp. 269–276.

Booth, Anne, and R.M. Sundrum. 1984. *Labour Absorption in Agriculture*. Oxford: Oxford University Press.

Boyer, Robert. 2006. Employment and Decent Work in the Era of Flexicurity. Paris-Jourdan Sciences Economiques. *Working Paper* No. 2006-21.

Braverman, Harry. 1998. *Labor and Capital Monopoly*. (25th anniversary edition). New York: Monthly Review Press.

Briones, Roehlano, and Jesus Felipe. 2007. Does Agriculture (Still) Matter? Agricultural Transformation and Economic Development in Asia. Mimeograph.

Brown, Ian. 1997. *Economic Change in South-East Asia, c.1830–1980*. Oxford: Oxford University Press.

Brunner, Karl. 1986. Fiscal Policy in Macro Theory. In Hafer, Rik, ed., *The Monetary versus Fiscal Policy Debate: Lessons from Two Decades*. Totowa, NJ: Rowman and Allanheld.

Bruno, Michael. 1995. Does Inflation Really Lower Growth? *Finance and Development*. September.

Bruno, Michael, and William Easterly. 1998. Inflation Crises and Long-Run Growth. *Journal of Monetary Economics*. 41. pp. 2–26.

Chang, Ha-Joon. 2002. *Kicking Away the Ladder*. London: Anthem Press.

Chaudhry, Muhammad Aslam, and Munir A.S. Choudhary. 2006. Why the State Bank of Pakistan Should Not Adopt Inflation Targeting. *SBP Research Bulletin*. 2 (1). pp. 195–209.

Chenery, H.B., S. Robinson, and M. Syrquin. 1986. *Industrialization and Economic Growth*. Oxford: Oxford University Press.

Chin, Kok-Fay. 2005. East Asian Monetary and Financial Cooperation: The Long Road Ahead. In Rochon, Louis-Philippe, and Sergio Rossi, eds. *Monetary and Exchange Rate Systems: A Global View of Financial Crises*. Northampton, MA: Edward Elgar.

Cho, Y.C., and D. Khatkhate. 1990. Financial Liberalization. *Economic and Political Weekly*. May 20.

Cline, W.R., 1982. Can the East Asian Model of Development be Generalized? *World Development*. 10 (2). pp. 81–90.

Cohen, Daniel. 1998. *The Wealth of the World and the Poverty of Nations*. Cambridge, MA: MIT Press.

Colander, David, and Peter Hans Matthews. 2006. Integrating Sound Finance with Functional Finance. In Vernengo, Matias, and Per Gunnar Berglund, eds. *The Means to Prosperity*. London and New York: Routledge.

Commission on Growth and Development. 2008. *The Growth Report. Strategies for Sustained Growth and Inclusive Development*. Washington, DC: World Bank.

Commonwealth of Australia. 2006. *Pacific 2020. Challenges and Opportunities for Growth*. www.ausaid.gov.au/publications/pdf/pacific2020.pdf

Coronel, Sheila S., Yvonne T. Chua, Luz Rimban, and Booma B. Cruz. 2004. *The Rulemakers. How the Wealthy and Well-Born Dominate Congress*. Manila: Philippine Center for Investigative Journalism.

Dasgupta, Partha. 1995. Economic Development and the Environment: Issues, Policies, and the Political Economy. In Quibria, M.G., ed. *Critical Issues in Asian Development: Issues, Policies and Experiences*. Hong Kong, China, and Oxford: Oxford University Press.

Davidson, Paul. 2006a. Can, or Should, a Central Bank Inflation Target? *Journal of Post Keynesian Economics*. 28 (4). pp. 689–703.

———. 2006b. Keynes, Post Keynesian Analysis and the Open Economies of the Twenty First Century. In Arestis, P., J. S. L. McCombie, and R. Vickerman, eds. *Growth and Economic Development*. Cheltenham, UK: Edward Elgar.

De Grauwe, P., and M. Polan. 2005. Is Inflation Always and Everywhere a Monetary Phenomenon? *Scandinavian Journal of Economics*. 107. pp. 239–59.

Department of Agrarian Reform (Philippines). 2002. *Agrarian Reform Accomplishments*. Quezon City: Department of Agrarian Reform Planning Service.

Deshpande, L. K. 2004. *Liberalization and Labor: Labor Flexibility in Indian Manufacturing*. New Delhi: Institute of Human Development.

Dew-Becker, Ian, and Robert Gordon. 2005. Where Did the Productivity Growth Go? Inflation Dynamics and the Distribution of Income. *NBER Working Paper* 11842. National Bureau of Economic Research. December.

Deyo, F., ed. 1987. *The Political Economy of the New Asian Industrialism*. Ithaca, NY: Cornell University Press.

Dobb, Maurice. 1959. *Economic Growth and Planning*. New York: Monthly Review Press.

Doctor, Kailas C., and Hans Gallis. 1964. Modern Sector Employment in Asian Countries: Some Empirical Estimates. *International Labor Review*. 89 (December).

Domar, E.D. 1946. Capital Expansion, Rate of Growth and Employment. *Econometrica*. 14 (2). pp. 137–47.

Dornbusch, Rudiger. 2000. Containing High Inflation. In Dornbusch, Rudiger, ed. *Keys to Prosperity. Free Markets, Sound Money, and a Bit of Luck*. Cambridge, MA: MIT Press.

Easterly, William. 2002. *The Elusive Quest for Growth. Economists' Adventures and Misadventures in the Tropics*. Paperback edition. Cambridge, MA, and London: MIT Press.

———. 2006. Planners versus Searchers in Foreign Aid. *Asian Development Review*. 23 (1). pp. 1–35.

———. 2008. Hayek vs. the Development Experts. The Hayek Lecture. The Manhattan Institute for Policy Research. The Fourth Annual Lecture, 23 October 2008.

The Economist. 2007. Does America Need a Recession? 25–31 August. p. 76.

———. 2008a. From Mao to the Mall. 16–22 February. p. 86.

———. 2008b. The Next Green Revolution. 23–29 February. pp. 67–68.

———. 2008c. What Is Holding India Back? 8–14 March. p. 11.

———. 2008d. Winners and Losers. 1–7 March. p. 54.

Einhorn, B. 2006. China. *BusinessWeek*. 6 November.

Eisner, Robert. 1995. Our NAIRU Limit: The Governing Myth of Economic Policy. *American Prospect*. Spring. (21). pp. 58–63.

———. 1997. US House of Representatives, Committee on Banking and Financial Services, Subcommittee on Domestic and Monetary Policy. Full Employment and Inflation: Where We Stand and Where We Can Go. 23 July. financialservices.house.gov/banking/72397re.htm

Engardio, P., and D. Roberts. 2004. The China Price. *BusinessWeek Online*. 6 December.

Ertuk, K. 2001–2002. Overcapacity and the East Asian Crisis. *Journal of Post Keynesian Economics* 24 (2). pp. 253–76.

Espinosa-Vega, Marco A., and Steven Russell. 1997. History and Theory of the NAIRU: A Critical Review. *Federal Reserve Bank of Atlanta Economic Review*. Second Quarter.

Fagerberg, J. 2000. Technological Progress, Structural Change and Productivity Growth: A Comparative Study. *Structural Change and Economic Dynamics*. 11. pp. 393–411.

Fardmanesh, Mohsen, and Li Tan. 2005. *From Command to Market: A Performance Perspective for Transition Economies*. New Haven, CT: Economic Growth Center, Yale University.

Felipe, Jesus. 2000. On the Myth and Mystery of Singapore's "Zero TFP." *Asian Economic Journal*. 14 (2). pp. 187–209.

———. 2003. Is Export-Led Growth Passé? Implications for Developing Asia. *ERD Working Paper* 48. Manila: ADB.

———. 2006. A Decade of Debate about the Sources of Growth in East Asia: How Much Do We Know about Why Some Countries Grow Faster Than Others? *Estudios de Economía Aplicada*. 24 (1). pp. 181–220.

―――. 2007. A cautionary note on the interpretation of unit labor costs as an indicator of competitiveness, with reference to the Philippines. *Philippine Journal of Development* No. 63. Vol. XXXIV, No. 2. pp. 1–23.

―――. 2008. What Policymakers Should Know About Total Factor Productivity. *Malaysian Journal of Economic Studies*. Vol. 45. No. 1.

Felipe, Jesus, and Gemma Estrada. 2008. Benchmarking Developing Asia's Manufacturing Sector. *International Journal of Development Studies*. Vol. 7, No. 2: 97–119.

Felipe, Jesus, and Rana Hasan. 2006. *Labor Markets in Asia: Issues and Perspectives*. Basingstoke, UK: Palgrave Macmillan.

Felipe, Jesus, Editha Laviña, and Emma Xiaoqin Fan. 2008. The Diverging Patterns of Profitability, Investment and Growth of China and India, 1980–2003. *World Development*. 36 (5). pp. 741–74.

Felipe, Jesus, Miguel León-Ledesma, Matteo Lanzafame, and Gemma Estrada. 2007. Sectoral Engines of Growth in Developing Asia: Stylized Facts and Implications. *ERD Working Paper* 107 (November). Manila: ADB. Forthcoming 2009, *Malaysian Journal of Economic Studies*.

Felipe, Jesus, and Joseph Lim. 2005. Export or Domestic-Led Growth in Asia? *Asian Development Review*. 22 (2). pp. 35–75.

Felipe, Jesus, and J. S. L. McCombie. 2001. Biased Technical Change, Growth Accounting, and the Conundrum of the East Asian Miracle. *Journal of Comparative Economics*. 29 (3). pp. 542–65.

―――. 2003. Some Methodological Problems with the Neoclassical Analysis of the East Asian Miracle. *Cambridge Journal of Economics*. 27 (5). pp. 695–721.

―――. 2008a. What Can the Labour Demand Function Tell Us About Wages and Employment? The Case of the Philippines. In Berg, Janine, and David Kucera, eds. *In Defence of Labour Market Institutions: Cultivating Justice in the Developing World*. Basingstoke, UK: Palgrave Macmillan.

―――. 2008b. Are Estimates of Labor Demand Functions Mere Statistical Artefacts? *International Review of Applied Economics*. Forthcoming.

Felipe, Jesus, John McCombie, and Kaukab Naqvi. 2009. Is Pakistan's Growth Rate Balance-of-Payments Constrained? Policies and Implications for Development and Growth. Manuscript. Manila: ADB.

Felipe, Jesus, William Mitchell, and Randall Wray. 2009. A reinterpretation of Pakistan's "economic crisis" and options for policy makers. Manuscript. Manila: ADB.

Felipe, Jesus, and Norio Usui. 2008. Rethinking the Growth Diagnostics Approach: Questions from the Practitioners. *ADB Economics Working Paper* 132. Manila: ADB.

Felipe, Jesus, and Matias Vernengo. 2002. Demystifying the Principle of Comparative Advantage: Implications for Developing Countries. *International Journal of Political Economy*. 32 (4). pp. 49–75.

Fields, Gary. 1995. Income Distribution in Developing Economies; Conceptual, Data, and Policy Issues in Broad-Based Growth. In Quibria, M. G., ed. *Critical Issues in Asian Development: Issues, Policies and Experiences.* Hong Kong, China, and Oxford: Oxford University Press.

Foley, D., and A. Marquetti. 1999. Productivity, Employment and Growth in European Integration. *Metroeconomica.* 50 (3). pp. 277–300.

Foley, D., and T. Michl. 1999. *Growth and Distribution.* Cambridge, MA, and London: Harvard University Press.

Forstater, Mathew. 1998. Flexible Full Employment: Structural Implications of Discretionary Public Sector Employment. *Journal of Economic Issues.* 32 (2). pp. 557–63.

———. 1999. Public Employment and Economic Flexibility: The Job Opportunity Approach to Full Employment. *Public Policy Brief* 50. New York: The Jerome Levy Economics Institute of Bard College.

Frenkel, Roberto, and Jaime Ros. 2006. Unemployment and the Real Exchange Rate in Latin America. *World Development.* 34 (4). pp. 631–46.

Friedman, Milton. 1968. The Role of Monetary Policy. *American Economic Review.* 68 (1). pp. 1–17.

Fry, Maxwell. 1997. In Favour of Financial Liberalisation. *Economic Journal.* 107 (442). pp. 754–70.

Galbraith, James K. 1997. Dangerous Metaphor: The Fiction of the Labor Market. *Public Policy Brief* 36. New York: The Jerome Levy Economics Institute of Bard College.

Galbraith, James K., L. Randall Wray, and Warren Mosler. 2009. The Case against Intergenerational Accounting. The Levy Economics Institute of Bard College. *Public Policy Brief* No. 98.

Galbraith, John Kenneth. 1979. *The Nature of Mass Poverty.* Cambridge, MA: Harvard University Press.

———. 1996. *The Good Society.* Boston: Houghton Mifflin Co.

Gereffi, Gary. 1996. Commodity Chains and Regional Divisions of Labor in East Asia. *Journal of Asian Business.* 12 (1). pp. 75–112.

Gerschenkron, A. 1962. *Economic Backwardness in Historical Perspective: A Book of Essays.* Cambridge, MA: Belknap Press of Harvard University Press.

Gupta, K.L. 1987. Aggregate Savings, Financial Intermediation and Interest Rates. *Review of Economics and Statistics.* 69 (2). pp. 303–11.

Habito, C., R. Briones, and C. Pater. 2003. Investment, Productivity and Land Market on the Comprehensive Agrarian Reform Program. *CARP Impact Assessment Studies.* 4. Department of Agrarian Reform, Quezon City.

Hamilton, C. 1986. *Capitalist Industrialization in Korea.* Boulder, CO: Westview Press.

Haque, Nadeem Ul. 2006. Beyond Planning and Mercantilism. An Evaluation of Pakistan's Growth Strategy. *The Pakistan Development Review.* 45 (1). pp. 3–23.

Haque, Nadeem Ul, and Ratna Sahay. 1996. Do Government Wage Cuts Close Budget Deficits? Costs of Corruption. *IMF Staff Papers*. 43 (1). pp. 754–78. Washington, DC: International Monetary Fund (IMF).

Harberger, Arnold. 1998. Monetary and Fiscal Policy for Equitable Economic Growth. In Tanzi, Vito, and Ke-young Chu, eds. *Income Distribution and High-Quality Growth*. Cambridge, MA: MIT Press.

Harrod, Roy. 1939. An Essay in Dynamic Theory. *The Economic Journal*. 49 (33). pp. 14–33.

Hausmann, Ricardo, Jason Hwang, and Dani Rodrik. 2005. *What You Export Matters*. John F. Kennedy School of Government, Harvard University. ksgnotes1.harvard.edu/Research/wpaper.nsf/rwp/RWP05–063

Hausmann, Ricardo, Francisco Rodriguez, and Rodrigo Wagner. 2006. Growth Collapses. *Working Paper* No. 136. Center for International Development, Harvard University.

Hausmann, Ricardo, and Bailey Klinger. 2006. Structural Transformation and Patterns of Comparative Advantage in the Product Space. Draft. John F. Kennedy School of Government, Harvard University. idbdocs. iadb.org/wsdocs/getdocument.aspx? docnum=773109

Hausmann, Ricardo, and Dani Rodrik. 2006. Doomed to Choose: Industrial Policy as Predicament. Draft. John F. Kennedy School of Government, Harvard University. ksghome.harvard.edu/~drodrik/doomed.pdf

Hausmann, Ricardo, Dani Rodrik, and Andres Velasco. 2005. Growth Diagnostics. Draft. John F. Kennedy School of Government, Harvard University.

Hayami, Yujiro. 1997. *Development Economics*. Oxford and New York: Oxford University Press.

Herrera, Ernesto. 2008. More Than Common Economic Indicators. *The Manila Times*. 18 March.

Herrin, Alejandro, and Ernesto Pernia. 2003. Population, Human Resources and Employment. In Balisacan, A., and Hal Hill, eds. *The Philippine Economy: Development, Policies and Challenges*. Quezon City: Ateneo de Manila University Press.

Hidalgo, C., B. Klinger, A.L. Barabási, and R. Hausmann. 2007. The Product Space Conditions the Development of Nations. *Science*. 317. pp. 482–87.

Hill, Hal. 2003. Industry. In Balisacan, Arsenio, and Hal Hill, eds. *The Philippine Economy. Development, Policies and Challenges*. Quezon City: Ateneo de Manila University Press.

Hirschman, A. 1958. *Strategy of Economic Development*. New Haven, CT: Yale University Press.

Hobday, Michael. 1995a. East Asian Latecomer Firms: Learning the Technology of Electronics. *World Development*. 23 (7). pp. 1171–93.

————. 1995b. *Innovation in East Asia: The Challenge to Japan*. Aldershot, UK: Edward Elgar.

Hobday, Michael, Howard Rush, and John Bessant. 2004. Approaching the Innovation Frontier in Korea: The Transition Phase to Leadership. *Research Policy*. 33. pp. 1433–57.

Hoddinott, John, John A. Maluccio, Jere R. Behrman, Rafael Flores, and Reynaldo Martorell. 2008. The Impact of Nutrition during Early Childhood on Income, Hours Worked, and Wages of Guatemalan Adults. *The Lancet*. 2 February. pp. 411–16.

Husain, Ishrat. 2005. Keynote Address. *SBP-Research Bulletin*. 2 (1). pp. 1–4.

Hwang, Jason. 2006. Introduction of New Goods, Convergence and Growth. Mimeograph. Department of Economics, Harvard University.

Imbs, Jean, and Roman Wacziarg. 2003. Stages of Diversification. *The American Economic Review*. 93 (1). pp. 63–86.

Ito, Motoshige, and Jun Shibata. 1996. The Role of Cross-Border Division of Labor and Investment in Promoting Trade: Two Case Studies from East Asia. In Quibria, M.G., and J. Malcolm Dowling, eds. *Current Issues in Economic Development: An Asian Perspective*. Hong Kong, China, and Oxford: Oxford University Press.

Jacobsson, Staffan, and Ghayur Alam. 1994. *Liberalization and Industrial Development in the Third World: A Comparison of the Indian and South Korean Engineering Industries*. New Delhi: Sage Publications.

Jaumotte, Florecen, and Nikola Spatafora. 2007. Asia Rising: A Sectoral Perspective. *IMF Working Paper* 07/130. Washington, DC: IMF.

Jayadev, Arjun. 2006. The Class Content of Preferences Towards Anti-Inflation and Anti-Unemployment Policies. Manuscript. Political Economic Research Institute. University of Massachusetts, Amherst.

Jha, Raghbendra. 2006. Inflation Targeting in India: Issues and Prospects. Manuscript. Political Economic Research Institute, University of Massachusetts, Amherst.

Johnson, Simon, Kalpana Kochhar, Todd Mitton, and Natalia Tamirisa. 2006. Malaysian Capital Controls: Macroeconomics and Institutions. *IMF Working Paper* 06/51. Washington, DC: IMF.

Jomo, K.S., and Kock Wah Tan, eds. 1999. *Industrial Policy in East Asia. Lessons for Malaysia*. Kuala Lumpur: University of Malaya Press.

Journal of Economic Perspectives. 1997. Symposium on NAIRU. Winter.

Kaboub, Fadhel. 2007. ELR-Led Economic Development: A Plan for Tunisia. *Working Paper* 499. New York: The Jerome Levy Economics Institute of Bard College.

Kaka, N.F., S.S. Kekre, and S. Sarangan. 2006. Benchmarking India's Business Process Outsourcers. *The McKinsey Quarterly*. July. pp. 20–21.

Kaldor, Nicholas. 1937. Annual Survey of Economic Theory: The Controversy on the Theory of Capital. *Econometrica*. 5. pp. 201–233.

————. 1966. *Causes of the Slow Rate of Growth in the United Kingdom.* Cambridge: Cambridge University Press.

————. 1967. *Strategic Factors in Economic Development.* Ithaca, NY: New York State School of Industrial and Labor Relations, Cornell University.

————. 1970. The Case for Regional Policies. *Scottish Journal of Political Economy.* 17. pp. 337–348.

Kalecki, Michał. 1939. *Essays in the Theory of Economic Fluctuations.* London: Allen and Unwin.

————. 1943 [1971]. Political Aspects of Full Employment. In Kalecki, M., *Selected Essays on the Dynamics of the Capitalist Economy.* Cambridge, UK: Cambridge University Press.

————. 1944. Three Ways to Full Employment. In Balogh, T., ed. *The Economics of Full Employment.* Oxford: Basil Blackwell.

————. 1954 [1991]. The Problem of Financing Economic Development. In Osiatyński, Jerzy, ed. *Collected Works of Michał Kalecki.* Oxford: Clarendon Press.

————. 1966a [1991]. The Difference Between Crucial Economic Problems of Developed and Underdeveloped Non-Socialist Economies. In Osiatyński, Jerzy, ed. *Collected Works of Michał Kalecki.* Oxford: Clarendon Press.

————. 1966b [1991]. Forms of Foreign Aid: An Economic Analysis. In Osiatyński, Jerzy, ed. *Collected Works of Michał Kalecki.* Oxford: Clarendon Press.

Kaplinsky, R. 2000. If You Want to Get Somewhere Else, You Must Run at Least Twice as Fast as That: The Roots of the East Asian Crisis. *Competition and Change: The Journal of Global Business and Political Economy.* 4 (1). pp. 1–30.

Kapur, Basant K. 1996. Ethic, Values, and Economic Development. In Quibria, M.G., and J. Malcolm Dowling, eds. *Current Issues in Economic Development: An Asian Perspective.* Hong Kong, China, and Oxford: Oxford University Press.

Keynes, John M. 1930. *A Treatise on Money.* New York: Harcourt, Brace.

————. 1936 [1961]. *The General Theory of Employment, Interest and Money.* London: Macmillan and Co.

————. 1972. *The Collected Writings of John Maynard Keynes, IX: Essays in Persuasion,* Donald Moggridge, ed. London and Basingstoke: Macmillan/Cambridge University Press.

Khan, Ali. 1996. Population and Economic Development. In Quibria, M.G., and J. Malcolm Dowling, eds. *Current Issues in Economic Development: An Asian Perspective.* Hong Kong, China, and Oxford: Oxford University Press.

Khan, M., and A. Senhadji. 2001. Threshold Effects in the Relationship between Inflation and Growth. *IMF Staff Papers*. 48. pp. 1–21.

Kim Jung Min. 2003. A New Spring in Its Step. *Far Eastern Economic Review*. 13 February. pp. 30–33.

Kim, L. 1997. *From Imitation to Innovation: Dynamics of Korea's Technological Learning*. Boston: Harvard Business School Press.

Kochhar, Kalpana, Utsav Khumar, Raghuram Rajan, Arvind Subramanian, and Ioannis Tokatlidis. 2006. India's Pattern of Development: What Happened, What Follows? *IMF Working Paper* 06/22. Washington, DC: IMF.

Kremer, Michael. 1993. The O-Ring Theory of Economics Development. *Quarterly Journal of Economics*. 108 (3). pp. 551–75.

Krueger, A., 1997. Trade Policy and Economic Development: How We Learn. *American Economic Review*. 87 (1). pp. 1–22.

Krugman, Paul. 1994. The Myth of Asia's Miracle. *Foreign Affairs*. November–December. pp. 62–78.

———. 1996. Making Sense of the Competitiveness Debate. *Oxford Review of Economic Policy*. 12 (3). pp. 17–25.

———. 1999. *The Accidental Theorist*. New York: Penguin Books.

Kuijs, Louis. 2007. How Will China's Saving–Investment Balance Evolve? *World Bank Policy Research Working Paper* 3958. Washington, DC: World Bank.

Kuijs, Louis, and Jianwu He. 2007. Rebalancing China's Economy— Modelling a Policy Package. *World Bank China Research Paper* 7. Washington, DC: World Bank.

Lall, Sanjaya. 2000. The Technological Structure and Performance of Developing Country Manufactured Exports, 1985–98. *Oxford Development Studies*. 28 (3). pp. 337–69.

Landes, David. 1998. *The Wealth and Poverty of Nations*. London: Abacus.

Lau, Lawrence. 1990. *Models of Development. A Comparative Study of Economic Growth in South Korea and [Taipei,China]*. San Francisco: ICS Press.

Lawrence, Robert, and David Weinstein. 2001. Trade and Growth: Import-Led or Export-Led: Evidence from Japan and Korea. In Stiglitz, Joseph E., and Shahid Yusuf, eds. *Rethinking the East Asian Miracle*. New York: Oxford University Press.

Lee, Joseph S., ed. 2007. *The Labour Market and Economic Development of [Taipei,China]*. Cheltenham, UK: Edward Elgar.

Leontief, W. 1953. Dynamic Analysis. In Leontief, W., ed. *Studies in the Structure of the American Economy*. New York: Oxford University Press.

Lerner, Abba. 1943. Functional Finance and the Federal Debt. *Social Research*. 10. pp. 38–51.

———. 1961. The Burden of Debt. *Review of Economics and Statistics*. 43 (2). pp. 139–41.

Levine, Ross, and S. Zervos. 1993. What We Have Learned about Policy and Growth from Cross-Country Regressions. *American Economic Review Papers and Proceedings*. 83 (2). pp. 102–6.

Lewis, Arthur W. 1954. Economic Development with Unlimited Supplies of Labor. *The Manchester School*. 22. pp. 139–91.

———. 1978. *Growth and Fluctuations 1870–1913*. London: Allen and Unwin.

Lewis, William W. 2004. *The Power of Productivity*. Chicago: The University of Chicago Press.

Lian, D. 2003. Asia Pacific: In Search of Synthesis in Southeast Asia. www.morganstanley.com/GEFdata/digests/latest-digest.html

Lin, J. Y., and M. Liu. 2003. Development Strategy, Viability and Challenges of Development in Lagging Regions. Paper presented at the Annual Bank Conference on Development Economics, 21–23 May, Bangalore, India.

Llanto, G., and M. Ballesteros. 2003. Land Issues in Poverty Reduction Strategies and the Development Agenda: Philippines. *Discussion Papers Series* 2003–03. Makati City: Philippines Institute of Development Studies.

Lucas, Robert. 1988. On the Mechanics of Economic Development. *Journal of Monetary Economics*. 22 (July). pp. 3–42.

Macours, Karen, and Johan F. M. Swinnen. 2005. Agricultural Labor Adjustments in Transition Countries: The Role of Migration and Poverty. *Review of Agricultural Economics*. 27 (3). pp. 405–11.

Magnoli Bocci, Alessandro. 2008. Rising Growth, Declining Investment: The Puzzle of the Philippines. *Policy Research Working Paper* 4472. Office of the Chief Economist, East Asia Pacific Region, World Bank.

Magtibay-Ramos, Nedelyn, Gemma Estrada, and Jesus Felipe. 2008. An Analysis of the Philippine Business Process Outsourcing Industry. *Asian-Pacific Economic Literature*. 22 (1). pp. 41–56.

Marquetti, A. 2003. Analyzing Historical and Regional Patterns of Technical Change from a Classical–Marxian Perspective. *Journal of Economic Behavior and Organization*. 52 (2). pp. 191–200.

Mattick, Paul. 1969. *Marx and Keynes. The Limits of the Mixed Economy*. Boston: Porter Sargent, Extending Horizons Books.

McCombie, J. S. L., M. Pugno, and B. Soro, eds. 2002. *Productivity Growth and Economic Performance: Essays on Verdoorn's Law*. Basingstoke, UK: Palgrave Macmillan.

McCombie, J. S. L., and A. P. Thirlwall. 1994. *Economic Growth and the Balance of Payments Constraint*. New York: St. Martin's Press.

McDougall, P. 2006. IBM Expands India and China Operations in Quest for Growth. *InformationWeek*. 6 November.

McGregor, R. 2004. Philips on Track to Double Revenues in China. *Financial Times*. 3 September.

Mehta, Aashish, Jesus Felipe, Pilipinas Quising, and Sheila Camingue. 2007. Changing Patterns in Mincerian Returns to Education and Employment Structure in Three Asian Countries. *Institute for Social, Behavioral, and Economic Research, Center for Global Studies Working Paper* 06. University of California, Santa Barbara.

Meier, G.M. 1995. *Leading Issues in Economic Development*. 6th ed. New York and Oxford: Oxford University Press.

Mellor, J. 1998. The Effect of Family Planning Programs on the Fertility of Welfare Recipients: Evidence from Medical Claims. *Journal of Human Resources*. 33 (4). pp. 866–95.

Midelfart-Knarvik, K.H., H.G. Overman, S.J. Redding, and A.J. Venables. 2000. The Location of European Industry. *Economic Papers 142*. European Commission Directorate-General for Economic and Financial Affairs.

Minsky, Hyman. 1965. The Role of Employment Policy. In Gordon, Margaret S., ed. *Poverty in America*. San Francisco: Chandler Publishing Co.

———. 1968. Effects of Shifts of Aggregate Demand upon Income Distribution. *American Journal of Agricultural Economics*. 59 (2). pp. 328–39.

———. 1973. The Strategy of Economic Policy and Income Distribution. *The Annals of the American Academy of Political and Social Science*. 409 (September). pp. 92–101.

Mitchell, William F. 2003. The Job Guarantee Model—Financial Considerations in an Open Economy. In Nell, E.J., ed. *Functional Finance and Full Employment*. New York: Edward Elgar.

Mitchell, William F., and J. Muysken. 2008. *Full Employment Abandoned: Shifting Sands and Policy Failures*. Cheltenham, UK: Edward Elgar.

Mitchell, William F., and Randall Wray. 2005. In Defense of Employer of Last Resort: A Response to Malcolm Sawyer. *Journal of Economic Issues*. 39 (1). pp. 235–45.

Mitra, Pradeep. 2006. Productivity Growth and Job Creation in Eastern Europe and the Former Soviet Union. Presentation made at the State University Higher School of Economics, Moscow.

Morgan Stanley. 2004. India and China: New Tigers of Asia. Part I. Special Economic Analysis.

———. 2006. India and China: New Tigers of Asia. Part II. Special Economic Analysis.

Myrdal, G. 1957. *Economic Theory and Underdeveloped Regions*. London: Duckworth.

Nayyar, Deepak. 2008. Macroeconomics of Structural Adjustment and Public Finances in Developing Countries: A Heterodox Perspective. *International Journal of Development Issues*. 7 (1). pp. 4–28.

Nelson, R.R. 1956. A Theory of the Low-Level Equilibrium Trap in Underdeveloped Economies. *American Economic Review*. 46. pp. 894–908.

Nelson, R. R., and G. Wright. 1992. The Rise and Fall of American Techno-logical Leadership: The Post-war Era in Historical Perspective. *Journal of Economic Literature*. 30. pp. 1931–64.

Nerlove, Marc. 1996. Reflections on Agricultural Development, Population Growth and the Environment. In Quibria, M. G., and J. Malcolm Dowling, eds. *Current Issues in Economic Development: An Asian Perspective*. Hong Kong, China, and Oxford: Oxford University Press.

Neumann, J. V. 1945–1946. A Model of General Economic Equilibrium. *The Review of Economic Studies*. 13 (1). pp. 1–9.

Ng, Thiam He. 2002. Factor Endowments and the Distribution of Industrial Production across the World. *Statistics and Information Working Paper* 6. Vienna: United Nations Industrial Development Organization (UNIDO).

Ofreneo, Rene. 2003. *An Economic Reform Agenda for the Next Administration*. A "think paper" contributed in a debate on the role of elites in the Philippine economy in a forum held at the George Washington University Inn, Washington, DC.

Olson, Mancur Jr. 1996. Big Bills Left on the Sidewalk: Why Some Nations Are Rich, and Others Poor. *Journal of Economic Perspectives*. 10 (2). pp. 3–24.

Oulton, Nicholas, and Mary O'Mahony. 1994. *Productivity and Growth. A Study of British Industry, 1954–1986*. Cambridge: Cambridge University Press.

Oxfam. 2005. *Photo Voices. Shezhen Workers Speak*. Hong Kong, China: Oxfam.

Pacheco-López, P., and A. P. Thirlwall. 2007. Trade Liberalisation and the Trade-Off Between Growth and the Balance of Payments in Latin America. *International Review of Applied Economics*. Vol. 21. pp. 469–490.

Pack, Howard, and Kamal Sagi. 2006. Is There a Case for Industrial Policy? A Critical Survey. *World Bank Research Observer*. 21. pp. 267–97.

Pakistan Institute of Development Economics (PIDE). 2006. *Science and Technology-Based Industrial Vision of Pakistan's Economy and Prospects of Growth*. www.hec.gov.pk/htmls/about_hec/Technology%20Based%20Vision.pdf

Palley, T. I. 2002. A New Development Paradigm: Domestic Demand–Led Growth. Why It is Needed & How To Make it Happen. *Foreign Policy in Focus Discussion Paper*. September. www.fpif.org/papers/development.html

Park, Donghyun. 2007. Beyond Liquidity: New Uses for Developing Asia's Foreign Exchange Reserves. *ERD Working Paper* 109. November. Manila: ADB.

Pasha, Hafiz A. 2007. Inclusive Growth: The Asian Experience. Mimeograph.

Pasinetti, Luigi L. 1962. Rate of Profit and Income Distribution in Relation to the Rate of Economic Growth. *The Review of Economic Studies*. 29 (4). pp. 267–79.

————. 1981. *Structural Change and Economic Growth*. Cambridge: Cambridge University Press.

Pau, Eva. 2005. *Foreign Investment, Development, and Globalization*. Basingstoke, UK: Palgrave Macmillan.

Perotti, Roberto. 2007. Fiscal Policy in Developing Countries: A Framework and Some Questions. *World Bank Policy Research Working Paper* 4635. September. Washington, DC: World Bank.

The Philippine Star. 2008. Cost of Corruption: Gov't Projects overpriced by 20%. 9 February.

Pollin, Robert. 1998. The "Reserve Army of Unemployed" and the "Natural Rate of Unemployment": Can Marx, Kalecki, Friedman, and Wall Street All be Wrong? *Review of Radical Political Economics*. 30. pp. 1–13.

Pollin, Robert, and Andong Zhu. 2006. Inflation and Economic Growth: A Cross-Country Non-Linear Analysis. *Journal of Post-Keynesian Economics*. 28 (4). pp. 593–614.

Prasad, Eswar S., and Raghuram G. Rajan. 2007. Practical Approaches to Capital Account Liberalization. Manuscript.

Prebisch, Raul. 1959. Commercial Policy in the Underdeveloped Countries. *American Economic Review Papers and Proceedings*. 49 (2). pp. 251–73.

Prichett, Lant. 2003a. A Conclusion to Cross-National Growth Research: A Foreword "To the Countries Themselves." In McMahon, Gary, and Lyn Squire, eds. *Explaining Growth. A Global Research Project*. Basingstoke, UK: Palgrave Macmillan.

————. 2003b. A Toy Collection, a Socialist Star, and a Democratic Dud? In Rodrik, Dani, ed. *In Search of Prosperity. Analytic Narratives on Economic Growth*. Princeton, NJ, and Oxford: Princeton University Press.

Quibria, M.G., ed. 1995. *Critical Issues in Asian Development: Issues, Policies and Experiences*. Hong Kong, China, and Oxford: Oxford University Press.

Quibria, M.G., and J. Malcolm Dowling, eds. 1996. *Current Issues in Economic Development: An Asian Perspective*. Hong Kong, China, and Oxford: Oxford University Press.

Raj, K.N. 1978. Preface. In Ishikawa, S. 1981. *Essays on Technology, Employment and Institutions in Economic Development: Comparative Asian Experience*. Tokyo: Kinokuniya.

Rajan, Raghuram G. 2009. Rent Preservation and the Persistence of Underdevelopment. *American Economic Journal Macroeconomics*. Vol. 1, Issue 1. pp. 178–218.

Rajan, Raghuram G., and Luigi Zingales. 2003. *Saving Capitalism from the Capitalists*. New York: Random House Business Books.

Ramaswamy, K.V. 2006. *Global Opportunity and Domestic Constraints in Textile and Apparel Industry in South Asia: Analysis and Strategic Response of Firms in India*. Mumbai, India: Indira Gandhi Institute of Development Research.

Rampa, Giorgio, Luciano Stella, and A. P. Thirlwall, eds. 1998. *Economic Dynamics, Trade and Growth. Essays in Harrodian Themes*. New York: St. Martin's Press.

Rao, V. K. R. V. 1959. Population Growth and Its Relation to Employment in India. In Agarwala, S. N., ed. *India's Population: Some Problems in Perspective Planning*. London: Asia Publishing House.

Rashid, Salim, and M.G. Quibria. 1995. Is Land Reform Passé? With Special Reference to Asian Agriculture. In Quibria, M.G., ed. *Critical Issues in Asian Development: Issues, Policies and Experiences*. Hong Kong, China, and Oxford: Oxford University Press.

Rawls, J. 1971. *Theory of Justice*. Cambridge, MA: Harvard University Press.

Reinert, Erik S. 2007. *How Rich Countries Got Rich...and Why Poor Countries Stay Poor*. London: Constable.

Roberts, W. 2006. First Class to China. *Electronic Business*. 9 January.

Robinson, William I. 2002. Remapping Development in Light of Globalization: From Territorial to a Social Cartography. *Third World Quarterly*. 23 (6). pp. 1047–71.

Rodriguez, Francisco. 2005. Comment on Hausmann and Rodrik. Mimeograph. Department of Economics and Latin American Studies Program. Wesleyan University.

Rodriguez, Francisco, and D. Rodrik. 2001. Trade Policy and Economic Growth: A Skeptic's Guide to Cross-National Evidence. In Bernanke, B., and K. S. Rogoff, eds. *Macroeconomics Annual 2000*. Cambridge, MA: MIT Press.

Rodrik, Dani. 1999. Globalisation and Labour, or: If Globalization Is a Bowl of Cherries, Why Are There So Many Glum Faces around the Table? In Baldwin, Richard, Daniel Cohen, Andre Sapir, and Anthony Venables, eds. *Market Integration, Regionalism and the Global Economy*. New York: Cambridge University Press.

———. 2003. *Growth Strategies*. John F. Kennedy School of Government, Harvard University. www.ksg.harvard.edu/~drodrik/GrowthStrategies. pdf

———. 2004. *Industrial Policy for the Twenty-First Century*. John F. Kennedy School of Government, Harvard University. ksghome.harvard. edu/~drodrik/UNIDOSep.pdf

———. 2006a. *Industrial Development: Stylized Facts and Policies*. John F. Kennedy School of Government, Harvard University. ksghome.harvard. edu/~drodrik/ industrial%20development.pdf

———. 2006b. The Social Cost of Foreign Exchange Reserves. *International Economic Journal*. 20 (3). pp. 253–66.

———. 2007. The Real Exchange Rate and Economic Growth: Theory and Evidence. Mimeograph.

————. 2008. Second-Best Institutions. Mimeograph.

Rodrik, Dani, and Arvind Subramanian. 2008. Why Did Financial Globalization Disappoint? Mimeograph.

Roemer, J.E. 2006. Economic Development as Opportunity Equalization. *Cowles Foundation Discussion Paper* 1583. New Haven, CT: Yale University.

Rogers, S., and M. Stone. 2006. On Target? The International Experience with achieving inflation targets. *IMF Working Paper* 05/163. Washington, DC: IMF.

Rogoff, Kenneth. 1996. The Purchasing Power Parity Puzzle. *Journal of Economic Literature*. XXXIV (June). pp. 647–68.

————. 2006. Impact of Globalization on Monetary Policy. Harvard University. Manuscript (August 28 draft).

Ros, Jaime. 2000. *Development Theory and the Economics of Growth*. Ann Arbor: University of Michigan Press.

Rowthorn, R., and R. Ramaswamy. 1997. Deindustrialization: Causes and Implications. *IMF Working Paper* 97/42. Washington, DC: IMF.

————. 1999. Growth, Trade and Deindustrialization. *IMF Staff Papers*. 46 (1). pp. 18–41.

Roy, S. Dutta. 2004. Employment Dynamics in Indian Industry: Adjustment Lags and the Impact of Job Security. *Journal of Development Economics*. 73 (1). pp. 233–256.

Sachs, J., and A. Warner. 1995. Economic Reform and the Process of Global Integration. *Brookings Papers on Economic Activity*. pp. 1–118.

Samuelson, Paul. 2004. Where Ricardo and Mill Rebut and Confirm Arguments of Mainstream Economists Supporting Globalization. *Journal of Economic Perspectives*. 18 (3). pp. 135–46.

Schaaf, J. 2005. *Outsourcing to India: Crouching Tiger Set to Pounce*. Frankfurt: Deutsche Bank Research.

Schultz, T.P. 1994. Human Capital, Family Planning and their Effects on Population Growth. *American Economic Review*. 84 (2). pp. 255–60.

Sen, Amartya. 1999. *Development as Freedom*. New York: Alfred A. Knopf.

Setterfield. M. 2007. Is There a Stabilizing Role for Fiscal Policy in the New Consensus? *Review of Political Economy*. 19 (3). pp. 405–418.

Shaikh, Anwar. 1996. Free Trade, Unemployment, and Economic Policy. In Eatwell, John, ed. *Global Unemployment. Loss of Jobs in the '90s*. Armonk, NY, and London: M.E. Sharpe.

————. 1999. Explaining Inflation and Unemployment: An Alternative to Neoliberal Economic Policy. In Vachlou, A., ed. *Contemporary Economic Theory*. London: Macmillan.

Shapiro, Carl, and Joseph Stiglitz. 1984. Equilibrium Unemployment as a Worker Discipline Device. *American Economic Review*. 74 (3). pp. 433–44.

Shiller, R.J. 1997. Why do people dislike inflation? In Romer, C.D., and D.H. Romer, eds. *Reducing Inflation: Motivation and Strategy*. Chicago: University of Chicago Press.

Siddiqa, Ayesha. 2007. *Military Inc*. London: Pluto.

Skarstein, Rune. 2007. Free Trade: A Dead End for Underdeveloped Economies. *Review of Political Economy*. 19 (3). pp. 347–367.

Sleigh, A., and H. von Lewinski. 2006. Moving Up the Value Chain. *Outlook*. 3. Accenture Report.

Smith, Adam. 1776 [2003]. *The Wealth of Nations*. New York: Bantam Classic Edition.

Snower, Dennis. 1996. The Low-Skill, Bad-Job Trap. In Booth, Alison L., and Dennis J. Snower, eds. *Acquiring Skills: Market Failures, Their Symptoms and Policy Responses*. Cambridge: Cambridge University Press.

Solow, Robert. 1956. A Contribution to the Theory of Economic Growth. *Quarterly Journal of Economics*. 70. pp. 65–94.

———. 1997. What Is Labour-Market Flexibility? What Is It Good For? *Keynes Lecture 1997 Working Paper* 98–06. The World Economy Laboratory, MIT.

———. 2004. Is Fiscal Policy Possible? Is it Desirable? In Solow, Robert, ed. *Structural Reforms and Economic Policy*. Basingstoke, UK: Macmillan Palgrave.

Stiglitz, Joseph. 1976. The Efficiency Wage Hypothesis, Surplus Labor and the Distribution of Income in L.D.C.'s. *Oxford Economic Papers*. 28 (2). pp. 85–207.

———. 1998. The Role of Government in the Contemporary World. In Tanzi, Vito, and Ke-young Chu, eds. *Income Distribution and High-Quality Growth*. Cambridge, MA: MIT Press.

———. 2005. Finance for Development. In Ayugu, Melvin, and Don Ross, eds. *Development Dilemmas: The Methods and Political Ethics of Growth Policy*. London: Routledge.

Stiglitz, Joseph, Jose Antonio Ocampo, Shari Spiegel, Ricardo Ffrech-Davis, and Deepak Nayyar. 2006. *Stability with Growth*. Oxford: Oxford University Press.

Tatom, John A. 2006. Not All Deficits Are Created Equal. *Financial Analysts Journal*. 62 (3). pp. 12–19.

Taylor, Lance. 1995. Pasinetti's Processes. *Cambridge Journal of Economics*. 19 (5). pp. 697–713.

Teves, Margarito. 2008. New Entries Outstrip Jobs. Interview to Margarito Teves. *Development Asia*. No. 2 (December). p. 24.

Thirlwall, A.P. 1987. *Keynes and Economic Development*. New York: St. Martin's Press.

———. 1994. *Growth and Development*. 5th ed. London: Macmillan.

———. 2007. Keynes and Economic Development. *Economia Aplicada.* 11 (3). pp. 447–457.

Thirlwall, A.P., and P. Pacheco-López. 2008. *Trade Liberalisation and the Poverty of Nations.* Edward Elgar.

Timmer, M.P., and A. Szirmai, A. 2000. Productivity Growth in Asian Manufacturing: The Structural Bonus Hypothesis Examined. *Structural Change and Economic Dynamics.* 11. pp. 371–92.

Tobin, James. 1965. The Burden of the Public Debt: A Review Article. *Journal of Finance.* 20 (4). pp. 679–82.

United Nations Conference on Trade and Development (UNCTAD). 2007. *Trade and Development Report.* New York and Geneva: United Nations.

United Nations Industrial Development Organization (UNIDO). 2005. Industrial Statistics (INDSTAT) 2005 Database: 3-digit Level of International Standard Industry Classification (ISIC) Code Revision 2. Strategic Research and Economics Branch, UNIDO, Austria.

Vickrey, William. 1992. Chock-Full Employment without Increased Inflation: A Proposal for Marketable Markup Warrants. *The American Economic Review.* 82 (2). pp. 341–45.

———. 1993. Today's Task for Economists. *The American Economic Review.* 83 (1). pp. 1–10.

———. 1996 [2000]. Fifteen Fatal Fallacies of Financial Fundamentalism: A Disquisition on Demand Side Economics. In Warner, Aaron W., Mathew Forstater, and Summer M. Rosen, eds. *Commitment to Full Employment: The Economic and Social Policy of William S. Vickrey.* Armonk, NY: M.E. Sharpe, Inc.

———. 1997. A Trans-Keynesian Manifesto (Thoughts on Assets Based Macroeconomics). *Journal of Post Keynesian Economics.* 19 (4). pp. 495–510.

Wade, R. 1988. The Role of Government in Overcoming Market Failure: [Taipei,China], Republic of Korea, and Japan. In Hughes, H., ed. *Achieving Industrialization in East Asia.* Cambridge: Cambridge University Press.

Wan, Henry Y. 2004. *Economic Development in a Globalized Environment. East Asian Evidences.* Norwell, MA: Kluwer Academic Publishers.

Wang, Huijong, and Shantong Li. 1995. *Industrialization and Economic Reform in China.* New World Press: Beijing.

Weintraub, S. 1958. *An Approach to the Theory of Income Distribution.* Philadelphia: Chilton.

Willard, Luke B. 2006. Does Inflation Targeting Matter? A Reassessment. *CEPS Working Paper* 120. Princeton University.

Williamson, J. 1990. What Washington Means by Policy Reform. In Williamson, J., ed. *Latin American Adjustment: How Much Has Happened?* Washington, DC: Institute for International Economics.

Wong, Douglas. 2003. Singapore's Research Heaven Lures Scientists. *Financial Times*. 24 January.

World Bank. 2002. *Globalization, Growth and Poverty: Building an inclusive world economy*. Oxford: World Bank and Oxford University Press.

———. 2005. *Enhancing Job Opportunities in Eastern Europe and the Former Soviet Union*. Washington, DC: World Bank.

———. 2006. *Doing Business in 2006*. Washington, DC: World Bank.

———. 2008. *World Development Report: Agriculture for Development*. Washington, DC: World Bank.

———. 2009. Swimming Against the Tide: How Developing Countries are Coping with the Global Crisis. Background paper prepared by the World Bank staff for the G20 Finance Ministers and Central Bank Governors Meeting, Horsham, United Kingdom on 13–14 March 2009.

Wray, Randall. 1998. *Understanding Modern Money: The Key to Full Employment and Price Stability*. Cheltenham, UK: Edward Elgar.

———. 2007a. Employer of Last Resort: Strategies for Combating Poverty. *Development*. 50 (2). pp. 96–102.

———. 2007b. The Employer of Last Resort Programme: Could it work for Developing Countries? *Economic and Labor Market Papers* 2007/5. Geneva: International Labour Organization. www.ilo.org/public/english/employment/download/elm/elm07-5.pdf

———. 2008a. The Commodities Market Bubble. Money Manager capitalism and the Financialization of Commodities. The Levy Institute of Bard College. *Public Policy Brief* No. 98.

———. 2008b. An Alternative View of Finance, Saving, Deficits, and Liquidity. University of Missouri–Kansas City. Mimeograph.

Young, Alwyn. 1992. A Tale of Two Cities: Factor Accumulation and Technical Change in Hong Kong and Singapore. *National Bureau of Economics Research Macroeconomics Annual 1992*. pp. 13–63.

Author Index

Subject Index